Ninth edition © The Association for Physical Education and Coachwise Ltd, 2016

ISBN: 978-1-909012-35-6

Authors: Angela James and Jill Elbourn
Parts of this text have been developed from *Safe Practice in Physical Education and Sport*
© The Association for Physical Education, 2012, and other national safety and employment guidance written by Peter Whitlam.
afPE project lead officer: Sue Wilkinson
afPE technical subject expert: Peter Whitlam
afPE appreciates the contributions through review made by:

Tom Bunner and Adam Burgess – Sportshall Athletics
Neil Burton – British Gymnastics
Peter Davidson – Education Manager, Sports Science, Council for the Curriculum Examinations and Assessment (CCEA), Northern Ireland
Denise Fountain – Head Teacher, Dame Ellen Pinsent School
David Gent – British Weight Lifting
Jon Glenn – ASA
Justin Hampson – Teacher, Scissett Middle School, Huddersfield
Owen Hayward – Head of Outdoor Education Service, Conwy County Borough Council
Michael Hunt and David Brown – UK Athletics
Emma Hutchinson – Teacher, Worcesters Primary School, Enfield
Dan Keefe – Teacher, Clare Mount Specialist Sports College

Graham Lodge – Adviser – Outdoor Learning, Norfolk County Council
Adrian Lole – Royal Life Saving Society
Richard Painter – Chair, OEAP National Guidance Working Group
Jan Parker – PE and School Sport Programme Manager, Livewire, Warrington
Glenn Price – Head of PE, Thomas Keble School, Gloucestershire
Martin Smith – SOLAR Services Manager, Education Partnerships, Nottingham City Council
Glenn Swindlehurst – Head of Primary PE, School Sport and Outdoor Education, Lancs County Council
Ryan Trumpeter and Theo Millward – Swimming Teachers Association
Hannah Vecchione – Director of PE and Sport, St John's Catholic Primary School, Manchester
Dr Jes Woodhouse – Senior Lecturer in Education (Physical Education), University of Cumbria

Coachwise editor: Chris Stanners
Coachwise designer: Matthew Dodd
Cover photo © Coachwise/SWpix
Indexer: Paul Douch

Room 117
Bredon
University of Worcester
Henwick Grove
Worcester WR2 6AJ
Tel: 01905-855 584
Fax: 01905-855 594

Published on behalf of afPE by

Coachwise Ltd
Chelsea Close
Off Amberley Road, Armley
Leeds LS12 4HP
Tel: 0113-231 1310 Fax: 0113-231 9606
Email: enquiries@coachwise.ltd.uk
Website: www.coachwise.ltd.uk

Foreword

With this, the ninth edition of *Safe Practice: in Physical Education, School Sport and Physical Activity*, the Association for Physical Education (afPE) have once again provided an essential resource for all those involved in the teaching of physical education, school sport and physical activity. I am delighted to have been offered the opportunity to provide a foreword.

Improving PE and school sport is a key priority for this government. Since 2013, through the primary PE and sport premium, we have invested over £450 million into improving the PE and sport provision in primary schools. We have committed to continue this funding until 2020 and the 2016 budget announcement went further – revenue from the soft drinks industry levy will be used to double the primary PE and sport premium from September 2017. It will also provide funding to enable up to a quarter of secondary schools to extend their school day to offer a wider range of activities, including sports clubs. This will enable further improvement to the quality and breadth of PE, school sport and physical activity currently offered, and this resource perfectly complements this changing landscape by ensuring schools can continue to have access to expert guidance on safe practice.

This book builds upon previous editions to offer a near complete collection of advice, instruction and information. Spread across four sections, this handbook is clearly structured in a straightforward and simple way, making it equally accessible for Governor and teacher alike. It is fully updated to reflect recent developments in legal practice, national guidance, and statute law. It is also underpinned throughout by reference to relevant case law, used to illustrate key principles, assisting the reader in applying theory to actual situations. afPE have worked tirelessly with partners across the sector, incorporating the newest guidance available, including the latest concussion guidelines as agreed by both national governing bodies and independent medical experts.

Edward Timpson, Minister of State for Children and Families

Contents

Contents

Important information

Any updates or amends to this ninth edition will be published online.

If you register for the online version, you will receive email notifications of any updates.

Alternatively, to view the updates, visit www.pesafepractice.com/9/updates

You should visit this page to print out any updates and attach them to this hard copy edition.

26779196

Introduction

About this resource

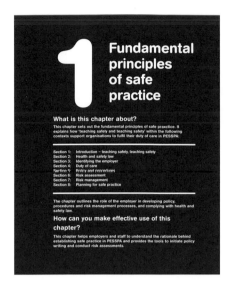

This resource is organised into four chapters, each of which addresses a key aspect of teaching safely or teaching safety.

Chapter 1 sets out the fundamental principles of safe practice. It explains how organisations are best placed to fulfil their duty of care and comply with other health and safety law through 'teaching safely and teaching safety'. The chapter explains the role of the employer and the importance of developing useful and relevant policy and procedures, and the processes of risk management and risk assessment.

Chapter 2 focuses on 'teaching safely' through the principles of organisation and management. It considers what employers and staff need to know and understand about a wide range of physical education, school sport and physical activity (PESSPA) health and safety issues in order to fulfil their duty of care, with a strong focus on how to apply this knowledge to practical 'everyday' situations.

Chapter 3 focuses on promoting relevant and effective student learning about risk management and keeping safe in and through PESSPA. It provides examples of objectives, outcomes and tasks to support staff to promote effective learning about safeguarding, assessment and risk, first aid, safe exercise practice and safe practice in relation to the use of space, tasks, equipment and working with people.

Chapter 4 focuses on 'teaching safely' and provides additional information about safe practice that is relevant to specific practical PESSPA activities. The chapter applies the principles and processes set out in **Chapter 1: Fundamental principles of safe practice** and Chapter 2: Teaching safely – principles of organisation and management. Knowledge and understanding of the content of **Chapters 1** and **2** will facilitate more accurate interpretation of the activity-specific guidance included in this chapter.

Each chapter is divided into several **sections**, each of which addresses a key component associated with the focus of the chapter. Examples of **case law** and **frequently asked questions** are included in many of the sections.

Case law

Throughout the resource, **case law** is used to illustrate how principles of health and safety law have been established or how they have been applied to different cases. Learning gained from relevant case law should inform and improve safe practice in PESSPA.

Health and safety legislation applies to all the home countries in the United Kingdom. However, other specific legislation may vary. Although the position in each of the home countries is broadly similar, those involved in the delivery of PESSPA in England, Northern Ireland, Scotland and Wales are recommended to visit the following websites for details of specific legislation and policy:

www.legislation.gov.uk/browse (UK-wide information covering England)
www.legislation.gov.uk/browse/ni
www.legislation.gov.uk/browse/scotland
www.legislation.gov.uk/browse/wales

A list of all the case law used in the resource can be found on page 463.

A case in point

The examples included use case law and information from legal inquiries and hearings to illustrate key principles and help readers to apply the theory to actual situations.

FAQ

Frequently asked questions (FAQs) are included throughout the resource to support readers to develop their understanding of how principles can be applied in practice.

Many of the tables, charts and templates in the resource are available to download from www.pesafepractice.com

Readers can adapt these to make them specific to their own situations.

Throughout the resource, web links are provided to enable the reader to refer to the source of information or access additional information.

How to use this resource

This resource helps readers to address specific questions about safe practice in physical education, school sport and physical activity (PESSPA). Figure 1 illustrates two different routes.

The left hand arrow illustrates an individual seeking to address their safe practice question by referring initially to information in **Chapters 1** and **2**. This route can provide reliable answers that are underpinned by a firm understanding of the fundamental principles of safe practice and principles of safe organisation and management, ie 'teaching safely'.

The right hand arrow illustrates an individual seeking to address their safe practice question by referring initially to the chapter focusing on activity-specific information (**Chapter 4**). This route may produce 'quick fix' answers, but these should be treated with caution as they may lack rigour if not rooted in a firm understanding of the fundamental principles of safe practice and principles of safe organisation and management.

A clear understanding of the fundamental principles of safe practice and principles of safe organisation and management are essential for promoting learning about safety with students. **Chapter 3** supports this process.

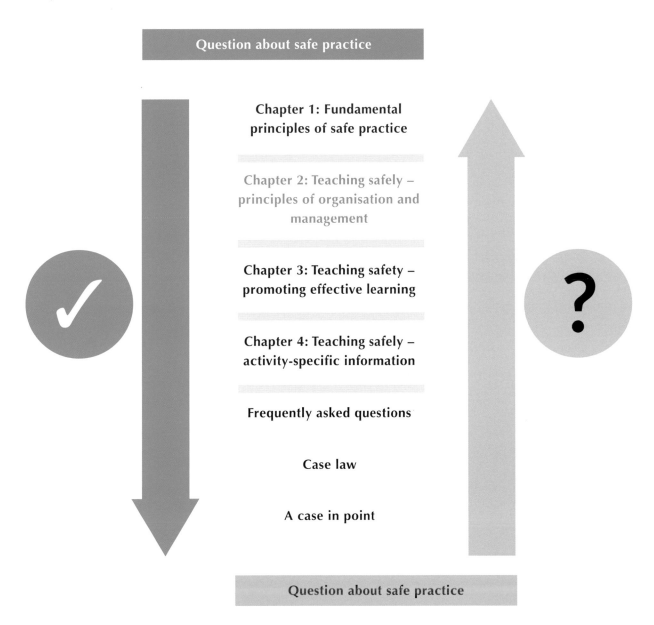

Figure 1: Using this resource to address specific questions about safe practice in PESSPA

How specific terminology is used in the context of this resource

Safe practice is where the risks for those involved in **PESSPA** sessions are deemed to be acceptably low.

PESSPA sessions include physical development activities, physical education lessons, organised sport and/or physical activity sessions beyond the curriculum both within school settings and in the community.

Risk refers to the likelihood of harm occurring from a hazard.

Hazard refers to something with the potential to cause harm.

Physical education is planned, progressive learning for all students that takes place within the school curriculum and involves both 'learning to move' (ie becoming more physically competent) and 'moving to learn' (eg learning through movement and the development of a range of competencies beyond physical activity, such as cooperating with others). The context for the learning is physical activity, with children experiencing a broad range of activities, including sport and dance.

School sport is structured learning that takes place beyond the curriculum but within school settings. The context for learning is physical activity that has the potential to develop and broaden the learning that takes place in physical education and form vital links with community sport and activity. School sport is sometimes referred to as extracurricular or out-of-school-hours learning.

Physical activity is a broad term referring to all bodily movement that uses energy. It includes all forms of physical education, sports and dance activities. However, it is wider than this as it also includes indoor and outdoor play, work-related activity, outdoor and adventurous activities, active travel (eg walking, cycling, Rollerblading, scootering) and routine, habitual activities such as using the stairs, doing housework and gardening.

Must is only used where the situation described relates to a statutory requirement, **or when the employer sets out what must be followed by the employees. Should** is used in this resource to illustrate regular and approved practice.

PESSPA activities include all practical learning contexts that are part of physical development activities, physical education lessons, organised sport and/or physical activity sessions beyond the curriculum both within school settings and in the community.

Parent refers to any person, a natural parent or not, who has care and parental responsibility for a child or young person, ie the child lives with and is looked after by that person, irrespective of their relationship.

Head teacher refers to the most senior teacher, leader and manager of a school.

Staff a term used to refer to adults leading PESSPA sessions in schools with the approval of the head teacher. This commonly includes qualified/registered teachers (with or without specialism in physical education), teaching assistants (TAs) and sports coaches.

Students refers to all children and young people attending school.

Support staff is a term used to refer to adults without qualified/registered teaching status (QTS) who contribute to the teaching of students in schools (eg TAs, cover supervisors, volunteers, sports coaches). Support staff do not include trainee teachers.

Fundamental principles of safe practice

What is this chapter about?

This chapter sets out the fundamental principles of safe practice. It explains how 'teaching safely and teaching safety' within the following contexts support organisations to fulfil their duty of care in PESSPA:

Section 1:   Introduction – teaching safely, teaching safety
Section 2:   Health and safety law
Section 3:   Identifying the employer
Section 4:   Duty of care
Section 5:   Policy and procedures
Section 6:   Risk assessment
Section 7:   Risk management
Section 8:   Planning for safe practice

The chapter outlines the role of the employer in developing policy, procedures and risk management processes, and complying with health and safety law.

How can you make effective use of this chapter?

This chapter helps employers and staff to understand the rationale behind establishing safe practice in PESSPA and provides the tools to initiate policy writing and conduct risk assessments.

Chapter 1/Section 1: Introduction – teaching safely, teaching safety

1.1.1   We live in a world where we are advised to move more and to be more physically active in order to benefit our health. Physical activity can range from brisk walking to playing games, to climbing a mountain. Once we start to be more physically active, we become involved in a range of movement challenges such as changing speed, moving in different directions, moving with and around objects or people, or using equipment to help us move. Within physical education, students learn to move, improving their physical competence, and use movement to learn through a range of different physically active contexts. As we move more, we need to consider ways in which we can move safely and reduce the likelihood that involvement in such movement might cause harm to ourselves or others.

1.1.2   Teachers and staff delivering physical education, school sport and physical activity (PESSPA) aim to encourage students or participants to increase their activity levels in ways that are enjoyable and beneficial for health, and that can contribute to improving learning. This needs to be achieved within safe environments and using safe practice.

1.1.3   To achieve acceptable safety standards, those leading practical activities and those participating have a responsibility to undertake actions that will minimise the likelihood of harm occurring. Where such measures are taken in a sensible, proportionate way using appropriate **forethought** (see 2.2.11), they contribute to fulfilling the principle of **duty of care** and attaining safe outcomes. **'Teaching safely, teaching safety'** is the framework that this resource exemplifies to summarise the principles of safe practice and to support all those teaching and managing PESSPA sessions for children and young people in schools in their quest to achieve and maintain acceptable safety standards.

1.1.4   **'Teaching safely, teaching safety'** is often misinterpreted, with an emphasis on the 'teaching safely' aspect, and with little attention paid to 'teaching safety'. However, student learning about safety is very important, and provides knowledge, understanding and skills for young people to adapt and apply throughout their lives. In addition, progressive learning about safety is an expectation of the school curriculum and inspectorate.

1.1.5   Achieving safe delivery of, and promoting learning through, a broad PESSPA programme involves schools meeting a number of requirements, established through statute, case law or best practice, as well as the expectations and statutory requirements of a national curriculum (for those schools that choose to follow one).

1.1.6   afPE recognises good practice as **'teaching safely' and 'teaching safety', which can be achieved through effective teaching and management, and effective student learning about safe practice. Figure 2, page 7, summarises how** afPE's PIE process (preventing, informing and educating) offers an approach to implementing safe practice principles.

Safe Practice Principles	Framework for Safe Practice in PESSPA	Processes for Safe Practices in PESSPA (PIE)	Processes Achieved through	Guidance to Support and Develop Safe Practice in PESSPA
Fundamental principles of safe practice	Teaching safely	Preventing harm	Recognising and managing risk effectively	Chapters **1**, **2** and **4**
Principles of safe organisation and management	Teaching safety	Informing	Good teaching, organisation and management	
		Educating	Promoting relevant and effective student learning about risk management and keeping safe	**Chapter 3**

Figure 2: Safe practice in PESSPA – overview of principles, processes and guidance

1.1.7   In reality, it is not always possible to prevent harm in PESSPA situations, but harm can often be minimised through recognising and managing risk; good teaching, organisation and management; and informing students about the potential hazards and risks.

1.1.8   **P**reventing and **I**nforming through the PIE process demonstrate **'teaching safely'**.

Guidance on 'teaching safely' can be found in Chapters 1, 2 and 4.

1.1.9   Staff delivering school PESSPA sessions have a duty to **educate** students about being and feeling safe. They fulfil this duty through a combination of informing and educating students about the safety standards and procedures that will help them to safely participate in PESSPA activities while at school and throughout their life, and about the risk management process that will help them to make safe decisions and choices.

1.1.10   **I**nforming and **E**ducating through the PIE process demonstrate **'teaching safety'**.

Guidance on 'teaching safety' can be found in Chapter 3.

1.1.11   Professional learning about safe practice and risk management in physical education are available through afPE (email cpd@afpe.org.uk).

1.1.12   As schools embrace teaching safely and teaching safety, they should do so on the understanding that there is no one perfect approach, and that staff need to work within **a 'range of reasonable options'** (see Woodbridge School 2002 **case law** below). Every PESSPA session will pose different circumstances and different decisions to be made. The minutiae of all the possible answers cannot be set out in any one resource. Developing a sound knowledge and understanding of **safe practice principles** and applying the guidance to each situation and setting will support this process.

Case law

1.1.13   **Woodbridge School versus Chittock (2002):**

*This established the principle of a 'range of reasonable options' being acceptable in dealing with issues, recognising that **no single response was the correct way to deal with a situation;** rather that some degree of flexibility according to the circumstances was a more appropriate professional response.*

Chapter 1/Section 2: Health and safety law

1.2.1   Health and safety statute, supported by civil case law, places ultimate responsibility for health and safety on the **employer**. This includes the duties to:

- have a written health and safety policy

- initiate procedures to ensure satisfactory implementation of the policy, and regular reviews (typically annually, but also following any incidents)

- provide a safe place of work

- assess and manage the risks of all activities

- inform employees of measures to make situations safe

- provide training and supervision, where appropriate

- monitor implementation of the procedures.

1.2.2   Further information relating to these points can be found within the following legislation:

- Health and Safety at Work etc Act 1974

- Management of Health and Safety at Work Regulations 1999

- Management of Health and Safety at Work Regulations (Northern Ireland) 2000.

© Alan Edwards

Case law

1.2.3 **R versus Essex County Council (2012):**

A pupil nearly drowned during a swimming lesson in a local authority school's swimming pool. The local authority (LA) was investigated and prosecuted by the Health and Safety Executive (HSE) on the basis of inadequate supervision.

The LA was alleged to have failed to provide schools with adequate up-to-date information, guidance and training on the safe management and running of its pools. The LA was also challenged for failing to monitor where schools did not follow guidance and for failing to initiate remedial steps to rectify failings.

All of these factors are statutory requirements within the Health and Safety at Work etc Act 1974 and the Management of Health and Safety Regulations 1999. Within this legislation, a school authority has a duty to provide policy, procedures and training, where appropriate, and to monitor whether procedures are applied and safe standards maintained.

The prosecution was successful, and the LA was fined £20,000.

1.2.4 **McErlean versus Governors of St Bride's Primary School (2014):**

This ruling highlights the point that an employer is under a duty to take reasonable care for the safety of their employees, and that activities usually carry some risk of injury. In this instance, the head teacher had checked the route, considered it reasonably safe and, therefore, complied with the requirement for the governing body to take reasonable care for its students and staff. A risk assessment had previously been carried out for the route, concentrating mainly on risks from road traffic.

A teacher sustained a fractured forearm, having slipped on the icy path while on the route, escorting a group of students to an off-site event.

On the day of the accident, the head teacher had walked the route to ensure it was safe. He maintained that it was, but the teacher had disagreed, saying it was too dangerous in the severe weather conditions.

The judge said a different head teacher might have considered the safety of the route differently, but that did not indicate this head teacher's conclusion was wrong or negligent. There was no history of anyone slipping on the path, and the risks were obvious to everyone. The claim was dismissed on the basis that accidents happen but the teacher's fall was not due to any breach of duty by the governing body (the employer).

1.2.5 Where **employers** (see **Chapter 1, Section 3, page 13**) produce policy, directives and guidance, these **must** be followed and applied by employees within the organisation, in the same way that laws and statutes must be applied. Ignoring these may result in the employee becoming individually responsible.

1.2.6   Effective health and safety practices are integral to good management. Head teachers (HTs) have a responsibility for everything over which they have control. This includes all day-to-day health and safety issues within and outside the curriculum, including weekends and during the holidays, **where activities are organised by the school**.

1.2.7   The ultimate accountability to meet these responsibilities cannot be devolved, but tasks can be delegated to others within the organisation and to commissioned third party providers such as coaches or swim schools.

1.2.8   In schools, this delegation would normally be from the HT to the leadership team, and in some cases, to subject leaders or other staff. All teachers and support staff are expected to know and apply the school policy, report any concerns to the leadership team, and take reasonable steps to control any existing risks of which they become aware.

1.2.9   Within PESSPA, heads of physical education, subject leads and other staff members are likely to have aspects of these responsibilities delegated to them. As **employees**, they are required to:

- take reasonable care of the health and safety of themselves and others

- cooperate with the employer on health and safety issues

- know and apply the employer's policy for health and safety, and incorporate this into PESSPA policy

- carry out their work as directed by the school leadership team

- report any concerns about health and safety

- do what is within their power to prevent further injury from reported concerns

- not place themselves or others at risk (such as students and colleagues)

- ensure they do not interfere with or misuse items for health and safety, such as fire extinguishers or safety signs

- participate in safety inspections.

1.2.10   Where games activities, tournaments and events are **organised** by a **governing body of sport**, their rules and regulations will be enforced. Where activities are organised by schools or other non-governing body of sport organisations, school rules will apply. Where governing bodies of sport are involved in delivering activities at events organised by schools or other agencies (eg the School Games), organisers are advised to ensure that both schools and governing bodies of sport are clear about which rules should be applied.

1.2.11   While laws and regulations **must** be followed, within PESSPA, there are guidelines for safe practice that **should** also be followed. These might include:

- national guidance such as that offered in this resource by the Association for Physical Education (afPE) or by local schemes

- rules and regulations set out by governing bodies of sport. These should be noted and applied where practical and workable within the context. For example, while it is good practice, it may not be financially practical to make the wearing of mouth guards compulsory in all school hockey curriculum lessons. In this case, the teacher must take action to ensure that the activities within the lesson are safe for all participants whether or not they are wearing a mouth guard. It may, however, be possible to enforce the wearing of mouth guards within club, match and other competitive situations, where students have chosen to take part.

1.2.12   In most cases, employer's guidance is drawn from, and makes reference to, reputable national guidance. However, there may be cases where **local** circumstances mean that guidance differs, and this **must** be acknowledged and followed.

1.2.13   **Wherever guidance is issued by the employer, this must always take precedence over national guidance, such as that issued by afPE.**

1.2.14   Staff should ensure that:

- safe-practice requirements are proportionate to the identified risks of an activity through appropriate risk assessments

- common sense is used in assessing and managing the risks of any activity

- they are aware of their legal duty to be proactive in establishing and maintaining a safe learning environment

- they recognise that accident prevention is desirable for health, economic and legal reasons

- they understand that the existence of risk and exposing someone to that risk are sufficient for liability to be established, and that injury is not a necessary outcome in health and safety law (though it is for civil claims for compensation)

- they initiate where needed, and take part in, any appropriate professional learning.

(Information relating to these requirements is addressed in **Chapter 1, Section 3, page 14.**)

1.2.15   Schools have a **duty**, by law, to provide a safe working environment and safe systems of work for staff, students and other visitors, as well as a responsibility to ensure that learning about safe practice is promoted with students.

1.2.16   Students are entitled to be taught in a safe and healthy environment. In addition, there are considerable benefits for students of identifying and applying consistent, safe standards.

1.2.17   Students should:

- be able to experience a wide range of PESSPA activities/situations in which safe-practice measures enable opportunities rather than prevent them

- feel empowered to manage their own safety in order to become progressively more independent in lifelong participation in physical activity

- experience high quality PESSPA that involves appropriate challenge and progression.

Chapter 1/Section 3: Identifying the employer

1.3.1   Overall legal responsibility and accountability for all health and safety lie with the employer, and staff must follow the policy and guidance set by their employer. For this reason, it is essential to be clear about who the employer is.

1.3.2   The Health and Safety Executive (HSE) provides a summary of this information at http://goo.gl/jvTZwf

1.3.3   Table 1 below presents this information, and includes the latest changes in Northern Ireland.

Table 1: Identifying the employer

In England and Wales	
The local authority (LA) is the employer in:	• community schools • community special schools • voluntary controlled schools • maintained nursery schools • pupil referral units.
The governing body or the board of trustees is the employer in:	• foundation schools • foundation special schools • voluntary aided schools • academies • free schools.
The proprietor is the employer in:	• independent schools.
In Scotland	
The LA is the employer in:	• the majority of schools that are state owned.
The governing body, or equivalent, is the employer in:	• the few grant-aided schools that are independent of LAs, but that are supported financially by the Scottish Government.
The proprietor, Board of Trustees or equivalent is the employer in:	• independent schools.
In Northern Ireland	
The Education Authority* is the employer in: *Until recently there were five Education and Library Boards. These have now been amalgamated into the one body.	• controlled schools (nursery, primary, special, post-primary and grammar schools).
The Council for Catholic Maintained Schools (CCMS) is the employer in:	• maintained schools (nursery, primary, special and post-primary).
The Board of Governors is the employer in**: **Arrangements for employment can vary. In some cases in these schools, the Education Authority is the employer for ancillary staff, while the governing body is the employer for teaching staff.	• voluntary schools (grammar) • integrated schools (primary and post-primary).

1.3.4   The landscape within education continues to change, and the management and governance of different types of schools vary.

1.3.5   Schools need to be very clear about the health and safety requirements of their employer. For LA schools as long as they remain, this will mean keeping up to date with guidance issued from their LA. Where the **governing body** is the employer, the governors have **full legal responsibility** to ensure compliance with health and safety law. Governors can find details regarding their responsibilities in:

- Department for Education (DfE) (2015) 'Governance handbook: For trustees of academies and multi-academy trusts and governors of maintained schools', http://goo.gl/Gu3tmL

- DfE (2014) 'Health and safety: Advice on legal duties and powers for local authorities, school leaders, school staff and governing bodies', http://goo.gl/pMhfRN

1.3.6   Where schools with greater autonomy are required to make their own health and safety arrangements independently of LAs, they should be clear about what health and safety law requires of them.

1.3.7   Some schools choose to 'buy back' into LA services where they are still available, while other schools opt to use the services of private commercial companies. Whichever route is taken, the employer remains responsible when things go wrong, other than when an individual is prosecuted.

For more information, see Section 4 in this chapter.

1.3.8   Where commercial health and safety companies are used by schools, the guidance offered within this resource will be useful when discussing PESSPA issues with them.

1.3.9   Where no additional detailed guidance is provided by the employer, it would be wise to follow the standards and practice contained in this resource.

1.3.10   While the directives set by the employer may vary across schools, the head teacher needs to be aware of and approve any significant change to PESSPA policy or procedure before presenting it to governors and communicating the changes to staff, pupils and parents.

For more information, see Chapter 1, Section 5, page 27.

Chapter 1/Section 4: Duty of care

1.4.1   Everyone has a **duty of care** to ensure the safety and well-being of others. Under this premise, all staff working in schools must demonstrate this duty of care. Where the professional standards of care expected are not met (that is an individual is **'careless'**), and as a result, **damage** is an outcome (ie harm or injury in physical education, school sport and physical activity [PESSPA] contexts), and the outcome was reasonably **foreseeable**, it is possible that an allegation of **negligence** could be pursued.

1.4.2   **Negligence** may be defined as 'careless conduct which injures another and which the law deems liable for compensation' (Frederick Place Chambers, 1995*).

1.4.3   Within education, such allegations of negligence are very rare in relation to the number of students being educated, and significant levels of protection exist for staff, as employees, against such allegations.

1.4.4   Injuries will occur in PESSPA simply because of its active nature. These may be 'no-fault' accidents. It is the element of **carelessness** that may impose a liability of negligence.

1.4.5   Compensation for injury caused by the careless, unintentional actions of staff, officials or participants in PESSPA is usually obtained through a claim of negligence made by the parents of the student against the **employer** of the teacher concerned.

1.4.6   School staff continue to exercise a duty of care for all students aged 18 when under school regulations. This duty of care applies to any school student until they have reached the age of 19, at which stage a young person ceases to have the legal status of being a registered school student.

1.4.7   Originally, the **standard of care** expected of school staff only applied to qualified class teachers and was described as being **in loco parentis**: in place of a prudent parent.

1.4.8   This standard has been modified and updated to acknowledge both the context of a school rather than a home, because a class teacher clearly has responsibility for more children at any one time and in a different environment, and also the changing school workforce where this level of professional responsibility has broadened to include **all adults** who work with young people.

 Case law

1.4.9   **Williams versus Eady (1893):**

*This described the expected standard of care as that of a **careful parent**.*

1.4.10   **Lyes versus Middlesex County Council (1962):**

*This case extended the 'careful parent' standard to being in the **context of a school** rather than a home because a teacher clearly has responsibility for more children at any one time and in a different environment than the home.*

* Frederick Place Chambers (1995) *Negligence at Work: Liability for Injury and Disease*. St Albans: XPL Publishing. ISBN: 978-1858110-31-8

1.4.11 Any adult involved in PESSPA sessions, whether working alongside or at a distance (remotely) from the teacher, is expected to show the same standard of care. In a school-organised activity, which is delivered by an external agency, on or off site, the school's duty of care to students continues whether or not the teacher is involved in the delivery of the session.

 Case law

1.4.12 **Gower versus LB of Bromley (1999):**

This ruling broadened the scope of the standard of care to encompass 'a duty to exercise the skill and care of a reasonable member of the teaching profession', thus expanding the standard of **in loco parentis to all adults** *involved in teaching young people and not simply qualified teacher status (QTS) teachers.*

1.4.13 Where a teacher has knowledge and experience that is higher than that expected of a 'reasonably competent person' acting in their position or capacity, they are judged by that **enhanced standard of foresight**. This defines a **higher duty of care**, in that a teacher with specialist expertise, qualifications or responsibility is expected to have a greater insight and awareness of the consequences of their actions. All specialist physical education teachers are deemed to possess **specialist expertise** within their profession and thus a higher duty of care as are well-qualified and experienced coaches in their specific activity.

 Case law

1.4.14 **Stokes versus Guest, Keen and Nettleford (Bolts and Nuts) Limited (1968):**

This case determined that, where someone has knowledge and experience that is higher than that to be expected of a reasonable person acting in their position or capacity, they are judged by that enhanced standard of foresight, in other words a **higher duty of care** *due to specialist skills and experience.*

1.4.15 'Specialists' in a particular PESSPA activity, those who lead higher-risk PESSPA activities (such as trampolining or outdoor adventurous activities), or those responsible for very young children or young people with limited abilities are also deemed to have a higher duty of care (ie a higher level of responsibility) for those in their care. They will be judged as having a greater degree of insight relating to the consequences of their actions and against the common standard of others in the profession. This standard considers whether people in the same profession, working at the same level, would have carried out the same action, ie whether their action is **regular and approved practice** in the profession. Action is regular and approved if it is common and accepted across a wide geographical area as being safe.

1.4.16   This being the case, a qualified teacher, other member of school staff, visiting coach or volunteer who is inexperienced would be judged **by the same standard** as more experienced colleagues to avoid **inexperience** being frequently used as a defence against an allegation of negligence. Head teachers (HTs), on behalf of the employer, should be aware of this when deploying a range of staff.

 Case law

1.4.17   **Bolam versus Friern Hospital Management Committee (1957):**

*This established that a person who possesses **specialist skills in a profession** is not judged by the standard of the reasonable man ('on the street') but by the standard of people within the same profession, ie teachers.*

1.4.18   Courts recognise, however, that there is no single answer to a situation. Teachers are expected to operate '**within a range of reasonable options**'. The teaching profession is therefore judged according to what would be **common** practice across the profession, with no single remedy deemed to be the answer to an issue.

 Case law

1.4.19   **Shaw versus Redbridge LBC (2005):**

*An allegation of negligence was dismissed because the teacher's action was **typical** of what would be seen across the profession – judged to be 'proper professional judgement' – ie regular and approved practice.*

1.4.20   A fair and realistic view of responsibility is usually taken as not expecting perfection, but requiring a standard appropriate to a competent professional person. There is no distinction in the standard of care expected between teachers and others working with students, other than that set by the level of expertise the individual offers and the circumstances within which they work.

1.4.21   All teachers of physical education have a duty to **work within** a system that anticipates and manages risks. HTs must ensure such a system is operable, even by recently appointed staff and any visiting staff.

 For more information, see Sections 5, 6 and 7 in this chapter.

1.4.22 The duty and standard of care are **continuous** and cannot be diluted or removed by any association with the terms **holiday, abroad, weekend** or similar terms. The school retains a responsibility for whatever it organises. A simple question can help to establish whether the school holds a responsibility: 'Who invited the students to participate in the activity?' If the school has played **any part** in that invitation being expressed and accepted, then the school carries some responsibility for the outcomes.

1.4.23 While this clearly applies to **all mandatory curricular situations**, it also applies to **activities the school deems important to provide for the students**, including those organised beyond the curriculum and outside the normal timetabled day, such as extracurricular clubs, fixtures, sports festivals and visits to adventure activity centres. Where specialist staff (such as those at residential activity centres) are responsible for the technical aspects of the experience, school staff maintain overall duty of care for the students, and clarity of roles and responsibilities in such situations is essential.

1.4.24 For these activities, the school is providing experiences that it believes to be an essential aspect of school life and **'assumes the duty'** to provide such experiences, albeit optional, as part of an extended day or on a residential basis.

1.4.25 Assuming such an obligation indicates that the school maintains a duty of care for the students. This is because it is the school that is placing the students in these contexts, even where a third party is contracted to deliver the activity on behalf of the school. While this interpretation of the case law is offered here, school staff are advised to **clarify with their employer's legal advisers** whether they take a different view, and to agree in what circumstances activities outside the curriculum are deemed to be an 'assumed duty to provide'.

1.4.26 Case law arising from the 'case in point', 1.4.28, sets out the following contexts where the school authority would not be held liable for any negligent act of an independent contractor, establishing a distinction between provision and responsibility for the students, ie:

where the school's duty is not to perform the relevant function but only to arrange for its performance.

1.4.27 For example, a school has no duty to provide transport for an event but chooses to arrange it for the convenience of the students, in which case, the transport is arranged but the students remain the responsibility of the school staff.

The defaults of an independent contractor providing extracurricular activities outside school hours, such as school trips in the holidays.

This can be interpreted as follows. Where a school allows an independent provider to organise sports activities on its site, or allows advertising for the independent activity through school channels, but has no direct involvement in the activity, it is likely that the independent provider would have the responsibility for the children rather than the school. This must be clearly set out and agreed.

Not liable for the negligence of those to whom no control over the child has been delegated, such as bus drivers or theatres, zoos or museums to which the children may be taken by school staff in school hours.

Under occupiers' liability law and other relevant statute, the provider would have an independent responsibility unless the school had made an arrangement for the bus driver or zookeeper (for example) to take direct responsibility for pupils on behalf of the school.

A case in point

1.4.28   **Woodland versus (1) Swimming Teachers Association, (2) Stopford (trading as Direct Swimming Services), (3) Maxwell, (4) Essex County Council and (5) Basildon District Council, 2011:**

In July 2000, a student from an LA school attended a swimming lesson that had been contracted out to a swimming services company [2]. The company hired a pool and provided a qualified swimming teacher and lifeguard [3]. The class teacher and district council swimming staff were also present on poolside.

During the lesson, the student was found 'hanging vertically in the water'. Poolside resuscitation was administered, but the student suffered permanent brain damage. Other students reported seeing the injured student in distress, but any further details or facts were debated.

The claim made was one of inadequate duty of care, and was brought against several of the parties involved.

The school employer, Essex County Council, claimed that duty of care had been delegated to the swimming provider, once the lesson had begun, and that they had no liability for the actions of the commercial company.

The student's father claimed that Essex County Council maintained a **'non-delegable duty of care'** – ie that they remained legally responsible for the outcome despite outsourcing the tuition and water safety to a separate commercial party.

The High Court ruling in 2011 confirmed that Essex County Council was not liable, stating that:

> *Where a school must take their pupils to other premises, they discharge their duty of care if they know the premises and if the premises are apparently safe, and if they know that the premises are staffed by competent and careful persons.*

This outcome clearly went **against** the long-held common understanding and practice that schools could not transfer their duty of care. In 2012, the Appeal Court upheld the High Court's decision, and it seemed as though this would be the new standard to work to when using external organisations to provide activities off site. However, in 2013, the issue was taken to the Supreme Court, where these original decisions were overturned.

The outcome confirmed that the **school authority** (an LA, a board of governors or a trust) **is responsible in situations where a duty is provided through a third party, whether on or off site**.

This responsibility remains with the school authority because the external agent contracted to provide the service does this **on behalf of** the school authority. Therefore, duty of care remains with the school authority and **cannot be delegated**:

> The **work required to perform such a duty may well be delegable... But the duty itself remains the defendant's**. *Its delegation makes no difference to his legal responsibility for the proper performance of a duty which is in law his own.*

This ruling brings the application of duty of care for schools back to the long understood standard. As the highest court in the land has made **this decision, it is now common law**. It impacts on all maintained schools, including LA schools, academies and free schools. Fee-paying schools perform similar functions under contract rather than common law.

In summary:

- **LAs, governors or trusts remain liable for any negligent act relating to their services and programmes, including where these are contracted out to a third party** to use technical expertise not necessarily available within the direct workforce of school staff.

- Where the external agency is found to be negligent, the school authority would be in breach of its duty of care to the students.

- The school must continuously **monitor and manage** that whoever carries out duties on its behalf does so without fault, and not simply rely on pre-check competence.

Based on summary of case by Peter Whitlam, afPE Project Manager for Health and Safety, November 2013.

Negligence claims

1.4.29   When civil claims for compensation alleging negligence are made, the required level of proof is that of **'probability'** that the act or omission would probably and foreseeably lead to harm. This standard of the likelihood is much higher than simply 'likely' to occur.

1.4.30   Defences against such charges include the following principles:

1.4.31   **Vicarious liability:** An employer is responsible for the acts of an employee when they are acting in the proper course of their employment. This would apply to anything undertaken as part of any contractual or sanctioned voluntary duty. For this reason, those working in PESSPA are expected to:

- work within guidelines and policies laid down by the employer

- obtain permission for particular activities

- follow regular and approved practice

- maintain an up-to-date awareness of the subject through professional learning (PL).

1.4.32   **Contributory negligence**: Any act or omission by the injured party seeking compensation that contributes to the injury may be taken into account when compensation is determined. The level of compensation may then be reduced according to the claimant's percentage of responsibility for contributing to the harm. In these cases, the younger the person harmed, the less likely they are to be considered to have an awareness of their contribution to the situation. A similar decision is likely to be made for those with some form of learning difficulty.

1.4.33 **Voluntary assumption of risk**: This principle allows the court to provide no compensation to a claimant whatsoever. It is based on the premise that the participant knowingly **accepts the possibility of harm** through taking part in an activity within the laws, spirit or common practice of that activity. It does not allow for the infliction of harm outside the laws and spirit of a game so any intentional or reckless infliction of injury cannot be defended under this principle.

1.4.34 This is a concept that more commonly applies to adult participation in sport, or may apply to voluntary participation by young people but only in very specific circumstances. It would be difficult to apply this defence to a student in physical education lessons as this participation is part of a prescribed curriculum. It would also be difficult to show that young people were fully cognisant of the risks involved and legally competent to accept them.

1.4.35 The only consent to injury parents have to accept on behalf of their children is that which arises as a result of an unforeseeable accident.

1.4.36 Ongoing preparation for defending any allegations of negligence might include maintaining a 'portfolio' of support information. This could comprise documents including:

- policy and guidelines
- schemes of work and lesson plans
- registers of attendance (detailed enough to illustrate what content would have been missed through non-attendance)
- assessment records
- medical information
- risk assessments
- equipment maintenance reports
- minutes of meetings highlighting discussion of safe practice
- professional learning records
- emergency action procedures
- special educational needs and disabilities (SEND) register
- out-of-hours club registers
- accident management and reporting systems and analysis
- health and safety audits
- school procedures – fire safety/first aid/evacuation/critical incidents.

 FAQ

1.4.37 **What is meant by 'a duty of care'? Can I be blamed (sued) if a child is hurt while they are my responsibility?**

Everyone has a duty of care to ensure the safety and well-being of others. School staff, as professionals, are deemed to have a professional responsibility, and should display a duty of care of a standard equal to that of a competent person in the same position as them within their profession.

Physical education teachers are considered to possess specialist skills in the profession of teaching, and individuals would therefore be judged against the standards expected of a competent person working at the same level as a physical education teacher. Breaching their duty of care could arise if they were judged to be failing to work at the standard typical of others in that role within the profession, ie failing to display regular and approved practice associated with that position within the profession.

Within a teaching situation, where these standards were not met, and as a result, damage occurred (eg an injury in PESSPA), and this was reasonably foreseeable, then an allegation of negligence on the teacher's part could apply.

Foreseeability could be in relation to the teacher's decision to use within a lesson an item of equipment known to be damaged. If the use of the equipment resulted in an injury occurring, this could have been foreseeable.

Within education, allegations of negligence are very rare in relation to the number of students participating in PESSPA sessions. Significant levels of protection exist against allegations of negligence by staff as employees.

 ## Case law

1.4.38   **Blairford versus CRS Adventures Ltd (2012):**

A teacher took a group of students to an outdoor centre for a week of adventure experiences. On the last evening, a series of fun activities was held. One activity involved throwing a wellington boot backwards through their legs – a game called 'welly wanging'. The teacher joined in and threw the boot, but as he let go, he fell forwards on to his head, suffering a catastrophic spinal fracture.

He claimed damages, alleging that the game was unsafe and his injury foreseeable in throwing the boot in that way. He also claimed that a suitable risk assessment had not been carried out. The adventure centre staff denied the allegations, claiming that reasonable risk assessments had been carried out, that the likelihood of injury in the way the teacher was injured was not foreseeable, and that there had been no previous injuries in 'welly wanging' games.

*The claim was dismissed on the basis that this type of injury **was not foreseeable**, it was simply a freak but tragic accident. The adventure centre staff were not bound to assess the risk of an injury occurring, only a risk of serious injury based on the specific circumstances.*

1.4.39   **Bolton versus Stone (1951) and Harrison versus Wirral MBC (2009):**

*These two cases also determined that, where it was foreseeable that someone may be injured by an activity but there was **no record of previous injuries** in the same circumstances (making the outcome **rare** rather than probable), there was no negligent liability.*

Chapter 1/Section 5: Policy and procedures

Introduction

1.5.1　Policy and established procedures provide order, and a secure learning and work environment for students and staff. Policy should be relevant to a school's particular circumstances and help to ensure that students feel safe, are safe, and learn how to be safe during any physical education, school sport and physical activity (PESSPA) session.

1.5.2　Schools **must** implement the **employer's policy** and requirements. These cannot be ignored, but school policy may add to an employer's requirements.

Why PESSPA policy and procedures are needed

1.5.3　Clear policy is useful within a school to enforce standards and expectations. For example, policy regarding acceptable clothing, footwear, jewellery and personal protective equipment can be set out in school communications such as a prospectus, newsletter, school website or in letters to parents.

1.5.4　When parents choose to send their children to the school, it is useful for them to know exactly what is required in PESSPA. Equally, when students arrive for PESSPA without the correct kit or equipment, the policy can be used to remind them and their parents about the requirements they 'signed up to'. Students might also become involved in influencing policy that directly affects them as part of learning about safety.

1.5.5　Policy and procedures are **likely to be requested** in the event of an accident or incident at a school as part of the portfolio of evidence required for any investigation.

1.5.6　Accidents happen occasionally in PESSPA. Many cannot be anticipated and arise from unforeseen circumstances. Some accidents could have been **foreseen**, and as such, lessons can be learnt from them, which can in turn inform future policy.

1.5.7　All accidents and incidents in PESSPA are **management** issues. Safe practice embeds the premise that effective management will be safe management.

1.5.8　When an accident, incident or 'near miss' occurs, **analysis** should consider not only the immediate causes but also the origin of the causes and whether or not **management systems (policy and procedures)** were sufficient. **See Table 2, page 24.**

Table 2: Analysing an accident or 'near miss'

Undesired event	Accident, incident, injury or 'near miss'.
Immediate causes	For example, improper technique, equipment not checked.
Origin of the causes	For example, lack of skill/competence, lack of supervision, inadequate forethought.
Real cause – insufficiencies in management systems	For example inadequate programme, policy or procedures; inadequate standards; lack of forward planning; inadequate risk assessment; a lack of monitoring of competence and application of procedures.

1.5.9 Such an analysis can lead to improvements in safety standards through upgrading **documented policy and procedures,** improving communication, conducting thorough risk assessments and by ensuring that all involved in teaching the PESSPA programme consistently apply safety standards. In essence, subject leaders should constantly ask, in relation to safety standards in PESSPA:

- **What do we say we do?**

- **Do we do what we say we do?**

 Case law

1.5.10 **R versus Leisure Connection Ltd (2013):**

A leisure centre operator was ordered to pay more than £190,000 in fines and costs after a seven-year-old girl drowned in a swimming pool during a public swimming session. The Health and Safety Executive (HSE) found serious failings with lifeguard cover.

*The HSE investigation concluded that the company involved had failed to ensure that sufficient, suitably positioned lifeguards were always on poolside duty to ensure the safety of pool users. The leisure centre was considered **not to be compliant with its own procedures**, and the procedures in place at the site were considered inadequate.*

Characteristics of PESSPA policy and procedures

1.5.11 **Case law** indicates that the policy and procedures should be:

- in written form
- specific to the school
- reasonably comprehensive
- regularly reviewed (typically annually)
- regularly communicated
- consistently applied by **all staff** contributing to the PESSPA programme.

1.5.12   Many **whole-school** policies, procedures and routines will be relevant to PESSPA, such as those for dealing with first aid and emergency situations. PESSPA staff should be responsible for ensuring that all aspects of PESSPA are adequately covered by policy and, where this is not the case, establish additional policy and procedures specific to PESSPA, referencing school policy where appropriate.

1.5.13   For example, the PESSPA policy may need to consider situations where PESSPA staff and students are working at the extremities of a large school site or where PESSPA activities are happening off site and/or outside normal lesson times. Staff may also need to identify whether the first aid policy adequately covers procedures for administering first aid at a PESSPA event held at a weekend or at another school.

1.5.14   Where concerns are identified about the scope of existing whole-school policy, the subject leader or teacher should discuss this with the leadership team, and produce additional relevant procedures.

1.5.15   Subject leaders need to know what requirements are imposed by the employer, and ensure that these are widely understood by all school and visiting staff contributing to the PESSPA programme. The employer must make available all school policy that impacts on PESSPA, and would expect the subject leader to monitor that it is applied.

Writing a policy

1.5.16   A policy should explain through an initial statement **why** a common understanding and consistent application of safety standards are important. All policy is deemed to be the policy of the governing body, and as such, the policy statement should be fully understood by the governing body, as well as the leadership team, school staff and visiting staff.

1.5.17   The policy statement should be supported by more **detailed guidance** about the procedures through which the policy is put into effective practice.

1.5.18   Subject leaders and school leadership teams may wish to review and possibly develop their existing documentation for PESSPA by drawing on the guidance in this resource, which is appropriate to their specific circumstances. Chapter 2 is particularly relevant as it provides guidance to support the safe teaching and management of PESSPA, and considers what staff need to know and understand about a wide range of PESSPA health and safety issues in order to fulfil their duty of care and establish a safe PESSPA programme. There is a strong focus on how to apply this knowledge to practical 'everyday' situations, which helps to clarify why common practices in PESSPA have become established as professional 'norms'.

 See Chapter 2, Section 1, page 64, for additional guidance.

1.5.19   All policy and supporting documentation relating to safe practice in PESSPA should be **dated** in order to aid a schedule of regular review.

1.5.20   Whenever health and safety procedures or practices are **amended**, the school has a duty to inform all those affected. This may be done verbally, pictorially and/or in writing, and a record kept detailing that this has happened.

An exemplar generic policy statement for PESSPA

1.5.21   Safe-practice standards, consistently applied by staff, students and other visitors across all aspects of the school's PESSPA programme, are important. The **purpose** of documented safe-practice standards in PESSPA is to:

- offer PESSPA within a well-managed, safe and educational context

- set out the responsibilities for health and safety in PESSPA at all levels

- establish common codes of practice for staff and students

- provide common administrative procedures

- ensure statutory and local requirements are followed, and other national guidelines, such as codes of practice, are considered

- ensure school health and safety policy and procedures adequately address the PESSPA context of working on and off site and outside normal lesson times

- aid the recording and reporting of accidents and incidents

- audit and achieve consistent safety standards.

1.5.22   The **outcomes** of establishing and applying safe-practice standards in PESSPA are to:

- enable students to participate in PESSPA that provides appropriate challenge with acceptable risk

- promote student learning about risk management, and their responsibility in this, in order for them to participate independently in physical activity later in life

- fulfil the provision of a broad, balanced and relevant curriculum for physical education through:

    - an environment that is safe for the activity
    - adequately supervised activities
    - the use of regular and approved practice
    - progressive stages of learning and challenge
    - building a system of advice and the practice of warning
    - the use of equipment for the purpose for which it was intended
    - provision of basic care in the event of an accident
    - the use of forethought and sound preparation
    - involvement of students in the process of risk management

- ensure clear management responsibilities and organisation provide for safe systems of work

- identify and provide for any professional learning needs the staff are likely to encounter in their work.

Communicating policy and procedures

1.5.23   The consistent application of safety standards is an essential aspect of maintaining a safe learning environment. **Regular discussion** between staff helps achieve such consistency.

1.5.24   Staff and departmental meetings are good contexts for the regular reporting and discussion of safe-practice standards and routines. Where meetings are minuted, this provides recorded evidence of such professional learning taking place. Safe practice should be a standing item on a staff or departmental meeting agenda so that concerns can be shared, clarification provided and instruction agreed.

1.5.25   Circulating minutes of staff meetings to the school leadership and governing body ensures that they are kept informed of professional learning relating to safe practice, provides a system for reporting concerns about health and safety, and confirms that school policy and procedures are being appropriately applied in the PESSPA context.

1.5.26   Information contained within records of such discussions may also be used as part of the portfolio of information requested in the case of an accident investigation.

 A case in point

1.5.27   **Inquest into student killed by polar bear, 2014:**

In August 2011, a 17-year old student was killed by a polar bear while on an adventure holiday with the British Schools Exploring Society (BSES). Four other members of the group were badly injured. In summing up the inquest, Sir David Steele said of this case: 'It was a remote possibility but not unforeseeable.'

The case can be analysed using the framework in Table 3 below.

Table 3: Analysing the incident, 2014

Undesired event	• A boy is killed by a polar bear. • Four others are seriously injured.
Immediate causes	• Rifle and flare gun failed to fire. • Warning tripwire had failed to go off.
Origin of the causes	• Rifles not checked and had been set up incorrectly. • Insufficient flares available. • Tripwires were found to be missing parts. • Inadequate maintenance of safety equipment. • Camp set-up was unsuitable – in a circle formation. • No guard or bear watch rota (not required by law but highly recommended). • Lack of forethought and consideration of the hazards/risks.
Real cause – insufficiencies in management systems	• Leaders ignored expert advice. • Failure to comply with standard practice. • Lack of frequently updated risk assessment by the group. • Lack of application of procedures.

The group knew the system was unsatisfactory because a team member had tripped the wire a few days before when he went to the toilet in the night, but it had not activated the alarm.

Bears had been seen in the area, and pack ice drifting close to shore increased the likelihood of their presence.

Recommendations were that tents should be in a line rather than a circle, to avoid a trespassing bear feeling trapped.

At the inquest, the parents reported that they had carefully examined a risk assessment document before the trip, and believed a number of safety procedures would be in place to protect the group.

It was suggested that the risk assessment outlined actions that were not actually followed through (**What do you say you do? Do you do what you say you do?**). It is the teacher's job to foresee what could happen, and to produce procedures that are followed to prevent accidents happening.

In this case, the organisers of the trip were cleared of neglect. While items of equipment were considered to be missing, the coroner at the inquest decided that a combination of reasons led to the fatal outcome, but that the organiser's failure was not seen as 'total or complete'. The analysis of the failings, however, is useful to highlight the importance of applying procedures thoroughly and systematically.

 FAQ

1.5.28   **I have recently started my first teaching job. There doesn't appear to be any health and safety policy available to look at. Should I ask to see one?**

Yes. Making you aware, and providing you with a copy, of the policy should be part of your induction programme, and you are required by law to read, understand and apply the policy. The school or physical education department is likely to have an additional policy that references information in the school policy, but that is more pertinent to a PESSPA context. This document should help you to plan safe and approved practices into your teaching.

 FAQ

1.5.29   **I have been asked to produce a physical education policy for my school. How should I go about this? Do you have a template to help me?**

The most important thing to remember when writing a physical education policy is that it must be specific to your school. There is no 'one size fits all'. However, the generic policy statement provided (1.5.21) can be adapted to set out the purpose and aim of your policy, and what you hope it will achieve. Having established this, you can use Chapter 2 of this resource to consider all the areas that your policy might cover. Table 6 in Chapter 2, Section 1, pages 64–67, can be used as a checklist to help you carry this out.

Chapter 1/Section 6: Risk assessment

Introduction

1.6.1 Risk is about the likelihood that a person may be harmed. The more frequent the exposure to uncontrolled high-risk situations, the higher the probability, or likelihood, of harm occurring.

1.6.2 Risk assessment (RA) is central to safe practice and is a judgement about whether a situation is safe within established practice and procedures, or whether additional precautions are required.

1.6.3 Under the terms of the Management of Health and Safety at Work Regulations 1999 (MHS Regs), employers have a duty to ensure periodic formal, **activity- or site-specific risk** assessments are carried out in the establishments for which they are responsible.

 See Chapter 1, Section 2, page 9, and Chapter 1, Section 3, page 14.

1.6.4 The Health and Safety Executive (HSE) has the power to **confirm** that risk assessments have been carried out, and instigate action against those organisations that fail to do so.

1.6.5 Written risk assessments for physical education, school sport and physical activity (PESSPA) should be available in all schools and physical education departments, and should be accessible to all who contribute to teaching the PESSPA programme. Individual staff should be informed of any significant risks requiring action, and advised as to how to manage the risk safely. Where such information is not provided, staff are recommended to ask about the contents of the written risk assessment.

1.6.6 All risk assessments need to be **specific** to the school, reasonably detailed and **reviewed regularly**. A 'regular' review is frequently interpreted as annually. The MHS Regs 1999 use the term 'periodic', but the HSE is keen to point out that there is no legal requirement to **redo** risk assessments annually, and that they only need to be reviewed if there have been significant changes (eg learning from an accident or injury). While a 'typical' practice, they advise avoiding a blanket annual review that is in danger of becoming a 'box-ticking' exercise, and recommend proper consideration as and when circumstances change. In ensuring that risk assessments are kept up to date, schools are recommended to identify a review date for their risk assessment that is typically annual, but to be mindful of the advice from the HSE regarding 'box ticking'.

1.6.7   It is preferable that all PESSPA staff, or as many as possible, are involved in the process of completing the written risk assessment as this helps establish consistent safety standards and safe practices.

1.6.8   Risk assessment in PESSPA involves:

- deciding what to assess in terms of risk (eg the PESSPA programme as a whole or each activity, facility or special event)

- identifying the hazards that could cause harm

- judging whether or not existing safety precautions are sufficient to provide a safe learning environment

- deciding whether there is any significant risk of harm remaining

- identifying who could be harmed by the significant risks

- minimising any remaining significant risk of harm to an acceptable and reasonable level by some additional form of corrective action or control measure

- recording the findings of the risk assessment and implementing them

- informing participants, staff and any other relevant people about any changes (additional controls and procedures) that have been implemented to make any situation safer

- reviewing and updating the risk assessment regularly.

1.6.9   The case law outlined below (Edwards versus the National Coal Board) is still cited as that which sets out the ruling in respect of assessing whether the degree of risk is **'reasonably practicable'**. In this case, the 'sacrifice' or costs are not something that an individual employee can use as a reason for not addressing the risk, but applies more at organisational level, ie the cost to the school as a whole, and should be 'weighed up' accordingly.

 Case law

1.6.10   **Edwards versus National Coal Board (1949):**

This case set the ruling on **'reasonably practicable'** *as being a term narrower than 'physically possible'. The interpretation is a calculation of the degree of risk against the 'sacrifice' in terms of time, trouble (effort) and financial cost involved in averting the risk. Where this is clearly disproportionate, with the* **risk being insignificant in relation to the 'sacrifice' (cost)***, there is no requirement to address the risk.*

1.6.11   In some cases, voluntary aided schools, academies and foundation schools 'buy in' to local authority (LA) insurance provision (where this is still available), and consequently comply with LA health and safety regulation, but this does **not abnegate their responsibility** for maintaining up-to-date policy. Academies that buy into the risk protection arrangement (RPA) (see Chapter 2, Section 3, page 86) can source risk management advice and training through this plan.

1.6.12   Dependent on the type of school (see **Chapter 1, Section 3, page 13**), on a day-to-day basis, responsibility for health and safety is usually delegated from the employer to head teachers. The head teacher delegates to appropriate staff members the tasks to examine what might cause harm to students, staff and visitors during all activities organised by the school, and to put in place measures to mitigate and manage the potential for such harm.

1.6.13   Under the terms of the Regulatory Reform (Fire Safety) Order 2005, schools are obliged to include a specific, written **fire risk assessment** within their overall risk management provision. The fundamental purpose is to establish measures to minimise the risk of fire and ensure safe evacuation in the event of fire. Within a physical-education-specific risk assessment, fire-related issues also need to be addressed, including:

- the identification of escape routes from designated working areas
- safety procedures relating to enclosed areas from which there is no escape (eg storerooms)
- the safe storage of flammable items (eg mats)
- the clear display of, and easy access to, fire extinguishers
- contingency planning for any emergency evacuation in cold or inclement weather.

 For more information on the Regulatory Reform (Fire Safety) Order 2005, see http://goo.gl/AuH32h

 Also see Fire safety in Chapter 2, Section 13, page 226.

 ## Case law

1.6.14   **R versus Chargot and Ruttle Contracting (2008):**

*This case reinforced the principle that the HSE focuses on the **leadership** in relation to safety standards and accidents. The duties set out in the Health and Safety at Work etc Act 1974 were described by the judge as 'responsibilities imposed on employers as results to be achieved or prevented' and therefore cannot be ignored or dismissed. It also confirmed the **common sense standard** of a reasonable response to health and safety concerns as being 'a material risk to health and safety which any reasonable person would appreciate and take steps to guard against'.*

Different types of risk assessment

1.6.15 **Dynamic risk assessment** (sometimes referred to as ongoing or continuous risk assessment) is carried out before an activity or event takes places and while it is taking place, identifying and responding to unforeseen issues, such as an unsafe response to a task, sudden illness, changes in climatic conditions or ineffective officiating.

1.6.16 This type of risk assessment is based on a teacher's **expertise** and previous experience, and can also be used to inform future planning. It is **unwritten** and represents an ongoing process where staff remain vigilant, constantly reassessing the precautions they have put in place. Planning should include evidence of dynamic risk assessment such as **forethought**, and anticipation of what could go wrong and how it might be managed.

1.6.17 Students should also be taught to be vigilant for risk during activity, and to report any concerns.

 See Chapter 3, Section 3.

1.6.18 **Generic risk assessment** – This considers the general principles that apply to an activity wherever it may take place. A generic risk assessment is usually the starting point and is generally provided in a **written format** by the employer, governing body of sport or similar organisation. Generic guidance needs to be amended to make it applicable to a school's particular circumstances, and will be used to inform both ongoing risk assessment and the written risk assessment for the site or activity.

1.6.19 **Site- or activity-specific risk assessment** is usually carried out for each location, facility or activity, and is specific to the venue, type of event and people involved. This is usually in a **written format** and regularly reviewed.

 See Table 4, page 36, in this section.

1.6.20 **Near misses** – These are incidents that have occurred in a PESSPA lesson or session, in which an individual could have suffered harm but fortuitously did not. Near misses should be recorded and analysed. Staff should look for any trends that might indicate unsafe practice or procedures, and use these to instigate a change in practice and inform future risk assessment.

1.6.21 **Where any staff member is not confident in their ability to carry out the types of risk assessment processes detailed above, they should consult their leadership team for guidance and any additional professional learning in this area.**

Case law

1.6.22 **R versus Porter (2008):**

*A young child fell down some school steps. The Court of Appeal dismissed the allegation of negligence by distinguishing between **real risk and fanciful or hypothetical risk**. One of the criteria for establishing whether real risk exists is whether there is evidence of similar accidents in normal circumstances. No history of accidents in the same context is a strong indicator that real risk is manageable.*

Carrying out a written risk assessment

1.6.23 Risk assessments are most effectively carried out:

- as a team exercise using collective expertise

- in or around the facility/location in which the activity is planned to take place

- referring to **existing documentation**, procedures and practice, and establishing whether any additional precautions are necessary over and above those currently in place.

1.6.24 All risks should be evaluated during the risk assessment and an **informed judgement** made about whether an identified hazard is capable of causing harm or injury in some way.

1.6.25 Findings should be **recorded** as the risk assessment is carried out. There is no set format for a formal written risk assessment. The statutory requirements are that a risk assessment document should:

- demonstrate that the assessment has been carried out

- identify any significant risks

- identify who is affected by them

- identify what action is to be taken to reduce risk to an acceptable level.

1.6.26 Risks can be categorised simply as **safe or unsafe**, based on using one's professional judgement. Some organisations may prefer the slightly expanded form of high, medium or low risk. It is not necessary to rate risks in any more complex manner than these. Staff should check with their employer what method of risk rating and recording they wish to be used.

1.6.27 The **level of risk** in a particular environment or setting is determined by a number of contextual and organisational features, including the:

- extent of unpredictability in the task, event or activity

- speed of decision making required to stay safe

- complexity of the task or activity

- severity of any potential injury, should things go wrong.

1.6.28   All risks should be identified. Those felt to be low or medium risks should be **monitored** to ensure that they do not develop into significant risks. Those already identified as high risk or unsafe require control measures to be put in place to manage them.

1.6.29   Written risk assessments should be **reviewed** on a regular basis (see 1.6.6 in this section), typically annually but also following a near miss or injury, or when circumstances change. The date of review should be indicated and the report signed off by the person(s) responsible.

1.6.30   All staff should know the location of and read the written risk assessments. It is increasingly common for schools to require all staff to sign to confirm they have read the risk assessments and all other safety-related documentation.

Case law

1.6.31   **Uren versus (1) Corporate Leisure (UK) Ltd, (2) Ministry of Defence (2013):**

An RAF technician sustained catastrophic injuries while taking part in recreational games organised at an RAF base. One of the games involved participants entering a shallow pool of water, collecting a floating toy and dropping it into a bucket. The man entered the pool head first, the same way as many others, but he went in at a steep angle and broke his neck.

He alleged the game carried an unacceptable risk of injury to participants and that there had been insufficient risk assessments to highlight the risk of serious injury. The response from the organisers was that the risk of serious injury was very slight and that his injury was caused by a freak accident.

The High Court rejected the argument that the risk of serious injury was slight. They suggested that a proper appraisal of the game before it began would have established the possibility, and risks, of participants entering the pool head first. Steps could then have been taken to avoid that risk. Prohibiting head first entry would not have spoiled the game but would have prevented the accident. The court concluded that this accident arose from the failure of organisers to carry out 'a considered and conscientious risk assessment' of the recreational games.

Completing a risk assessment for PESSPA

1.6.32   Table 4 on the pages that follow provides a typical range of **generic issues** that might be helpful in compiling PESSPA risk assessments.

1.6.33   The risk assessment (RA) form should be adapted to meet the specific requirements of the school.

- In column 1, use the chapter and additional references to find information to help complete the RA. The questions raised are not an exhaustive list. Add any school-specific additional questions to this column.

- Indicate in column 2 where the question raised in column 1 has already been actioned appropriately and is therefore considered **'safe'**.

- Indicate in column 3 where the question raised in column 1 still requires action to be taken. If this is the case, the situation is considered **'unsafe'**.

- Where action is required, indicate in column 4 who may be harmed by the identified risk: students, staff and/or visitors. It could affect more than one group.

- In column 5, list the action needed, over and above what is already in place, to reduce the risk to acceptable levels.

- Column 6 should be dated and signed when appropriate action has been taken to make the issue safe.

Table 4: Exemplar risk assessment form for PESSPA

1	2	3	4	5	6
PESSPA Issues	Appropriate Action Taken (Safe)	Appropriate Action Required (Unsafe)	Who is Affected (Students Staff Visitors)	Appropriate Action Needed to Reduce Risk to Acceptable Levels	Action Taken (Date and Sign)
Policy and procedures (**Chapter 1, Section 5**) • Are all procedures monitored adequately?					
Competence, qualifications and professional learning (Chapter 2, Section 2) • Do staff feel confident/competent/ have adequate qualifications and experience to fulfil their teaching commitments safely? • Has the teaching and discipline capability of all staff been checked? • Does anyone require some form of professional learning or support for reasons of safe teaching? • Do all staff know their role and responsibilities?					
Insurance (Chapter 2, Section 3) • Do all adults teaching groups have appropriate insurance cover where necessary?					

(continued)

1	2	3	4	5	6
PESSPA Issues	Appropriate Action Taken (Safe)	Appropriate Action Required (Unsafe)	Who is Affected (Students Staff Visitors)	Appropriate Action Needed to Reduce Risk to Acceptable Levels	Action Taken (Date and Sign)
Safeguarding (Chapter 2, Section 4) • Have disclosure certificates been seen for all support staff? • Are safeguarding procedures and training in place? • Does the play schedule allow appropriate activity/recovery periods? • Are rehydration/sun protection planned for? • Are overplay/ overtraining implications checked/known?					
Programme management (Chapter 2, Section 5) • Is a register check taken for every session/lesson in secondary and where applicable in primary? • Have extreme weather conditions been considered and contingency arrangements put in place?					
Sports fixtures, festivals, tours and club links (Chapter 2, Section 6) • Has the head teacher been made aware of/approved all activities offered? • Has preparation for off-site visit requirements been completed – lists, first aid etc? *(For an off-site RA template, see 1.6.35 in this section.)*					

(continued)

1	2	3	4	5	6
PESSPA Issues	**Appropriate Action Taken** (Safe)	**Appropriate Action Required** (Unsafe)	**Who is Affected** (Students Staff Visitors)	**Appropriate Action Needed to Reduce Risk to Acceptable Levels**	**Action Taken** (Date and Sign)
Parental consent (Chapter 2, Section 7) • Have parents been informed of any off-site visits and activities, and any necessary permission/consent obtained?					
Group Management (Chapter 2, Section 8) • Are group numbers always known/checked? • Are group sizes and teacher:student ratios always safe? • Is staff supervision of students appropriate to their behaviour, age and development stage, and the facility layout? • Are there any times when additional supervision is required but not provided? • Are there any times when students are not supervised that give cause for concern? • Do staff have sufficient knowledge of individuals and groups they teach to maintain a safe situation? • Are there any control/discipline/ behaviour problems with any student/group and any adult teaching them that cause safety concerns?					

(continued)

1	2	3	4	5	6
PESSPA Issues	Appropriate Action Taken (Safe)	Appropriate Action Required (Unsafe)	Who is Affected (Students Staff Visitors)	Appropriate Action Needed to Reduce Risk to Acceptable Levels	Action Taken (Date and Sign)
• Is relevant information (including medical) always passed on to visiting staff before they teach a group? • Is the school policy on physical contact (supporting) and substantial access (one-to-one) known and applied effectively? • Do staff regularly scan or do head counts at the beginning/during/at the end of lessons? • Are group organisation/management procedures safe and consistently applied? • Are physical support and manual handling techniques known and applied, where appropriate? • Do staff know the limits of their involvement in games, practices and demonstrations involving students? • Are staff observation and analysis skills adequate? • Do all staff operate optimum teaching positions in relation to participants? • Is effective communication between the teacher and support staff evident?					

(continued)

1	2	3	4	5	6
PESSPA Issues	**Appropriate Action Taken** (Safe)	**Appropriate Action Required** (Unsafe)	**Who is Affected** (Students Staff Visitors)	**Appropriate Action Needed to Reduce Risk to Acceptable Levels**	**Action Taken** (Date and Sign)
Safe exercise practice (Chapter 2, Section 9) • Do lessons provide appropriate and effective warm-up/ cool-down? • Are staff confident that exercises used in activities are developmentally appropriate? • Is student-led warm-up monitored by staff?					
Clothing, footwear and personal effects (Chapter 2, Section 10) • Are staff clothing and personal effects appropriate for teaching PESSPA? • Are student clothing and footwear appropriate for each activity? • Is the policy on jewellery and other personal effects applied consistently?					
Personal protective equipment (Chapter 2, Section 11) • Is safety equipment/personal protective equipment (PPE) available and used where needed (eg shin pads)? • Are staff clear about school policy where students do not have the PPE required?					

(continued)

1	2	3	4	5	6
PESSPA Issues	Appropriate Action Taken (Safe)	Appropriate Action Required (Unsafe)	Who is Affected (Students Staff Visitors)	Appropriate Action Needed to Reduce Risk to Acceptable Levels	Action Taken (Date and Sign)
Equipment (Chapter 2, Section 12) • Is equipment used for the purpose for which it was designed? • Is all equipment in good condition and used safely, including electrical items? • Are goalposts/nets etc safe, secure and in good condition? • Is equipment suitable in size, type, weight and quality for the age, build and strength of students? • Have students been taught to carry, move, place and retrieve equipment safely? • Is supervision of the carrying/placing of equipment managed, where appropriate? • Do staff check equipment before use by participants? • Do staff regularly check equipment before use and report any faults found? • Is a system for reporting faults in place? • Is equipment easily accessed and safely stored? • Are routines for the collection, retrieval and changing of equipment known and applied by staff and students?					

(continued)

1	2	3	4	5	6
PESSPA Issues	**Appropriate Action Taken** (Safe)	**Appropriate Action Required** (Unsafe)	**Who is Affected** (Students Staff Visitors)	**Appropriate Action Needed to Reduce Risk to Acceptable Levels**	**Action Taken** (Date and Sign)
• Are there any other concerns about equipment handling, carrying or siting in any activity? • Is there an annual gymnastics, play and fitness equipment inspection check by a specialist company? • Is all required safety and rescue equipment present?					
Facilities (Chapter 2, Section 13) • Is the changing area safe (space, pegs, floor surface, supervision)? • Have safeguarding issues in relation to changing been addressed as far as practical (eg separate changing areas, away from windows)? • Is the route from the classroom/changing room to activity area safe, especially for young/disabled students? • Is access to each facility safely managed? • Are safety information notices evident, clearly positioned, effective, shared and applied? • Are emergency evacuation procedures known?					

(continued)

1	2	3	4	5	6
PESSPA Issues	Appropriate Action Taken (Safe)	Appropriate Action Required (Unsafe)	Who is Affected (Students Staff Visitors)	Appropriate Action Needed to Reduce Risk to Acceptable Levels	Action Taken (Date and Sign)
• Do emergency evacuation procedures take account of evacuation in inclement weather and when students have bare feet? • Is access to the facility safe (steps, doors, disability issues)? • Are fire exits clear, with emergency routes out passable? • Are fire extinguishers/notices etc present? • Are safety signs present, in correct locations and illuminated? • In case of emergency evacuation, are doors unlocked? • Is the first aid provision/system suitable for the facility/students etc? • Does the playing/work surface provide secure footing? • Is the work area an optimum size for the group/activity/ organisation? • Are there any obstructions (heating, columns, piano etc)? • Is the lighting safe and adequate for activities? • Does the location of windows cause sunlight/glare on to the work area?					

(continued)

1	2	3	4	5	6
PESSPA Issues	**Appropriate Action Taken** (Safe)	**Appropriate Action Required** (Unsafe)	**Who is Affected** (Students Staff Visitors)	**Appropriate Action Needed to Reduce Risk to Acceptable Levels**	**Action Taken** (Date and Sign)
• Do any other display and furniture items present obstacles? • Are the storage space, system and routines safe? • Are there any obvious entrapments? • Are there plastic/glass/stone/hole problems on pitches? • Are there any activity-specific safety concerns?					
Special educational needs and disabilities, and medical conditions (Chapter 2, Section 14) • Are student medical conditions known by any adult teaching an individual? • Are there any concerns about Equality Act requirements for access and involvement in PESSPA for those with cognitive, visual, hearing or motor impairment? • Are any individual care issues met? • Are students with visual, hearing, motor or cognitive impairment catered for appropriately to enable them to participate safely?					

(continued)

1	2	3	4	5	6
PESSPA Issues	Appropriate Action Taken (Safe)	Appropriate Action Required (Unsafe)	Who is Affected (Students Staff Visitors)	Appropriate Action Needed to Reduce Risk to Acceptable Levels	Action Taken (Date and Sign)
First aid (Chapter 2, Section 15) • Is first aid equipment provided, and are procedures and responsibilities known by staff and (where appropriate) students? • Are accident and emergency procedures to address potential incidents during lessons and visits set out, known and applied by all? • Can first aid support be summoned and provided quickly? • Are contingency plans to address potential incidents during lessons and visits set out, known and applied by all staff?					
Digital technology (Chapter 2, Section 16) • Is the policy on digital imagery known and applied, and have the required permissions been obtained?					

(continued)

1	2	3	4	5	6
PESSPA Issues	**Appropriate Action Taken** (Safe)	**Appropriate Action Required** (Unsafe)	**Who is Affected** (Students Staff Visitors)	**Appropriate Action Needed to Reduce Risk to Acceptable Levels**	**Action Taken** (Date and Sign)
Transport (Chapter 2, Section 17) <ul><li>Is movement to the work area safe and orderly?</li><li>Is a clear policy applied where any form of transport is used?</li><li>Are school vehicles checked for roadworthiness before use?</li><li>Is a reputable coach/taxi company used?</li><li>Are there clear procedures about the use of parents' cars?</li><li>Are embarkation points safe?</li><li>Are seat belts always used?</li><li>Are booster seats available where required?</li><li>Is there always a check on numbers leaving and returning to the transport?</li><li>Are driver requirements and responsibilities known and applied?</li><li>Is there an emergency contact system in place?</li><li>Are there any concerns about supervision while driving?</li></ul>					

(continued)

1	2	3	4	5	6
PESSPA Issues	Appropriate Action Taken (Safe)	Appropriate Action Required (Unsafe)	Who is Affected (Students Staff Visitors)	Appropriate Action Needed to Reduce Risk to Acceptable Levels	Action Taken (Date and Sign)
• Is there a procedure for dismissing students after an event away from school that is understood, accepted and applied by all staff, students and parents? • Are procedures in place in the event of a transport problem arising?					
Teaching safety: Promoting effective practice (Chapter 3) • Do the students know and safely apply PESSPA routines and procedures appropriate to their age/ability?					
Teaching safely: Activity-specific information (Chapter 4) • Are there any safety issues about participation in any specific activity?					

Risk assessment completed by: _____

Date: _____

Next planned review date: _____

Risk assessment for off-site activities

1.6.34   An exemplar RA template and information about issues to consider when carrying out an RA for **off-site fixtures, centrally organised events and sports tours** are set out below.

> **Table 11 –** Chapter 2, Section 6, page 132 – **can also be used to support the questions raised in this off-site RA template.**

Exemplar risk assessment form for off-site school sport fixtures and events

1.6.35   The RA form should be adapted to meet the specific requirements of the school.

- In column 1, use the chapter and additional references to find information to help complete the RA. The questions raised are not an exhaustive list. Add any school-specific additional questions to this column.
- Indicate in column 2 where the question raised in column 1 has already been actioned appropriately and is therefore considered **'safe'**.
- Indicate in column 3 where the question raised in column 1 still requires action to be taken. If this is the case, the situation is considered **'unsafe'**.
- Where action is required, indicate in column 4 who may be harmed by the identified risk: students, staff and/or visitors. It could affect more than one group.
- In column 5, list the action needed, over and above what is already in place, to reduce the risk to acceptable levels.
- Column 6 should be dated and signed when appropriate action has been taken to make the issue safe.

Table 5: Exemplar risk assessment form for off-site school sport fixtures and events

1	2	3	4	5	6
Off-site Issues	**Appropriate Action Taken** (Safe)	**Appropriate Action Required** (Unsafe)	**Who is affected?** (Students Staff Visitors)	**Appropriate Action Needed to Reduce Risk to Acceptable Levels**	**Action Taken** (Date and Sign)
Pre-event • Has the head teacher approved the fixtures programme or event? • Is approval needed from the governors or other employer authority? • Have all paperwork or online approval forms been completed and submitted?					

(continued)

1	2	3	4	5	6
Off-site Issues	**Appropriate Action Taken** (Safe)	**Appropriate Action Required** (Unsafe)	**Who is affected?** (Students Staff Visitors)	**Appropriate Action Needed to Reduce Risk to Acceptable Levels**	**Action Taken** (Date and Sign)
• Are school policy and procedures for taking groups off site known and applied? • Has any additional insurance been obtained if needed? • Are consent forms required? If so, have they been obtained? • Is there a procedure for non-returned consent forms? • Where required, have expiry dates of passports been checked to allow for sufficient time before expiry as set by the country to be visited? • Are parents aware of the venue address, itinerary, programme, particular needs and conditions, insurance provision and emergency contact system (eg a 'telephone tree')? • Are staffing levels sufficient for supervision and officiating? • Do staff know their roles and responsibilities? • Do staff have adequate group-management and leadership skills and knowledge of the group (eg for students with SEND)?					

(continued)

1	2	3	4	5	6
Off-site Issues	**Appropriate Action Taken** (Safe)	**Appropriate Action Required** (Unsafe)	**Who is affected?** (Students Staff Visitors)	**Appropriate Action Needed to Reduce Risk to Acceptable Levels**	**Action Taken** (Date and Sign)
• Do staff have any of the specific skills required (eg swimming, adventure activities)? • Have student size, experience and ability been considered in the selection process? • Do staff:student ratios reflect the needs of the students? • Is a group register available? Has it been taken to the event? • Are medical backgrounds known by the staff involved? • Are any reciprocal arrangements with the host school clarified/known? • Has contingency planning been thought through and communicated? • Have the school's crisis-management plan requirements been taken into account? • Has a pre-event visit been made to the venue? • Has a venue RA been received from the event host, or completed during the pre-event visit, and taken into account?					

(continued)

	1	2	3	4	5	6
	Off-site Issues	**Appropriate Action Taken** (Safe)	**Appropriate Action Required** (Unsafe)	**Who is affected?** (Students Staff Visitors)	**Appropriate Action Needed to Reduce Risk to Acceptable Levels**	**Action Taken** (Date and Sign)
	• Have safeguarding issues been checked where required (eg centre staff, host families)? • Are first aid arrangements and responsibilities at the event known and understood, including knowledge of dealing with incidents of concussion? • Have any injections required prior to a trip been explained and completed? • Has a student code of conduct specific to the type of trip been developed and communicated? • Are students prepared for the event/trip physically, emotionally and behaviourally?					
	Assembly • Is it a continuous duty of care, or broken where parents take responsibility for the journey? Is there clarity about where this duty begins/ends? • Have parents been made fully aware of meeting times and what to do if they miss the transport?					

(continued)

1	2	3	4	5	6
Off-site Issues	**Appropriate Action Taken** (Safe)	**Appropriate Action Required** (Unsafe)	**Who is affected?** (Students Staff Visitors)	**Appropriate Action Needed to Reduce Risk to Acceptable Levels**	**Action Taken** (Date and Sign)
• Has a register been taken and a corresponding register left at school? • Have numbers in the group been checked at departure and during the journey? • Has kit/footwear been checked? • Have medication and other personal needs been checked? • Do relevant students understand their own responsibility to administer their required medication, where appropriate? • Is emergency contact information to hand during the journey? • Do the students know and apply the school's code of conduct? • Are mobile phones available to use in an emergency? • Have large groups been subdivided into smaller groups, with a designated adult responsible for each subgroup? • Where required, have methods for supervising groups at airport, ferry or train terminals been decided?					

(continued)

1	2	3	4	5	6
Off-site Issues	Appropriate Action Taken (Safe)	Appropriate Action Required (Unsafe)	Who is affected? (Students Staff Visitors)	Appropriate Action Needed to Reduce Risk to Acceptable Levels	Action Taken (Date and Sign)
Outward and return journeys • Does the form of transport chosen meet legal and employer requirements, including volunteer cars? • Where required, have international driving requirements been considered? • Has it been decided whether the driver will supervise and drive, or drive only with additional staff to supervise? • Are additional drivers required? • Has the driver carried out a vehicle check? • Is a first aid kit available, and are arrangements for administering first aid known? • Are the register and head count consistent before setting out on journeys, including after any break during the journey? • Are arrangements in place to manage journey breaks (eg motorway service areas)? • Has it been decided what information might be carried by students in case of separation from the main group?					

(continued)

1	2	3	4	5	6
Off-site Issues	**Appropriate Action Taken** (Safe)	**Appropriate Action Required** (Unsafe)	**Who is affected?** (Students Staff Visitors)	**Appropriate Action Needed to Reduce Risk to Acceptable Levels**	**Action Taken** (Date and Sign)
• Are embarkation and disembarkation points safe? • Is contingency action planned in the event of illness or incident on the journey? • Are the emergency action plan and critical incident arrangements known? • Are arrangements in place if parents are delayed in collecting their children? • Are arrangements in place to alert parents of any delay? • Has the anticipated dispersal time been communicated to parents?					
Venue/competition • Has the venue/facility been risk assessed by the home team/organiser/yourself and informed this RA? • Are there any group or activity management issues (eg one member of staff with two teams/officiating and supervising)? • Is acceptable behaviour assured? • Are periodic head counts carried out? • Is there equality in size/experience/ confidence between teams?					

(continued)

1	2	3	4	5	6
Off-site Issues	Appropriate Action Taken (Safe)	Appropriate Action Required (Unsafe)	Who is affected? (Students Staff Visitors)	Appropriate Action Needed to Reduce Risk to Acceptable Levels	Action Taken (Date and Sign)
• Are kit and footwear requirements appropriate to the weather/playing surface, and consistently applied by all? • If participants need to change at the event, are facilities and supervision appropriate? • Have personal effects been removed for the competition? • Is relevant PPE worn (eg pads/helmets/mouth guards)? • Has the equipment been checked before use as part of the host school RA and agreed as safe by users? • Does the programme allow sufficient rest/recovery periods? • Is the total playing time within the capability of the students involved? • Are officials competent/qualified? • Are young sports leaders supervised by competent staff? • Have consent arrangements for any photography been obtained?					

(continued)

1	2	3	4	5	6
Off-site Issues	**Appropriate Action Taken** (Safe)	**Appropriate Action Required** (Unsafe)	**Who is affected?** (Students Staff Visitors)	**Appropriate Action Needed to Reduce Risk to Acceptable Levels**	**Action Taken** (Date and Sign)
• Have first aid cover/reciprocal arrangements with the host been confirmed (eg in relation to first aid, supervision, taking pupils to hospital, staff sickness)? • Is the emergency action plan clear, and has it been communicated to all staff involved and to students? • Have weather conditions been considered (sun protection/rehydration/ storms/other seasonal considerations), and contingency plans communicated?					
Post-event evaluation • Are there any near misses/incidents to review? • Have injuries been recorded and the outcome followed up? • Can any improvements be made for the next event? • Is any feedback necessary to head teacher (HT)/subject leader (SL)/staff/activity leaders/students/ parents? • Are any adjustments to the RA necessary to inform future planning?					

RA completed by: _____

Date: _____

Next planned review date: _____

 These templates are available to download from www.pesafepractice.com

 ## Case law

1.6.36   **Liverpool City Council versus the Adelphi Hotel (2010):**

*A hotel guest went swimming in the hotel pool and drowned. There was no lifeguard present. The hotel had carried out an RA seven years before that identified the risk of drowning but had not determined that lifeguard supervision was necessary. A breach of section 3(1) of the Health and Safety Act was found – **failing to ensure a customer's safety**. The hotel was fined £65,000 plus costs.*

Reporting and communicating risk

1.6.37   All staff **must report any concerns** about hazards of which they are aware to the appropriate person in school. Schools have different arrangements for such reporting requirements. It is advised that an individual teacher makes a written note/email copy of any concern reported and dates the note in case there should be a need to provide evidence that this statutory action was carried out.

1.6.38   Any identified risks should be communicated to all staff and, where appropriate, to students. Whenever any amendments to procedures or practices are made as a result of the assessments of risks, the school has a duty to inform all those affected. This can be done verbally, in writing, and/or through diagrams and pictures.

Chapter 1/Section 7: Risk management

Understanding risk management

1.7.1   Everyday living and working present potential risks, but these risks are managed by adopting strategies learnt from a range of experiences. Staff have a responsibility to employ methods to control and manage risk as part of good teaching and management.

1.7.2   Establishing and maintaining a safe working environment is something that all staff delivering or teaching physical education, school sport and physical activity (PESSPA) need to aim to achieve, and is a statutory requirement of the **Teachers' Standards** (see Chapter 2, Section 2, page 73), and of Level 2 coaching qualifications.

1.7.3   Figure 3 shows how the likelihood of injury might be anticipated as one progresses along the continuum from a totally safe situation to one that is considered dangerous.

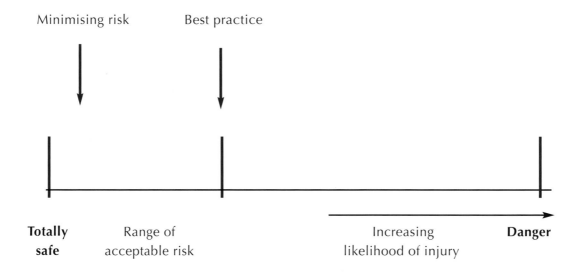

Figure 3: Managing risk

Whitlam, P. (2004) *Case Law in Physical Education*. Leeds: afPE/Coachwise Ltd. ISBN:1-902523-77-6.

1.7.4   Thorough planning and preparation of their PESSPA sessions will help staff to anticipate the level of **potential risk**, and they should proceed with the session only when the level is acceptable. An activity may be extremely challenging on the continuum in Figure 3, but planning and effective management will help maintain a safe learning environment.

 See Chapter 1, Section 8: Planning for safe practice, page 61.

1.7.5   Trying to eradicate all risk in PESSPA in order to achieve a 'totally safe' PESSPA environment (as suggested on the left of the diagram) is not only unrealistic, but could also result in sessions that present little challenge to students. This may limit the level of work expected of students and hamper their progress. Low-risk teaching is usually demonstrated by individuals who lack competence, and therefore confidence, in managing risk.

Case law

1.7.6   **Flint versus Cornwall Academies Trust (2015):**

A 10-year-old student was injured during a race where two teams were to jump over stools. As the student jumped, one of her legs caught the stool, resulting in her tripping and being injured.

The student alleged that the lesson was inadequately devised, that the risks of the activity were inadequately assessed, that the lesson was inadequately supervised, and that safety matting – known as 'crash mats' – was not provided.

The defendant argued that, had crash mats been provided, they would have created a tripping hazard thus increasing the risk of injury, and if the stools had been placed on them, there would have been a risk of the stools slipping. It was demonstrated that appropriate risk assessments for gymnastics, general sports and physical education had been carried out, that equipment is checked annually, the sports hall has an annual certificate of safety inspection, and the teacher supervising the lesson was fully qualified.

The judge accepted that the defendant had taken all reasonable steps to devise and supervise the lesson safely, despite not having carried out a formal risk assessment of the specific activity. The claim was dismissed.

1.7.7   The Royal Society for the Prevention of Accidents (ROSPA) – www.rospa.com – offers a sensible measure of the level of safety required, as that which is **'as safe as necessary, not as safe as possible'**. Figure 3, page 58, shows how 'best practice' involves working at the upper end of a range of acceptable risk that can enable students to work with an appropriate level of challenge and motivation, and assist their progress.

1.7.8   At Key Stage 1, the expectation of the National Curriculum (NC) in England is that pupils should be able to engage in physical activities 'in a range of increasingly challenging situations' (Department for Education [DfE] [2013] 'The national curriculum in England: Key stages 1 and 2 framework document: Physical Education' [pages 198–200]). This reinforces that challenge is an essential element of making learning fun, exciting and more likely to result in students progressing.

For more information on the National curriculum in England: Physical education programmes of study, see https://goo.gl/czlX2y

1.7.9   When students are not challenged sufficiently, they are more likely to struggle to stay on task, and a decline in standards of behaviour can result, which might in itself lead to a situation becoming less safe.

Risk-benefit analysis

1.7.10   Risk-benefit analysis is a comparison of the level of risk against the benefits. It aims to balance acceptable risk with appropriate challenge, and in doing so, considers whether the benefits of participation outweigh the likelihood of harm occurring.

1.7.11   If the risk is equal to or outweighs the benefits, the activity/experience or situation should be considered 'high risk' and should not be undertaken. It might be possible to adapt the activity/experience or situation in order to reduce the level of risk while retaining the same or similar benefits and still setting an appropriate level of challenge.

1.7.12   Staff need to determine, through ongoing observation and risk assessment, when an activity or task is becoming unsafe, and take steps to manage the risks or decide to end the activity if the risk becomes too great. This is 'best practice'. However, the point at which 'best practice' occurs is not set.

1.7.13   There may be times when, despite the quality of planning, a session does not develop in the way intended. This could be due to a number of variables, for example:

- an event that has happened before the session

- a new student in the group

- a last minute change in the facility or equipment available

- a change in weather.

1.7.14   A competent member of staff will be aware of the impact of these variables on the group and the task. In this situation, they will recognise if the activity is moving beyond the cusp of 'best practice' and will stop it. After conducting an 'on the spot' risk-benefit analysis, they will either bring the learning environment back to a safe point or end the activity.

 Case law

1.7.15   **R versus HTM (2008):**

*This case determined that **foreseeability** relates to the likelihood of the risk being realised (ie the injury occurring) and not simply the test for the existence of risk (ie the potential to cause harm – a hazard). Foreseeability (the likelihood of harm) only becomes relevant when it is established that a risk exists.*

Chapter 1/Section 8: Planning for safe practice

1.8.1   The principles for managing risk presented in this resource are designed to help staff to plan safe physical education, school sport and physical activity (PESSPA) sessions/situations. As part of the planning process, the safety of each aspect of the session should be considered and checked against the relevant guidance. A logical and structured approach to preparation, referred to as **'forethought'**, is an essential part of effective teaching, managing and learning.

 See 2.2.11–2.2.16 in Chapter 2, pages 70–71.

1.8.2   There are a number of important elements that can impact on the safety of any planned session. For example, the unexpected poor behaviour of a student within a session or a change in the weather conditions can sometimes lead to the situation becoming less safe.

1.8.3   Good teaching and therefore safe teaching in PESSPA are achieved where a balance between appropriate challenge and acceptable risk is illustrated and the likelihood of injury occurring is minimised. Anticipating possible risks can help in the planning of effective risk management strategies. Where this process reveals a risk that cannot be sufficiently managed, then the planning needs to be reviewed.

1.8.4   Figure 4, page 62, illustrates some of the important factors that need to be taken into account when planning a PESSPA session. These are addressed in detail in Chapter 2.

Forethought

Appropriate Challenge
How have you planned to ensure that the learning tasks are appropriately challenging and take account of students' ability and prior learning?

Progression
How have you planned to check that students are competent, confident and appropriately prepared before moving on to more complex and demanding tasks?

Knowledge of Students
How will you find out about, and act on, key information (eg medical information, special educational needs and disabilities [SEND], prior experience/learning, confidence and competence)?
Have any students been absent? What did they miss? How do you plan to catch them up?

Observation and Analysis Skills
How will you respond to and adapt what you see, to ensure that the activity remains safe?

Teaching Safety
How have you planned to involve students in learning, and making decisions, about their own safety?

Equipment
Have you planned how you will ensure appropriate equipment is available for use, has been checked, and is used for the purpose it was designed for? Has faulty equipment been removed from use?

Regular and Approved Practice
Is your planning based on practice that is common and accepted across a wide geographical area as being safe?

Learning objectives and learning outcomes

Relevant and effective warm-up

Progressive and appropriately challenging learning activities

Relevant and effective cool-down

Learning

Applying School Policy
Do you know, and can you effectively implement, school policy pertinent to your session (eg behaviour policy, emergency procedures, first aid)?

Learning Environment
How have you planned to provide clear explanations/demos, check understanding, and amend or develop tasks to make them safe and appropriately challenging for individuals?

Personal Effects
Have you planned how to check that long hair is tied back, jewellery and religious adornments are removed, fingernails appropriately short and chewing gum removed?

Rules
Are you competent in the rules of the game you are teaching or officiating, and can you apply them to maintain a safe environment?

Facility
What procedures will you use to check that the space is sufficient, and the facility is safe? Is movement to and from, and around, the area safe?

Groupings
Have you planned how to group and match pupils appropriately and safely to promote effective learning (eg by size, confidence, ability) in relation to learning objectives?

Kit and Personal Protective Equipment (PPE)
Have you planned how to check that kit and PPE are appropriate? How will you manage if not? Are you dressed appropriately for the activity?

Figure 4: Examples of factors to consider when planning for safety in PESSPA

2 Teaching safely – principles of organisation and management

What is this chapter about?

This chapter focuses on 'teaching safely' through the principles of organisation and management. It considers what employers and staff need to know and understand in order to fulfil their duty of care.

How can you make effective use of this chapter?

This chapter helps employers and staff to develop a clear understanding of what safe practice means in the context of PESSPA. This understanding will help them to make well-informed decisions about safe practice in their daily work, and fulfil both their duty of care and their commitment to 'teaching safely'. The information included can be used to support the development of effective policy and procedures required to achieve safe practice in PESSPA.

Chapter 2/Section 1: Introduction – teaching and managing safely

2.1.1   Table 6 highlights sections of this resource that can be used to inform planning, teaching and managing safe physical education, school sport and physical activity (PESSPA). The list can be referred to when developing documented safe practice policy and procedures (see **Chapter 1, Section 5, page 23**), or relevant aspects can be applied to individual sessions or series of sessions.

Table 6: How to locate information about teaching and managing safely in this resource

Aspects of Safe Practice in PESSPA	Where Can I Find this Information?
The employer's and/or school's **policy and procedures** relating to PESSPA are known and applied, such as dealing with emergencies or physical contact (touching) with students.	**Chapter 1, Section 5**
Ongoing safety checks are maintained throughout the lesson, and consideration is given to how the planned activity or organisation can be amended to maintain that safe standard where doubt is established. This is sometimes referred to as a **dynamic risk assessment**.	**Chapter 1, Section 6**
Relevant aspects of the school PESSPA **risk assessment** or the normal operating procedures (NOP) and emergency action plans (EAP) for off-site facilities are known.	**Chapter 1, Section 6**
Duty of care is understood and demonstrated by all adults and teachers delivering PESSPA.	**Chapter 1, Section 4**
All staff delivering PESSPA have sufficient knowledge (competence) to teach the activity safely in relation to the ability levels of the students and demands of the activity.	Chapter 2, Section 2
Forethought is evident in planning for, and thinking logically through, PESSPA sessions.	**Chapter 1, Section 8** Chapter 2, Section 2
All staff delivering PESSPA have observation and analysis skills sufficient to ensure that what is going on is safe, and if it is not, to know what to do to make it safe.	Chapter 2, Section 2
All staff delivering PESSPA have adequate discipline, control, behaviour and group management skills to organise and maintain a safe learning environment for all.	Chapter 2, Section 2 Chapter 2, Section 8
All staff delivering PESSPA have relevant knowledge of the students in order to cater for their individual needs, confidence, previous experience, behaviour, abilities, medical conditions, stage of development, religious and cultural needs, vulnerability and understanding of their safety awareness.	Chapter 2, Section 2 Chapter 2, Section 8
All those managing support staff involved in the lesson know and understand their role and responsibilities, and keep up to date with relevant student and school information.	Chapter 2, Section 2

(continued)

Aspects of Safe Practice in PESSPA	Where Can I Find this Information?
Insurance arrangements are in place to ensure that staff and students are adequately covered in a range of different situations.	Chapter 2, Section 3
Safeguarding procedures are followed (eg in terms of physical contact, recognising signs of abuse, disclosures of abuse, travel, residential visits).	Chapter 2, Section 4
Accurate **demonstrations** and explanations are provided to develop understanding and competence in a form that accommodates individual perceptual preferences (eg visual, aural and kinaesthetic).	Chapter 2, Section 5
Rules are strictly applied in all games and sports.	Chapter 2, Section 5 **Chapter 4**
Provision for rehydration and procedures for sun protection are in place.	Chapter 2, Section 5
Students are monitored for signs of **fatigue**, and level of demand and participation are adjusted accordingly.	Chapter 2, Section 5
Contingency planning is built into preparation for on-site and off-site PESSPA activities, to be used in the event that a situation arises where the possibility of injury increases.	Chapter 2, Section 5
A well-structured and differentiated **scheme of work** is used to set appropriately challenging work.	Chapter 2, Section 5
Lesson structure is consistent and includes introductory activity (including appropriate warm-up), technical development, consolidation of skills and concluding activity (including appropriate cool-down).	Chapter 2, Section 5 Chapter 2, Section 9
Clear **learning objectives and outcomes/success criteria** are identified and shared with the students, with safe strategies to achieve these whereby the benefits of the experience outweigh the likelihood of injury occurring.	Chapter 2, Section 5
Progression and pitch (level of demand) of the activity are carefully planned and developed, checking that students are competent, confident and appropriately prepared before moving on to more complex or demanding tasks.	Chapter 2, Section 5
Regular and approved practice is used (ie that based on local authority, professional association, governing body of sport or other reliable guidance) so that any improvisation strategies are rare, used with caution and only after due forethought about the possible safety factors.	Chapter 2, Section 5 **Chapter 4**
Registers and records of attendance and non-participation are kept in order to maintain knowledge of how many are present and who is participating in the lesson, and to monitor and adjust the programme, where necessary, when students rejoin after injury or absence.	Chapter 2, Section 5
The head teacher (HT) is made aware of all **trips, visits, fixtures** and off-site events, and these are well planned and managed.	Chapter 2, Section 6
Parental consents are obtained, where relevant to the activity.	Chapter 2, Section 7

(continued)

Aspects of Safe Practice in PESSPA	Where Can I Find this Information?
Staff participation in student activities is restricted to a role enabling increased fluency in a game situation, such as pausing the flow to establish better positions to receive passes. Any necessary physical contact between the teacher and students is conducted in an appropriate manner that cannot be misconstrued or misused.	Chapter 2, Section 8
A **safe learning environment** is established through a clear explanation of the task, checking understanding, observing the students' initial response for safe standards, and then reinforcing the instructions and amending or developing the task for individuals in order to maintain a safe but challenging learning experience.	Chapter 2, Section 8
The extent, form and procedure for appropriate safe **supervision have been decided for every PESSPA situation** in accordance with the gender mix, age, behaviour and experience of the group, and changing provision.	Chapter 2, Section 8 Chapter 2, Section 13
Students are matched in terms of size, ability, confidence, and previous experience in teaching situations and the first stages of competition, particularly where weight bearing, physical contact or 'accelerating projectiles' apply. Any implications for managing **mixed-gender** activities have been considered.	Chapter 2, Section 8
All staff delivering PESSPA assume appropriate **teaching or observation positions** that enable frequent scanning of the whole class to ensure safe practice is maintained, particularly when teachers are moving into the work area to support and develop a small group.	Chapter 2, Section 8
Students perform a **warm-up** to prepare for the lesson. This is sufficient for the weather conditions and demands of the activity, specific to the activity, where appropriate, and performed with safe technique in order to be effective in preparing the body and mind for the physical activity to follow.	Chapter 2, Section 9
Staff footwear and clothing are suitable for teaching the specific PESSPA activities.	Chapter 2, Section 10
Students' clothing is appropriate for the activity and weather conditions.	Chapter 2, Section 10
Students' footwear (including barefoot work) is appropriate for the activity and work surface, and provides traction. Any implications of mixed footwear are considered.	Chapter 2, Section 10
Long hair is tied back, and students' **fingernails** are appropriately short to prevent injury to themselves or others.	Chapter 2, Section 10
Students' personal effects, including jewellery and cultural or religious adornments, have been removed or the situation adjusted to make it safe for participation if they cannot be removed. Students who cannot remove or make safe personal effects are effectively and safely involved in the learning activities.	Chapter 2, Section 10

(continued)

Aspects of Safe Practice in PESSPA	Where Can I Find this Information?
Personal protective equipment (PPE) is worn by students where it is deemed necessary for safe participation, or the activity is amended to enable safe participation without the PPE.	Chapter 2, Section 11
Equipment practicalities are considered, including storage, accessibility, condition, carrying, positioning, being fit for purpose, using only for the purpose it is designed for, retrieval systems (eg in athletics throwing events).	Chapter 2, Section 12 **Chapter 4**
Safety and rescue equipment is readily to hand throughout the session.	Chapter 2, Section 12
Electrical equipment has been certified as safe to use by the school's system for testing such equipment (eg PAT testing).	Chapter 2, Section 12
Changing provision is checked in terms of safety, security and supervision appropriate to the age and/or development stage of the students.	Chapter 2, Section 13
Movement to the work area, whether on or off site, is orderly and safe.	Chapter 2, Section 13
The **work space** is visually checked to ensure it is sufficient for the group size, nature and demands of the activity, and the skill levels of the students, noting any obstacles, damaged areas or leakages.	Chapter 2, Section 13
Fire safety provision and evacuation routes are checked as a facility is entered and before the lesson commences.	Chapter 2, Section 13
Particular students are monitored closely, such as those with **visual, hearing, cognitive, behavioural, confidence or any other individual needs**, to check they understand tasks. Where additional needs are identified, reasonable adjustments to tasks are made, and support and guidance provided as necessary, creating a safe learning environment that enables all students to participate fully.	Chapter 2, Section 14
Injury, emergency evacuation or critical incident procedures are known and applied as relevant whether on or off site.	Chapter 2, Section 15
Both students and staff are aware of and implement the policy and procedures relating to the use of digital technology in PESSPA.	Chapter 2, Section 16
Walking routes taken by students going off site are known and checked, and safety procedures are adequate.	Chapter 2 Section 17
School procedures for the safe use of any **transport system** are known and followed when taking groups off site. These include safe embarkation points, legal driving requirements, and passenger lists available to ensure immediate emergency contact with parents.	Chapter 2, Section 17
Students' involvement in, and responsibility for, their own safety relevant to their age, ability, experience and awareness are encouraged by checking their understanding, providing opportunities to assume appropriate levels of responsibility and giving clear instructions.	**Chapter 3**

Chapter 2/Section 2: Competence, qualifications and professional learning

Competence

2.2.1   Anyone teaching a physical education, school sport and physical activity (PESSPA) session should be **competent** to do so safely.

2.2.2   The Health and Safety Executive (HSE) highlights four means of demonstrating **competence**:

- hold a relevant qualification

- hold an equivalent qualification

- have received appropriate in-house training

- be competent through experience.

2.2.3   These are not totally discrete. Qualifications, experience and training overlap to produce expertise in a particular field or aspect of PESSPA.

2.2.4   Employers have a legal duty under Section 3 of the Health and Safety at Work etc Act 1974 to ensure that, so far as is reasonably practicable, others not in their employment (in schools, this is interpreted as the students) are not exposed to risks to their health and safety.

For more information on the Health and Safety at Work etc Act 1974, see http://goo.gl/4yjWmf

2.2.5   Part of this duty requires the employer to ensure that students are taught by adults competent to fulfil the demands of the tasks to which they are deployed. If a member of staff is not competent to undertake the responsibility placed on them, but has been placed in that situation by the employer, or by the employer's representative (eg a head teacher [HT]), the employer may be **directly liable** for any negligence.

2.2.6   An HT, as the manager technically deploying staff, must ensure that those delivering PESSPA sessions are competent, and carries responsibility on behalf of the employer should a teacher be placed in a situation where they **do not have the skills** to fulfil the requirements of the deployment safely.

2.2.7   Where teachers feel they do not have an appropriate level of confidence, knowledge or expertise, they should discuss the issue with their line manager in order to determine what should be done to maintain safe situations in lessons.

 Case law

2.2.8   **Jones versus Manchester Corporation (1958):**

*This case established that, where someone is **not qualified or competent** to undertake the responsibility placed on them but has been placed in that situation by the employer or the employer's representative, such as an HT, the employer and manager may be directly liable for negligence.*

2.2.9   **R versus Thornton Grammar School (2014):**

A physical education resources and equipment manager suffered multiple fractures when he fell nine metres from a climbing wall, breaking a forearm and elbow and fracturing two vertebrae. He had gradually become more involved in helping out with student lessons and had learnt the basics of climbing a rigged wall and belaying techniques.

Working with a colleague, the technique he had adopted to rig the wall for a lesson failed, and the equipment manager fell, hitting the gymnasium floor below. There were no mats or padding, and he was not wearing a helmet. The HSE found the management of the wall and the safety system regarding it almost non-existent. The competence of the staff using it and providing instruction to others was an afterthought and not effectively put in place.

The school was fined £5000 after admitting breaching Section 2(1) of the Health and Safety at Work etc Act 1974. In the report, an HSE inspector stated that those who provide climbing tuition should be properly trained and certificated. The training and development of staff using the climbing wall in this situation were judged to be inadequate. Staff were allowed to undertake tasks on it that they had not been trained for.

2.2.10 An effective **assessment of competence** to teach PESSPA establishes that a member of staff:

- understands the importance of considering forethought in their planning

- can teach the relevant techniques, tactics or compositional skills safely, accurately and at a level that is appropriate to the ability, confidence and previous experience of the students involved

- provides appropriate progressive practices to enable and support student improvement

- effectively applies the safety issues relevant to the specific activity

- has a secure knowledge of, and can appropriately apply, the rules if the activity is a sport

- knows the abilities, confidence and particular needs of the students

- has well-developed observational and analytical skills to ensure that what is going on is safe, and amend or stop anything that is deemed unsafe

- has effective class control.

Elements of competence for safe teaching

Forethought

2.2.11 Forethought or forward planning involves anticipating what may happen, and requires teachers to think about where harm is likely by considering:

- what they want students to learn

- how they will support students to achieve desired outcomes

- how to organise the lesson prior to physical engagement in the activity.

2.2.12 An important aspect of forethought is providing **clear instructions** to students so that there is no misunderstanding of what is expected of them.

2.2.13 As well as anticipating what may cause injury in a planned PESSPA activity, staff should think beyond the activity itself to the **organisation and logistics** of a whole event. For example, this may include any implications for transporting students (see Chapter 2, Section 17, page 286) and possible external causes that may impact on the event, such as being delayed by heavy traffic or a road traffic accident.

2.2.14 It is also important to plan for possible illness or injury to participants or staff. Such **contingency planning** is likely to ensure that incidents that are not part of a planned event can be managed safely and efficiently.

2.2.15 Very occasionally, something may occur that could not reasonably be anticipated (eg a sudden change in weather conditions). In such circumstances, the teacher needs to **manage the situation** by pausing the activity and considering if and how the situation can be managed to make it safe once more. If no additional precautions or controls can be identified to adjust the situation to enable continuing safely, then the activity must be abandoned because the law requires teachers **not to knowingly place others in unsafe situations.**

Case law

2.2.16 **Denbighshire County Council versus McDermott (2005):**

*An experienced climber, but inexperienced leader, gave **unclear instructions** when he told a hesitant climber to 'let go of the rope' while she was abseiling down a rock face with two colleagues roping from the top. The instruction was intended to encourage the hesitant climber, by reinforcing that she was being supported by her colleagues. The two colleagues at the top of the rock face thought the instruction was directed to them, as did the climber, and all three let go of the supporting ropes, resulting in no control over the descent. The climber fell 10m on to rocks.*

Knowledge of the students

2.2.17 It is important that all staff have relevant knowledge of the students they teach. Where the member of staff is not the usual adult responsible for the students (eg they are a visiting coach or cover supervisor), it is essential that they are provided with key information about the students with whom they will be working. This should include:

- medical information (on a need-to-know basis)

- behavioural information

- previous experience/prior learning

- confidence and competence

- any special educational needs and disabilities (SEND)

- individual needs or specific personal circumstances that might affect a student's performance, health or emotional well-being, such as a recent bereavement.

2.2.18 This information helps staff to pitch the challenge of the activity more accurately for all students, and to ensure that expectations are appropriate and within their ability.

2.2.19 Students with **visual, hearing, motor or cognitive impairment** needs should be considered and catered for appropriately to enable them to participate safely. All staff, regular or visiting, need to be fully aware of the implications of the ability and needs of any student in order to provide a worthwhile and safe learning opportunity.

2.2.20 PESSPA staff should think through any possible safety implications, and the efficiency of amending **group sizes during lessons** before initiating the change. Changes may be required because of available space, behaviour, or the mobility of specific students. Where staff choose to **combine classes** to provide a PESSPA activity for students whose usual member of staff is absent, they should carry out a risk analysis to determine whether it is safe to proceed in the circumstances.

Observation and analysis skills

2.2.21   The ability to **analyse and evaluate** student response to particular tasks is essential to safe teaching, as well as to improving performance.

2.2.22   PESSPA staff need to check constantly whether the activity taking place is safe, and **if not, to intervene or stop it** in order to make it safe. This requires them to have expertise to make adjustments (eg to technique, skill, task, intensity, equipment) in order to make it safe.

2.2.23   For example, staff should be confident to identify the onset of fatigue, which might impact on students' concentration levels. This is particularly important in activities such as swimming, gymnastics, trampolining and sustained running. Similarly, staff should be confident to make accurate judgements about whether the space available to students is sufficient for the safe execution of specific tasks or skills.

2.2.24   Poor control, discipline and behaviour management, or inadequate group-management skills by PESSPA staff may adversely affect the standard of safety in any situation.

Officiating

2.2.25   Officiating at a sports event carries a dual role of duty of care and duty of control. The duty of control includes the requirement for staff to know and apply the rules stringently. The duty of care applies to the safety of the players within a competition and any spectators within a playing area. It is thus important that officials seek to ensure that spectators do not 'spill' on to the playing area, and that a suitable run-off area is maintained as a buffer zone between spectators and the playing area for the protection of both groups.

 Case law

2.2.26   **Smolden versus Whitworth (1996):**

*A player was paralysed during a rugby match when the scrum collapsed. The referee was judged to have been negligent by **not applying the laws** of the game consistently. He allowed 32 scrums to collapse (a potentially dangerous event) without taking action to prevent further occurrences.*

2.2.27   **Wooldridge versus Sumner (1962):**

*This case reinforced the principle that a spectator injured during the normal course of events in a competition cannot claim negligence on the part of the players, officials or organisers, provided the spectator has been made aware of the need to remain **outside the playing area** and any run-off zone.*

Competence of students to support other students in PESSPA activities

2.2.28 Individuals holding the legal status of a registered school student (this can be up to the age of 19), on a school roll, **cannot be legally responsible for other students**, and their role in 'running' PESSPA activities should always be supervised.

2.2.29 The member of staff providing such supervision should be able to oversee, monitor and intervene immediately, if necessary. If the responsibility for this supervision falls to playground supervisory staff, they must be adequately competent to fulfil this role. Where this is not the case, the teacher responsible for the young leaders must provide the supervision.

2.2.30 It is not necessary for a young person to hold an award such as the **PlayMaker or Young Leader** Award in order to participate in such activities, although this would be good practice.

Qualifications that contribute towards competence for safe teaching

Teachers' standards

2.2.31 Teachers' standards (TS) for England, Northern Ireland, Scotland and Wales all share a common commitment to raising standards of teaching in order to improve learner outcomes.

2.2.32 The distinct frameworks for each country set out standards within which all teachers at all stages of their careers should operate, and these are used to assess those who are training and those completing their 'induction' period. The standards are used to promote the ongoing professionalism and proficiency of qualified/registered teachers.

2.2.33 All frameworks of TS highlight the importance of creating and maintaining safe learning environments for all learners, for example, in relation to:

- developing and maintaining positive attitudes, value and behaviour

- setting appropriate goals and challenges for students that take account of their prior learning

- promoting students' progress

- having a secure knowledge of physical education

- planning and teaching well-structured lessons

- adapting teaching and strategies to respond to the needs of all students

- giving students regular feedback

- managing behaviour effectively.

This list of examples is by no means exhaustive.

2.2.34 The TS frameworks highlight that appropriate self-evaluation, reflection and professional development are critical to teachers developing their practice at all career stages. The standards identify the key areas in which teachers should be able to assess their practice and receive feedback from colleagues. More experienced teachers are expected to extend the depth and breadth of knowledge, skill and understanding that they demonstrated in meeting the standards, and in accordance with the role they are fulfilling or the context in which they are working.

2.2.35　Professional values are at the core of all TS frameworks. The educational experiences of students are shaped by the values and dispositions of all those who educate them. Values are complex, as are the ideals by which teachers shape their practice. Starting with teachers, values extend to all students for whom they are responsible. Teachers' professional values drive their personal commitment to all learners' intellectual, social and ethical growth and well-being. A teacher's professionalism has close links with their duty to ensure the health, safety and well-being of children in their care and, within the law, to do what is reasonable in all circumstances for the safeguarding or promotion of their welfare.

2.2.36　Accurate interpretation of TS is essential in relation to developing and maintaining safe practice in PESSPA. This will require teachers to develop a sound understanding of the fundamentals of safe practice and safe teaching and management principles, as well as information about specific PESSPA activities and students' involvement in learning about safe practice. Therefore, a thorough knowledge and understanding of the information in this resource is a key reference, not only for those involved in teaching PESSPA, but also for those involved in initial teacher education.

Information regarding the standards for teachers in each of the home countries can be found at:

England

Department for Education (DfE) (2011) 'Teachers' Standards':
https://goo.gl/YrE1zP

Northern Ireland

General Teaching Council of NI (GTCNI) (2011) 'Teaching: The reflective profession – promoting teacher professionalism':
http://goo.gl/hrARIQ

Scotland

General Teaching Council for Scotland (2012) 'The Standards for Registration: Mandatory requirements for registration with the General Teaching Council for Scotland':
http://goo.gl/gCtQv1

Wales

Welsh Government (2011) 'Revised professional standards for education practitioners in Wales':
http://goo.gl/11G7m8

Initial teacher education

2.2.37　**Initial teacher education (ITE) providers** recommend trainees for the award of qualified/registered teacher status (QTS). Therefore, the assessment of trainees must be accurate and reliable in establishing, consistently over time, whether or not trainees satisfactorily meet all of the TS.

2.2.38　Where such accreditation is given and the new teacher's lack of experience and competence contributes to a foreseeable injury, the ITE provider may be deemed liable for erroneous accreditation.

2.2.39　The education white paper 'Education excellence everywhere' (DfE, 2016) states that QTS in England will be replaced with a stronger, more challenging accreditation based on teachers' effectiveness in the classroom, as judged by great schools. This accreditation will only be achieved after teachers have demonstrated their proficiency – including the strength of their subject knowledge – over a sustained period in the classroom.

 For more information on 'Education excellence everywhere', see https://goo.gl/BRv5kL

2.2.40 **School placements** form a fundamental part of ITE. Trainees are not 'signed off' as competent to teach until they have satisfactorily met all of the TS and, as such, should not be given full, unsupervised responsibility within a practical PESSPA setting for any group during a placement. In addition, their placement in schools is primarily for their professional learning, and they should therefore not be considered as support staff for class teachers. Trainees should be appropriately supervised, managed and monitored throughout their training period when they are delivering physical education lessons. Arrangements for trainee placements should be clearly set out by the ITE provider in a contract with the placement school. Employers and HTs of trainees employed on the school staff are responsible for deciding the trainees' competence to teach during their training period.

2.2.41 **Qualified/registered primary teachers and secondary physical education teachers** may be required to teach all aspects of the physical education curriculum. Having satisfactorily completed their initial training, qualified/registered teachers should look to access further professional learning, particularly in specific PESSPA activities in which they feel less competent, but are required to teach.

Teaching PESSPA in academies and free schools

2.2.42 Currently, academy employers are responsible for the quality of teaching in their schools and determine their own requirements for any potential teacher they employ or promote, including whether they need to be qualified/registered.

2.2.43 Given this, it is possible that non-qualified teachers will teach physical education in academies or free schools. The white paper for education 'Educational excellence everywhere' (DfE, 2016) states that schools in England will have more scope to bring experts in from other fields and put them on a pathway to full accreditation. Where this is the case, the HT, on behalf of the employer, will need to have undertaken a full competency assessment with the staff member employed, and satisfied him/herself that they are competent to undertake all aspects of the role.

2.2.44 Currently, local-authority (LA)-run state schools must have a fully qualified/registered teacher assigned to every timetabled PESSPA class. A non-qualified teacher can only be assigned a class for a 'temporary' period, when the school is actively in the process of recruiting a qualified/registered teacher.

PESSPA awards, qualifications for specific activities

2.2.45 Primary school staff and specialist PESSPA staff are not legally obliged to hold activity-specific qualifications or awards in order to teach specific PESSPA activities unless required to do so by their employer. However, some LAs, school trusts or school governing bodies establish their own policies and insist on minimum training, experience or qualifications before allowing staff to teach PESSPA activities that involve greater risk. Staff should be aware of **local employer requirements** and ensure that they meet these before teaching the activities concerned.

2.2.46   Examples of potentially **higher-risk** activities include adventurous activities, aquatic activities, athletics throwing events, combat sports, contact sports, aspects of gymnastics, trampolining and working with free weights in a fitness room. Those leading sessions in schools in these contexts should hold recognised and current qualifications (eg governing body of sport qualifications. (See **Chapter 4, page 351**, for more information about qualifications and training required for specific PESSPA activities.) In the absence of such qualifications, it is strongly advised that significant, recent and relevant experience or training is required to demonstrate an individual's competence to teach these activities safely.

2.2.47   Some governing bodies of sport and other awarding organisations require qualifications to be revalidated periodically. This is not simply to endorse previous requirements, but to inform learners of changes and developments that may have occurred in the interim period. Guidance should be obtained from the relevant governing body of sport, awarding organisation or LA, the Education Authority in Northern Ireland or an expert consultant.

2.2.48   The standards of expertise, discipline, relationships and risk management expected of all adults working with students need to be consistent with providing a safe working environment. This level of competence applies to all who contribute to PESSPA activities as part of a school-organised programme, and at all times when they are delivering the activities (eg during activities which take place inside and outside of lessons; on or off the school site; in term time or holidays).

2.2.49   afPE's **Quality Mark** (http://goo.gl/xi7VgO) recognises high quality PESSPA in schools, and evaluates the competence of the PESSPA workforce and the work they do through PESSPA to make a difference to students' learning within the subject and more widely across the curriculum. Safeguarding and the promotion of health and safety are important aspects of the Quality Mark criteria, as well as the effective deployment of competent support staff.

Ongoing professional learning for staff

2.2.50   Health and safety law includes a **requirement** that employees receive the professional learning necessary for them to fulfil the demands of the work they are deployed to do by managers. Professional learning opportunities in safe-practice procedures are therefore a necessity and an entitlement where any lack of confidence or competence is evident. Otherwise, alternative staffing arrangements need to be made. Those involved in delivering PESSPA need to undertake professional learning in order to keep abreast of what is acceptable and safe.

2.2.51   A rolling programme of professional learning in relation to safe practice, evidenced through a personal or collective **training log**, would indicate that the required qualifications and experience, relevant to the PESSPA programme being offered, remain current.

2.2.52   **Primary teachers** with little or no ITE in physical education may be at risk. Where this is the case, they should undertake appropriate professional learning before being allowed to teach a full range of activities. HTs must be satisfied that all those who are required to teach PESSPA are able to do so in a safe manner, with a sound understanding of the needs and stages of development of all the students in their charge.

2.2.53   **Primary staff** with QTS can now access the afPE and Sports Leaders UK:

- Level 5 Certificate in Primary School Physical Education Specialism

- Level 6 Award in Primary School Physical Education Subject Leadership.

2.2.54   **Support staff** contributing to the PESSPA programme can also access the Level 5 Certificate in order to increase their competence in promoting learning through PESSPA activities.

For more information on this qualification, see http://goo.gl/k2H0Tq

2.2.55   Coaches supporting PESSPA provision in schools can also access the following qualifications:

- Level 2 Certificate in Supporting Learning in Physical Education and School Sport

- Level 3 Certificate in Supporting the Delivery of Physical Education and School Sport

- Level 3 NVQ Diploma in Supporting the Delivery of Physical Education and School Sport

For more information on these qualifications, see http://goo.gl/OaxB0G

- Level 3 Certificate in Supporting Physical Development and Physical Activity in the Early Years

For more information on this qualification, see http://goo.gl/aump71

These qualifications help to improve delegates' knowledge and understanding of PESSPA, and cover learning about safe practice.

 FAQ

2.2.56   **I am a qualified secondary physical education specialist. Do I need a formal fitness industry qualification in order to teach my students in a fitness room facility?**

No, full QTS and a specialism in physical education are sufficient to be able to teach your students in a fitness room, although additional professional learning is recommended. As a member of staff teaching or supervising in this environment, you should be competent to do so. An assessment of such competency should confirm that you are:

- well informed and up to date in terms of knowledge about safe exercise practice for young people

- sufficiently experienced and confident in using a range of fitness room equipment

- able to lead, demonstrate, observe and correct safe exercise technique

- able to manage group circulation and practice within the facility.

If a teacher needs to develop/update any of these competencies further, it is recommended that additional appropriate professional learning is undertaken, such as:

- Level 2 gym instructor qualification (eg www.ymcafit.org.uk/courses/gym-instructor)

- training course: Promoting effective learning about healthy active lifestyles in fitness rooms at Key Stages 3 and 4 (www.learningabouthal.co.uk).

 Case law

2.2.57   **Kenyon versus Lancashire County Council (2001):**

*A student was injured performing a back drop on a trampoline. She claimed **incorrect tuition** and succeeded in the claim. Care needs to be taken when teaching technical skills.*

Use of support staff in PESSPA

2.2.58   For a number of reasons, students may be taught in schools by adults who are not qualified teachers. Generally, these are referred to as **'support staff'** – a term used for all adults, other than trainee teachers, without QTS who contribute to the teaching of students in schools. Support staff include regular staff on the school roll such as **classroom assistants, teaching assistants, cover supervisors, learning mentors and volunteer parents, as well as visiting staff, whether occasional or regular contributors, such as coaches, and physical education apprentices.**

2.2.59   The 2013 Supreme Court decision (see **Chapter 1, Section 4, page 19**) established in common law that the school employer (LA, governors or trust) maintains the responsibility for students where a duty is provided through a third party, such as an individual coach or coaching agency. This is because the agency or coach provides the teaching service **on behalf of** the school employer, and the responsibility for the care of students **cannot be delegated**. The HT, as manager of the school, technically deploys all staff, whether on the school roll or visiting, and as such, it is their duty to ensure that all staff, including all support staff, are competent to fulfil the demands of the tasks to which they are deployed.

2.2.60   Support staff can add to the quality of a PESSPA programme through their expertise, encouragement and support. In addition, teachers can develop their own knowledge by **learning from support staff** who have particular expertise in a specific PESSPA activity. This can be achieved if:

- provision is made for teachers to **work alongside support staff** whenever possible

- support staff are committed to imparting information through such a joint working arrangement.

2.2.61   The use of support staff can also help to broaden the PESSPA programme, increase the quality of learning and challenge, and provide greater flexibility in staffing.

2.2.62 The **physical education and sport premium funding** for primary schools in England (https://goo.gl/W0YNR1) has enabled many primary schools to engage the support of coaches and physical education apprentices to enhance their PESSPA offer where a need has been identified. However, in line with national partners (sports coach UK, Sport England, Youth Sport Trust, the County Sport Partnership Network and UK Active), afPE maintains the position that **coaches should not be used to replace teachers in curriculum time.**

2.2.63 At no time should support staff **displace a qualified teacher from the staffing roll.** Their role is to complement the qualified teacher timetabled to a class. In some cases where support staff are assessed as competent, they may work alone 'at a distance' from the assigned class teacher, but must be managed effectively by that teacher, **who remains legally responsible for the students in their care**, whether through direct or remote supervision. Such management involves ongoing responsibility for what is taught, and the conduct, health and well-being of the students involved, as well as ensuring that support staff are aware of the limits of their role and responsibilities in relation to applying school policy and procedures.

Support staff in planning, preparation and assessment time

2.2.64 Where support staff (either internal staff or external coaches) teach a group during a class teacher's **planning, preparation and assessment (PPA) time**, another member of staff with QTS must take responsibility for the duty of care, and effectively supervise and direct the support staff in question. Once again, the HT (on behalf of the school authority) is responsible for assessing the competence of the support staff deployed to deliver these lessons.

Cover supervisors delivering practical physical education

2.2.65 Careful thought should be given before allowing **cover supervisors** to supervise practical lessons for absent physical education staff. Where cover supervisors have the necessary competence to deliver the activity being covered (ie a combination of qualifications and/or recent and relevant knowledge and experience in that activity), this could be possible. Where these requirements are not satisfied, the cover supervisor should only be permitted to cover a classroom-based lesson.

Assessing the suitability of support staff in PESSPA

2.2.66 The school procedures for engaging support staff, such as coaches, should address three essential questions:

- **Is it legal** to engage this person? This will be determined by the requirements of a broad range of legislation that sets out whether particular individuals are prohibited from working with children and young people. The relevant **vetting** and background checks need to be completed carefully. (See Chapter 2, Section 4, page 105.)

- **Is it safe** to employ this person? **Safe recruitment** procedures include checking and confirmation of disclosure certification, qualifications and authenticity of identity, and a relevant governing body of sport coach licence (where relevant).

- **Is it effective** to engage this person? This will be determined by the expertise the person brings to the school, how their expertise may **add** to the professional learning of the school staff, how the quality of student learning experiences will be improved, and whether the PESSPA programme will be beneficially broadened.

2.2.67　In undertaking a **competence assessment**, it is good practice for class teachers to **directly supervise during the initial phase of support staff teaching**. Direct supervision involves support staff working alongside a class teacher in order that the teacher can intervene at any time, as necessary. At a later stage, **distant supervision** of support staff might be appropriate, according to their competence and the level of responsibility assigned. This would allow support staff to work at some distance (remotely) from a class teacher, possibly out of sight, in a different facility or even off site. However, frequent monitoring by the teacher would be part of good management. (Where physical education and sport premium funding for primary schools is being used to employ support staff in curriculum time, the support staff should always teach alongside the class teacher to satisfy the criteria of this funding.)

2.2.68　It is good practice for schools to keep a **register** of any support staff used who are not on the school roll, such as individual coaches or coaching agencies, including contact details and work undertaken, for future reference.

2.2.69　The level of supervision required for support staff should be determined by a thorough competency and risk assessment. Support staff can be judged on the **national standards** for higher level teaching assistants (HLTAs) or, alternatively, on competences specific to PESSPA to determine the eventual level of direct or remote supervision required.

Case law

2.2.70　**R versus Kite (1996)**:

*This case was known as the Lyme Bay canoeing tragedy. The managing director of the adventure company was convicted of manslaughter on the basis that he had not established **proper safety standards**, including a failure to appoint staff with adequate experience for the demands of the activity.*

© Alan Edwards

2.2.71   Table 7 provides guidance for HTs and other managers to use to recruit, induct, and assess the competence of support staff:

Table 7: Assessing the competence of coaching and other support staff in PESSPA

1 Safe Recruitment

a   **Arrange a face-to-face interview** with each coach to confirm that they are at least 18 (ie an adult) and confirm their identity using original documents (passport, driving licence, recent service provider bill confirming current home address).

b   **Make the decision about whether the coach will be engaged in regulated activity.** (See Chapter 2, Section 4, page 105.) If yes, request information from the Disclosure and Barring Service (DBS) barred list. If the coach will not be in regulated activity, there is no right to access information from the barred list. Decide whether a disclosure certificate is needed where the coach will operate alone with students in some context. (If the coach is to work alone with students, enhanced disclosure certification is necessary. If the coach will be supervised at all times by a member of staff who holds enhanced disclosure, the coach does not need disclosure certification, but the employer has discretion in this decision.) If disclosure is required, the employer should see the original disclosure certificate and record the number. (Do not photocopy it without the applicant's consent.) Decide if portability applies and is acceptable. Check whether additional information is on the disclosure form that may influence any decision to accept the coach into school.

c   **Check qualifications** – see the originals. Accept a Level 2 award as the normal baseline qualification for each PESSPA activity the coach is expected to teach, diverting from this standard only if the coach is observed prior to acceptance and demonstrates good coaching qualities and is working towards a Level 2 qualification, where appropriate.

d   **Check the coach's training in, and experience of, working with children and young people** (eg attendance at safeguarding and concussion awareness and management workshops).

e   **Explore the coach's motivations to work with children, and attitudes towards children and young people**.

f   **Check original reference(s)** – investigate any gaps in coaching employment and any conditional comments in the reference.

g   **Check, if relevant, with the appropriate governing body of sport that the coach is currently licensed to coach**. (A qualification cannot be rescinded, but a governing body of sport licence to coach can be if any poor practice or abuse issues have arisen.)

h   **Ensure correct employment status and employment rights are made known to the coach**. Provide a written summary and include in contract as appropriate.

i   **Ensure the coach is fully aware of what, if any, insurance provision is made** by the school and what aspects he/she needs to provide for him/herself (according to employment status) re:

    i   employers' liability (compulsory by law) – legal liability for injuries to employees (permanent/temporary/contracted for services) arising in the course of employment

    ii   public liability (essential but not compulsory through law) – to meet the responsibility for 'third party' claims against the activities of the individual/group and legal occupation of premises

(continued)

1 Safe Recruitment (continued)

    ii   professional liability (desirable) – legal cover against claims for breaches of professional duty by employees acting in the scope of their employment (eg giving poor professional advice)

    iv hirers' liability (desirable) – covers individuals or agencies that hire premises against any liability for injury to others or damage to the property while using it

    v   libel and slander insurance (optional) – cover against claims for defamation (eg libellous material in publications)

    vi personal injury – accidental bodily injury – or deliberate assault (desirable) – arranged by individual or employer

    vii miscellaneous – a variety of types of insurance such as travel (compulsory or required for best practice) or motor insurance (compulsory – minimum of 'third party') – check personal exclusions and excesses individual carries. (For more information regarding insurance, see Chapter 2, Section 3, page 86.)

j   **Set out a clearly defined role, identifying any limits of responsibility, lines of supervision, management and communication, and specialist expertise needed** (eg children with individual special needs), and ensure that the coach is appropriately qualified/experienced to undertake the role.

k   **Determine an agreed period of probation**, and monitor the coach's performance and attitude closely during this period.

l   **Check that all of the above have been addressed by the agency or by the school before a self-employed or agency-appointed coach begins work.**

m **Agree an appropriate induction package that must be fulfilled**.

2 Induction

a   The HT or their representative presents the coach with a summary of relevant school policy and procedures, including risk assessments, emergency evacuation, referral and incentives, behaviour management, first aid, managing suspected concussion, safeguarding procedures and something about the ethos of the school – how staff work with children and young people (such as looking for success in young people, rewarding achievement).

b   Identify a member of staff to manage induction into school procedures who will:

    i   arrange a meeting with the SEND designated person and class teacher(s) as appropriate for specific information about students

    ii monitor and assess the competence of the coach through observations and discussions with students and other staff

    iii determine the coach's role in contributing to the overall assessment of students.

(continued)

3 Qualifications, Experience and Qualities Necessary for a Coach to Work Alone

a   Expect a Level 2 award as the normal baseline qualification for each activity the coach is expected to teach. Divert from this standard only if the coach is observed prior to acceptance, demonstrates good coaching qualities and is working towards a Level 2 qualification where appropriate or where a coach holds a recognised multi-games qualification and will be teaching generic skills to a basic level.

NB: In addition to activity-specific qualifications, afPE's good practice expectation is that coaches supporting curriculum time physical education should hold or be working towards a 1st4Sport/afPE Level 2 or 3 qualification in supporting physical education and school sport.

b   Check previous experience in working with small/large groups.

c   Check behaviour management skills.

d   Check their:

   i   quality of relationships – the way the coach cares for and respects students, is an appropriate role model and promotes the ethos of school

   ii   developing knowledge of the students – their levels of confidence, ability, individual needs, medical needs and behaviour

   iii student management skills – how they match students' confidence, strength and ability in pair and group tasks, maximise participation, have strategies for effective student control and motivation, apply the school's standard procedures and routines (eg safeguarding, emergency action, managing suspected concussion, jewellery, handling and carrying of equipment)

   iv   knowledge of the PESSPA activities – appropriate level of expertise to enable learning to take place in the activities being delivered, use of suitable space for the group, differentiated equipment, differentiated practice, evident progression and application of rules

   v   observation and analytical skills – providing a safe working and learning environment, ability to identify faults and establish strategies for improvement

   vi   clear understanding and application of risk management principles.

4 Day-to-day Management of the Coach

a   Check that the coach has received a summary of school and subject procedures, and understands what is required (including clear guidelines in relation to handover of responsibility at the start and end of lessons/sessions).

b   Ensure the coach receives relevant information on students/groups (eg medical conditions that may impact on participation, illness, family bereavement, behaviour issues, pupils recovering from injury, including concussion).

c   Monitor promptness.

d   Establish regular review and evaluation of the coach's work.

e   Determine who assesses students' work.

f   Ensure the coach is supported and valued, and accepted as a member of staff.

g   Monitor dialogue and relationship between class teacher and coach.

(continued)

5 Monitoring Quality and Effectiveness

a Ensure direct monitoring of the coach for an agreed period – use criteria set out in 3 above.

b Set up continual indirect monitoring to ensure students make progress and enjoy lessons.

c Ensure that students are engaged in consistent high quality learning, using challenging and stimulating activities that support them to achieve their potential, not just activities that keep them 'busy, happy and good', and that sessions have an educational focus and are not used simply for 'talent spotting'.

6 Identification and Provision of Continuing Professional Learning

a Evaluate the coach's abilities against appropriate standards.

b Arrange attendance on afPE/sports coach UK 'Adults Supporting Learning' (ASL) induction course.

c Agree essential qualifications and desirable qualifications – plan and provide for a personal development programme beyond governing body of sport coach qualifications to enable the coach to proceed from emerging to established, and advanced ratings.

7 Dealing with Inadequate Performance by the Coach

a Proactively monitor the coach's work, as set out in 5 above.

b Intervene immediately if a coach's performance is inadequate and poses a health and safety risk to the students or has the potential to impact on their welfare.

c Review the situation with the coach after any lesson in which their performance is technically inadequate.

d Agree and provide supportive continuing professional development to improve inadequate aspects of performance.

e Monitor for improvement.

f Terminate a short-term contract if little or no improvement occurs, or initiate competency procedures if a longer-term contract exists.

g Terminate a longer-term contract where competence does not improve.

Adapted from Whitlam, P. (2016) 'Best practice guidance on the effective use of individual and agency coaches in physical education and sport'.

FAQ

2.2.72   **Can an HLTA or cover supervisor teach a practical physical education lesson?**

If an HT makes this decision, they must be satisfied that the HLTA or cover supervisor is competent to do so. A competency assessment needs to be undertaken to ascertain whether the HLTA or cover supervisor is sufficiently competent to teach the **specific PESSPA activity** required. The assessment will consider aspects such as qualifications, experience, reputation, knowledge of the children, and should include observing this member of staff.

If an accident occurred during a PESSPA lesson that the HLTA or cover supervisor was leading, the HT must be satisfied that they could justify their decision that allowed this to happen. The HT would do this by presenting evidence that a thorough and accurate positive competence assessment had been carried out that reported the HLTA or cover supervisor as a competent deliverer, and that the students in their sessions are achieving and making progress. This type of evidence would then be considered. If they cannot justify their decision, then the situation should not continue.

The National Agreement of 2003 covering England and Wales, and related to regulations made under Section 133 of the Education Act 2002, places a duty on HTs to ensure that each class or group timetabled for core and foundation subjects, and each class or group in the foundation stage has a qualified teacher assigned to teach it. Provided this requirement is met, an HLTA or cover supervisor performing the role of a teacher can be a long-term arrangement.

If the class being covered is accommodating the class teacher's PPA time, the responsibility for the class must be transferred to another qualified teacher or to the HT.

Case law

2.2.73   **Norfolk County Council versus Kingswood Activity Centre (2007):**

*An eight-year-old was injured when he fell six metres from a climbing wall. The investigation established that the screw of a karabiner (metal loop) had not been tightened, allowing the karabiner to open and free the safety rope when a weight was applied. It also found that the **training and supervision** procedures were not sufficient for the activities being carried out and were not being routinely followed on the ground. It was described as 'an accident that could have been prevented had the correct safety procedures been followed and the staff undertaking the activities been trained and supervised'.*

Chapter 2/Section 3: Insurance

Provision of insurance

2.3.1   School status (see **Chapter 1, Section 3, page 13**) impacts on how schools source their insurance. Some local authorities (LAs) continue to provide comprehensive cover and support for LA schools.

2.3.2   Academies and other non-LA eligible schools may choose independent insurance providers, or opt for the government's risk protection arrangement (RPA) scheme (https://goo.gl/3kcRLP), which aims to protect academy trusts against losses due to any unforeseen and unexpected event. As a minimum, the RPA is intended to cover risks normally included in a standard schools insurance policy, where there is not an alternative valid insurance policy already in place.

2.3.3   Whatever choice is made, academies and other non-LA eligible schools must ensure that they have adequate insurance cover to comply with their legal obligations.

2.3.4   Staff should **check** with their head teacher and/or employer to clarify precisely what insurance cover is provided, under what circumstances the cover applies and whether it is advisable to initiate additional cover for themselves or for any volunteer or visiting staff who may be self-employed. This information needs to be shared with any such volunteers or visiting staff.

2.3.5   Employers may or may not insure staff for **extension** work outside their normal school role, such as when coaching or managing regional representative teams. Where this is not provided, similar cover will need to be sought through the relevant governing body of sport or sourced personally by the member of staff in question.

2.3.6   The following aspects of insurance need to be considered:

Employer's liability insurance

2.3.7 Employers are responsible for the health and safety of their employees while they are at work. It is a statutory requirement for employers to insure against liability for **injury or illness that may occur to their employees** while they are working within the remit of a contract, whether permanent, temporary or for specific services. LAs are exempt from this requirement, but need either to act as the insurers or make alternative insurance arrangements to cover the potential liabilities of their employees.

2.3.8 **Schools not maintained by an LA are not exempt** and must therefore comply with these employer requirements.

2.3.9 The **RPA is not an insurance**. However, those schools that have opted for it are exempt by virtue of the fact that the Secretary of State has certified that any claim against an academy from an employee will be satisfied out of moneys provided by Parliament. In practice, claims will be met by the RPA from moneys provided by Parliament, which means that academies that are relying on the RPA for employer's liability cover are compliant with the law.

2.3.10 The only deviation to the extent of this cover occurs in the case of church academies, where the RPA will cover losses and liabilities incurred by the trustees in respect of the academy trust's operations **on their property**, and allow the trustees to make claims on behalf of an RPA member in respect of losses and liabilities incurred by the trustees relating to trust property made available to the member by the trustees.

2.3.11 Employer's liability insurance does not apply to students in schools as they are visitors to school, rather than employees.

Public liability insurance

2.3.12 Schools are expected to obtain public liability insurance that covers them against claims made by others who have suffered injury or damage to property in connection with the school. This would include:

- death or injury to students, volunteers, coaches and other support staff, during school activities on and off school premises as a result of the school's negligence (where any of these parties are on the school staffing roll – ie are employees – they are likely to be covered by the employer's liability insurance)

- injury or damage to third parties (this includes visitors), including that caused through student **negligence** within the scope of the school's provision for their education.

Professional liability insurance

2.3.13 This insurance for staff is advisable. It provides cover against claims for **breaches of professional duty** by employees acting in the scope of their employment, such as giving poor professional advice.

2.3.14 This type of cover is also particularly important for anyone working in a self-employed capacity, such as a visiting coach or physical education professional development provider.

Personal injury insurance

2.3.15   This insurance for staff is desirable. It provides cover against accidental bodily injury or deliberate assault by someone.

2.3.16   Personal injury insurance might be arranged by the employer or may need to be provided by individual members of staff.

2.3.17   **It is a parental responsibility to provide personal injury insurance for students.** Some schools choose to make this facility available collectively to parents, but there is no requirement to do so.

Hirer's liability insurance

2.3.18   This covers individuals or agencies that hire premises against any liability for injury to others or damage to the property while using it.

2.3.19   This type of insurance is recommended due to the increase in initiatives that encourage schools to hire out their premises for community use.

2.3.20   Where hirers do not already have such a policy, schools can organise this on their behalf from their insurers or through the RPA.

Libel and slander insurance

2.3.21   This is an optional insurance. It provides cover against claims for defamation (eg libellous material in publications).

Other types of insurance cover

2.3.22   There might also be a range of **miscellaneous aspects** that require insurance cover, according to the particular role of individuals. These range from compulsory to merely advisable and may include travel or motor insurance.

2.3.23   Where cover is not provided, it is the responsibility of the individual member of staff to ensure that adequate provision is made where appropriate to their work circumstances.

Transport-related insurance

2.3.24   The provision and requirements for **transport** insurance **will** vary. Staff need to check that:

- commercial transport companies have the appropriate range of insurance cover

- the school minibus insurance policy is appropriate for the journey being undertaken (eg there are additional insurance and licence requirements for travelling abroad that require staff to take the school minibus insurance certificate, or a copy, on their journey)

- they have read the employer's policy on the use of private cars to transport students; local requirements vary considerably – some employers do not allow it (eg the RPA does not cover staff intending to use their own or others' private cars on occasional business use)

- they understand the insurance procedures required to use private cars for school business, and obtain confirmation from other drivers that their insurance covers the risk involved.

Insurance for PESSPA events

2.3.25 Insurance cover relating to the use of physical education, school sport and physical activity (PESSPA) **facilities** is relevant to the employer or owner of the facility, and should be checked. It should be clearly understood who is financially responsible and under what circumstances, should any claim arise.

2.3.26 It is important that adequate risk assessment of school PESSPA activities and events is made in order that appropriate insurance cover can be arranged where necessary.

2.3.27 The employer's insurance provision needs to cover all PESSPA **events organised by the school**, whether on or off site, in lesson time or outside, in term time or during holidays, provided the head teacher is fully aware of the events that are taking place. The head teacher will then determine whether the governors and/or the employing authority need to be informed. Staff should check what documentation needs to be completed, and ensure that this is in place prior to the event.

2.3.28 All **special events**, such as 'one-off' sports trips, or sports tournaments will need appropriate insurance. Staff should check with the head teacher, to clarify what provision is in place and whether any additional cover needs to be arranged. Sports tours arranged wholly by the school are likely to be covered in part by the employer's insurance provision, but some additional aspects of cover might need to be arranged specifically.

2.3.29 Sports tours, ski trips and other excursions arranged as a **package** through a commercial provider usually have a full range of insurance cover built in. Staff need to check carefully the detail of the insurance provided, particularly the levels of compensation offered and any particular exclusions to the cover. Parents should be provided with full details of the insurance cover in order that they can make additional arrangements in relation to personal injury cover for their child should they wish to do so.

For more information on sports tours, see Chapter 2, Section 6, page 131.

2.3.30 **Overseas trips are not covered by the RPA.** Only United Kingdom travel is included, and academy trusts should take out their own overseas travel policy where required in the same way that all schools would ensure the correct level and type of insurance.

2.3.31 **Appropriate insurance cover is needed for centrally organised events, such as sports festivals**, in which students from a variety of schools take part. It is important that the organiser for the managing agency, such as a county sports partnership (CSP), governing body of sport, schools association or LA, makes clear who is providing essential insurance, and clarifies what schools and even individual parents might need to consider in terms of providing additional cover. The organiser for the managing agency should check that:

- the venue used for the event has its own public liability insurance that covers any accident involving a person due to a fault with the venue

- there is adequate third party liability to cover any accident arising from negligence by the managing agency, or as a result of a student participant causing injury to another participant or spectator

- parents know that it is their responsibility to take out personal injury insurance for their child should they feel that this is necessary, based on information they have received about the event.

More information regarding insurance requirements and planning a sports event can be found in afPE (2011) 'Safe practice for the school games – Guidance for local organising committees and schools', http://goo.gl/3ALIfM

FAQ

2.3.32 **As a physical education teacher, I have been asked to take a group of students to a sports event on a Saturday. Does my school insurance cover me to do this?**

If this is a school-organised and approved activity, then employers are expected to provide sufficient and appropriate insurance to cover their staff for the range and type of activities they might be asked to carry out within their contract of employment. Where it is commonplace for teachers to lead fixtures and activities on a Saturday, it is likely that the employer has included cover for this, but this should be confirmed.

Academies or free schools are responsible for arranging their own insurance. Those sourcing insurance cover therefore need to be clear about exactly the extent of cover required, ie including at weekends if the employer requires attendance at events by teachers.

Where the event or activity is not organised and approved by the school (eg it is a request by parents), if the teacher decides to go ahead, they must make their own insurance arrangements.

Case law

2.3.33 **van Oppen versus the Clerk to the Bedford Charity Trustees (1988):**

*The court established that it is the school's duty to insure against negligence, and it is the **parents' responsibility** to consider personal injury insurance for their children because it is a matter of choice or discretion.*

Chapter 2/Section 4: Safeguarding

Introduction

2.4.1   Safeguarding is action that is taken to promote the welfare of children, and protect them from harm. The concept is enshrined in statute based on the principle that the health, safety and welfare of the child are paramount. The definition provided in the most recent statutory guidance suggests that this should be achieved by:

> *protecting children from maltreatment; preventing impairment of children's health or development, ensuring children grow up in circumstances consistent with the provision of safe and effective care; and taking action to enable all children to have the best outcomes.*
>
> Department for Education (DfE) (2016) 'Keeping children safe in education: Statutory guidance for schools and colleges', https://goo.gl/U9MLH9

2.4.2   All who work with students have a duty to ensure the health, safety and well-being of those in their care and, within the law, may do what is reasonable in all circumstances for the safeguarding or promotion of students' welfare. Staff have a duty to **pass on concerns** about possible abuse (including suspected cases of female genital mutilation [FGM]) to the dedicated safeguarding lead within their organisation or school. There is no requirement to find evidence to support any concern, nor to have to be certain that significant harm may have, or has, occurred in order to report the concern. Where required, schools need to work with social care, the police, health services and other services to promote the welfare of children and protect them from harm.

2.4.3   Schools are required to have clear safeguarding **policy and procedures**. Employers must ensure that all staff are aware of and apply the necessary policy and procedures relating to the prevention of **intentional and unintentional harm of their students**. Within physical education departments, subject leaders need to check that the relevant school policy and procedures adequately cover the physical education, school sport and physical activity (PESSPA) context and, where they do not, discuss how these might be added from the relevant physical education documentation.

For further information regarding schools' responsibilities for safeguarding, see:

Ofsted (2015) 'Inspecting safeguarding in early years, education and skills settings: Guidance for inspectors undertaking inspection under the common inspection framework', https://goo.gl/e6GGSO

DfE (2016) 'Keeping children safe in education: Statutory guidance for schools and colleges', http://goo.gl/3ALIfM

HM Government (2015) 'Working together to safeguard children: A guide to inter-agency working to safeguard and promote the welfare of children', https://goo.gl/mefUFS

Understanding intentional harm

2.4.4 Safeguarding in some schools may be limited in scope to protecting students from **deliberate harm**, including physical, emotional or sexual abuse, neglect, bullying (including online or cyberbullying), racist abuse, harassment, discrimination and the potential for abuse of trust by adults working with children and young people. *The Teachers' Standards in England* (DfE, 2012), for example, state that teachers, including head teachers, should safeguard children's well-being, and maintain public trust in the teaching profession as part of their professional duties.

For more on *The Teachers' Standards*, see Chapter 2, Section 2, page 73.

2.4.5 All staff need to know about **indicators of intentional harm**, the school's systems for reporting causes for concern, and how to deal with students **disclosing** information about intentional harm to themselves or others.

2.4.6 It is important that PESSPA staff are aware of the general **signs and symptoms** of intentional harm, such as non-accidental bruising, and identifying changes in the mood or personality of students who may be affected by any such harm.

For information about identifying signs of abuse or neglect, recognising signs of child grooming or exploitation, and raising concerns, see the National Society for the Prevention of Cruelty to Children (NSPCC) website: www.nspcc.org.uk

Case law

2.4.7 The following cases were brought under the principle of **'abuse of a position of trust'**. (It is an offence under the Sexual Offences Act 2003 for a person over the age of 18, such as a teacher, to have a sexual relationship of any kind with a child under 18 where that person is in a position of trust in respect of that child, such as in teaching, even if the relationship is consensual.)

2.4.8 **R versus Drake (2011)**:

A physical education teacher who was also a deputy head teacher was sentenced to six years' imprisonment for maintaining sexual relationships with two 14-year-old students and one 16-year-old student.

2.4.9 **R versus Brooks (2007)**:

A physical education teacher received a five-year prison term for having an affair with a 14-year-old student.

2.4.10 **R versus Thompson (2008)**:

A physical education teacher groomed a 17-year-old student through texts and telephone calls. He was sentenced to a nine-month prison sentence, to be listed on the sex offenders register for 10 years and is not allowed any unsupervised access to a child under 18.

2.4.11 **R versus Lister (2005)**:

A physical education teacher was jailed for 15 months for using mobile phone calls and texts to groom young girls.

2.4.12 PESSPA staff should also be aware of specific PESSPA-related incidences of intentional harm such as staff intentionally:

- overplaying and overtraining talented students, using inappropriate training methods and imposing physical punishment for not carrying out a task or for being last to complete a task as **forms of physical abuse**

- depriving students of rehydration during physical activity in hot weather or adequate clothing during cold weather as forms of **neglect**

- encouraging or allowing violent play.

Safeguarding students by preventing violent play

2.4.13 Injuries occur in sport because of bad luck, careless acts or unacceptable violence on the pitch. Violence in sport may cause injury inflicted **outside the laws and spirit of the game**. This is assault, which is defined as the fear of or actual infliction of force. Dangerous play in sport represents unacceptable risk.

2.4.14   Violence in sport is not confined to adult participation. It is thus relevant to staff, coaches and managers in school situations because they have a **secondary, vicarious liability** for the actions and behaviour of their students 'on the pitch'. This is because they are the final adult to place the students in a competitive situation.

2.4.15   There is, as yet, no reported case of such criminal vicarious liability in PESSPA in the UK, but it could occur if a team manager has knowledge of a student's proven violent sporting offences and fails to apply sanctions. Continued selection of this player may provide evidence of **condoning violent play**.

2.4.16   Staff who teach, encourage or accept **over-aggressive play** may be held liable if their players go beyond the rules and spirit of the game. Failure to exercise control of a team is the responsibility of the team manager and one they cannot afford to ignore.

2.4.17   It is therefore important that schools have a procedure for monitoring students' fair play in competition. Where violent or reckless play occurs outside the rules and spirit of the game, immediate corrective action during the game should be implemented. For example, if the official does not remove the 'offending' player from the game, then the team manager should ensure the player takes no further part in the game because the likelihood of a similar incident occurring becomes foreseeable. In this case, the team manager could be deemed to have condoned the violence and be held vicariously criminally responsible for it.

2.4.18   Staff should also encourage students to report any occasion in which they feel threatened or intimidated as a result of violence or reckless play.

2.4.19   Further investigation will then be needed to establish whether the player has a propensity towards violence or reckless play, or whether the incident in question is deemed to have been isolated. This will determine whether that player is selected in future. Where there is the probability of repetition, the team manager selecting the player may be judged to condone violent play and be criminally prosecuted should there be any repetition of reckless or violent play by the player in question that results in causing injury.

2.4.20   It is good practice to design a 'fair play' **code of conduct** that is developed in collaboration with students. This should be communicated to and agreed by students, staff and parents. The code should outline the expectations of all concerned, and make clear any sanctions that might be imposed on those failing to respect its requirements.

For more information, see Chapter 2, Section 7, page 146.

Case law

2.4.21 **Hattingh versus Roux (2011, South Africa):**

*A hooker in the front row of a rugby scrum received a severe neck injury in a school match. The opposing hooker and prop both intentionally placed their heads together in the same gap when engaging in a scrum, instead of interlocking, to exert increased pressure on the opposing hooker. This is **illegal and dangerous**. The judge confirmed that players could not seek to deliberately injure opponents.*

2.4.22 **R versus Weston (2012):**

During a rugby match, a player hit an opponent, breaking his jaw, during an on-pitch fight about a tackle. The player was sent off by the referee. In court, the player was found guilty of grievous bodily harm and sentenced to six months' imprisonment.

2.4.23 **Gravil versus Carroll (1) and Redruth RFU Club (2) (2008):**

*A player admitted punching the claimant in an off-the-ball incident following a scrum during a semi-professional rugby match. The injured party needed facial surgery and was out of the game for six months. The offending player was suspended for eight weeks. The injured player alleged that the club (the second defendant) had encouraged aggressive play through a results-based bonus system. The Appeal Court ruled that it was 'fair and just' to hold semi-professional and professional clubs liable for their players' illegal or violent actions, establishing **'a vicarious responsibility for the injury'**.*

2.4.24 **R versus Chapman (2010):**

*During a football match, the injured player, while lawfully shielding the ball, was tackled from behind by the accused with raised studs. The accused claimed the tackle was not reckless but admitted grievous bodily harm. The judgement referred to the offence as **'a very deliberate criminal act'**. This was the first prison sentence (six months) given for a 'reckless tackle'.*

2.4.25 **R versus Stafford (2009):**

A golfer was jailed for nine months for causing actual bodily harm when he hit another player about the head in a 'golf rage'.

2.4.26   Poor behaviour by parents and other spectators at sports events and matches can be a concern for schools and have a detrimental effect on students. In its tool kit 'It's our game not yours', the NSPCC Child Protection Unit in Sport provides useful information to help organisations manage these concerns by:

- encouraging positive parental participation through clear communication, information and expectations

- managing challenging parental behaviour through promoting codes of conduct for parents, developing a clear process to respond to concerns or complaints

- promoting values such as respect and listening to each other, ensuring a designated safeguarding officer is known to all, and reminding parents to be positive role models for their children

- establishing sanctions for parents through monitoring behaviour, and carrying through to barring individuals from attending, while ensuring that the child's participation is not affected.

 To access 'It's our game, not yours', visit: https://goo.gl/Vdb0HB

Understanding unintentional harm

2.4.27   In addition to addressing the prevention of intentional harm, schools have a duty to ensure that students are safe and feel safe through protection from unintentional harm. Many of these issues are central to safe teaching and form part of relevant school policy and procedures. However, in PESSPA contexts, there are a number of more specific aspects of safeguarding that should be considered, and good practice indicates that these should be documented in PESSPA procedures and risk assessments.

2.4.28   Table 8, page 97, provides a checklist of aspects of safeguarding issues that are relevant to PESSPA and directs the user to where relevant information can be found in this resource.

2.4.29   The essential outcome is that intentional harm is effectively responded to and eradicated, and unintentional harm is avoided so that students **feel safe and are safe** within the broader consideration of safeguarding.

Table 8: Safeguarding issues within a PESSPA context

Indicators of Effective Safeguarding	Supporting Information
Students:	
• feel knowledgeable, comfortable and confident in PESSPA (ie caring ethos, safeguarding context and staff relationships)	Chapter 2, Section 4
• are appropriately matched, for example, in terms of group/team sizes, match ability, physical size, age, maturation	Chapter 2, Section 8
• are given consideration in specific situations as to whether they are likely to feel intimidated, threatened or harmed by others during activity	Chapter 2, Section 4
• are given opportunities to lead aspects of PESSPA sessions	Chapter 2, Section10
• wear clothing and footwear appropriate for the activity and conditions	Chapter 2, Section 10,
• remove/make safe jewellery and other personal effects • have access to PPE that is adequate for activity demands	Chapter 2, Section 11
• with cognitive, visual, hearing or motor impairment can access and be involved in PESSPA in line with requirements of the Equality Act	Chapter 2, Section 14
• with English as an additional language (EAL) are supported to understand safety procedures	Chapter 2, Section 14
• are knowledgeable about procedures and routines.	**Chapter 1, Section 5**

(continued)

Indicators of Effective Safeguarding	Supporting Information
Staff:	
• recruitment procedures are safe and followed for all PESSPA appointments	Chapter 2, Section 2
• competence to teach activity to the level of student ability is checked and monitored	
• requirement for a licence to coach (this is a requirement of some governing bodies of sport/local authorities) is checked before employment commences	
• observation and analysis skills are effective to ensure safe practice	
• control, discipline and organisational skills are adequate	
• project a positive, encouraging, educational manner, and establish appropriate relationships with, and respect for, students (and any other adults) who are teaching, training or instructing the same group of students unsupervised frequently, ie once a week or more often, or on four or more days in a 30-day period or overnight (ie are in regulated activity) have an enhanced Disclosure and Barring Service (DBS) disclosure and a barring check confirmed and accepted by the school, and those who are constantly supervised (not in regulated activity) have an enhanced disclosure accepted by the school if the school has decided to request one	Chapter 2, Section 4
• satisfy all disqualification checks	
• who are coaches need to be thoroughly vetted before starting work in schools to ensure they are not barred from working with children and young people	Chapter 2, Section 2
• delivering PESSPA should remove/make safe their jewellery and personal effects	Chapter 2, Section 10
• professional learning needs are identified and supported with regular training	Chapter 2, Section 2
• know and consistently apply school procedures to deal with observation or disclosure of possible abuse	Chapter 2, Section 4
• always supervise young sports leaders	
• avoid one-to-one situations with students wherever possible	
• should know which member of the senior staff has designated safeguarding responsibility.	

(continued)

Indicators of Effective Safeguarding	Supporting Information
Protecting children from deliberate harm:	
• School safeguarding procedures adequately address PESSPA situations.	Chapter 2, Section 4
• School procedures and codes of conduct are known and consistently applied by all staff and students.	**Chapter 1, Section 5**
• Checks are made with all club links/outdoor activity centres/other organisations that are used by the school/signposted to students, and their protocols are known and monitored.	Chapter 2, Section 6
• Staff have good awareness of contexts and opportunities in PESSPA and sports trips for bullying/racist incidents (including cyberbullying) and monitor these closely. • General and PESSPA-specific indicators of neglect, and physical, emotional and sexual abuse are known and regularly monitored by all staff. • Staff responses to disclosure of abusive experiences/knowledge are consistent with school reporting policy.	Chapter 2, Section 4
Medical conditions:	
• Staff know that administration of medicines is a voluntary activity that cannot be enforced. • Parents are asked for relevant medical information about their child. • Relevant medical information about students is known by the school, regularly updated, and always communicated to the class teacher and other adults teaching the student. • PESSPA-related individual health-care plans are in place, where appropriate. • Student medications are available to use in different PESSPA locations. • School policy on removal/wearing of medical bracelets is known and applied. • School policy on medication management is followed. • Staff are trained in specific medical situations as necessary (eg administering EpiPens). • School-parent agreements on administration of medicines are checked and applied to individuals.	Chapter 2, Section 14

(continued)

Indicators of Effective Safeguarding	Supporting Information
First aid provision:	
Provision for first aid must be available at all times for employees, and within a school situation, it is accepted that students are also included in such provision. Appropriate provision comprises: • clear, detailed and effective school procedures for managing first aid/emergency situations • staff who know and apply these school procedures • strategies to address time implications to respond to illness/injury at extremes of the school site • an effective emergency contact system • a travelling first aid kit being taken on all off-site visits • a trained first-aider or appointed person accompanying any group going off the school site, or alternative arrangements	Chapter 2, Section 15
• agreed reciprocal arrangements for use of the host school's first aid provision, equipment and facilities when injury occurs at away fixtures/off-site events	Chapter 2, Section 6
• keeping injury records according to school procedures • knowing and monitoring recovery and return procedures following concussion • discussion of near misses to improve safety standards • following school procedures for informing parents and keeping in touch regarding the student's recovery • making community users aware of limitations of first aid provision by the school.	Chapter 2, Section 15

(continued)

Indicators of Effective Safeguarding	Supporting Information
Digital technology:	
• School policy and strategy on Internet safety are applied consistently in PESSPA.	Chapter 2, Section 16
• All PESSPA staff are trained in Internet safety.	
• Students are reminded about Internet safety during PESSPA sessions and must be safeguarded from potentially harmful and inappropriate online material.	
• A school policy on staff contacting students by phone, email or text is known and applied by all.	
• Parents are involved in any electronic communication about fixtures/visit arrangements, and only via a disclosed list.	
• Photography and filming are used only within a clear learning context, and parents are made aware of such use within school policy.	
• Procedures and protocols to ensure ethics and security of digital imagery are known by all PESSPA staff, applied consistently and communicated to parents.	
• Access to images held by the school is controlled by a password/authentication process.	
• Clear procedures and agreement exist about when and where it is appropriate to use imagery across groups of schools.	
• Staff apply general safeguarding considerations in use of imagery (eg students cannot be identified, consideration of filming angles, general shots, particular care in swimming and gymnastics contexts).	
• School policy is applied on parental consent for digital imagery in education contexts.	
School/department security:	
• All adults involved in PESSPA programme wear identification and/or are known to students.	Chapter 2, Section 8
• Facilities not in use are locked, wherever possible, to prevent unauthorised access.	Chapter 2, Section 13
• Facilities are checked before locking to ensure that nobody is locked in.	
• High risk equipment is disabled/locked, or prohibition signs, where preventing access cannot be assured, are in place to prevent unauthorised use.	
• Equipment and facilities are checked periodically for continued safe use.	
• Routes to outside areas are safe and lit at night.	

(continued)

Indicators of Effective Safeguarding	Supporting Information
Drug and substance misuse:	
• Staff are trained in recognising symptoms of drug misuse. • School strategies to identify and support students with drug problems are known and applied. • Club links are checked for inclusion of anti-doping education and strict application of policies in written and practical procedures. • Implications of doping to enhance performance are communicated to students and monitored by staff. • School policy on advising about sports supplements is followed.	Chapter 2, Section 14
Transporting students:	
• School/employer policies on the use of cars, taxis, coaches and minibuses are clear for PESSPA activities. • Seat belts are always worn in any vehicle where belts are provided. • Child restraints are made available and used where required. • Roadworthiness of any vehicle used is checked. • Appropriate and current documentation (eg insurance, MOT) is in place. • Any driver has DBS clearance that has been checked and approved by the school/local authority. • No adult travels alone in any vehicle with an individual student other than their own children, unless required to do so in an emergency. • Emergency contact information is either carried by the group leader or held at school with access ensured at any time. • Safe embarkation/disembarkation points are identified and used. • There are no distractions for the driver of any vehicle other than in an emergency. • Adult supervision ratios are considered pre-journey. • Reciprocal arrangements are in place. (Through such an arrangement, the host school would agree to supervise students from a visiting school should an emergency require the supervising teacher from the visiting school to accompany a student to hospital. Another member of staff would be called from the visiting school to go the host school to take over this supervision.) • Accredited/well-known taxi, bus and coach companies are used. • Parents are informed where their child is to be transported in another parent's car arranged by the school, and their agreement is obtained. • A section 19 standard permit is displayed in the minibus if any form of charge is made by the school. • School/employer requirements for driving a minibus are fully met. • A minibus driver's legal responsibilities are known and met. • The school system for management of minibuses is compliant, effective and ensures safe use. • Trailer towing regulations are met. • Passenger access/exit is unobstructed when luggage/equipment is carried.	Chapter 2, Section 17

(continued)

Indicators of Effective Safeguarding	Supporting Information
Health and safety:	
• Good teaching standards are applied.	Chapter 2, Section 8
• There is good organisation (management) of lessons by the teacher and of the subject by the physical education subject leader.	
• Consistent safety standards are applied across the team of staff delivering the PESSPA programme.	
• School policy, procedures and standards are applied in PESSPA.	**Chapter 1, Section 5**
• Written risk assessments and documentation, specific to the school, are reasonably comprehensive and reviewed regularly.	**Chapter 1, Section 6**
• All necessary health and safety management documents are accessible to all staff.	
• Students are involved in their own safety at a level compatible with their age, understanding and ability.	**Chapter 3**
• Potentially hazardous PESSPA equipment (eg trampolines, climbing/traverse walls, resistance equipment, swimming pools) is used safely.	Chapter 2, Section 12 and Section 13
Use of appropriate physical intervention and support:	
• Exercise is not used as punishment.	Chapter 2, Section 4
• Stage/age/physical size/experience is matched in contact sports and in dance/gymnastics when lifting/supporting others' weight.	
• No adult participates fully in contact sports, weight-bearing activities or PESSPA activities that involve 'accelerating projectiles'.	Chapter 2, Section 8
• Students are informed about how manual support will be given (eg in dance or gymnastics). Manual support is provided using only appropriate techniques, and only when student consent has been given.	
• Spotters in trampolining are well trained, effective and limited in number.	Chapter 2, Section 12

(continued)

Indicators of Effective Safeguarding	Supporting Information
Overplaying and overtraining:	
• Staff demonstrate awareness of governing body of sport requirements/guidance in this area.	Chapter 2, Section 8
• Careful consideration is made about the size of court/pitch/hall and type of equipment appropriate for each group of students.	
• Students/teams are matched in terms of comparable age, standard, ability and confidence in early stages of competition.	
• Fixtures are stopped if a significant imbalance in size, age, ability or capability of students is observed.	
• Fixtures are rearranged to reflect better balance and matching of participants.	
• The appropriateness of activities is considered where boys and girls compete or take part together in fixtures or competition.	
• Programming and scheduling ensure that students' participation is not more than one full sports fixture in any given day, or in cases where a student participates in more than one game, their match preparation and training, and levels of fitness and skill are considered appropriate to ensure safe participation.	
Intimate care issues within PESSPA:	
• School policy addresses the PESSPA context adequately.	**Chapter 1, Section 5**
• Staff are trained and assessed as competent (eg at manual handling, administration of specific medicines).	Chapter 2, Section 14
• Gender staffing implications are considered where intimate care applies.	
• Dignity, decency and respect are consistently evident.	
Responding to weather conditions:	
• Measures to reduce overexposure to sun/heat are effective.	Chapter 2, Section 5
• Rehydration systems are in place.	
• Staff teaching position avoids students looking directly into sun.	
• Appropriate additional clothing is allowed in cold conditions.	Chapter 2, Section 10
• Security of footing on playing surfaces is considered.	
• Students are taught a safe response if caught in a sudden thunderstorm.	

Vetting and barring – the Disclosure and Barring Service process

2.4.30   School appointment procedures, including those for visiting coaches and other volunteers who will be in 'regulated activity', must include **vetting** to ensure that the person appointed is not barred from working with children and young people.

2.4.31   The Protection of Freedoms Act became law in May 2012. A key purpose of this legislation in relation to safeguarding is to clarify checking procedures and reduce the number of applications for checks, while still maintaining safe standards of protection.

For more information on the Protection of Freedoms Act 2012, see http://goo.gl/1hP89N

2.4.32   **For most appointments in schools** and settings working with children, an enhanced DBS check with barred list information will be required as the majority of staff will be engaging in **regulated activity**. For those appointed who will not be in regulated activity, a DBS check is not a requirement, but is considered to be good practice. (See Table 10, page 107.)

For more information on the DBS, see https://goo.gl/WAlp6i

2.4.33   Regulated activity is defined in Table 9 below.

Table 9: Regulated activity

a   Unsupervised activities: teach, train, instruct, care for or supervise children, or provide advice/guidance on well-being, or moderate a public electronic interactive communication service likely to be used wholly or mainly by children, or drive a vehicle only for children.

b   Work for a limited range of establishments ('specified places'), with the opportunity for contact (eg schools, children's homes, childcare premises). Not work by supervised volunteers.

Work under a or b is regulated activity only if done **regularly**.

Regularly is defined as:

carried out by the same person frequently (once a week or more often), or on four or more days in a 30-day period or overnight. 'Overnight' would be (even once) at any time between 2am and 6am where there is an opportunity for face-to-face contact with children.

Additional statutory guidance is being published by the government on supervision of activity that would be regulated activity if unsupervised.

c   Relevant personal care (eg washing or dressing; or health care by or supervised by a professional).

d   Registered childminding; and foster care.

Personal care includes helping a child, for reasons of age, illness or disability, with eating, drinking, or in connection with toileting, washing, bathing or dressing.

Health care means care for children provided by, or under the direct supervision of, a regulated health-care professional.

Defining 'supervision'

2.4.34   When appointing **support staff** to a PESSPA programme in schools, a number of recommended checks, observations and assessments should be carried out in addition to the DBS checking procedure. Further details of these are set out in Table 7, page 81, including the need to ensure the identity of the person, their actual qualifications, relevant courses attended and current licensing to coach from a governing body of sport.

2.4.35   When the head teacher or employer is satisfied with the initial checks, they must put in place the supervision required.

Condition of Supervision	What Does This Mean?
Must be provided by a person who is in regulated activity (see Table 9).	This is a staff member who meets the definition set out in a or b in Table 9.
Must be regular and day-to-day.	It must occur on an ongoing basis, and not only take place in a concentrated 'block' (eg at the start of the activity).
Must be 'reasonable in all the circumstances to ensure the protection of children'.	It must take into account the number, ages, abilities and special needs of children, and any additional support.

2.4.36   Once the head teacher or employer has established that the newly appointed support staff member will not be working in regulated activity (see Table 9, page 105), and that the scope and frequency requirements are met, they can request that the appropriate DBS check is undertaken. When completed, the DBS certificate is sent to the applicant, who is obliged to show this to their potential employer or contractor. (Employers may use the online update checking system if the applicant has previously subscribed to this through the DBS update service – see 2.4.43.)

 For more information on the DBS update service, see https://goo.gl/MnZwcA

2.4.37   Volunteers and coaches should never be used to displace teachers within the school curriculum, and always require a level of supervision as the class teacher remains responsible for the children in their group. (See Chapter 2, Section 2, page 79.) This being the case, volunteers and coaches delivering on the PESSPA programme and supervised at all times are unlikely to ever be in regulated activity, and schools will only need to request an enhanced level DBS check from them (where the scope and frequency are met). If, however, the extent of the supervision is only 'managerial' (ie overseen and directed) and the volunteer or coach is left alone with the students, then an enhanced check with barring information will be required.

2.4.38   The minimum age at which a DBS check can be requested is 16.

2.4.39   In the case of **trainee teachers salaried** by a school or college, the school must ensure that all necessary checks are carried out. If the school decides that these trainee teachers are likely to be engaging in regulated activity, an enhanced DBS certificate (including barred list information) must be obtained.

2.4.40   Where **trainee teachers** are **not salaried**, it is the responsibility of the initial teacher education (ITE) provider to carry out the necessary checks. Schools should obtain written confirmation that this has been done.

2.4.41   It must, however, be remembered that **trainee teachers are not fully competent to teach** until they are **'signed off'** as having reached the required level of competence against the Teachers' Standards (TS). This being the case, until that time, they should not be given full, unsupervised, responsibility within a practical PESSPA setting for any group, and are therefore unlikely to be deemed to be in regulated activity.

Table 10: Categories of vetting and barring checks

Type of Check	Extent of Check	Eligibility for Check to be Carried Out	Required for
Standard check	A check of the Police National Computer (PNC) records of convictions, reprimands and warnings	To be eligible for a standard level DBS certificate, the position must be included in the Rehabilitation of Offenders Act (ROA) 1974 (Exceptions) Order 1975	Those who may be working in a school setting but have no contact or direct dealings with students (eg maintenance workers, engineers, tradespersons) A standard DBS check is not appropriate for anyone working with children or young people
Enhanced check	A check of the PNC records as above, plus other information held by the police that is deemed by them to be relevant	To be eligible for an enhanced level DBS certificate, the position must be included in both the ROA Exceptions Order and in the Police Act 1997 (Criminal Records) regulations	Staff working in schools, but who are fully supervised at all times, and are therefore not in regulated activity (see Table 9, page 105)
Enhanced criminal record check with children's and/or adults' barred list information	Checks of the DBS children's and adults' barred lists, as well as the enhanced check	To be eligible to request a check of the children's or adults' barred lists, the position must be eligible for an enhanced level DBS certificate as above and be specifically listed in the Police Act 1997 (Criminal Records) regulations as able to check the appropriate barred list(s)	The majority of posts within schools where staff are left alone with students, and are considered to be in regulated activity (see Table 9, page 105)

Details relating to the legislation listed in the table can be found at www.legislation.gov.uk

Arrangements for the self-employed

2.4.42 Current legislation in England does not allow self-employed individuals to apply for a DBS check on themselves. Where a self-employed person (eg educational consultant, sports coach) needs to obtain a DBS check, they have the following options:

- **Contracting organisations** – if an organisation contracts a self-employed person for the delivery of a service, this organisation may apply for the DBS certificate on the self-employed person's behalf.

- **Endorsement organisations or umbrella bodies** – some professional bodies apply for DBS checks on behalf of their members (eg governing bodies of sport). The government provides a database of DBS umbrella bodies.

- **Disclosure Scotland** – the government's own advice suggests that a 'basic check' can be obtained from Disclosure Scotland (the sister organisation of the DBS), whether an individual lives in Scotland, England or Wales.

- **Subject access request** – this is an option where the local police force provides a certificate with similar information to a DBS certificate at the cost of £10. Since local arrangements vary for obtaining an application form, it is advised that applicants telephone the police and ask to speak to the data protection team. In order to complete the form, two sources of identification must be provided, one with a name and a photograph (passport or driving licence) and the other with a current address (a recent utility bill or bank statement), and a cheque or postal order for the appropriate sum.

- A **recruitment agency** can apply for a DBS check for self-employed people who register with them. The agency would be eligible to ask an exempted question as it would be the agency assessing the individual's suitability. The agency could countersign the application form.

Disclosure and Barring Service update service

2.4.43 Membership of this service enables the DBS holder to keep their certificate up to date, and allows employers to check a certificate online with the owner's consent. Through this method, the certificate can be used again when applying for a position within the same workforce group, where the same type and level of check is required.

2.4.44 Employers should ensure that where a previous volunteer moves into a paid role, a full reapplication is completed.

2.4.45 The update service can either be taken up when applying for the DBS certificate or within 19 days of receiving the certificate. Application is not possible outside of these times. For this reason, if the certificate has been applied for through an employer, it is important that it is passed to the applicant as soon as possible so they can commence the process.

More information can be found at https://goo.gl/2G7TyT

FAQ

2.4.46 **I currently teach in a secondary school and am moving to a new post in further education. Will I need to have a new DBS check carried out?**

If you signed up to the DBS update service when your previous DBS check was carried out, your new employer should be able to access and check, with your permission, your DBS certificate online. You will need to show your new employer your original certificate, and they will take the necessary details from it. This is possible because you are moving **within the same workforce**, and the type and level of check required is the same.

When your new employer checks your certificate with the online service, they should be able to satisfy themselves of your eligibility to work within the terms of your new post, provided that the certificate does not reveal any criminality or barring information and remains current, ie there is no outstanding information to be updated to it.

This service is designed to reduce the need to apply for additional DBS checks. Without signing up to the service, repeated checks are likely to be required.

Disqualification

2.4.47 Under government regulation, all teachers and support staff, and those who supervise activities out of school hours with pupils up to the age of eight, such as childminders and nursery staff, can be disqualified from their employment if they have, or live with someone who has, committed a serious violent or sexual crime, or has been banned from working with children.

2.4.48 Staff within this category can be asked to go through the process of declaring this information.

2.4.49 Where a staff member is affected, they may be suspended and will need to apply to have the disqualification waived. Anyone who is disqualified (or disqualified by nature of association) should not be employed. In these cases, it is understandable that the employer should suspend them until the waiver is granted. It is then the employer's decision about whether they wish to continue to employ them.

Procedures across the UK

The procedures outlined above are as set out by the DBS and apply in **England and Wales**.

In **Northern Ireland, AccessNI** provides the information required to consider a person's suitability for a post working with children and vulnerable adults. They will issue the necessary DBS information.

In **Scotland**, the **Protecting Vulnerable Groups Scheme** (PVG Scheme), managed by Disclosure Scotland, makes decisions about who is barred from working with children.

For further information on this area, see:

DBS: https://goo.gl/WAlp6i

Child Protection in Sport Unit and Sport and Recreation Alliance (2013) 'Defining "supervision" and regulated activity: Sport and recreation sector guidance', https://goo.gl/Memkrx

DfE (2015) 'Disqualification under the Childcare Act 2006: Statutory guidance for local authorities, maintained schools, independent schools, academies and free schools', https://goo.gl/p8boVC

Safeguarding considerations when planning for students to stay with host families – sporting events or tours abroad

2.4.50   Whatever the event, the health, safety and well-being of the student remains paramount in law. It cannot be assumed that similar checks will be made in other countries as those made by the DBS under UK safeguarding systems, policies and procedures. The culture of safeguarding young people may therefore be very different in foreign countries.

2.4.51   Staff should establish what control is possible over decisions made in the foreign country prior to and during the visit, and then confirm with the host school whether there is an equivalent system to the DBS in the host country. If there is, the host school should confirm in writing the checking process, and confirm that it has **carried out checks** for the host families. The DBS cannot access criminal records held overseas. The school can also contact the relevant foreign embassy or high commission of the country in question to find out if similar checks to the DBS can be conducted in the country they will be visiting.

2.4.52   In situations where no checks have taken place, the Outdoor Education Advisors' Panel (OEAP) has produced a number of model forms, in a range of languages, that can be used to provide details of the family and home circumstances that are relevant to the stay.

These forms can be found on the OEAP National Guidance website at: http://goo.gl/Vd61os

2.4.53   Schools will also need to take into account any established guidance produced by their employer or governing body of sport that covers developing event **welfare plans** and duty-of-care requirements for taking children away.

2.4.54   If the host foreign school or sports club has no specific child-protection policy, the host school or commercial organising agency should be asked to ensure that they and all adult members of the host family adhere to the standard safeguarding procedures at all times when working with the students. Some key points that address this are provided here:

- UK minimum standards (ie the operating standards within the UK school) are ensured and will not be compromised.

- Hosting arrangements have been made prior to departure, and host families have been checked by the host organisation or school, for suitability.

- Students share placements that are carefully matched with regard to gender, age, diet, religious beliefs, special needs and any other stated preferences.

- Where possible, two students stay with the same host family. If this is possible, two same-gender and similar-age students should share a room.

- The UK school has received confirmation in writing from the host school of the arrangements and approved the host families.

- The host family is provided with a key point of contact and a clear means of communicating any concerns that might arise.

- Arrangements are in place for host families to be informed of any special information about the placed student with regard to dietary and medical needs, access needs, and acceptable levels of supervision, free time and disciplinary sanctions.

- Host families are made aware of arrangements for collecting and transporting students throughout the trip.

2.4.55   Arrangements, such as an agreed code word, should enable students to **speak to a member of their school staff** confidentially, should they feel uncomfortable in the host-family home. All staff should have a list of the visiting group, with the names, addresses and telephone numbers of the families with whom they are staying.

2.4.56   A contingency fund may be advisable should an urgent need arise to re-accommodate a student.

Further guidance on exchanges and home stays (including a document outlining the key questions to consider when organising home stays and how to best manage the issue of vetting) is available on the OEAP National Guidance website: http://goo.gl/fvKJnv

2.4.57   The status of any members of the party who may not be a British national, or who may be in the process of obtaining that status, or who are not members of a European Union member state should be checked, including reference to the Home Office UK Border Agency, concerning the right of re-entry.

2.4.58   If a young person is flagged on a police watch list (eg where there are concerns that they may be at risk of sexual exploitation or abduction), the airport police may wish to interview them and see evidence of consent for them to travel abroad, prior to their being allowed to board an aeroplane. If a school knows (or suspects) that a young person in the group might be flagged, they are advised to ring 101 in advance of the visit. They will be directed to the appropriate police section to pre-empt any flagging issues at the airport.

Further guidance when planning a visit abroad can be obtained from the OEAP National Guidance for overseas visits: http://goo.gl/k6ImNz

For additional information from the Child Protection in Sport Unit regarding away trips and hosting, see https://goo.gl/KMUkAB

Safeguarding considerations when planning for students to stay with host families – residential events in the UK

2.4.59   Procedures should be the same as existing in-school arrangements, and minimum operating standards should be applied in the same way. If a central residential venue is used, then accreditation, safeguarding policies, procedures and good-practice guidance should be in place, but it is wise never to make assumptions.

2.4.60   The vetting of host families in the UK has been seen as good practice for some time. Requirements within the Safeguarding Vulnerable Groups Act 2006 make the vetting of host families in the UK mandatory. If the school is responsible for making the arrangement, and the host family is being paid, then the school can be seen as the regulated activity provider. Such a provider would be committing an offence if they knowingly allowed a person to carry out a regulated activity while barred. (Even where the family was not being paid, checking this would be good practice.) This being the case, they would need to request a DBS certificate with barred list check for those hosting students.

2.4.61   Where parents make the arrangements and select the hosts themselves, the school is not deemed to be the regulated activity provider. In these cases, the home stay forms on the OEAP National Guidance website can be helpful as these are also available in English.

The National Society for Prevention of Cruelty to Children (NSPCC) Child Protection in Sport Unit document 'Safe sports events, activities and competitions' covers all aspects of safeguarding responsibilities for events in the UK, as well as the planning required for residential events in the UK and abroad: https://goo.gl/XYYAgZ

Use of supplements in PESSPA

2.4.62   In recent years, the use of sports supplements by young athletes has increased dramatically. In the past, their use may have been focused on talented sports students. However, today, overt, widespread advertising has made these products obtainable, and appear more desirable for many young people.

2.4.63   The use of sports supplements should never be recommended to students by school staff.

2.4.64   Claims are made that the variety of chemicals in these products, such as minerals, vitamins, caffeine, creatine and glutamine, promote body development and, subsequently, enhance sports performance.

2.4.65   While the risk of taking vitamin supplements is relatively low, there is some concern that young athletes may then progress to taking more dangerous substances under the impression that they are as harmless as vitamins and minerals. However, overdose with vitamins and minerals cannot be ruled out, and some vitamins can be toxic when taken in vast quantities (such as iron and vitamin A) and may interact with other vitamins or drugs.

2.4.66   Sports supplements have not yet been tested on young people. Studies on adults indicate that many supplements provide no benefit to physical capacity or performance. As supplements are not classified as drugs, there is no regulation in their manufacture, often resulting in contamination with other chemicals, such as banned substances, during the manufacturing process. In addition, there are no formal guidelines for dosage so there could be adverse side effects if too much is inadvertently taken.

2.4.67 Protein powders are a commonly used supplement in the form of shakes, bars and capsules, and claim to promote muscle growth, and aid metabolism, hence assisting with weight loss. Again, these are not recommended for young people due to the lack of research into long-term effects.

2.4.68 Where staff are asked about the use of sports supplements, or they become concerned that students may be putting themselves at risk through the use of such substances, they should provide students with clear information:

- There is no clinical evidence that a young person who already eats a healthy, well balanced diet comprising plenty of fruit and vegetables, and keeps hydrated before, during and after exercise will improve their physical capacity or performance further by taking supplements.

- If used alongside a healthy diet, supplements will be excreted by the body as being 'surplus to requirements'.

- Supplements can place young people at risk and cause serious health problems.

- Higher risk supplements have been found in some products – these include androstenedione and other 'prohormone' precursors of testosterone, yohimbine and products containing cava. Tests on the effects of these products on the body have shown evidence of:

  - headaches
  - hair loss
  - raised cholesterol
  - stress on the liver
  - high blood pressure
  - heart palpitations
  - hallucinations.

Anti-doping

2.4.69 The UK anti-doping organisation (UKAD) – www.ukad.org.uk – provides information for schools, parents and sporting bodies to promote 'clean sport' and to help athletes to comply with the world anti-doping code.

2.4.70 Recently, UKAD has launched an accreditation process for schools that involves training for staff and students to promote a 'clean' approach to competition, and discourage the use of banned substances. Areas such as nutrition, physiotherapy and strength and conditioning are also covered, with the aim of educating potential 'athletes' early in their sporting careers.

 For more information, see http://goo.gl/2OAsWL

Chapter 2/Section 5: Programme management

Planning and preparation

2.5.1   **Well-prepared, structured lessons contribute to safe learning situations.** There is clear evidence that there are more injuries in unstructured situations than structured ones. **Planning** is therefore essential to safe practice, using whatever method the individual teacher needs, prefers or is required to use.

2.5.2   **Throughout the planning stage**, staff should think through the following process:

* This is what I want students to learn. This is how I plan for the learning to take place. **Is this learning experience safe?**

* If something happened to make the learning experience unsafe, what could I do to maintain the safety of the students?

* If I cannot introduce a safe alternative, I will have no option but to abandon the learning experience.

2.5.3   Staff should assess students' **learning needs** against well-structured **schemes of work (SoWs)** that set out progressive learning targets, essential techniques and skills, and relevant safe-practice information. SoWs should make reference to relevant aspects of the risk assessment for physical education, school sport and physical activity (PESSPA), which should include guidance on the organisation and teaching of safety so that safe practice is embedded in the learning process and addressed and implemented in every lesson.

2.5.4   It is important for all schools to have **schemes of work** that inform lesson planning, fulfil the statutory requirements of any curriculum being followed (eg national curriculum – NC) and meet local circumstances and needs.

2.5.5   In cases involving negligence, the issue of whether students have experienced the appropriate **stages of development** through a particular physical task is frequently raised.

2.5.6   Reference to a planned and progressive SoW that has been methodically followed helps to respond to such investigation.

2.5.7   Planning should take account of, and accommodate, all levels of competence and confidence to ensure effective, meaningful, relevant and inclusive content.

2.5.8   **Matching student capability** to an appropriately challenging task is enhanced when founded on progressive and structured learning experiences.

2.5.9   'Doubling up' of classes to provide some form of activity should be planned and managed with care, with particular thought being given to relevant aspects of safety such as space, student ability and teacher experience.

Contingency planning

2.5.10   Despite careful pre-planning, there are occasions when the planned PESSPA task, activity or session cannot proceed for reasons of safety. Alternative plans need to be considered and applied where possible, or when unavoidable, the session may need to be abandoned.

2.5.11   Contingency plans should be identified by asking 'what if' questions, throughout the planning process. This will ensure a more rapid and appropriate response to incidents such as sudden inclement weather, injury or mismatch between student ability and the demand of an activity.

 Case law

2.5.12   **R versus Ellis (2003)**:

*A teacher was convicted of manslaughter and a failure to provide adequate care for the rest of the group when a student died during a pool plunging activity where the prevailing conditions required the activity to be cancelled and **adequate contingency planning** to be in place.*

Learning objectives and outcomes

2.5.13   Planning clear learning objectives/intentions and outcomes/success criteria contributes to safe experiences, as well as to learning about safety.

2.5.14   Learning objectives/intentions are a key aspect of structured lessons, and these should be planned and made clear to students. Students should know what they are learning, how this will build on their prior learning, and why this learning is relevant and important to them.

2.5.15　In addition, learning outcomes and/or success criteria need to be planned and/or negotiated with students so that these are appropriate for their stage of learning, and students are clear about what will indicate learning progress. Well-planned learning outcomes/success criteria will help students and teachers to judge when and how it is appropriate and advisable to make further progress, which is a key element of ensuring a safe learning environment.

2.5.16　It is important that teachers:

- include explicit learning about safety in appropriate lessons

- monitor students' understanding of, and ability to apply effectively, principles of safe practice.

2.5.17　This is key to students becoming progressively more independent in relation to keeping themselves safe when engaged in independent physical activity.

 For guidance regarding student learning about safety, see Chapter 3, page 299.

Appropriate preparation/recovery

2.5.18　Preparation for physical activity can reduce the likelihood of injury, as well as ensure that the activity experience feels more comfortable. Helping the body to recover gradually after intense physical activity is also important and can combat problems such as muscle stiffness and soreness, and dizziness, fainting and nausea, which may occur if a gradual easing-off process is not followed.

2.5.19　An appropriate **warm-up** and cool-down should be included in every lesson, and should be relevant to the activity and appropriate for the learning environment/weather conditions. Students should learn about the purpose of the components and about how to perform warm-up and cool-down exercises, paying attention to the principles of **safe exercise practice.**

2.5.20　Progressively, students should take responsibility for planning and carrying out their own warm-ups and cool-downs as a step towards independent activity in later life. However, the content should be closely **monitored** by the teacher, to ensure that it is safe, effective and appropriate.

 For more information on warming up, cooling down and safe exercise practice, see Chapter 2, Section 9, page 170, **and Chapter 3, Section 5, page 320.**

Progression

2.5.21　Progression is about the **staged development** of knowledge, skills and understanding in accordance with confidence, ability and successful prior experience. Carefully planned and graduated progression is fundamental to enabling students to improve safely their skill and understanding in PESSPA. Planning learning outcomes/success criteria (as described on page 115) is an important element of ensuring appropriate and safe progression.

2.5.22　Progressive practices enable students to develop or proceed competently and confidently to more complex movement and skills application over time.

2.5.23   Staff intervention in students' practical work leads on from sound planning. Appropriate **adjustment, modification or conditioning** of PESSPA activities should attempt to accommodate the ability range, previous experience, confidence or group size in lessons, thus improving the overall safety of the experience for all.

2.5.24   Applying the **'STEP'** framework can help to achieve such modifications by making appropriate changes to the:

- **s**pace –where the activity is happening

- **t**ask – what is happening

- **e**quipment – what is being used

- **p**eople – who is involved.

2.5.25   By using this approach, all students can be enabled to achieve success in an environment that safely meets their needs.

2.5.26   Staff should check that students have competently and confidently achieved each stage of learning before moving on to more complex or demanding tasks. Well-planned learning outcomes/success criteria should support these judgements and enable students to become increasingly involved in making appropriate decisions about their own progress. Careful management of the lesson should prevent peer pressure resulting in students progressing on to tasks beyond their capability until they are sufficiently prepared to do so.

2.5.27   In addition, it is an essential element of safe provision for staff to be knowledgeable about, and able to organise, PESSPA activities that are developmentally appropriate. They should understand how to apply 'overload' (working the body beyond its normal everyday level) appropriately in physical activity programmes, and take account of developmental needs when 'staging' and organising specific sport events (eg in terms of pitch size, duration and equipment used). This contributes to safe teaching and the setting of physical challenges at an appropriate level.

2.5.28   Safe and appropriate progression within a PESSPA session may be developed through various **strategies**, including progressing from:

- single to combined tasks

- non-contact to contact situations

- simple to more complex tasks

- copying to practising and then to refining, adapting and varying movements, skills and tasks

- identifying and describing to comparing, to analysing and evaluating performance

- familiar to unfamiliar situations

- set to negotiated tasks and possibly to self-determined tasks

- individual to pair and small-group activities

- large spaces to more restricted spaces (or vice versa depending on the specific nature of the activity)

- cooperative to competitive tasks

- closely supervised to remotely supervised activity.

2.5.29 Staff should assess an individual's **mental and physical readiness** before introducing a new skill or progressing to greater complexity. Staff should also be confident that they are themselves competent to progress the teaching safely. Where this is not the case, they should seek further professional learning.

 ## Case law

2.5.30 **Heffer versus Wiltshire County Council (1996):**

*A student was injured in a gymnastics lesson while attempting a straddle vault over a buck. The class had progressed from performing leapfrog with support to performing the same skill using the buck. Support was withdrawn when using the buck, unless it was requested by the students. The student in question was hesitant and refused his first attempt, unseen by the teacher. On the second attempt, he managed to clear the buck but used a one-foot take-off, allowing the swing of his leg to dislodge his supporting arm, causing him to fall to the floor, injuring himself. In allowing compensation for the claimant's injury, the court judged that the student was supported throughout the leapfrog activity and that support should not have been withdrawn on the buck. It should **not** have been left to the student to 'opt in' for support (peer-group pressure may have prevented opting in). Reduction in support was judged to be premature and total, rather than gradual, and it was deemed that progression to the buck constituted a new activity requiring a continuation of support.*

2.5.31 **Jones versus Hampshire County Council (1997):**

A vaulting table had been introduced into the school about 3–4 weeks before the incident occurred. The class had not used this before in the way they were being asked to use it during this gymnastics lesson. It was alleged they were not told precisely what to do with it, that no task had been set.

One pupil rolled along the table, and the claimant copied, twice successfully but on the third attempt, fell and broke her arm. The pupil alleged inadequate instruction and supervision, and an unsafe system being used by the teacher.

The claimant in this case was 24 years old. They were making a claim against this incident that had happened 13 years before, when they were 11.

The Court of Appeal said that 'it may be perfectly reasonable for a teacher to allow children to engage in an activity which, on the face of it, is fraught with danger if that teacher has made an assessment of those children and come to the conclusion that the activity is reasonably safe for them'. On the evidence provided, no such judgement had been made. The pupils were 'simply left to get on with it'.

A breach of duty was evident. The teacher should have seen that the particular activity was beyond the competence of this particular pupil.

2.5.32 **R versus Manningtree High School (2013):**

In a prosecution brought about by the Health and Safety Executive (HSE), a secondary school was fined for safety failings after a 14-year-old boy fell more than four metres from a climbing wall.

The teenager was on his first ever 'lead climb' – a more advanced rock-climbing technique – during a physical education lesson. He had managed to clip on to three points as he ascended the climbing wall but struggled with the fourth. A fellow student, similarly inexperienced, had been told to 'belay' the rope for the boy. After the climber grew tired, the teacher told him to let go of the climbing wall, which he did. However, instead of being supported by the belay technique, he fell unrestrained and hit the safety mat on the floor, fracturing a heel bone.

The HSE investigation found that, prior to the lesson, none of the students involved were aware what lead climbing was or the risks involved, and none had been properly trained or prepared for the more advanced type of climbing that was being attempted.

The school failed to have an adequate safety management system in place for lead climbing by failing to adequately protect the students against the risk of falls. In addition, the teacher was not competent to teach or supervise lead climbing.

Personalised learning

2.5.33   Individual students have variable levels of prior experience, ability and confidence. They need provision to make safe progress at individual or small-group rates. No class has a uniform level of ability or need to progress at the same rate, even if grouped or 'streamed' according to ability.

2.5.34   All students can learn if they are provided with appropriate learning conditions. Differentiated work, or **personalised learning,** involves matching the tasks to the students to enable progress at an appropriate pace within lessons, over a series of lessons and throughout a programme of study.

2.5.35   In addition, the range, quality and availability of age- and ability-related equipment for most activities should enable schools to meet the specific needs of students without risking injury through the use of items of inappropriate size, weight or design.

2.5.36   Staff should understand that individuals may need to work differently and the implications of this on safe practice, and should respond by **adjusting the demand of the activity,** making it easier or more difficult according to the specific requirements of the individual.

2.5.37   Safety may be compromised where a student or group of students cannot match the demand or pitch of a task or activity. Equally, work that is **not sufficiently challenging** may lead to boredom and casual application by the student that compromises safe practice.

2.5.38   To provide **personalised learning,** staff should know:

- what is to be achieved

- students' ability levels and prior experience

- students' stage of development

- how students prefers to learn

- how to extend a student's response in an appropriate and safe manner

- how to manage groups so that individuals can function individually as and when necessary.

2.5.39   Personalised learning can be addressed through:

- enabling or extension activities, such as modifying the general task

- setting different tasks for different students

- providing different levels of information, support and intervention

- providing more teacher time for some students than others

- allowing more or less time to complete a task

- using modified equipment and resources to promote success

- modifying the playing area or work space for some students

- modifying the task

- modifying the language used

- responding to an individual's ability, such as in challenging some for more creative or complex responses.

2.5.40   The STEP framework (page 117, 2.5.24) is commonly used to support effective planning of personalised learning in PESSPA.

 Case law

2.5.41   **Anderson versus Portejolie (2008):**

*A skier was seriously hurt when taken off-piste during a ski-school lesson. He was successful in claiming negligence on the part of the instructor, arguing that he was **not experienced** enough to have been taken off-piste and that the instructor should have realised the demand of the task was beyond some in the group.*

Regular and approved practice

2.5.42   Regular and approved practice is that which is **common and widely practised** as safe, as opposed to an idiosyncratic practice adopted by individuals or organisations.

2.5.43   Following regular and approved practice is good practice and provides a strong defence against a charge of alleged negligence as this practice is typical of what the profession would utilise across the country in delivering aspects of the PESSPA programme.

2.5.44   When choosing not to follow practice that is generally accepted as regular and approved, organisations should be able to justify clearly their reasons for this decision.

2.5.45   **Typical sources** of widely used, established practice include guidelines provided by local authorities, governing bodies of sport, government agencies, professional associations (eg afPE, BASES) or respected and acknowledged experts in a particular field.

2.5.46   **Improvisation** of equipment, or improvised use of equipment for purposes other than those it was designed for, is not widely held to be good practice and should be considered only with great care and forethought.

 For more information, see Chapter 2, Section 12, page 191.

2.5.47   It is recognised within law, however, that there is no one set response to situations, but that acceptable practice can be achieved within a number of appropriate choices, ie there are a **'range of reasonable options'**.

 ## Case law

2.5.48   **Woodroffe-Hedley versus Cuthbertson (1997):**

*An experienced alpine guide caused the death of a client by not following the **established climbing procedure** (regular and approved practice) of providing a strong enough anchor point, by using only a single ice-screw instead of two, in order to save time. A sheet of ice gave way, and the client was swept away as the single ice-screw came loose.*

2.5.49   **Shaw versus Redbridge LBC (2005):**

*An allegation of negligence was dismissed because the teacher's action was **typical** of what would be seen across the profession and judged to be 'proper professional judgement', ie regular and approved practice.*

2.5.50   **Woodbridge School versus Chittock (2002):**

*This case established the principle of a 'range of reasonable options' being acceptable in dealing with issues and recognised that **no single response was the correct way to deal with a situation.** In other words, some degree of flexibility according to the circumstances was a more appropriate responsible response.*

Introducing new activities

2.5.51   Where staff plan to introduce a new activity into the PESSPA programme, they should:

- consult with the head teacher and employer

- check insurance arrangements in relation to the activity

- where the sport or activity has a recognised governing body or national association, make use of information and guidance it offers, either through its website or by contacting it directly

- check on the governing body website, or during a visit to a local club, that all necessary policies are in place

- meet with any development officers available for that activity

- consider staff expertise and any professional learning requirements

- talk to other schools that have introduced the activity and learn from their experiences

- carry out a risk-benefit analysis.

For more information, see Chapter 1, Section 7, page 60.

Keeping registers and records

2.5.52   It is a legal requirement that a school records the presence or absence of students.

2.5.53   It is important to maintain evidence of students' **participation** by recording their presence, extent of participation or absence from physical education lessons.

2.5.54   Where a student has been absent from physical education lessons for a period of time, staff need to **reintegrate** that student with care. Extra observation is important to ensure that the student can cope with the pitch and pace required to catch up on the progression made during their absence. The same principle applies where a student joins a group part way through a lesson.

2.5.55   For the same reasons, schools should consider extending their policy of keeping registers to include extracurricular activity sessions run either by school staff or external coaches and volunteers. This practice is recommended.

2.5.56   Records of achievement and attainment also provide hard evidence of what individual students do or do not know, understand or are able to do. They indicate the extent to which individual students achieved the intended learning outcomes. These records enable the teacher to pitch the **demand of activity** at a level appropriate to the confidence, prior experience and ability of individual students and to take account of any work missed.

 Case law

2.5.57   **Moore versus Hampshire County Council (1981):**

*A student who was excused physical activity for medical reasons eventually persuaded a teacher to allow her to take part. During her first gymnastics lesson, she fell and broke her ankle while attempting a handstand. The teacher had **not supervised her closely** in what was her introduction to work that the other students in the class had experienced over a series of lessons. The teacher failed to cater for that student's individual needs and background.*

Practical demonstrations

2.5.58 Students' perceptual preferences differ in terms of the extent to which they favour **visual, auditory and kinaesthetic** experiences in movement-related learning (ie learning through seeing a movement, hearing information about how it should be performed, or placing the body or relevant part into the desired position[s]). Practical demonstrations provide one or more of these experiences.

2.5.59 During practical demonstrations and when this is necessary, students might need to be agreeable to the use of appropriate physical contact to enable a staff member to demonstrate correct positioning. In the case of students with SEND, appropriate communication and response methods will need to developed between staff and the student over time. Staff should be aware of **safeguarding procedures** with regard to appropriately positioning parts of a student's body correctly.

For more information about physical contact from adults in student activities, see Chapter 2, Section 8, page 157.

Rules

2.5.60 All sports have rules. These have evolved to make competition **fair and safe.** Anyone involved with officiating games has a duty of care and a duty of control. They need to **know the rules** relevant to the specific PESSPA activity and must **apply** the rules stringently in order to avoid unnecessary, foreseeable injury.

2.5.61 Where activities have a governing body of sport to administer the way they operate, the rules of those activities are set by that body. School PESSPA, in many aspects, acknowledges and reflects these rules. However, in an educational setting, it is not always practical or possible to apply the rules of the governing body of sport, and schools need to consider adjustments that they can make to enable maximum participation while retaining the safety of the activity (eg in relation to the wearing of personal protective equipment [PPE]).

For more information, see Chapter 1, Section 2, page 11, 1.2.10–1.2.11, and Chapter 2, Section 11, page 189, **from** 2.11.51 **onwards.**

Fatigue, injury and exhaustion

2.5.62 **Fatigue, injury and exhaustion** may occur when students are required to use equipment or attempt a task:

- that is inappropriate to their age, stage of development or ability

- where they are required to play on pitches and courts that are inappropriate for their level of fitness or disability

- where they are required to carry out events over longer distances than those recommended for their age or stage of development.

2.5.63   Age-appropriate sized pitches/courts should be made available, either in a permanent or temporary form (such as using marker discs). Information regarding recommended pitch and court sizes is available on governing body of sport websites and home country sport agency technical websites and publications; for example, Sport England (2015) 'Comparative sizes of sports pitches and courts':

- outdoors – https://goo.gl/vN8jYk

- indoors – https://goo.gl/vkzJXA

For more information, see Chapter 2, Section 13, page 216.

2.5.64   Staff should constantly **monitor** students to check that the demand of a PESSPA activity does not create an unacceptable level of physical or emotional stress on any individual. Increased demand should be progressive and at a rate and level of challenge appropriate for the individual.

2.5.65   **Physical signs** are evident in students as fatigue and exhaustion occur. These may vary, but a flushed face, rapid shallow breathing, wide eyes, frantic or disjointed movements and loss of performance are frequent indicators.

2.5.66   PESSPA staff should familiarise themselves with any additional 'elite' or community sports club training that students may be undertaking outside school that may increase the likelihood of fatigue. In cases where possible fatigue is identified, discussions should take place with the student to consider reducing the level of exertion from school PESSPA sessions to accommodate external training expectations that may put additional physical demands on them.

See also fatigue through fasting in Chapter 2, Section 5, 2.5.74, page 126.

Weather conditions

2.5.67   Before PESSPA sessions commence, forethought should be given to the **weather conditions** (for sessions on or off site). There is always the potential for **adverse** weather to affect lessons. Careful and thoughtful planning of safe indoor alternatives is important, where these can be accommodated.

2.5.68   The physical demands of athletics, games and adventure activities are such that the body is often moving quickly so it is essential that the weather conditions do not impede safety. On damp or frosty mornings, the risk of slipping on a **grass or painted court surface** is increased and needs to be carefully assessed.

2.5.69   The position and brightness of the sun in relation to the students and types of activities they undertake can also impact on safe performance. The risks associated with overexposure to the two bands of ultraviolet light (from the sun) are well documented.

See also Chapter 2, Section 11, 2.11.50, page 189.

2.5.70   It is unreasonable to try to base decisions about carrying out PESSPA activities on specific maximum temperatures as there are no specific recommendations about this. However, during periods of unusually hot weather, teachers should monitor students for signs of heat exhaustion (eg headaches, dizziness, nausea, cramps, muscle weakness or pale skin).

2.5.71   Staff should be particularly mindful of a range of precautions for ensuring the well-being of students when working outside in hot/sunny conditions. Staff should ensure that:

- lengthy periods in direct sunlight, particularly around midday when the sun is at its hottest, are avoided whenever possible; this may occur when students have a physical education lesson outside followed or preceded by an outdoor lunchtime practice

- there is a system for providing access to drinking water in a way that is manageable for staff (eg students might provide their own water bottles when outside)

- they handle body image issues sensitively with students (eg with overweight or obese students wearing unnecessary layers of clothing in hot temperatures)

- students are taught how to screen themselves from the harmful effects of the sun through wearing light clothing and using sunscreen products; parents should be reminded about the need for students to use sunscreen products, and asked to provide these

- students are permitted to wear hats as long as they pose no danger to the wearer or other participants in terms of the quality of the items and the nature of the activity; some primary schools purchase sun hats for pupils, which are then kept in school

- additional shaded areas are provided during sports days, or when attending tournaments, festivals and other events, where students may be exposed to the sun for long periods of time (eg by using gazebos or tents)

- students showing early symptoms of heat exhaustion are moved into a cool area and rehydrated.

Additional guidance is provided by the National Institute for Health and Care Excellence (NICE) at https://goo.gl/Hiko4G

Also see information provided by the Outdoor Kids organisation at www.oksunsafetycode.com

© TinnaPong/Shutterstock.com

FAQ

2.5.72   **I have heard that school staff should not assist students in applying suncream. Some younger students struggle to manage this on their own. Should they be helped?**

School policy on the use of suncream often specifies that students must apply their own suncream, or that the parents do so before the child arrives at school. The HSE suggests that the real issue to address is about teaching young people at an early age how to take sensible precautions against the sun, which is learning they can make use of throughout their lives. The HSE does not consider it helpful or proportionate for schools to insist on students wearing long sleeves and sun hats as some students will find this very uncomfortable. The HSE also clarifies that **there is no legal obstacle to school staff helping children to apply sunscreen**. Schools are able to make their own decisions about this, and where they do decide to assist students, they should do so observing correct procedures regarding physical contact. Whichever route a school decides to take, as with all policy, it should be clearly communicated to all staff, students and parents.

Considering religious and cultural issues when managing a programme

2.5.73   The broad religious and cultural demographics in schools present a range of health and safety issues that need to be managed within a PESSPA programme to enable all students to take part safely. The most frequent health and safety **questions** arise in relation to:

- the wearing of certain items of clothing and/or religious artefacts (see Chapter 2, Section 10, pages 175 and 179)

- the impact of religious/cultural festivals (eg Ramadan – Muslim month of fasting, which changes from year to year)

- cultural expectations relating to PESSPA activities and procedures

- participation in single- or mixed-gender groups (see Chapter 2, Section 8, page 156)

- language issues, which may put newly arrived students for whom English is an additional language (EAL) at risk due to difficulties in understanding the requirements of the task, safety procedures and expectations relating to conduct, and may affect their ability to stop work immediately in the event of danger or emergency.

2.5.74   Staff should be aware that religious and cultural **festivals** (eg Ramadan, which involves fasting from dawn to dusk over the period of a month) may require some students to engage in specified dietary regimes. As a result, energy levels may be low and the risk of dehydration increased. In such situations, staff expectations relating to participation in physical activity (eg sustained running) may need to be reviewed and levels of physical demands adjusted to accommodate individual needs.

2.5.75   Younger students, particularly, may be prone to a lowering of concentration levels if **fasting**. This has clear implications for the supervision and management of physical activity, and care needs to be taken in maintaining a safe working environment. For example, work on apparatus in gymnastics may require modification, and intensity levels in games activities may need to be reduced to a point where fasting students may continue to participate safely.

2.5.76   Staff need to remain responsive to student needs at all times. However, particular care needs to be taken when Ramadan or similar festivals fall in the summer months, which may exacerbate the risk of dehydration and fatigue.

2.5.77   Religious and cultural customs and beliefs fundamental to certain faiths may initially be seen to conflict with the demands made by some PESSPA activities within a prescribed curriculum. **Swimming**, for instance, presents particular issues for some communities (possibly from the Hindu and Muslim faiths), associated with unacceptable exposure of the body, mixed-gender settings or the wearing of adornments.

2.5.78   As well as being a statutory requirement in some contexts (eg the primary NC in England and Wales), swimming is a potentially lifesaving skill that all children have an entitlement to access. In securing this access, school staff should apply all practical means to respect any religious or cultural sensitivities, while providing a swimming programme that at least meets the requirements of the curriculum being followed. To enable this, staff should try to:

- establish ongoing discussion with local faith leaders and parents so that policies concerning swimming provision are effectively communicated and understood

- accommodate adjustments in swimming attire to satisfy religious and cultural sensitivities while maintaining safe practice

- ensure that changing arrangements take into account any mixed-gender issues and provide acceptable levels of privacy

- operate a swimming programme that builds in single-sex teaching, whenever practical and wherever this preference is feasible.

2.5.79   EAL students may not fully understand the requirements of, or how to set about, a particular physical activity. This could potentially pose a risk to themselves and the rest of the group. It cannot be assumed that the complexity of the language used in PESSPA activities is any less demanding than elsewhere in the curriculum, and the speed of response often required puts further pressure on the ability of such students to comprehend. PESSPA staff should ensure that:

- where learning support staff are available, they should be effectively briefed about the learning outcomes of the lesson and alerted to any safety features

- time should be taken, initially, to ensure individual EAL students clearly understand the command 'Stop!' and know that an immediate response to cease activity is required, should this command be necessary; over time, other key phrases, identified through risk assessment procedures, can be introduced into EAL students' vocabulary

- all staff are familiar with the names of EAL students in order that they can quickly attract and maintain their attention

- focused demonstrations are used, when appropriate, to attempt to overcome linguistic difficulty – linked to an acknowledgement by the students that they have understood what is required

- a 'buddy' system is used, where necessary, in which an EAL student is paired with another student known to have a responsible and mature disposition; this reflects good practice.

Chapter 2/Section 6: Sports fixtures, festivals, tours and club links

Sports fixtures

2.6.1 Sports fixtures held at and away from the school site are common practice. Procedures for these events should be routine, and all staff and students who participate in them should be familiar with these. The head teacher (HT), on behalf of the employer, must be aware of, and **approve**, all activities that students undertake within a school sport programme.

2.6.2 Safety issues relating to **home fixtures** should be addressed within the risk assessment for physical education, school sport and physical activity (PESSPA) as normal procedures should apply.

> **i** **See the exemplar risk assessment template for PESSPA in Chapter 1, Section 6, Table 4, page 36.**

2.6.3 **Away fixtures** often fall within a school's procedures for **regular off-site visits**. As school fixtures generally follow the same organisational procedures, it is acceptable for a single risk assessment to cover the whole off-site school-sport fixture list for a full year, or it may be reviewed on a seasonal basis. **It is not necessary for every individual sports fixture to have a written risk assessment**.

> **i** **See the exemplar risk assessment template for off-site fixtures and events in Chapter 1, Section 6, Table 5, page 48.**

2.6.4 Normal school procedures for informing parents, and requirements for consent forms should be followed.

> **i** **See information about parental consent in** Chapter 2, Section 7, page 143.

2.6.5 When operating a fixtures programme, planning and procedures should follow those set out in the checklist in Table 11, page 132, in this section.

FAQ

2.6.6 **I understand that I need to carry out a risk assessment for away sports fixtures with other schools. Is it necessary to do this for every fixture?**

The decision regarding when and how risk assessment should be carried out depends to a large extent on the requirements of the employer. While employers are tasked to undertake risk assessments under the Management of Health and Safety at Work Regulations (1999), the type and frequency of these is generally a local decision. Guidance provided by the Department for Education (DfE) suggests a measured approach to risk assessment and that 'Sensible management of risk does not mean that a separate written risk assessment is required for every activity'.

DfE (2014) 'Health and safety: advice for schools', https://goo.gl/oyHvHU

The above information is relevant to daily school sports fixtures, and as such, it is considered acceptable for one risk assessment to cover all fixtures for the year unless the risk assessment needs to be reviewed following an incident or change of circumstances. In contrast, where a school decides to enter into a tournament off site in which they have previously not been involved, they would be wise to risk assess this activity separately.

In all cases, the employer needs to decide which approach is to be taken.

See the exemplar risk assessment template for off-site fixtures and events in Chapter 1, Section 6, Table 5, page 48.

Sports festivals and tournaments

2.6.7 These are examples of centrally organised events in which individual schools are invited to participate. In addition to working through the planning set out in the checklist in Table 11, page 132, such events need three separate planning and risk assessment responsibilities.

The venue risk assessment

2.6.8 The venue manager/owner/host needs to have completed a risk assessment that identifies the hazards, evaluates the risks and establishes appropriate controls to make the **venue** safe for the purpose for which it is being offered or hired out to the user group. This may be known as a risk assessment or normal operating procedures and emergency action plan. Swimming pools, leisure centres and independent arenas are usually thorough in doing risk assessments, but school venues can vary widely. Where the venue risk assessment is **lacking or not available**, the event organiser needs to complete a venue assessment prior to the event.

The organiser's event risk assessment

2.6.9   When an event organiser hires a facility to use for an event, they in effect become the legal occupier for the duration of that event. The event organiser needs to complete an event risk assessment that takes account of venue issues and the organisation of the planned event. Where possible and appropriate, a provider's or **hirer's contract** or questionnaire should be used to clarify these arrangements, and to secure confirmation and agreement regarding matters such as responsibilities of each party, and **public liability insurance**. The relevant issues from this assessment need to be clearly communicated to the staff who are managing groups attending the event, and should form part of the **pre-event guidance and information** provided to the schools, along with the event programming, procedures and any other essential information.

2.6.10   Organisers should also establish a **contingency date** that is acceptable to all to cover any situation where an event may need to be postponed (eg due to poor weather or exceedingly high temperatures).

School risk assessment

2.6.11   The school staff need to take account of the information received from the event organiser about the venue and organisation of the event, and carry out a **risk assessment for their group**. This risk assessment should consider preparing for the event, outward and return journeys, managing and supervising the group at the event, and returning them to their parents' care safely.

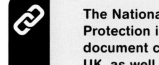

See the exemplar risk assessment template for off-site fixtures and events in Chapter 1, Section 6, Table 5, page 48.

The National Society for the Prevention of Cruelty to Children (NSPCC) Child Protection in Sport Unit 'Safe sports events, activities and competitions' document covers all aspects of safeguarding responsibilities for events in the UK, as well as the planning required for residential events in the UK and abroad: https://goo.gl/5malUh

Sports tours

2.6.12　The planning and management of sports tours in the UK and abroad is complex, whether they are arranged through a commercial company or by the school staff themselves.

2.6.13　The **employer's requirements** for events that take place at a considerable distance from the school base and/or are residential in nature should be part of an off-site and educational visits policy, and made known to, and applied by, all involved in the organisation.

2.6.14　Many overseas sports tour companies are accredited by the School Travel Forum, which is the awarding body for the Learning Outside the Classroom Quality Badge issued in this sector.

For more information on the School Travel Forum, see www.schooltravelforum.com

2.6.15　When schools include fixtures, attendance at school tournaments and festivals, and sports tours in their programme, planning should be methodical and precise. The advice for 'away fixtures' in the checklist in Table 11, page 132, should be followed, **plus** the additional requirements for festivals and tournaments, and sports tours set out in the adjacent columns. The planning process should consider:

- pre-event planning

- assembly

- outward and return journeys

- the venue and event

- post-event evaluation.

2.6.16　Table 11, page 132, suggests points for consideration by organisers of away fixtures, festivals and tournaments and sport tours.

2.6.17　These can be used:

- **to complement any additional documentation** and requirements set out by the school employing authority in respect of off-site and educational visits

- in conjunction with the exemplar risk assessment template for off-site school sport fixtures, events and tours (**Chapter 1, Section 6, Table 5, page 48**), which also indicates where relevant supporting information can be found in this resource.

2.6.18　In addition, and where appropriate, the educational visits coordinator should also be consulted.

2.6.19　**If organising an away fixture**, refer to the points in the Away Fixtures column only.

2.6.20　**If organising a festival or tournament**, refer to points in both the Away Fixtures and Festivals and Tournaments columns.

2.6.21　**If organising a sports tour**, refer to points in the Away Fixtures, Festivals and Tournaments, and Sports Tours columns.

Table 11: Points to consider when planning fixtures, festivals and tournaments, and sports tours

Stage of Planning	Points to Consider for Organisers		
	Away Fixtures	Festivals and Tournaments	Sports Tours
Pre-event	• Is the HT aware of the fixtures programme? • Are school policies and procedures known and applied? • Are consent forms required, and if so, have they been obtained? What is the procedure for non-returned consent forms? • Are parents aware of the itinerary, programme, particular needs and conditions, insurance provision, emergency contact system and venue address? • Have roles and responsibilities, ratios, competency, group management and knowledge of the group been discussed with the staff involved? Has this included, if relevant, discussion about equality in size, experience and confidence of participants? • Is a group register available to take to the fixture? • Are medical backgrounds known by staff involved?	• Is approval needed from the governors? • Is additional staffing needed (eg to cover supervision/ officiating)? • Have group issues been clarified (eg age, ability, behaviour, selection)? • Has a 'telephone tree' (cascading communication system to convey messages/delays back to parents) been organised? • Has a pre-event visit been made to venue? • Has the risk assessment been received from the venue host or completed during a pre-event visit? • What is the first aid order of responsibility (eg school, then host or private company)?	• Is employing authority approval needed and all requirements met? • Has all paperwork or online approval forms been completed and submitted? • Has a pre-visit been made to the area/venue where possible? • Have expiry dates of passports been checked to allow for sufficient time before expiry as set by the country to be visited? • Has any additional insurance been obtained if needed? (See 2.6.22 and Chapter 2, Section 3, page 86.) • What injections/ medication are required prior to, and during, the tour? • Has a student code of conduct been developed from basic school visit requirements (eg communication/ mountain code/country code/safety on water)? • Do parents have a copy of the itinerary, contact details and other relevant information?

(continued)

Stage of Planning	Points to Consider for Organisers		
	Away Fixtures	**Festivals and Tournaments**	**Sports Tours**
Pre-event (continued)	• Have first aid arrangements been made and agreed, including knowledge of dealing with incidents of concussion? • Have general school and PESSPA risk assessments been completed and requirements followed? • Are the school's crisis-management plan requirements built in to risk assessment and planning? • Are reciprocal arrangements with the host school clarified/known? • Have all other 'what ifs'/contingency planning been considered?		• Do accompanying staff and adults demonstrate appropriate leadership skills? • Have additional 'expert' staffing requirements been identified and met (eg for students with special educational needs and disabilities [SEND], residential/adventure activities/city tour/swimming involved)? • Have the implications of taking non-school staff been considered? • Have safeguarding issues been checked (eg non-school staff, centre staff, host families)? • Are students adequately prepared for the tour – physically, emotionally and behaviourally?

(continued)

Stage of Planning	Points to Consider for Organisers		
	Away Fixtures	**Festivals and Tournaments**	**Sports Tours**
Assembly	• When does the school duty of care begin and end? When does this take over from, and revert back to, the parents? • Has a register been taken and a corresponding register left at school? • Has kit/footwear been checked? • Do relevant students have their required medication with them, and understand their own responsibility to administer this? • Is emergency contact information to hand during the trip? • Do students know, and are they applying, the code of conduct? • Are mobile phones available to use in an emergency?	• If outside of the school day, do students and parents know what time to meet and what to do, for example, if they miss the coach? • Have large groups been subdivided into smaller groups for ease of management, with an adult designated to manage each subgroup?	• Have methods for supervising groups at airport, ferry or train terminals been decided?

(continued)

Stage of Planning	Points to Consider for Organisers		
	Away Fixtures	Festivals and Tournaments	Sports Tours
Outward and return journeys	• Does the form of transport chosen meet legal, employer and local requirements, including volunteer cars? • Has it been decided whether the driver will supervise and drive, or drive only with additional staff to supervise? • Has the driver carried out a vehicle check? • Is a first aid kit available, and are arrangements for administering first aid known? • Have safe embarkation and disembarkation points been decided? • Are the register and head count before leaving consistent? • Are the emergency action plan and critical incident arrangements known? • Are arrangements and communication plans in place to alert parents of any delay? • Have strategies for dealing with illness or incident on the journey been decided?	• Are additional drivers needed? • How are breaks in the journey to be managed (eg motorway service areas)? • Was a head count completed after any break in journey?	• What are the package tour conditions? Will Package Travel, Package Holidays and Package Tours Regulations 1992, and the Package Travel Directive 2015 apply? (See 2.6.23.) • Have the implications of foreign law, standards, health and language been considered? • Have the international driving requirements been considered? • What information will be carried by students, in case of separation from the main group?

(continued)

Stage of Planning	Points to Consider for Organisers		
	Away Fixtures	**Festivals and Tournaments**	**Sports Tours**
Venue and event	• Has a venue risk assessment been supplied to visitors by the host team? (If not, carry out a visual check on arrival.) • Have any reciprocal arrangements agreed been reconfirmed (eg in relation to first aid, supervision, taking pupils to hospital, staff sickness)? • Have any group or activity management and supervision issues been established (eg one staff with two teams/officiating and supervising)? • Are officials competent and/or qualified? Are any young sports leaders supervised by competent staff? • What is the procedure for assuring acceptable behaviour? • Are periodic head counts carried out? • Is equality in size/experience/confidence monitored? • Are kit and footwear appropriate to the weather/playing surface, and consistently applied by all teams?	• Does the programme allow sufficient rest/recovery periods? • Is total playing time within the capability of those students involved? • Has it been decided who provides refreshments and rehydration? Are additional supplies available? • Is there a contingency plan in case of early completion/abandonment of the programme (eg telephone tree)? • Is there a system for granting consent if necessary for any photography that may be involved? • Is sunshade/rain cover available, or is additional portable cover required (eg gazebos or tents)? • Do participants need a change of clothes? • Is supervision appropriate where changing is involved?	• Is the itinerary decided and agreed as appropriate? • Is security sufficient and appropriate at the accommodation? • Are home care abroad standards, including safeguarding requirements, being met? • Is the student code of conduct being applied? • Is additional insurance needed? • Have down/free-time issues been considered? • Has a policy on student use of mobile phones been decided? • Do students have an accessible point of contact in the host country? • Have reciprocal arrangements been clarified if hosted by another school/group?

(continued)

Stage of Planning	Points to Consider for Organisers		
	Away Fixtures	Festivals and Tournaments	Sports Tours
Venue and event (continued)	• Has responsibility for managing personal effects been established? • Have PPE requirements been agreed (eg pads/helmets/mouth guards)? • Has the facility/equipment been checked before use as part of a host school risk assessment? Has this risk assessment been agreed by visitors? • Have weather issues been considered and well managed (eg sun/heat protection/rehydration/ storms/other seasonal considerations)?		

(continued)

Stage of Planning	Points to Consider for Organisers		
	Away Fixtures	**Festivals and Tournaments**	**Sports Tours**
Post-event evaluation	• Are there any near misses/incidents to review? • Have injuries been recorded and outcomes followed up? • Have improvements for the next event been identified? • Has any feedback been provided to HT/subject leader (SL)/staff/activity leaders/students/parents? • Have any adjustments to the risk assessment been formally recorded to inform future planning?		

Information for travel abroad

2.6.22   For many visits abroad, additional insurance cover is usually worth considering, such as:

- employer's liability insurance

- public liability insurance

- personal accident insurance

- comprehensive travel insurance

- tour operator insurance packages

- dual insurance.

Additional information regarding these types of insurance can be found in Chapter 2, Section 3, page 86, and in Outdoor Education Advisers' Panel (OEAP) national guidance: http://goo.gl/iU4T1L

2.6.23 When organising a tour abroad, consideration should be given to whether the Package Travel, Package Holidays and Package Tours Regulations 1992 will apply.

For more information on these regulations, see http://goo.gl/jcdTIF

2.6.24 The Package Travel, Package Holidays and Package Tours Regulations 1992 place certain legal obligations on organisers of package travel arrangements. It is unlikely that the regulations will apply to most establishment-organised visits, but there are some circumstances where they might.

The following document, available on the OEAP national guidance website, has been written to help organisers to consider whether the regulations might apply to their visit arrangements, and if so, what obligations the regulations place upon their organisation: http://goo.gl/f4Hauz

2.6.25 A new Package Travel Directive was issued on 31 December 2015, which will become applicable from 1 July 2018. Under this directive, a broader range of packages will be protected.

For details about how this might benefit school trips and tours, see http://goo.gl/s0Vi98

Resources available on the OEAP national guidance website include:

- **good practice basics – http://goo.gl/KxrbvG**

- **a visit leader checklist – http://goo.gl/06aEGX**

- **information on provider-led study and sports tours – http://goo.gl/wLmbVh**

- **guidance on overseas visits – http://goo.gl/PvdFzN**

Further good practice guidance in relation to planning visits and tours can be found in Chapter 4, Section 8, page 437.

Guidance on planning sports festival and events is also available in afPE (2011) 'Safe practice for the school games: Guidance for local organising committees and schools', which can be purchased and downloaded from www.afPE.org.uk

Case law

2.6.26   **Dickinson versus Cornwall County Council (1999):**

This case, involving the murder of a 13-year-old girl in a French hostel during a residential trip, established that knowledge or experience of something that was not a foreseeable possibility **becomes a foreseeable event once it has occurred** *and therefore needs to be taken into account with appropriate corrective action as part of the planning and management of similar future events.*

Club links

2.6.27   All schools should 'have in place arrangements for ensuring that their functions are exercised with a view to safeguarding and promoting the welfare of children' (section 175 of the Education Act 2002 – http://goo.gl/1h8mUz). It follows that it is essential that schools ensure that **safeguarding** is addressed in all school-club/community sport links in order to provide the best possible protection and fulfil their duty of care towards children and young people.

See Chapter 2, Section 4, page 91, **for further guidance.**

2.6.28   Clubs are likely to develop their guidelines for safeguarding children according to recommendations set out by organisations such as the Child Protection in Sport Unit and the Sport and Recreation Alliance, and using information supplied from governing bodies of sport. In addition, as part of their standard training, coaches and those volunteering in sports clubs will undertake training in child protection.

Child Protection in Sport Unit – https://thecpsu.org.uk
Sport and Recreation Alliance – www.sportandrecreation.org.uk

2.6.29   Using such information, the **link club** should have a regularly reviewed safeguarding policy, delegated officers to monitor this, and coaches and volunteers trained in child protection. It should also be clear about procedures for dealing with welfare and safeguarding issues. **When linking with a school, a club should acknowledge any additional, or variation in, requirements set out in the safeguarding policy of the school or organisation with which it is working.** For example, it may be more likely that, at the end of a club session, a child may be left alone with a coach while waiting to be collected by a parent. In school, the likelihood of a number of adults being in the building is higher. In such a situation, the coach needs to be clear about the policy to adopt. Both parties need to identify where club policy might vary from school policy, and agree which system is most appropriate within the school to club link arrangement.

2.6.30   The link club should:

- promote the policy and procedures to all club members and parents in order to demonstrate the club's commitment to a safe, friendly and supportive environment

- have guidance in place covering a range of practices and procedures relevant to the sport or activity

- provide appropriately qualified, trained and Disclosure and Barring Service (DBS)-checked coaches to work with children and young people

- ensure appropriate training is available for coaches and others working with children and young people

- consider the use of agreed codes of conduct that individuals can sign up to, and understand the sanctions imposed when failing to adhere to these; such codes of conduct may be aimed at:

  - parents
  - volunteers
  - coaches
  - students.

2.6.31   The **school** should ensure that safeguarding protocols are in place that clarify the shared roles and responsibilities in the event of a concern arising.

2.6.32   All of the above requirements, where relevant, apply to individual coaches and volunteers who are working with students. In addition, the adults who are responsible for **managing activities should be alert** for any of the following signs:

- activities where other adults are discouraged from staying to watch

- any individual who appears to ignore organisational guidelines

- staff who appear to show favouritism or personally reward specific students

- any engagement in inappropriate physical contact, such as taking part in physical activities other than demonstrations, or physically supporting where little or no support is necessary

- poor communication from the adults and negative responses to the students

- a 'win at all costs' attitude towards the sport or activity

- use of extreme additional activity as a 'punishment'

- students who drop out of an activity for no apparent reason (registers are important for curriculum, school sport and off-site activities)

- invitations offered to specific students to spend time alone with the adult, such as on the pretext of individual coaching.

2.6.33   Many sports have adopted a **club accreditation scheme**, and included within this are minimum standards for safeguarding that provide assurance for schools and others commissioning links. Clubmark is the Sport England cross-sport quality accreditation for clubs with junior sections, and governing bodies of sport accredit clubs that comply with minimum operating standards in four areas:

- the playing or participation programme

- duty of care and child protection

- sports equity and ethics

- club management.

For more information on Clubmark, see http://goo.gl/qA9DJq

2.6.34   At a more local level, many county sports partnerships (CSPs) have developed their own accreditation standards, and work with clubs in the area to help them reach this level. Clubmark, or a sport-specific version (eg The Football Association [FA] Charter Standard, Swim 21, Golf Mark) is an **indication of quality**, and schools should seek to build links with clubs that have achieved, or are working towards, achievement of club accreditation. As CSPs are tasked by Sport England to work with their local clubs and governing bodies of sport, help and guidance can be sought from them when trying to establish safe club links.

More information on sport-specific accreditations can be found on the following websites:

- **FA Charter Standard – http://goo.gl/qgRONB**

- **Swim 21 – http://goo.gl/A8LxXS**

- **Golf Mark – www.golfmark.org**

Coaches working alone

2.6.35   All coaches working in school clubs should be monitored on an ongoing basis. They should be informed and aware of all school procedures. Where schools feel that established coaches are regularly meeting the standards expected of them, the school may take the decision to allow the coach to work remotely from supervising staff.

For more details regarding the use of coaches and support staff in schools, see Chapter 2, Section 2, page 78.

Chapter 2/Section 7: Parental consent

Introduction

2.7.1   Support from parents and carers is helpful and often essential for establishing safe practice in school. Identifying reliable lines of communication and gaining consent between school and home can make it easier to enforce procedures that contribute to a safe and well-organised programme.

2.7.2   Physical education is currently a **statutory** part of the national curriculum for all age groups throughout the UK. In schools that are obliged to follow the national curriculum (eg local authority [LA] maintained schools in England), parents are not able to withdraw their children from physical education within curriculum time. Academies and other non-LA eligible schools can decide to follow the statutory requirements of the national curriculum and can choose to make physical education a compulsory part of their own programme, or may set up formal contracts with parents (as seen in the independent sector) regarding which elements of their 'broad and balanced' offer may be compulsory. In all schools, parents can choose whether their child takes part in **optional** physical education, school sport and physical activity (PESSPA) activities outside normal lesson times.

2.7.3   There is technically no requirement for schools to inform parents about how and where the curriculum is delivered. In cases where students are taken out of school during curriculum time for mandatory educational experiences at alternative facilities, there is no requirement for parental consent to be given. In practice, however, and in accordance with the school's duty of care, it is usual for schools to provide parents with sufficient information about any off-site activities within curriculum time so that they remain aware of their children's whereabouts, and advised of any additional safety measures that may be implemented.

2.7.4   When consent is required for participation in organised activities outside of curriculum time, the information provided to parents needs to be as **comprehensive** as possible in order for them to make informed decisions. Parents should be made fully aware of the itinerary, particularly the time at which the duty of care is transferred from the school to the parents. This will involve providing details about where and when the students will be dismissed.

2.7.5   Parents should be asked to confirm that they understand the risks involved in an activity and that they agree to comply with the conditions stated or that they choose to withdraw their child from the specific school event covered by the consent form.

2.7.6   Any student not providing a **signed consent form** should not take part in an optional school sport activity as there is no evidence that parents have given approval. Neither should students take part where the parent has crossed out any part of the consent form or amended the wording in any way as this could create difficulties should an emergency arise.

2.7.7   It is a common misconception that consent forms signed by parents **indemnify** the member of staff, school and employer against any claim for negligence. This is not so. Such **disclaimers** have no standing in law. The courts would not recognise anyone being absolved of their professional responsibility before an event takes place, thus making any such arrangement between the teacher and parent meaningless. Also, under the principles of the Unfair Contract Terms Act 1977 (http://goo.gl/1KfP51), minors have three years after reaching the age of consent (18 years old) to retrospectively file a claim in their own right for any injury suffered as a minor. This clearly sets a parental consent form as a participation agreement only. Such an agreement does not absolve responsibility. It is a signed statement indicating that the parent is willing for their child to take part in certain activities offered by the school, based on the information the parent has received.

2.7.8   Practice varies in schools. Some schools require parents to sign a **single consent form** to be effective throughout the student's whole school experience. This is currently a recommendation by the Department for Education (DfE) in England.

 A sample consent form for school trips and other off-site activities can be downloaded from the DfE here: http://goo.gl/0TtpcA

2.7.9   It is more common for schools to obtain one consent form at the beginning of each academic year. This might be sufficient, for example, to cover students taking part in after-school fixtures throughout the year. In some schools, more frequent responses from parents are required. The protocol for consent forms should **not be burdensome** on staff or parents but should ensure good communication, and fully **inform parents** of the schedules and organisation of any optional activities in which their child may be involved.

2.7.10   Parents can be kept informed about generic procedures relating to optional activities through the school's **normal communication systems,** such as the school prospectus, newsletter or website. However, the school should ensure that parents are aware of, and have access to, these methods. Specific information, such as that relating to dispersal procedures outside the school's normal practice or delays in journeys, needs to be relayed to parents via a reliable system that keeps them informed about the situation pertaining to their child.

2.7.11   Parents may be requested to complete consent forms about other aspects of PESSPA, such as permission to be photographed at PESSPA events or to be transported to activities.

 For a sample consent form for use of digital imagery, see Chapter 2, Section 16, page 284, **and in relation to transporting students, see** Chapter 2, Section 17, page 287.

Figure 5: DfE-recommended annual consent form for participation in optional school trips and other off-site activities

<Name of school>

Please sign and date the form below if you are happy for your child, *<name of the child>*, to:

- take part in school trips and other activities that take place off school premises

- be given first aid or urgent medical treatment during any school trip or activity.

Please note the following important information before signing this form:

- The trips and activities covered by this consent include:

  - all visits (including residential trips) that take place during the holidays or a weekend
  - adventure activities at any time
  - off-site sporting fixtures outside the school day
  - all off-site activities for nursery schools.

- The school will send you information about each trip or activity before it takes place.

- You can, if you wish, tell the school you do not want your child to take part in any particular school trip or activity.

Written parental consent will not be requested from you for the majority of off-site activities offered by the school (eg year-group visits to local amenities) as such activities are part of the school's curriculum and usually take place during the normal school day.

Please complete the medical information section below (if applicable) and sign and date this form if you agree to the above.

Medical information

Details of any medical condition that my child, *<name of child>*, suffers from and any medication my child should take during off-site visits:

....

....

Signed..

Date.............................

(as at 21 July 2014)

FAQ

2.7.12 **I will be taking a group of students from my school to compete in a school sports tournament next week. The organisers of the tournament have provided consent forms that they would like the parents of my students who are taking part to sign and return. Is this necessary? My school collects consent from parents at the start of each year to cover all trips and activities that the students may attend during that year. On the basis of this, can I inform the tournament organiser that all consents have been received?**

Yes. If the school has already requested this information for each student, then details can be passed on to the tournament organiser, thus avoiding the need for additional consent forms to be sent out, completed and signed. As part of your preparation for this event, you should have sent information about the tournament to the parents of students involved, informing them about arrangements in place (eg methods of transport being used; finishing time and arrangements for collection either at school or from the event). If, on receiving this information, a parent does not wish their child to take part, they can make this known to the school.

Codes of conduct

2.7.13 Another way to maintain good relationships with parents and pupils is through a **code of conduct**.

2.7.14 It is good practice for schools to agree a code of conduct with parents and students before students participate in sports activities and other educational visits. Codes of conduct set out the **expectations** placed on a student by the school, and are useful documents to make clear to students and parents the standards expected of those taking part. Acceptance of a code of conduct by parents and students will help staff to enforce the necessary authority to carry out their responsibilities.

2.7.15 While codes of conduct are key, in some circumstances, in setting out safe practices, they can also be used as the basis for administering discipline procedures stated within the code. For example, the decision to return a student home early from an event, such as a sports tour, might be made if their behaviour causes concern. The parents and student will have been made aware, through the code of conduct, and agreed to the premise that acceptable behaviour is a condition of taking part and that it will be the school's prerogative to judge the situation and to impose an early return home, if necessary, and at the parents' cost.

2.7.16 Breach of a code of conduct due to poor behaviour can have serious implications for the safety of that individual and others in the group, and should be effectively dealt with.

2.7.17 It is recommended that as part of **'teaching safety'**, students are included in the compilation of specific codes of conduct so that they have involvement in the process and more ownership of the outcome. It is considered effective practice for students to be asked to comply with a code of conduct that they have had some responsibility for producing.

For more information on 'teaching safety', see Chapter 3, page 299.

2.7.18   An agreed code of conduct should be formalised and sent to parents together with the medical and possibly photographic consent forms where these are required. These documents should be signed by parents and students.

2.7.19   The list below gives examples of behavioural standards that might be included in a code of conduct for an off-site visit, sports tour or residential trip.

2.7.20   Students are required to:

- observe normal school rules

- cooperate fully with all staff at all times

- consult with school staff if in doubt about any issues

- fulfil any tasks or duties set prior to and during the event

- participate fully in all activities and sessions during the event

- be punctual at all times

- ask permission before leaving group sessions or accommodation

- return to the meeting point or accommodation at agreed times

- remain in groups of no less than three students if granted indirectly supervised time

- avoid behaviour that may inconvenience others

- be considerate and respect others at all times

- observe rules relating to the use of mobile phones, filming and the use of social media

- behave at all times in a manner that reflects positively on themselves, the party and the school

- abide by the rules, regulations and laws of the school, venue or countries visited

- comply with customs and duty-free regulations when travelling abroad

- not purchase or consume alcohol or tobacco products, or purchase dangerous articles, such as explosives and knives, during a school excursion

- accept that a full written report of any misconduct will be forwarded to the school governors and leadership team, and their parents.

2.7.21   Staff might also explore the development of safe practice codes for the use of the school fitness room, behaviour in the changing rooms and other aspects of PESSPA where a code can help to establish expectations.

Chapter 2/Section 8: Group management

Ratios and supervising groups

2.8.1   Across the UK, class numbers vary, depending on legislation. Table 12 lists the current legislation:

Table 12: Legislation for class sizes for practical subjects in the UK

Scotland	All secondary practical classes should not exceed 20 students. (http://goo.gl/G0Yf2C)
Northern Ireland	Post-primary – practical group sizes should not exceed 20 students (statutory rule 2004). (https://goo.gl/Hy2Bb0)
England	There is currently no legislation regarding sizes of classes for practical subjects: *There is no legal limit to class size for health and safety reasons. To help raise standards in maintained schools, children between five and seven have a maximum class size of 30.* (https://goo.gl/SGa71F)
Wales	There is currently no legislation regarding sizes of classes for practical subjects.

2.8.2   In England and Wales, the school leadership team has responsibility for making decisions that group sizes and adequate workspace are safe, including the responsibility not to create situations that are overcrowded and thus unsafe. Dependent on the school authority, and their specific insurers, there may be additional factors regarding class sizes that would need to be adhered to. Where the Health and Safety Executive (HSE) becomes involved and determines that overcrowding is sufficient to cause injury, an improvement or prohibition notice could be served on the school. Information concerning such notices issued since 2006 is available on the HSE website (www.hse.gov.uk). An example provided on the site explains the inability of a school to keep a practical working area in a classroom free from materials and tools, presenting the possibility of potential slips, trips and falls. Space should be sufficient both for students to be accommodated and equipment to be used safely.

2.8.3   A class may be divided into smaller groups for reasons of safety, opportunity to progress, optimising activity levels or effective management of the available space. Group sizes and make-up will also vary according to age, experience, knowledge of the group and behavioural issues.

2.8.4   Teacher:student ratios may be determined on the basis of different reasons, including:

- staff competence and specific expertise

- student age

- student behaviour

- student ability levels

- previous experience of students and staff in particular circumstances

- a higher-risk environment (such as aquatics, adventure activities, trampolining)

- the nature of the activity

- the size and layout of the work area

- the condition of the facility

- the quantity of safety equipment available

- the type, location and amount of equipment in the work area

- the way the activity is most effectively organised

- any history of accidents and/or incidents occurring.

2.8.5   It is not advisable to define teacher:student ratios for school-organised PESSPA activities because of their highly contextual nature. For example, the same activity would merit more generous staffing levels if it were known that the teaching group involved presented challenging behaviour, had very limited experience or lacked confidence.

2.8.6   A rigorous risk assessment (RA) of the **particular circumstances** in question, culminating in a professional judgement by the head teacher (HT) and teacher involved, should indicate suitable staffing arrangements in terms of competence, number, type of activity and available space.

2.8.7   In order to maintain a safe learning environment, teachers need to consider how they will work with the **group numbers** assigned to them in the activity space provided. For example, when working in a restricted space, such as a small fitness room, the teacher needs to plan how students can be grouped to work on the equipment available, and how they can move safely around the space.

2.8.8   Where a teacher or subject leader believes group size may compromise safety in the work environment, they should consider whether the **organisation of the lesson** can be amended to establish a safe learning situation before approaching the leadership team to seek a reduction in the group size.

 ## A case in point

2.8.9   **Secondary school athletics, 2015:**

An experienced teacher took 24 students for an athletics lesson, with hurdles, long jump, triple jump, javelin, discus and shot-put activities going on in a rotational format that had been used regularly by the school in previous years. The arrangement of the activities meant that the end of the landing zone for the shot-put was only about three metres from the end of the triple jump sand pit, where the student was jumping. A whistle was blown to move stations, and the student left the triple jump and went across to the shot-put area to see how far a friend had thrown. At that point, another student launched a shot-put using a turning technique – his back was to the throwing area. The shot hit a 14-year-old student on the head, resulting in life-threatening injuries requiring emergency brain surgery. He returned to school after being in hospital for nearly a month.

The school's RA for physical education lessons referenced guidance from afPE, but had failed to note and follow their recommendation that such lessons be restricted to a maximum of four sports, with only one to be a throwing event. (See **Chapter 4, Section 2, 4.2.3 page 371**.) Six sports with three throwing events was deemed to have significantly increased the risks to students, as did the proximity of the triple jump activity to the shot-put landing area. The HSE inspector said the school put pupils at serious risk. The school was fined £10,000.

2.8.10 **Visiting coaches** working in schools may question the size of the group with whom they are asked to work. This could be because their insurance, if organised through a governing body of sport, may restrict their cover to a maximum group size. Some governing bodies of sport recommend or impose teacher/coach:participant ratios, particularly in potentially higher-risk activities, such as adventure activities, aquatic activities and some contact sports because of the type of environment. These ratios can be considerably less than the 'normal' school class size. Subject leaders and teachers responsible for liaising with coaching staff should be aware of these differences, and bring them to the attention of those planning the staffing.

2.8.11 Greater flexibility is possible where the coach works under the school or local authority (LA) insurance cover, ie in the same way as a member of the school staff. Subject leaders need to clarify with their employer whether a visiting coach operates under the employer's insurance or the coach's own insurance and, where the latter is the case, ensure that sizes of groups comply with any restrictions imposed by the coach's individual insurance.

 Case law

2.8.12 **Jones versus Cheshire County Council (1997):**

A teacher took a larger group to the swimming pool than the LA ratios allowed, but used a paired system, ie half the group were in the water at any one time apart from during 'free' time at the end of the lesson, when the whole group were in the water together. A child was injured during the 'free time', doing an activity that the group had not been taught. The teacher was held responsible for going beyond the **LA ratios** *and not limiting the end of lesson activity to pre-learnt skills instead of free time.*

Supervision

2.8.13 There is **no legal requirement** to supervise students all of the time, but schools should have a clearly stated position about supervision, both in changing areas and lessons. Teachers need to be aware of the school's requirements and follow them.

2.8.14 The level of supervision will be determined by the students' age, behaviour, ability, previous experience, work environment, identified risk and other contextual factors. However, analysis of case law provides a clear indication that the incidence of **injury** is much higher during **unsupervised** activities than supervised ones.

 Case law

2.8.15 **Harris versus Perry (2008):**

A child was injured on a bouncy castle. The parents alleged negligence due to lack of adequate supervision. The claim was dismissed. The court recognised it was 'quite **impractical to keep children under constant surveillance** *and it would not be in the public interest for the law to impose a duty to do so'.*

2.8.16 **Direct supervision** of students enables the teacher to intervene at any time. Their teaching **position** should enable them to observe clearly and intervene should it be necessary. This does not mean always being physically next to students, but rather to be able to attract attention and response from individuals even at a distance.

2.8.17 Decisions to supervise less directly should not be taken lightly.

Case law

2.8.18   **McDougall versus Strathclyde Regional Council (1995):**

*A teacher advised his students in a class not to attempt any exercise without his assistance if they were not sure whether it could be performed safely. One of the students was about to perform a vaulting exercise, which he had never performed on his own before, with the teacher in attendance. The teacher then moved to assist another student, but the first student went ahead with his performance and was injured. The Appeal Court found that it was not reasonably foreseeable that the student would attempt the exercise without the support of the teacher and that the teacher had not deliberately withdrawn support but had found himself in a situation in which he was required to assist someone else. Therefore, there had been **no failure** of supervision.*

2.8.19   **R versus Aberdeen City Council and Aberdeenshire Council (2012):**

An 11-year-old primary school student attended an open-air pool as part of an educational excursion. During the visit, he became submerged underwater and was recovered unconscious from the bottom of the pool by a member of the public. CPR was successfully administered by lifeguards, and the pupil has since made a full recovery.

*The investigation found issues with staffing levels and lifeguard **positioning** at the pool, as well as with the effective management of educational excursions at the school.*

Both parties pleaded guilty to breaching Section 3(1) of the Health and Safety at Work etc Act 1974. Aberdeen City Council was fined £9000 while Aberdeenshire Council was fined £4000.

2.8.20   Groups undertaking higher-risk situations, such as adventurous activities, aquatic activities, combat sports, contact sports, athletics throwing events, gymnastics, trampolining and free weights sessions, require closer supervision, and where possible, smaller groups should be considered.

2.8.21   The nature of the supervision needs to be clear. For example, it is recommended that trampolining activities are carried out with smaller groups, dependent on the number of trampolines and qualified teachers available. Safe practice is compromised where one teacher supervises half the class working on the trampolines as well as the other half doing a different activity, even when this is in the same space. Where this occurs, staff should be very experienced, students at a level where they can work independently, and the activity assigned should not distract the teacher from safe supervision of the trampoline.

A case in point

2.8.22   **Secondary fitness room activities (2011):**

A 13-year-old student was injured the first time he attended a health-related exercise lesson. While running on a treadmill, the student jumped off, wishing to alter the controls to reduce its speed. Believing he had slowed the speed, he jumped back on, but the treadmill had not slowed down. He lost his footing and fell, trapping his left hand in the treadmill's belt, resulting in friction burns to the hand. The treadmills were fitted with safety clips to be attached to the user's clothing, acting as stop mechanisms in an emergency.

The student alleged negligence on the basis of a failure to instruct him properly in the use of the treadmill, particularly with regard to attaching the safety clip to his clothing, and failing to supervise the class adequately. It was also alleged that a staff:pupil ratio of 1:12 was inadequate.

The teacher gave evidence that he had instructed the students in how to use a treadmill before any of them began, including a demonstration, and had emphasised that the safety clip must always be properly used. He had also made a detailed record of the accident immediately afterwards, emphasising that tuition had been provided. This record was given significant weight in court as evidence that such tuition had taken place. The judge also accepted that, given the absence of previous similar incidents, the staff:pupil ratio was adequate.

The judge considered whether the teacher should have seen that the student had jumped off then back on again, that the treadmill was going too fast and that the student had not used the safety clip. The judge held this would place too high a burden on the teacher in these circumstances. There was adequate instruction and supervision, and the claim was dismissed.

2.8.23   Older students may be given less supervision, but should not be totally independent as the teacher remains legally responsible for their well-being. Remote supervision may take different forms, such as during trips and tours, and should be progressively achieved and very carefully managed.

2.8.24   Careful thought should be given to **supervising changing rooms.** While there are a number of organisational tasks to be completed at the beginning of a lesson, it should not be forgotten that changing rooms are part of the area of learning.

Supervising mixed-gender student groups when changing

2.8.25   Where circumstances prevent full supervision, such as where a single staff member is responsible for a mixed group changing in separate changing areas, a clear, safe management procedure needs to be devised and communicated to the students. Methods can include appointing one or more responsible students to inform the member of staff should any disruptive or dangerous activity arise in the changing area. Where this and similar methods of supervision are relied on, the member of staff should be available at all times in the immediate vicinity of the changing rooms.

2.8.26   Using members of the opposite gender to supervise mixed groups is acceptable unless there are significant elements of relatively intimate contact that may affect the dignity, comfort and confidence of either students or staff.

 See Chapter 2, Section 13, page 223, **for more information about changing areas.**

Supervision of outdoor play and activity areas

2.8.27   Those responsible for supervising outdoor activity should be suitably trained and competent to do so. Clarification is required about exactly which aspects of supervision form part of their role, and how this should be carried out. This may involve break-time supervisory staff completing additional training in the supervision of playground activities, for example. Staff should be competent in setting out any equipment where required to do so.

2.8.28   The level and type of supervision to be undertaken should be clear and not exceeded. For example, it is highly recommended that younger primary-aged students on climbing equipment have dedicated supervision by at least one member of staff, or more if an RA identifies this as necessary. However, older students may be considered to need less supervision on low-level traverse walls. Where the need for a dedicated member of staff assigned to this role is identified, they should not then be required to supervise other areas of the playground at the same time.

2.8.29   Students should be **grouped** for practical activities according to age and developmental stage. The use of zoning areas of the playground for specific types of activity also acts as a useful supervisory strategy.

 See Chapter 2, Section 13, page 217, **for more information about playground areas for recreational use.**

2.8.30   The maximum number of students who can use different items of equipment, particularly in a climbing area at any one time, should be determined by an RA, and communicated to staff and students.

2.8.31   Any student given **leadership responsibility** for practical activities must work under the direct supervision of a member of staff, who should be present. The staff member should be clear about the extent and function of this supervisory role.

2.8.32   All supervisory adults should be fully aware of emergency procedures and how to rapidly access first aid in the event of an accident.

2.8.33   Students need to comply with behavioural expectations and any playground **code of conduct.** Where possible, they should be included in the design of such a code.

Case law

2.8.34   **Burton versus Canto Playgroup (1989):**

*Adult staffing of a playgroup was supplemented by a **14-year-old helper** who was left alone to supervise a climbing frame. She had been given no training, nor did she have the experience to anticipate the action of a young child who had not been on the apparatus before. The child jumped and injured herself. The playgroup was held responsible for inadequate supervision.*

2.8.35   **Palmer versus Cornwall County Council (2009):**

One lunchtime supervisor was responsible for about 200–300 students aged 11–15 in a field during lunch break. An older student was hit in the eye with a stone thrown by another student. The supervisor admitted to concentrating on the younger students with only an occasional glance at the older ones. The main issues were:

- *What should be the **proper ratio** of supervisors to students?*

- *Would the incident have happened irrespective of the number of supervisors present?*

*The Court of Appeal held that if there had been proper supervision, no stone would have been thrown, that one person supervising such a large number was **negligent at a management level,** and the purpose of proper supervision is to deter students from dangerous activity and to stop it if it occurs. This highlights the importance of adequate supervision of students in large numbers, and thorough RAs, guidance, warning and training regarding supervision of students.*

2.8.36   **Orchard versus Lee (2009):**

*A claim for negligence was dismissed when a student collided with, and injured, a lunchtime supervisor during a game of tag. The students were in a play area, playing the game in a typical manner and not breaking any rules. The court said that the student owed the adult a duty of care, but to establish a breach of that duty, the student would need to have been 'playing tag in a way that was to a significant degree **outside the norm** for 13-year-olds', and this was not the case. This case shows that the courts remain reluctant to impose liability for accidents in the playground so long as the school has taken **reasonable care** by applying a common sense approach with good risk management, including an RA of supervision levels.*

Matching students in groups

2.8.37   Students' individual levels of confidence, strength, prior experience, size and ability need to be accommodated in teaching contexts and at the earliest stages of competition. Grouping and pairing students according to any of these individual characteristics need to be considered in order to establish a safe learning environment.

2.8.38   Such group management is essential where the following form part of the learning experience:

- **weight bearing** (such as counterbalancing in gymnastics)

- **physical contact** (such as tackling in contact sports)

- **'accelerating projectiles'** (such as when a hard ball is thrown or bowled at an opponent, or throwing a javelin).

2.8.39   **Mixed-ability** pairing or grouping, as in peer teaching and learning, is acceptable where the outcome is clearly understood to be assisting and supporting cooperatively, rather than competing.

Mixed-gender group activities

2.8.40   Mixed-gender teaching and participation in activities have increased over the years. Potential advantages for safety include improved attitudes to learning, improved behaviour, and effective use of specific staffing expertise.

2.8.41   It is recommended that strength, confidence, previous experience, ability and attitude are key considerations in the need to match students in learning activities, whatever the gender involved. Age alone is not relevant to safe groupings unless it affects attitude and behaviour.

2.8.42   **Physical contact and strength** translated into power are fundamental considerations for safe groupings as students mature. In instances where bodily contact, support and power applied to actions such as tackling or hitting a ball form part of the context, separating the genders for practical experience does become a key consideration.

See Chapter 4, page 351, for activity-specific information about mixed-gender sanctions.

Schools that have pupils dealing with transgender or gender dysphoria concerns that affect how they will participate in PESSPA will find the Gender Identity Research and Education Society (GIRES) website very helpful: http://goo.gl/EjwQ7v

Mixed-age sport

2.8.43   Some governing bodies of sport stipulate team selection restrictions to **narrow age bands** for reasons of safety, particularly in contact sports, such as rugby, and martial arts activities, such as judo. This is intended to address possible differences in size, ability and confidence. Where any competitive situation occurs within the aegis of that governing body of sport, the requirement must be met.

2.8.44   While the principle to promote safe practice through **matching student size and experience** is generally sound, it is not necessarily appropriate to make decisions solely on chronological age due to variations in rates of physical development, confidence and skill.

2.8.45   On occasions, the principle of competing within the age group recommended by the governing body of sport might be considered in an RA but not applied as strictly as the governing body of sport sets out. This is acceptable if the safety and welfare of the students are maintained. For example, where a slightly younger but experienced, skilful and well-developed player would benefit from playing in an age band slightly outside their chronological age, a RA could determine that the selection is safe.

Case law

2.8.46   **Mountford versus Newlands School (2007):**

*A teacher played an **over-aged player** in an inter-school rugby match. An opposing player was badly injured when tackled within the rules of the game by this player. The court ruled that the teacher was negligent. In view of the difference in size and physique (178cm [five feet, 11 inches], 82kg versus 155cm [five feet, two inches], 45kg), the over-aged player should not have been allowed to play. Although there is no complete ban on players 'playing down' in terms of age group, and rugby is quite clearly a game designed for players of differing sizes and shapes, the fact that the over-aged player might cause harm to a far smaller opponent was foreseeable and preventable.*

Physical contact from adults in student activities

2.8.47   Physical contact, as defined in a safeguarding context, is 'intentional bodily contact initiated by an adult with a child'.

2.8.48   Staff should be aware of the limits within which such contact should properly take place, and ensure decency, dignity and respect are never compromised. Contact should remain impersonal and be made in a manner that cannot be misconstrued by the student, parent or observer, and only for the duration necessary for safe practice.

2.8.49   Any physical contact should be for the intention of **meeting a student's needs** in order to:

- develop techniques and skills safely

- treat injury

- prevent injury occurring

- meet any special educational needs and disabilities (SEND) needs

- prevent harm to the student or others.

2.8.50   All schools should have a clearly stated policy and **code of practice** about physical contact with students as part of their safeguarding policy. Aspects of this will apply to PESSPA contexts.

2.8.51   It is very likely that most students will need some form of manual support or physical contact from staff during their PESSPA experiences, and it is a school's responsibility to inform parents of this, and not that of the individual staff member.

2.8.52   Physical contact for reasons of safety, support, providing confidence or demonstration is typical within PESSPA situations (eg supporting a balance in gymnastics). It is important that the student is made aware beforehand of the purpose of such provision, what form it will take, and that they confirm that this is acceptable to them.

2.8.53   Staff should only ever deploy the degree of contact or physical force they genuinely believe to be necessary in order to safeguard a student against a hazard and/or for the purpose of restricting injury.

2.8.54   Where any **complaint** is made about a member of staff's physical contact with a student, the situation should be reported immediately to the staff member responsible for safeguarding in school, to explain the circumstances and obtain guidance and support.

2.8.55   Children with SEND may require a greater degree of support and proximity. Manual support should always take place in an open environment with no intimate touching at all, other than for specific care needs.

For information regarding manual handling of children with disabilities in swimming, see 'The inclusion of swimmers with a disability', www.swimming.org

Staff participation in student activities

2.8.56   Staff should be aware of the risks associated with **personal participation** while teaching or coaching PESSPA activities, particularly those involving physical contact or in which hard projectiles (eg cricket/rounders balls) are used.

2.8.57   Staff should **avoid** playing a full part as a participant in a game with students. Their involvement should be restricted to providing practical demonstrations in a controlled, essentially static way, or to bring increased fluency into a game situation.

2.8.58   It can be good practice for staff to take a limited role in a game periodically to set up situations that enhance the students' learning. This would exclude full practical involvement in activities such as tackling (other than static demonstrations), shooting with power and bowling or pitching with pace. Staff involvement should not compromise their ability to retain acceptable control of the whole group.

2.8.59   **Staff versus student matches are not advised,** whether in lesson time or extracurricular, competitive contexts, because of the likelihood that differences in size, strength, weight, ability and previous experience, plus the element of competition, could lead to injury.

FAQ

2.8.60   **At the end of term, we like to raise money for charity by having a staff versus students sports event. How is this practice viewed?**

Staff taking part in PESSPA activities should be limited to demonstration and learning purposes only. Participation situations should be generally static, or used in a controlled manner to provide a visual interpretation of the information being taught. The potential differences in ability, size, weight and experience between students and adults are further exacerbated when a 'competitive' element is introduced, such as in staff versus student games. While students find such events entertaining, it is highly recommended that they do not take place. An alternative could be considered (eg staff versus staff with students as the audience). On such occasions, the staff taking part would do so with their own consent (at their own risk). Any liability arising from personal injury would not be pursued through the employer, other than that arising from the facility used not being fit for purpose, unless this was considered to be a school organised event, and the staff involved were 'at work'.

 Case law

2.8.61 **Affutu-Nartay versus Clark (1994):**

*A student was injured during a rugby lesson when the teacher played a **full participative role** in a game. He tackled the student inappropriately 'in the heat of the moment', causing severe injury.*

Staff teaching PESSPA activities while pregnant

2.8.62 As soon as a member of staff knows that she is pregnant, it is best advice to let the HT know. At that point, it is the duty of the school to undertake a RA to consider how the pregnancy will affect the person's role.

2.8.63 Within PESSPA, there are obviously things to be careful about from the outset, but each pregnancy is different and will affect the member of staff differently. For this reason, the RA will need to be revised as things change at the different stages of the pregnancy.

2.8.64 In assessing, the following points should be considered:

- Lifting and carrying may become difficult. In some cases, students can be asked to assist under supervision.

- Certain activities are not advisable: teaching trampolining (from the bed or the floor); teaching activities in which a hard ball is involved (eg rounders, cricket, softball); high intensity demonstrations; or a sequence of moves.

- Officiating from the sides should be acceptable, particularly in the early stages, as long as the member of staff remains vigilant to projectiles.

- In the early stages of pregnancy, while physical size may not cause any issues, feeling nauseous during a lesson, and/or having to exit the lesson, may require certain procedures to be put into place (eg appointing a student to alert another member of staff, ensuring pupils know to stop all activity if the member of staff needs to leave the lesson urgently).

- It is sensible to share the news with the students so that they also take some responsibility for safety in the lesson.

Chapter 2/Section 9: Safe exercise practice

Assessing and managing risk

2.9.1   Staff should ensure that all physical activities and exercises taught as part of the physical education, school sport and physical activity (PESSPA) programme comply with principles of safe exercise practice in terms of:

- control

- alignment

- impact

- developmental appropriateness.

2.9.2   Children and young people should learn about the principles of safe exercise practice so that they are able to take part in PESSPA activities both at school and in the community with increasing independence and confidence and without personal physical injury either in the short or long term.

2.9.3   In order to make decisions about the safety of specific PESSPA exercises or movements, staff need to address the following questions relating to each of the four principles of safe exercise practice:

Principle of Safe Exercise Practice	Risk Assessment Question
Control	Can the exercise/activity be performed in a controlled manner?
Impact	Have any risks associated with high impact been minimised?
Alignment	Can the exercise/activity be performed with correct joint alignment?
Developmental appropriateness	Is the exercise/activity appropriate for the physical maturation of the student?

2.9.4   Staff should incorporate these principles of safe practice into their planning and implement them in their teaching. Tables 13–16, pages 161–166, provide information to help staff address these questions in order to make judgements about the safety of the activities and exercises they include in their PESSPA programmes.

Table 13: Making judgements about appropriate use of control for safe exercise practice

Control
Can the activity/exercise be performed in a controlled manner?

What is control?

Activities/exercises performed with control are easily stoppable and usually involve a smooth, continuous action. They are not necessarily slow.

What are the risks of performing physical activities/exercises without control?	How can the risk be reduced?
• Performing dynamic, explosive physical activity or 'full range' movements before an adequate warm-up can result in muscle tissue injuries. • Muscles may be tight and weak following a growth spurt and more susceptible to injury caused by activities involving flinging, bouncing or momentum.	• Include warm-up activities/exercises that become gradually larger and more energetic (dynamic). • Avoid momentum when lifting and lowering equipment or flinging and dropping when working against resistance. • Perform physical activities/exercises in such a way that the movement is 'stoppable'. • Avoid uncontrolled bouncing into stretches (ballistic stretches). • Provide children and young people with appropriate teaching points and clear practical demonstrations that reinforce and exemplify appropriate use of control. • Avoid practices that encourage children and young people to perform resistance exercises at speed (eg 'circuits' focusing on 'how many you can do in 60 seconds'). • Provide children and young people with a range of alternative physical activities/exercises that accommodate individual differences in terms of range of motion about joints. • Help children and young people to learn about the safety implications of performing exercise using control. • Encourage children and young people to evaluate appropriate use of control in their own and others' technique. For more information, see **Chapter 3, Section 5, page 321.**

Table 14: Making judgements about effective management of impact for safe exercise practice

Impact
Have any risks associated with high impact been minimised?

What is high impact?

High-impact activities/exercises involve a large amount of force against the floor (eg landing from jumping, springing, leaping activities).

High-impact activities/exercises performed with safe technique have many health benefits, particularly in terms of increasing bone strength and developing cardiovascular fitness.

What are the risks of performing activities/exercises without effective management of high impact?	How can the risk be reduced?
Injuries such as shin splints, stress fractures and joint (including back) problems may occur if high impact activities are performed frequently and for long duration: • on hard floors (eg concrete) • with poor technique (eg not bending the knees appropriately, landing on flat feet) • while wearing unsupportive footwear or in bare feet.	• Include a balance of high and low impact activities in sessions (eg jumping and non-jumping activities). • Promote learning about how to jump and land with safe technique. • Require that children and young people wear appropriate, supportive footwear when PESSPA activities involve frequent, long duration or very repetitive high impact activities, especially when working on hard floors. • Help children and young people to evaluate their own and others' jumping and landing technique. • Help children and young people to learn about safety implications associated with high impact activities. • Encourage children and young people to conduct their own risk assessments to decide if it is appropriate to wear supportive footwear. For more information, see **Chapter 3, Section 5, page 322.**

Table 15: Making judgements about correct joint alignment for safe exercise practice

Alignment
Can the activity/exercise be performed with correct joint alignment?

What is correct joint alignment?

Correct joint alignment is about moving or placing joints in anatomically correct ways (ie in ways they were designed to work).

What are the risks of performing activities/exercises without correct joint alignment?	How can the risk be reduced?
• Strain may be placed on ligaments and tendon insertions that are situated near the weak growth plates at the end of the bones. Over a period of time, this can result in joint laxity (instability). • Long-term and recurrent mobility problems and recurrent pain might develop in major joints, particularly the knee and spine.	• Emphasise correct movement and placement of joints when learning new skills/exercises (eg bend knees [no less than 90 degrees] and in line with toes on landing from a jump, knees in line with toes when running or jogging). • Discourage repetitive and/or forced hyperextension (locking out) of joints (eg pressing knees back when standing, locking elbows out when taking weight on hands, extreme/forced arching of the spine or neck). • Discourage hyperflexion (excessive bending) of joints when performing exercises (eg landing in a deep knee bend from a jump, straight leg toe touches, forcing chin to chest in a shoulder stand/backward roll). • Discourage knees knocking in when bending. • Provide practical demonstrations and teaching points that highlight correct joint alignment. • Help children and young people to learn about the safety implications of correct joint alignment. • Encourage children and young people to evaluate correct joint alignment in their own and others' technique. For more information, see **Chapter 3, Section 5, page 320.**

163

Table 16: Making judgements about the developmental appropriateness of physical activities/exercises for safe exercise practice

Developmental Appropriateness		
Is the activity/exercise appropriate for the physical maturation of the student?		

What is developmental appropriateness?

This refers to how appropriate the exercise/activity is for the physical maturation of the child or young person.

For the purposes of this table, children are 4–10 years and young people 11–18 years.

Fact	Risk Implication	Recommendations for Minimising Risk
Children's body proportions differ from adults (ie they are bottom-heavy with a weak upper body and big head).	Children's weak torso can struggle to support their weight, especially during actions that involve supporting long levers.	Use 'child-friendly' exercises. Avoid asking children to perform adult versions of exercises that incorporate long levers (eg side bends with arms stretched overhead, curl-ups with hands by ears).
Children have a lower rate of sweat production and a higher rate of heat production than adults. They also have a larger ratio of body surface area to weight.	Children cannot regulate their body temperature as efficiently as adults (ie they heat up rapidly, overheat easily and lose heat rapidly).	Ask children frequently how they are feeling, and monitor their response to activity and how they look. Implement the following measures to reduce overexposure to sun/heat: • Establish policies for wearing hats/caps and loose, light clothing. • Advise parents to provide suncream protection for their children to apply. • Reduce exercise intensity. • Provide frequent rest periods. • Have plenty of fluids available. • Continually monitor for signs of overheating.

(continued)

Fact	Risk Implication	Recommendations for Minimising Risk
		Implement the following measures to reduce overexposure in cold conditions: • Allow children to wear appropriate additional clothing, and keep them as active as possible. • Continually monitor for signs of the onset of hypothermia. Help children and young people learn to monitor and respond appropriately to how they feel when taking part in PESSPA activities. Help children and young people learn how to conduct their own risk assessments in relation to taking part in PESSPA activities in extreme temperatures. For more information, see **Chapter 3, Section 2, page 304.**
Children have less carbohydrate stored in their muscles than adults and a reduced ability to use it for energy production.	Children are less efficient at performing short burst, high intensity (anaerobic) activities than adults.	Ensure high intensity activities (eg fast running, jumping) are short and intermittent with adequate periods of active recovery.
In both children and young people, growth plates at the ends of bones are weak and soft.	Children and young people's bones are more susceptible to injury than adults', especially the ends of the bone where the growth plate is situated.	Encourage children and young people to place and move joints in correct alignment. Avoid exposing children and young people to physical activities that put bones and joints under excessive stress (eg falling on to hands, working against maximal resistance). Ensure high impact activities are performed with protective footwear, with safe and effective technique, and intermittently.

(continued)

Fact	Risk Implication	Recommendations for Minimising Risk
Young people of the same age and sex may be at very different stages of growth. Growth rates are not linear during adolescence.	Staff may assume one version of a physical activity/exercise: • is appropriate for all young people of the same age • can be performed at the same intensity, duration and level by all young people.	Include different versions of each exercise that fulfil the same purpose. Enable young people to decide the most appropriate level/intensity for them. Adapt physical activities/exercises to accommodate the needs of individual children and young people. Help children and young people learn to adapt physical activities/exercises to accommodate their individual needs.
Following a growth spurt, young people's muscles might be relatively thin, weak and tight.	Young people may have: • a restricted range of movement around some joints • an imbalance between flexibility and strength that may result in poor joint alignment. An exaggerated pull on the tendon-bone insertion may cause damage to a growth plate.	Ensure that during a growth spurt, young people are encouraged and helped to: • reduce muscle tightness, avoid muscle imbalance and maintain range of movement about joints by performing mobility exercises, resistance exercises and stretches as part of a regular exercise programme • perform exercises with correct alignment of joints • vary participation. Do not allow young people to take part in PESSPA activities when they are in pain.

Control remedies

2.9.5 **PESSPA staff will find that the majority of activities/exercises they wish to use with their students ARE safe and effective. In addition, some activities/exercises will only require minor adjustments to make them safer and more appropriate for specific groups or individuals.** It is possible, but unlikely, that a student will come to harm by performing simple activities/exercises with poor technique on a very few occasions. However, in the long term, if poor technique is not corrected and/or a student is allowed to continue to perform an exercise that is inherently at variance with safe practice principles, the risk of short- or long-term injury greatly increases.

2.9.6 Where ongoing (dynamic) risk assessment (**see Chapter 1, Section 6, page 32**) during the session identifies any areas of risk in terms of safe exercise practice, staff should take action to:

- adjust/adapt the physical activity/exercise to ensure that it does comply with all relevant safe exercise principles

or

- replace the physical activity/exercise with a safer alternative that fulfils the same purpose and complies with all the principles of safe exercise practice.

2.9.7 Table 17, page 168, provides some examples of risk assessments of safe exercise practice and shows how control remedies can be applied.

2.9.8 Where staff feel that they do not have a suitable vocabulary of exercises or the level of expertise to assess exercises in terms of correct joint alignment, they can seek this information from a Level 2 fitness instructor. However, Level 2 fitness instructors may not be able to give guidance about the developmental appropriateness of exercises unless their qualification is relevant to teaching children and young people.

For more information, see Chapter 2, Section 2, page 76.

© Alan Edwards

Table 17: Examples of risk assessment of safe exercise practice

	Straight leg toe touch to stretch hamstrings (back of upper leg)	Head circles to mobilise the neck in a warm-up	Sprinting at the start of a warm-up	Ladder activities (jumping, bounding, stepping) in bare feet
Control: Can the exercise/activity be performed in a controlled manner?	Yes	Yes	No – sprinting requires muscles to contract and lengthen at speed. If muscles are cold, they are less pliable and more likely to tear when this happens.	Yes
High impact: Can any risks associated with high impact be minimised?	N/A – this is a low impact activity.	N/A – this is a low impact activity.	Yes – if students are wearing appropriate footwear.	No – this activity involves repetitive and frequent high impact activity and might also be performed on a hard floor.
Joint alignment: Can the exercise/activity be performed with correct joint alignment?	No – the exercise involves hyperflexion of the spine, places stress on the ligaments in the base of the spine and can cause disc damage.	No – delicate cervical vertebrae may be damaged by this activity. Hyperextension of the neck may trap nerves and blood vessels.	Yes	Yes – if appropriate teaching points are provided.
Developmental appropriateness: Is the exercise/activity appropriate for the physical maturation of the student?	No – because of the alignment problems identified.	No – because of the alignment problems identified.	Yes – running is appropriate for most children and young people.	Yes – children and young people can all benefit from performing simple jumping and stepping activities.

(continued)

	Straight leg toe touch to stretch hamstrings (back of upper leg)	Head circles to mobilise the neck in a warm-up	Sprinting at the start of a warm-up	Ladder activities (jumping, bounding, stepping) in bare feet
Control remedy	**Change the exercise:** Stretch the hamstring in a seated or lying position.	**Adapt the exercise:** Mobilise the neck by gently and slowly: • tilting the head from one side to another • looking right and left, and up and down.	**Adapt the activity:** Start the warm-up with less intense, more controlled movements (eg jogging). Use sprinting at the end of the warm-up.	**Ensure correct footwear is worn:** This should be both supportive and cushioning. **Encourage correct technique:** For example, keeping light on the feet.

 FAQ

2.9.10 **Is there a list of exercises that are 'unsafe' for students in schools?**

No. The reason for this is that it would be impossible to decide which exercises should be included. Assessing the risks associated with a specific exercise depends on a lot of factors, including:

- who is performing the exercise (eg what is their physical maturity, experience, capability?)
- whether the exercise complies with the principles of safe exercise practice, ie control, impact, alignment and developmental appropriateness
- how well the exercise is taught
- how well the exercise is performed
- how frequently the exercise will be performed.

It follows that if there was a list of 'unsafe' exercises, an exercise not on the list could become high risk (eg if it was performed with incorrect technique).

It is the responsibility of PESSPA staff to make their own risk assessments of the exercises they wish their students to perform using the principles explained in this section. This will involve:

- clarifying the purpose of the exercise they wish to use with their students
- completing a risk assessment of the exercise using the principles of safe exercise practice (Tables 13–16, pages 161–164, and Table 17, page 168, in this section)
- applying the safe exercise practice control remedies.

Warming up and cooling down

2.9.11   The importance of warming up to prepare the body safely and effectively for exercise, and cooling down to recover afterwards, is well documented.

2.9.12   All PESSPA sessions should include appropriate and relevant warm-ups and cool-downs.

2.9.13   The components a warm-up/cool-down should include are outlined in Table 18 below.

Table 18: Components of warm-ups and cool-downs

Component	Purpose	Primary	Secondary
Mobility exercises or controlled movements of the joints (mobilising exercises)	**Warm-up:** To warm the synovial fluid and help joints move more freely. **Cool-down:** To calm students and prepare them to return to the classroom.	**Warm-up/cool-down:** Examples: • shoulder/arm circles • changing between simple body shapes • drawing shapes or letters in the air with limbs.	**Warm-up/cool-down:** Examples: • shoulder/arm circles • upper-body twists • knee lifts • side bends • gentle jogging/marching.
Pulse-raising or whole-body activities	**Warm-up:** To raise the body temperature, breathing and heart rate. These activities prepare the body gradually and comfortably to meet the energy requirements of activity to follow. Warm muscles are more pliable and less likely to be injured. **Cool-down:** To help breathing and heart rate recover. These activities help the body to recover effectively from activity and can help to prevent dizziness or nausea after very energetic activities.	**Warm-up/cool-down:** Examples: • travelling activities such as jogging, skipping, stepping • dribbling a ball • 'follow my leader' activities • copying simple dance movements led by the member of staff.	**Warm-up/cool-down:** Examples: • jogging • marching • dribbling a ball • controlled, low intensity rehearsal of sports/dance moves.

(continued)

Component	Purpose	Primary	Secondary
Stretches	**Warm-up:** To reduce the risk of injury to muscles. Stretches prepare muscles to contract and/or stretch at speed. **Cool-down:** To reduce 'next day' stiffness or soreness. A cool-down can provide an appropriate time to develop flexibility by performing stretches for muscles that tend to be tight (eg hamstrings, groin).	**Warm-up:** Children aged 4–8 years: Static whole-body stretches held for approximately six seconds – examples: • stretch tall (lying or standing) • stretch wide (lying or standing) • curl small (lying or crouching). Children aged 8–10 years: Simple static stretches held for 6–8 seconds for specific muscles – examples: • back of lower leg (calf) • back of upper leg (hamstring) • across chest (pectorals). **Cool-down:** Children aged 4–8 years: Static whole-body stretches held for up to 10 seconds. Children aged 8–10 years: Simple static stretches held for approximately 15–30 seconds for specific muscles.	**Warm-up:** Young people aged 11–18 years: Static stretches held for 6–8 seconds for specific muscles – examples: • back of lower leg (calf) • back of upper leg (hamstring) • across chest (pectorals) and/or dynamic stretches that build in range and energy. Students can progress to performing combined static stretches: • calf (soleus) and across chest (pectorals) • back of upper arm (triceps) and lower calf (soleus) **Cool-down:** Young people aged 11–18 years: Static stretches performed in lying, seated or relaxed positions (as appropriate) and held for approximately 15–30 seconds.
Sport/activity-related movements	**Warm-up:** To prepare the brain for the activity to follow and recap on previous learning.	**Warm-up:** Simple, low intensity, controlled versions of some of the skills/activities to be included in the activity to follow.	

2.9.14   Appropriate length of a warm-up depends on:

- the intensity and duration of the activity to follow (a more vigorous/very energetic activity may require a longer warm-up)

- the physical and psychological condition of the participants (eg children and young people who are sedentary may need a more gradual, longer warm-up)

- environmental factors such as temperature and humidity (a longer pulse-raising section may be required in colder temperatures and a shorter pulse-raising section in higher temperatures – however, **all components** should be included regardless of environmental factors).

2.9.15   Appropriate length of a cool-down depends on the:

- intensity and duration of the preceding activity (a more vigorous/very energetic activity may require a longer cool-down)

- physical and psychological condition of the participants (eg children and young people who are active on a regular basis will recover more quickly).

2.9.16   **All exercises and activities included in warm-ups and cool-downs should comply with the principles of safe exercise practice. (See 2.9.3.)**

2.9.17   Students need to acquire a practical knowledge and understanding of warming up and cooling down. This process starts with them following consistent good practice, and culminates in them designing their own relevant and appropriate procedures. Students should be progressively involved in designing, conducting and evaluating their own warm-ups and cool-downs.

For more information on this, see Chapter 3, Section 5, pages 324–328.

2.9.18   Staff should closely monitor student-led warm-ups and cool-downs to ensure that both choice of exercises/activities and performance are safe, effective and appropriate.

Case law

2.9.19   **A versus Leeds County Council (1999):**

An 11-year-old girl was injured during a warm-up activity that involved the class of 25 pupils running to touch all four corners of the gym before returning to the teacher. The girl was injured as the pupils criss-crossed on different paths of travel. The claim was upheld. The teacher was considered to be not in control of the exercise and unable to stop a collision once everyone had set off, and such a collision was 'foreseeable'. The responsible adult should ensure that pupils are able to stop or change direction in order to avoid collisions, and that the group has the ability to stop on command.

FAQ

2.9.20 **Should I include static or dynamic stretches in warm-ups?**

Static stretches involve stretching a muscle and then holding it still in a stretched position (eg static calf stretch or hamstring stretch). Research about the benefits of static stretches within warm-ups is largely inconclusive. It suggests that while static stretching might not be helpful in terms of preparing for highly dynamic performance, there are few indications that it is physiologically harmful as a component of a warm-up. Static stretches in warm-ups can be very useful in an educational context for helping students to learn about how to stretch, to identify where they can feel muscles stretching, to locate and/or name the muscles involved and to develop correct alignment in their technique.

Dynamic stretches involve active movements of muscles that cause them to stretch (eg lunges dynamically stretch quads and hamstrings). Dynamic stretches in warm-ups can be helpful, especially directly preceding very dynamic participation. It is advisable for dynamic stretches to be performed slowly and over a smaller range in the early stages of the warm-up. The speed and range of dynamic stretches should increase gradually and carefully as the warm-up progresses. Correct alignment of joints and appropriate use of control are requirements for safe and effective dynamic stretching, which is why they are more suitable for older students. Ballistic stretching, which involves bouncing while a muscle is at the end of its range, should be avoided due to the high risk of soft tissue injury.

2.9.21 **My year two class seem flexible enough. Do they need to stretch in warm-ups and cool-downs?**

You are correct in your observations – younger children are indeed more flexible than adults. While the benefits of stretching for this age group are debatable, it is beneficial to keep the messages about how to warm up and cool down consistent throughout their learning.

Whole-body static stretches held for about six seconds can be used with younger children. A good time to start learning some simple stretches for specific muscles might be towards the end of Key Stage 2.

Chapter 2/Section 10: Clothing, footwear and personal effects

Clothing for PESSPA – students

2.10.1   Students should wear clothing that is **fit for purpose** according to the physical education, school sport and physical activity (PESSPA) activity, environment and weather conditions. From the earliest ages, they should change into suitable PESSPA clothing (or 'kit') in order that they may participate safely and securely.

2.10.2   Clothing for PESSPA should be well suited to its function. For indoor sessions, it should be light and allow good freedom of movement, without being baggy or loose. **Loose clothing** in gymnastics, for example, may catch on equipment and cause injury. Any items of clothing for PESSPA, including those of cultural significance, need to be relatively close fitting, made safe or removed for reasons of safety of the individual.

For more information about religious and cultural clothing, see page 175.

2.10.3   Sportswear has become fashionable in recent years, and this is positive in cases where it encourages more students to engage in PESSPA activities. Care needs to be taken, however, to avoid unsuitable, long, wide-legged or loose items being worn, where they might be a safety hazard.

2.10.4   Although vest and pants were, in the past, an acceptable, easy and time-saving option for the youngest children, contemporary views on safeguarding, personal development and hygiene mean this is no longer advisable practice.

2.10.5   For classroom-based movement in a limited space or **playground activity** (eg 'wake and shake' type activities), it can be acceptable for students to remain in their everyday clothes or school uniform. During this type of activity, participants normally work within a small area or on the spot, and safety concerns linked with slips, trips and falls are reduced.

2.10.6   Students should wear sufficient and appropriate clothing according to the **weather conditions** in order to minimise the likelihood of injury or hypothermia in cold conditions, and illness or heatstroke in very hot conditions.

2.10.7   Clothing for outdoor lessons should allow good freedom of movement, but will also need to offer some insulation from **cold weather** in the winter months, when additional layers are advisable. Students who are insufficiently warm and experience discomfort will not be appropriately focused, and may lack concentration, leading to injury.

2.10.8   An increasing number of schools purchase kit including their school logo for students to buy. Hooded sweatshirts are popular, but care needs to be shown with these items. While useful for group trips, as team 'travelling' kit or wearing in warm-ups, staff should consider safe practice and recommend that students remove 'hooded' sweatshirts during contact or non-contact invasion games or similar activities.

2.10.9   When participating in **hot weather**, protection from the sun is advisable. Many schools have established policies for wearing caps and loose, light clothing, as well as advising parents to provide suncream protection for their children to apply.

For more information about weather conditions, see Chapter 2, Section 5, page 124.

2.10.10   In **specific activity** situations, adjustments to normal clothing guidelines may need to apply (eg wearing a long-sleeved top to prevent friction burns to the forearms when performing front drops in trampolining). Some decisions about clothing will require detailed risk analysis (eg deciding whether a fabric that reduces friction on gymnastic apparatus may cause slipping, particularly if working at height or in inverted positions).

2.10.11   Loose clothing for swimming is not advised (other than during personal survival skills tests in controlled situations) due to the drag created, which may adversely affect the confidence and buoyancy of weaker swimmers.

2.10.12   It is highly recommended that wetsuits are worn for activities where students are in open water for a long period of time.

2.10.13   When students arrive at a PESSPA session with clothing deemed to be inappropriate, strategies need to be applied to make their inclusion safe, or to limit the extent of the activity element of their participation.

Religious and cultural clothing

2.10.14   To maximise safe and meaningful participation, staff should use sensitive management when dealing with any concerns arising from the wearing of certain items of clothing specific to religious requirements. (See Chapter 2, Section 5, page 126.) Students should be able to experience a broad PESSPA programme whatever their cultural background, while schools must continue to have regard to health and safety and equality legislation.

2.10.15   Staff should ensure the following:

- Any clothing worn to comply with a faith commitment should be appropriate to the PESSPA activity. Clothing should be comfortable and allow for freedom of movement, while not being so loose as to become a hazard. A tracksuit is perfectly acceptable clothing for Muslim students and is not seen as offending the principles enshrined in *Haya* relating to modesty and decency.

- **Headscarves** (such as the **hijab**), where worn, should be tight, secured in a safe manner, particularly at the side of the face, and unlikely to obscure vision or catch on anything that may put the wearer at risk. Students can also consider obtaining a sports version of the hijab, for improved suitability. These are available from high street stores and on the Internet.

- In **swimming** lessons, unacceptable exposure of the body should be managed through adjustments in swimming attire to accommodate religious and cultural sensitivities while not compromising the safety of the students concerned.

Clothing for PESSPA – staff

2.10.16   Clothing and **correct attire** for a particular PESSPA activity represent important features of safe practice that apply in equal measure to both staff and students.

2.10.17   Staff should always endeavour to **change** into appropriate clothing for teaching physical education or leading PESSPA clubs and activities. It is becoming more common for teachers in primary schools to wear appropriate kit to school on days when they are teaching physical education so that they can model appropriate behaviour. On the rare occasions that this proves difficult or impractical, a change of footwear and removal of jewellery, at the very least, should always be undertaken.

Footwear

2.10.18   **Security of footing** is crucial in all situations. All **staff and students need to change** into footwear that is appropriate for the lesson location and, ideally, for the PESSPA activity being taught. This is a requirement for safe participation by students and safe supervision by staff. Staff may need to respond quickly to prevent a potential injury to a student, making effective mobility essential. Students need footwear that is capable of transmitting feel for the movement and the surface they are working on.

2.10.19   Footwear that is **fit for purpose** and appropriate to the surface conditions is essential for staff and student safety. Outdoor footwear should demonstrate effective grip and support, and reasonable protection for outdoor PESSPA activities and games.

2.10.20   In the same way, indoor footwear should demonstrate effective grip and support, and reasonable protection for indoor PESSPA activities and games.

2.10.21   In gymnastics, **barefoot work** is the safest, whether on floor or apparatus, because the toes can grip. Barefoot work in both gymnastics and dance can also improve aesthetics by allowing the foot and toes to move through a full range of flexion and extension, which in turn strengthens the muscles, bones and joints.

2.10.22   Decisions about the appropriateness of **bare feet for dance** should consider the type of contact with the floor by the feet, which is closely associated with the style of dance or nature of the movements being explored. **(See Chapter 4, Section 4, page 388.)** Where the floor condition is unsuitable for barefoot work, students should be permitted to wear clean sports footwear.

2.10.23   For **trampolining**, non-slip socks or trampolining slippers are necessary to prevent toes entering the gaps in the webbing. Cotton and wool socks are suitable, but nylon socks on a webbed nylon bed are unlikely to provide adequate traction.

2.10.24   Footwear is preferable for **indoor games** activities due to the higher frequency of sudden stopping and changing direction quickly where toes can be stubbed, and also for games that require the ball to be kicked (eg football) or involve a hard, fast-moving ball at ground level (eg indoor hockey). **Training shoes,** which provide good traction, will often prove effective for a range of indoor games and will also support the feet when carrying out activities that are largely high impact. Training shoes should not, however, be worn for gymnastics activities for the reasons of 'feel' described above.

2.10.25   Staff should try to avoid situations where a wet-weather indoor alternative activity means that some students wear training shoes and others have bare feet. This situation needs to be managed correctly (eg all students in bare feet or all students in trainers, or students being set different tasks that are appropriate for their footwear).

2.10.26   Neither staff nor students should ever participate in **socks** on polished wooden or tiled surfaces as the level of grip is poor. Well-fitting socks may be acceptable on a carpet surface if traction is not affected, and transfer between carpeted and wooden surfaces, such as benches, is not required.

2.10.27   **Outdoor footwear** for games and athletics may vary according to the playing surface, and according to the availability of particular footwear to some students. Studded, bladed or ribbed soles are beneficial in sports where the surface is soft or slippery and in conditions in which smooth soles would not provide secure footing. Security of footing is an essential requirement, along with consideration as to whether outdoor footwear presents any foreseeable risk to other participants.

2.10.28   Systems need to be in place whereby staff, officials and students regularly **check the safety** of their footwear. Procedures also need to be applied whereby students avoid, wherever possible, walking over hard surfaces to gain access to the playing area. This can result in studs and other traction devices becoming unacceptably rough and sharp, which might prove hazardous to opponents in competitive games and practices. It is likely that all PESSPA footwear will need some form of maintenance so as not to cause a hazard to anyone.

2.10.29   All footwear should be of the correct **size** and correctly **fastened** in the manner of its design to ensure appropriate support for the ankles. As fashion evolves, there are often items of casual or leisure footwear on the market that have the appearance of trainers. It is important that teachers check to ensure footwear has the required specification and provides the necessary support for safe participation.

2.10.30   Where a group presents a **variety of footwear** for outdoor lessons, the teacher has to determine whether the lesson can proceed as planned or whether some conditions need to be applied to maximise safety (eg splitting the group according to footwear and assigning different tasks as appropriate). For many reasons (eg financial pressures on families), students should never be excluded from taking part in a lesson due to not having the correct footwear. Every effort should be made to involve the student in as much of the physical part of the lesson as possible, and to provide alternative activity-related tasks when this is not possible.

2.10.31   **Students should be encouraged to take responsibility** for preparing and checking that all of their kit (clothing and footwear) is fit for purpose for the lesson being undertaken, and that it is safe. Work undertaken by afPE that involved students in designing their own safety posters illustrates how students can take increasing responsibility for their safety in this context.

 afPE students' safety posters are available to purchase and download from www.afPE.org.uk

FAQ

2.10.32 **I have a student who frequently fails to bring his kit for PESSPA activities. How can I try to address this? Should I provide him with kit?**

When students repeatedly 'forget' their PESSPA kit or seem reluctant to change for PESSPA activities, there are a number of things to consider and investigate. For some students, it may simply be a case of being disorganised, but for others, there may be more deep-rooted concerns, and staff should try to find out what these might be. They could range from difficulties at home to personal, medical or even abuse problems. In the shorter term, to manage the situation in the lessons, there are a number of strategies that staff may adopt:

- Depending on the PESSPA activity, can the student participate in parts of the lesson safely by removing some of their daily clothing (eg removing a jumper, taking part in bare feet)? This might not always be a satisfactory solution (eg if the student is in bare feet, repetitive high impact activities might need to be restricted; if the student is wearing loose clothing or items that are likely to cause slipping, use of gymnastics apparatus would not be acceptable). In addition, compromising on correct PESSPA kit should not appear as acceptable practice to other students. It is a temporary dispensation.

- Allow the student to take part in those elements of the lesson that can be carried out while not changed into physical education kit (eg listening to the learning, designing, planning and evaluating, and providing an alternative task during practical parts of the lesson).

- Provide the student with 'spare' physical education kit from the PESSPA department. When schools decide that they make 'spare' kit available to students, they should inform parents, through their policies and other forms of communication, that this will happen, and the format it will take.

Students should not be completely excluded from the PESSPA lesson on the basis of not having the correct kit (some students may be seeking this outcome). For efficient management, schools should outline clear policies regarding the handling of these situations, and the staff member must make the final decision regarding safe participation.

Case law

2.10.33 **Farmer versus Hampshire County Council (2006):**

A Year 1 class (5–6 years old) had been taught by an experienced teacher how to lift, carry and place gymnastic equipment. The class worked in **bare feet.** *A girl fractured her toe when a group dropped a low portable beam. A claim for negligence was based on the need for footwear to be worn when carrying equipment. The claim was dismissed on the basis that barefoot work in gymnastics is* **normal** *where the floor is suitable, the children had been taught how to carry the items, they were closely supervised by the teacher, footwear gives very little protection if a heavy weight is dropped on to the foot, and there is an inappropriate time factor for a whole class to put on and remove footwear during a lesson.*

2.10.34 **Villella versus North Bedfordshire Borough Council (1983):**

A young girl trampolining in bare feet caught her toe in the webbing and fractured her femur. The claim for compensation was upheld.

Personal effects, including jewellery and cultural or religious adornments

2.10.35 Personal effects, such as jewellery, (including body piercings), religious artefacts, watches, hair slides, and sensory aids including glasses, should ideally always be **removed** to establish a safe working environment.

2.10.36 Staff have a duty of care to ensure that students are able to participate actively without unnecessarily endangering themselves or those working around them. Systems and procedures need to be in place within the changing area to check that students fulfil this obligation to remove personal effects prior to participation.

2.10.37 The following procedure should be applied at the commencement of every lesson:

- **All personal effects** should be removed. Staff should always give a verbal reminder to students and, where necessary, visually monitor the group and/or individuals. Particular vigilance may be required when dealing with body jewellery.

- If items cannot be removed, staff need to take action to try to **make the situation safe**. In most cases, this may mean adjusting the activity in some way or, where a risk assessment allows, making the item in question safe.

  For example:

  Medical bracelets: Recent developments in the manufacture of **medical-aid wristbands** have resulted in products with an acceptably low risk factor (ie soft materials, Velcro fastenings). Such items should be acceptable for most PESSPA activities without need for removal. However, these bracelets need to be regularly checked by the owner to make sure there are no hard or sharp edges that may cause injury. Where there is any concern, the bracelet can be covered with tape, padding or a soft, sports-style wristband.

Wristbands monitoring **activity** and other health indicators have also become very popular. As above, these should be covered with a fabric sports wristband or similar padding.

Earrings: Students unable to remove earrings should be required to make them safe by taping, front and back, which may offer a measure of protection. The taping should be sufficient to prevent the stud post penetrating the bone behind the ear should an unintentional blow be received (eg from someone or from equipment such as a ball).

This taping may be done at home for younger children or prior to the lesson for older students. Staff are not required to remove or tape earrings for students.

Where taping is utilised, the teacher supervising the group maintains the legal responsibility to **ensure the taping is effective** for purpose. Where staff consider the taping to be unsatisfactory to permit safe participation, they will need to consider alternative involvement in the lesson for the student.

The use of **retainers** (flat studs that retain the piercing when earrings or studs are removed) is becoming more common as a form of acceptable substitution where total removal is not possible. Provided these are flat and cannot cause damage if a blow or ball hits the side of the head, the level of risk is clearly reduced.

Expander earrings are worn by some students. These are generally hollow circles used to stretch the piercing, making a large hole in the ear lobe. These are clearly not safe for close-contact physical activity, and should be taped effectively as described above.

Body jewellery: Staff should regularly ask whether any student is wearing body jewellery. The jewellery should be removed or taped to a safe standard. Where staff catch sight of body jewellery during any PESSPA activity, they should stop the activity and initiate procedures to make the situation safe.

Sensory aids: The decision as to whether it is safe or possible to wear **glasses** or **hearing aids** will usually be determined by the nature of the activity. Activities involving physical contact and full game situations may not be appropriate. For example, England Rugby (RFU) allows the wearing of glasses (in non-contact games) up to the under-8 age group, while The Football Association (FA) leaves this to the referee's discretion up to the age of 14. (See also sports goggles – Chapter 2, Section 11, 2.11.45–2.11.48, pages 188–189.)

Where the sensory aid needs to be worn for safe participation by the individual, then the staff, wherever possible, need to **amend** the activity (such as providing more space and time) or the equipment (such as using a soft ball instead of a harder one) in order to try to make participation while wearing a sensory aid as safe as possible for the wearer and others in the group.

2.10.38　In all cases, where removal of personal effects or making safe an item is not possible, strategies to enable safe participation in the lesson need to be introduced. The student should be involved in all the learning, but adaptations will need to be made in terms of how they take part in the practical aspects of the lesson. The student can contribute to group planning, designing and tactical discussions, but can have different tasks assigned to them during the practical elements of the lesson (eg individual skills practices, peer coaching, observation and feedback tasks, videoing others to analyse at a later stage, or officiating in a games context).

2.10.39   Ongoing risk assessment needs to determine what action will be appropriate. Staff should always try to avoid complete exclusion from a lesson due to the student being unable to remove personal effects.

2.10.40   **Staff** also need to be mindful of their own adornments, and remove them prior to teaching physical education. The wearing of **rings** and large hooped or drop earrings, for instance, has been responsible for unnecessary injury in the past, and represents a hazard to both staff and students involved in the lesson.

2.10.41   **Long hair** worn by both staff and students should always be tied back with a suitably soft item to prevent entanglement in apparatus and to prevent vision being obscured.

2.10.42   **Nails** for staff and students need to be sufficiently short to prevent injury to self and others.

2.10.43   Any **religious artefacts** should be removed or made safe. Where removal is expressly forbidden (eg the Sikh bangle, the kara), and the article cannot be made acceptably safe by taping, padding or covering, the activity and involvement of the wearer must be suitably modified to mitigate undue risk.

2.10.44   Case law relating to human rights legislation has established that a student does not have the right to manifest their belief at any time and place they choose at school, and this includes the wearing of jewellery. Generally, to attempt to succeed in making a claim on the grounds of human rights, there would be a commonly acknowledged religious obligation on a follower to wear the jewellery. However, where the safety of others is compromised through the wearing of such an item, the claim is unlikely to be successful.

2.10.45   In seeking, wherever possible, to respect any religious or cultural sensitivities, it is recommended that schools enter into discussion with local faith leaders and parents to establish and maintain constructive communication with them and the local community.

Establishing policy regarding clothing, footwear and personal effects

2.10.46   Clear expectations should be established throughout the school, and with parents, about the management of personal clothing, footwear and personal adornments, through the communication of a clear and unambiguous written policy. Such a policy should set out standards expected by the school for PESSPA, and should be provided to new parents on their child's entry to the school, as well as being easily available on the school's website or through school newsletters.

2.10.47   Any **changes to such a policy** need to be communicated to parents through the channels described above, with notice of the forthcoming changes and the reasons for them. Having well-communicated policies in place can help to support schools in their attempt to maintain high standards of safety in these areas.

 For more information about policy and procedures, see Chapter 1, Section 5, page 23.

2.10.48   **Disclaimers** from parents alleging the removal of responsibility from teachers in the event of an injury occurring while their child takes part while wearing jewellery, personal effects, or non-policy clothing or footwear should be declined.

2.10.49   Such indemnities have no legal status. The duty of care remains firmly with the school on such matters, as the student may take out independent action for compensation when they become an adult, thus nullifying any agreement made in good faith. Schools should work with parents to achieve a solution that does not compromise the safety of the student and others, nor the employer's duty of care.

 Case law

2.10.50   **R (ex parte Roberts) versus the Chair and Governors of Cwnfelinfach Primary School (2001):**

*The judge determined that the school was entitled to **exclude** the student from physical activity when she wore jewellery, which the parents refused to remove. This was on the basis of health and safety. A claim that the exclusion breached the European Convention on Human Rights was rejected.*

2.10.51   **Begum versus the Head Teacher and Governors of Denbigh High School (2006):**

*The outcome of this case, having progressed all the way to the House of Lords, was that a school had the right to set and enforce a **school policy on uniform**. The decision was based on the facts that the school had discussed the matter with the community and taken great pains to devise a policy that respected religious and cultural beliefs, and that the policy was in place when the student joined the school, therefore choosing to accept the rules in place at that time. It is important that **clothing for PESSPA seeks to respect religious and cultural beliefs without compromising health and safety standards**.*

2.10.52   **Watkins-Singh versus the Governing Body of Aberdare High School and Rhondda Cynon Taff Unitary Authority (2008):**

A claim for indirect racial discrimination was brought against a school because the governors' interpretation of the school's restrictive policy on wearing jewellery prevented a Sikh student attending school wearing the kara (a plain steel band about 5mm in width). The judgement for the student was based on the school's interpretation of the policy being 'procedurally unfair' and allowing no exemption at all. Consideration of the issue was totally about wearing the kara in school generally and not about the implications relating to a specific context of health and safety within PESSPA.

The student was prepared to remove or cover the kara with a sweatband during PESSPA where health and safety was an issue. The judge made particular reference to her willingness to do this in recognition of health and safety concerns in his summary of the judgement and thus acknowledged the need for exceptions to be made in specific health and safety situations.

*Another important consideration by the judge was that the restrictive school jewellery policy was formally recognised by the governors after the dispute had arisen. Prior to that, it was described as being in place but unsigned by the governors, incomplete in content and in a generic form from a neighbouring authority. Schools need to ensure that **all policies are specific to the school**, fairly detailed and approved by the governors before implementation.*

Chapter 2/Section 11: Personal protective equipment

Introduction

2.11.1   The use of personal protective equipment (PPE) is increasingly common in physical education, school sport and physical activity (PESSPA) sessions or situations. PPE refers to any device worn or held by an individual for protection against one or more health and safety hazards. The most common forms of PPE used in schools include mouth guards, shin pads, helmets, padding and swimming goggles.

2.11.2   Injury in PESSPA sessions most commonly occurs through physical contact with another individual, or contact of part of the body with:

- a hard ball

- an implement

- a rough surface or chemically affected environment.

2.11.3   PPE works by dissipating direct force relative to both time and impact, thereby offering a measure of protection to parts of the body.

2.11.4   In some sports, the legal principle of *res ipsi loquitor* – 'the thing speaks for itself' – applies. This is clearly relevant to sports such as fencing, boxing or taekwondo in which the wearing of protective items is inherent in the activity itself. This need, however, is not always obvious in other activities.

2.11.5   Wearing PPE will not guarantee protection from injury. It can though, in many cases, **mitigate** the severity of injury by reducing a high-risk situation to one of reasonable or acceptable risk.

2.11.6   PESSPA staff should **inform students** about the purpose, function and limitations of PPE in order to counteract any false sense of security that may arise as a consequence of wearing protective gear. In all PESSPA activities, it is the application of good technique and skill, and rigorous adherence to the rules that remain the most important features of safe participation.

2.11.7   It is a **parental responsibility** to provide PPE where the school has suggested it. However, it is insufficient for schools simply to tell students and to expect them to inform their parents. For this reason, it is recommended that well-communicated physical education policy and procedures should **strongly advise** the provision of particular PPE items, and outline the process for informing parents about providing them.

2.11.8   Communication to parents should include information about the range of PPE relevant to the PESSPA programme and about how staff will determine whether it is safe to continue or amend a planned session where students lack the necessary PPE.

2.11.9   Where schools decide to adopt a policy of **mandatory** usage of any PPE in physical-contact situations, their duty of care obliges them to ensure that **all participants** always have access to the PPE required.

2.11.10   Where mandatory policy exists, the member of staff is not absolved from any injury that occurs to a student as a result of them not using the PPE required.

 Case law

2.11.11   **G (a child) versus Lancashire County Council (2000)**:

*A student received a serious mouth injury in hockey while not wearing a mouth guard. The judge determined that, while the provision of personal protection is a parental responsibility, it is the responsibility of the school to ensure **parents receive critical information** about PPE and that simply passing on the information via students is insufficient.*

Managing the use of PPE

2.11.12   Within curriculum lessons, staff cannot exclude students from taking part on the basis that they do not have the correct PPE, even though its use has been recommended. The member of staff in charge must establish a safe playing environment.

2.11.13   When PESSPA staff believe that PPE for a specific activity is essential but their students do not have the necessary item(s), staff should **modify** how the activity is carried out in order to enable safe participation without the required item.

2.11.14   This may mean:

- providing PPE items where possible and practical for those who cannot provide them or have not provided them

- grouping together students who do not have the required PPE, and assigning them tasks that can be safely carried out without this equipment

- rotating groups to take part in different activities or tasks, some requiring PPE and some not requiring PPE

- changing the task for all students so that those without PPE are not put at risk

- if only one or two students do not have the required PPE, allowing them to take part in as much of the learning as possible, and assigning them a different role during any parts of the lesson where lack of PPE would put them at risk.

2.11.15   Staff should not proceed with the planned format of the PESSPA activity if their planning has identified, based on school policy, that PPE is required by all students, but that this requirement is not being met.

2.11.16   School fixtures, team practices and intra-school matches are generally situations where students have a choice and have opted to take part. These are also competitive situations in which it would be correct and safe practice to insist that the recommended PPE is worn. As within lesson times, staff could consider providing spare PPE, where possible, for any students who cannot supply this themselves, and who might otherwise be excluded from having the choice to take part.

2.11.17   As with all accidents and injuries, those relating to the use or lack of PPE should be recorded, and used to inform and add gravitas to future recommendations regarding the PPE policy.

 FAQ

2.11.18   **My primary school is considering making the wearing of mouth guards compulsory in all hockey sessions, both within the curriculum and at extracurricular clubs. Is this something we can do?**

Wearing mouth guards for hockey at all levels is highly recommended. A hockey stick in the hands of a beginner has the potential to do considerable damage to other players if control is poor.

If considering this course of action, you will need to inform parents in the first instance. You may be suggesting that the school provides all students with their own mouth guard, and following this, students will need to purchase a replacement, if they lose it. Alternatively, if you are asking parents to purchase the mouth guard, the school may decide to source them in bulk for this purpose.

If the decision for compulsory use of mouth guards is made within the school term, a letter communicating the proposed change to parents of those students affected is sufficient. However, in the longer term, the details should be built into the PESSPA kit policy, and communicated through the normal channels, such as the school newsletter, prospectus and website.

Staff will need to check who has their mouth guard at the start of each lesson, and in cases where students do not have their mouth guard with them, the member of staff needs to manage the situation using the methods set out in this section in order to make the activity safe for all participants. Students should not be completely excluded on the basis of not having the required PPE.

PPE guidance

2.11.19   Protective equipment should be **fit for purpose**. Manufacturers are encouraged to ensure that their products conform to specified standards, where these exist. British Standards Institute (BSI) and European (EN) standards are an advisory standard and not regulatory, but where any equipment is involved in an injury, these standards are considered to be a benchmark.

2.11.20   **Some specialist protective equipment**, such as that required for a **hockey** goalkeeper, may often be provided by the school, unless the student elects to participate to a high level in that position, in which case they may choose to obtain their own.

2.11.21   **Mouth guards** protect teeth and gums, and can reduce lacerations inside the mouth of the wearer and injury caused by teeth to an opponent in the event of unforeseen collision. There is also some evidence that mouth guards might reduce incidences of concussion, but this is less certain, and possibly only in situations where a bespoke personally fitted mouth guard is worn.

2.11.22   A mouth guard crafted and properly fitted by a dentist or dental technician offers the most effective protection. However, for some students, cost may be prohibitive. Relatively cheap, but less effective 'boil-and-bite' versions of mouth guards are now available. These should carry a European Conformity (CE) marking, which indicates that the product has been subject to some quality assurance in assessing its fitness for purpose. There is currently no British Standard available.

2.11.23   The safety benefits of wearing mouth guards for match play and competitive practices have been widely recognised for a considerable time, and schools are encouraged to consider introducing mouth guards as part of the **regular PESSPA kit requirements** both at primary and secondary levels. For hygiene reasons, mouth guards cannot be shared, but schools may consider purchasing them, and consider how their use is best managed.

2.11.24   **Shin pads** offer protection to the lower leg, and should be worn for competitive matches and whenever there is a risk of injury. It is recommended that students are encouraged to wear shin pads during lessons that involve game or match play. Better protection is provided where the pad covers much of the length of the leg between the knee and the ankle. However, the pad should not hinder performance. Some shin pads provide protection for the ankles as well as the shins, which can be particularly useful in hockey. Unlike mouth guards, shin pads can be 'shared' so while schools can include shin pads on their PESSPA kit list, they might also keep additional sets for students who 'forget' them or are unable to provide them.

2.11.25   **Protective helmets**, or **head guards**, are most commonly used in rugby, cricket, climbing and skiing.

2.11.26   The soft **rugby** headgear is considered to provide protection for the head against blood injuries and fractures, which are most likely to be sustained when taking the ball into contact situations. Helmets need to fit comfortably and can provide a sense of protection, with the contoured soft padding usually made of impact-resistant foam. However, head guards and helmets offer little added protection against concussion where the brain is shaken within the skull.

2.11.27   **Head protectors for cricket** have a rigid outer shell, which provides protection against higher-impact forces, and usually a grille or visor to protect the face. National cricket associations have made head protectors compulsory in under-19 cricket for all batsmen, wicketkeepers and any fielder within 14 metres of the bat, and schools would be wise to adopt this policy.

2.11.28   The latest standard-specification head protector, BS 7928:2013, has been on sale since spring 2014. It features improvements in the peak and face guard of the helmet that have been developed to reduce injuries incurred when the ball has penetrated the face guard and caused facial injury. From 30 June 2014, the old standard helmet, BS 7928:1998, was withdrawn. However, this does not mean that head protectors already purchased and tested against the old standard should no longer be used. They will continue to be available, and are perfectly acceptable. The England and Wales Cricket Board (ECB), however, has issued guidance regarding the new specification to inform future purchases.

For further information on the ECB guidance, see http://goo.gl/I5wuec

2.11.29 Helmets for pedal **cyclists, skateboarders and roller skaters** should comply with BS EN 1078:1997 (European Standard).

2.11.30 **Ski helmets** are becoming mandatory in several countries. Where the wearing of helmets is still a personal option, schools are advised to build provision for them into the required kit list, whether through hire or purchase, so that all students wear them. The employer's requirements and/or school or tour company insurance arrangements may also dictate this practice. Helmets (including those for snowboarders and snowbladers) should comply with the standard BS/EN 1077.

2.11.31 The decision to wear helmets for **climbing** varies depending on the setting. The British Mountaineering Council does not provide prescriptive policy or guidelines but suggests that staff should assess the requirements of the wall and whether helmet use is appropriate or not. Where staff feel unable to make this assessment, they should seek additional guidance from appropriately qualified practitioners.

2.11.32 When wearing helmets, users should be aware of any potential reduction in hearing and, in some cases, vision. A badly fitting helmet or one that is too large may reduce the level of protection provided, and may even add to the hazard or contribute to injury. Additionally, a helmet should be properly looked after. Dropping a helmet on a hard surface can significantly reduce the level of protection it would provide in the event of a fall.

2.11.33 **Padding, or body armour**, has developed from the traditional shoulder pads. It provides some protection to the shoulders, chest and back from the physical impact when tackling or being tackled in rugby.

2.11.34 **Swimming goggles** are recommended when swimming at competition level and for extended, regular training sessions. They can help to maintain the required body position and improve vision through the water. In contrast, within short curriculum swimming lessons (typically 20–25 minutes' water time) for beginners, or for single, short races in school galas, goggles are not considered to be necessary.

2.11.35 Students learning to swim or improving their swimming ability often do not swim in straight lines, and as a result, they might get close to, or come into contact with, other swimmers. If goggles are worn, any contact with others (eg the flailing arm of a beginner learning a new stroke) might result in injury to both the swimmers wearing the goggles and those who are not. Feeling confident and safe in the water, and swimming underwater, should not be dependent on wearing goggles, neither are goggles designed for such activity, as the eye pressure cannot be relieved.

2.11.36 When swimming goggles are used, they should be made of unbreakable plastic or rubber materials. The British Standard for the manufacture of goggles (BS 5883:1996) includes the requirement that the packaging should contain instructions regarding their putting on and removal. Students should be taught to remove goggles by slipping them off the head and not by stretching the retaining band as wet plastic is slippery and may cause injury to the eye area. Where goggles are not properly fitted, they may mist up and adversely affect visibility.

2.11.37   Given the potential for injury, the teacher responsible for the group should have the prerogative to require any student to remove their goggles for reasons of safety if they are constantly adjusting, removing and replacing them. The teacher is not responsible for fitting or adjusting a student's goggles. Where a student does wear goggles, they need to be able to carry out the task of fitting them independently.

2.11.38   As with the management of any risk in PESSPA, all aspects of the situation should be taken into consideration before the school, along with the provider (if lessons are taken externally), makes a decision about policy regarding the wearing of swimming goggles. Where any local authority (LA) or governors' policies regarding water safety exist, they should be adhered to. Having considered these, schools should fully inform parents of the points raised in the guidance, and the decision of the school in light of this.

2.11.39   In some cases, according to the stage and ability of the student, the use of goggles may be permitted. The reasons for the decisions either way should be fully explained in the risk assessment for that activity.

2.11.40   In a swimming pool environment, students who are very short-sighted may not be able to see the teacher's gestures or read any signage unless they are in extremely close proximity. Not being able to see the teacher clearly can also affect the clarity of receiving verbal instructions, which might impact significantly on safety. In cases of extreme short-sightedness (myopia), prescription goggles, which are now more widely available and reasonably priced, may result in a safer swimming experience for the student.

2.11.41   In cases of extreme short-sightedness or in rare instances where individuals have particularly sensitive eyes or wear contact lenses, schools should require a parental letter stating that the student has particular needs to warrant the use of goggles. Such a letter would have the status of simply being informative and **would not constitute any form of indemnity** should injury arise later through the misuse of the goggles. Additional medical certification about such particular needs is costly to obtain and should **not be sought** as this information is likely to have been previously set down in the student's records.

2.11.42   When students complain of eye irritation during swimming sessions, the cause, in almost all cases, is an incorrect chemical balance in the water. If several students are reporting eye irritation as a result of swimming, the pool provider should be informed. This imbalance can be eradicated. In other situations, from hospital records, irritation might result from a reaction to the chemicals used to clean the lenses of the goggles at home.

2.11.43   Swimmers who are training daily usually wear goggles because they are exposing their eyes for long periods to the effects of the chemicals in the water. In some cases, the tissue around the eyes does not dry out between training sessions and thus becomes more susceptible to infection. Goggles offer regular swimmers some protection against this happening.

2.11.44   When parents request the wearing of goggles because of their child's particular need, the school should inform them that the teacher in charge retains the prerogative to require the removal of the goggles for reasons of safety.

2.11.45   The use of **sports goggles for other sports and activities** has become increasingly common, with high profile sports players demonstrating their use in a wide range of sports, including squash, basketball, football, skiing and tennis.

2.11.46   Sports goggles may be used solely for protection, such as in squash where the likelihood of the ball hitting a player in the eye at speed is fairly high, but also for necessity, with prescription goggles providing a welcome improvement for participants with different eye conditions in sport.

2.11.47   Hard plastic resin (CR39), or even more durable polycarbonate or Trivex, is used to produce lenses that are far safer than glass and offer the necessary protection.

2.11.48   The European standard EN 166:2002 covers all protective eye wear, and Association of British Dispensing Opticians (ABDO) (2014) 'Protective eyewear' provides general information about sports goggles, as well as details about those best suited to different sports.

 For more information on the ABDO guidance, see http://goo.gl/QtmZi4

2.11.49   Local dispensing opticians can advise with regard to the most appropriate type of sports goggles whether for protection or with prescription.

2.11.50   **Exposure to the sun** is an aspect of personal protection that is increasingly important. The risks associated with overexposure to the two bands of ultraviolet light from the sun are well documented, and staff need to implement a range of necessary precautions.

 For more information about weather conditions, see Chapter 2, Section 5, page 124.

Governing bodies of sport and PPE

2.11.51   In some circumstances, governing body of sport requirements relating to the wearing of PPE may be directly adopted within educational settings. For example, during inter-school competitions or fixtures, the wearing of PPE may be mandatory.

2.11.52   However, a physical education risk assessment of a specific activity may result in some **flexibility in interpreting governing body of sport requirements** in order to achieve optimum levels of participation and involvement within the curriculum, such as modification of equipment, organisation of different groups, and non-contact versions of physical-contact games in order to remove the need for PPE.

2.11.53   A number of governing bodies of sport have introduced their own regulations, which impose the **mandatory** use of certain items of PPE. Students who are involved in competitions and events **organised and regulated by a governing body of sport** must comply with the governing body of sport's ruling in relation to use of PPE.

2.11.54   Governing body of sport regulations for the use of PPE apply to both boys and girls participating in the sport. Table 19 summarises a selection of these. Details are available on governing body of sport websites regarding any additional recommended items, or where they may differ between sexes.

Table 19: Governing body of sport requirements and recommendations relating to PPE

Similar requirements and recommendations are provided by governing bodies of sport in England, Northern Ireland, Scotland and Wales.

Governing Body of Sport	PPE Requirements
England and Wales Cricket Board	• Helmets and boxes are mandatory when batting using a hard ball and also when fielding close to the bat.
England Hockey	• Mouth guards and shin/ankle pads are recommended at all levels of participation. • Specialist protection for goalkeepers is mandatory.
England Lacrosse	• Mouth guards are mandatory at representative level. • Specialist protection for goalkeepers is mandatory.
Football Association (England)	• Shin pads are mandatory at all levels of participation.
Rugby Football League	• Mouth guards are recommended. • Shoulder pads are permitted at all levels of participation. • Padded helmets are permitted.
England Rugby (RFU)	• Mouth guards are mandatory for representative matches above school level. Otherwise, they are recommended. • Padded helmets are permitted. • Soft shoulder padding is permitted.
British Cycling	• All participants in a British Cycling cycle training session must wear a correctly fitting helmet, standard or full face, that conforms to recognised standards. • British Cycling strongly recommends that cyclists wear a cycle helmet when engaged in any cycling activity.
Archery GB	• It is good practice to fit pupils with arm guards to reduce the chance of bruising if the bow string catches, but it is not a requirement.
Baseball/Softball UK	• Rules for 'slow pitch' softball make the wearing of mitts for competitive softball mandatory.

2.11.55   Readers should continue to refer to the appropriate websites to keep up to date with ongoing changes in relation to the use of PPE.

Chapter 2/Section 12: Equipment

Managing equipment

2.12.1   Staff need to be confident that the physical education, school sport and physical activity (PESSPA) equipment they plan to use is of **acceptable quality** in terms of its design, manufacture and durability. Such assurance is given if equipment has a British and European Standards Kitemark (BS and BS EN respectively). PESSPA equipment is best purchased from a reputable and reliable company that assures such a quality standard. Not all equipment has provision for a BS EN standard, and if this is the case, staff should seek alternative confirmation that the products they intend to purchase and use with students are safe and well made. This could be achieved through discussion with other users and research of product reviews.

2.12.2   Reference to a particular BS or BS EN standard is a means of ensuring the consistency and fitness for purpose of certain products and procedures. However, compliance with a British Standard does not in itself confer legal immunity, although it will strengthen any defence against accusations of negligence in activities that use this equipment.

2.12.3   Accepting **used play items** from parents and other charitable sources, or purchasing from Internet sites, should be done only after careful consideration of the quality and condition of the items.

2.12.4   Recycled **tyres** are used in some playgrounds to add fun and interest. Where this is considered:

- Choose tyres that are intact, with no exposed wires.

- Test, using a white cloth, that the surface will not mark clothing too much.

- Check fixings regularly if tyres are bolted together.

- Supervise students carefully, particularly while they are developing the appropriate skills and awareness to use the tyres safely.

2.12.5   Equipment needs to be **fit for purpose**. Students of differing ages and abilities will benefit from different sizes and types of equipment. Students' individual needs may require adapted equipment in order to allow safe participation.

2.12.6   Equipment should be used for the purpose for which it is designed. **Improvisation** is rarely necessary due to the range, quality and quantity of equipment available to schools. Where a decision is made to use an item for a purpose it is not actually designed for, the member of staff would need to have a very strong justification for deciding to improvise.

2.12.7   On occasions, it may be appropriate to adapt the use of equipment, such as the use of cones to create mini goals, but this requires careful risk assessment. Some adaptations may be required when modifying a PESSPA activity for a particular playing surface or space (eg using lighter-weight balls for hockey on a hard court space).

2.12.8   Staff discussion about the use of particular items for any reason not directly related to design and purpose will be of benefit in eliminating extraordinary use, and establishing consistent practice and safety standards throughout the school.

2.12.9   Students should be taught how to **lift and carry** equipment safely from an early age. They should learn how many people are needed to lift, carry and place specific items of equipment safely, how to carry items correctly and about the importance of remaining focused on the task, ie to avoid tripping, falling or colliding that may be caused by lack of concentration. Teaching **correct lifting technique** should be an important part of a PESSPA curriculum and can encompass health messages about lifelong back care. Learning should start in the early years and progress to Key Stage 4/5.

 For more information about students learning to lift, move and place equipment safely, see Chapter 3, Section 8, page 341.

Checking PESSPA equipment prior to use

2.12.10   A minimum requirement is that equipment used in a physical education session should be **visually checked** prior to students using it, to ensure it is safe to use, assembled correctly and not damaged or faulty. While staff should make this practice part of their preparation, **students** should also become involved, reporting any faulty equipment at a level that is compatible with their age, ability and previous experience. In addition to the annual contractor inspections (see page 206 in this section), all schools should have a system for staff to report **faulty** equipment, and for ensuring that staff in turn are made aware of any faulty equipment.

2.12.11   Where schools take part in **centrally organised sports events** away from the school site, using equipment provided for them, staff and students should carry out their own checks prior to taking part, reporting any faults to the organisers.

2.12.12   Where organisers of off-site sports events have requested that schools bring equipment to be used at the event, this equipment should be checked by both the school providing the equipment and the event organiser together, establishing an agreement that all items are safe for use.

Table 20: Safety checklist for PESSPA equipment

Gymnastics Equipment	Check that:
Wooden rebound/springboards	• the board is stable on impact • the surface is non-slip and free from splinters • rubber feet are stable and are not worn through to the wood
Benches and planks	• the construction is not warped, and is free from splinters • rubber buffers on the supporting feet are secure and the bench is stable • the surface is clean and smooth • fixing hooks are intact and covered with leather or plastic • rubber pads on the top surface are in place if the bench is intended for use in an inverted position
Ropes and suspended apparatus	• ropes are not frayed or damaged • pull-out lines are not worn, and their securing wall cleats are secure and not broken or with sharp edges • the runway operates smoothly • ropes are knot-free, and the leather end caps are intact • rope ladder floor fixings are intact
Hinged apparatus fixed to a wall	• bracing wires are taut with no visible fraying at any point • castors run smoothly • floor sockets are clean and free from obstruction • securing bolts are firmly fixed, and engage properly with their floor and wall sockets • wooden components are free from cracks or splinters • painted components are well maintained, with no evidence of flaking • consideration is given to replacing traditional bare metal tension clamps with padded, boxed in versions
Single and double beams	• hauling cables are free running • trackways are well maintained, enabling smooth movement of the upright • there are sufficient pins and wedges • beam surfaces are clean and smooth • beams run smoothly when lowered and raised • floor sockets are clean
Vaulting equipment and movement platforms	• all wooden components are splinter-free • all covers – vinyl, material or hide – are free from tears, clean and, in the case of hide, suitably textured • construction is stable and solid with no weakness allowing dangerous movement on impact • wheeling mechanisms work efficiently.

(continued)

Games Equipment	Check that:
Outdoor socket-type goalposts	• they are correctly located • they are securely cemented into the ground, or wedged in to prevent unauthorised lifting out of the ground • they have protective padding in line with governing body of sport guidelines • they are regularly checked to ensure that bolts are in place, and that metal is not corroded • they meet British and European Standards (BS EN 748 and 8462), dependent on size
Goal netting	• it is stored and carried in a way that avoids it becoming a trip hazard • it is attached and dismantled using a stepladder, and never by jumping up to the crossbar • it is attached to both top corners before hooking along the crossbar • it is well fitting and does not extend beyond the area covered by the base of the posts • it is secured with plastic hooks or tape (metal cup hooks are banned, and should no longer be used) • it is secured firmly using metal pegs fully pushed into the ground
Portable or free-standing goalposts (used for football or hockey)	• they are obtained from a reputable manufacturer and comply with British Standard BS EN 8462 • they are made of lightweight construction and with integral wheels, where appropriate, in order to limit the lifting required • they are assembled in accordance with the manufacturer's instructions • they are smooth in construction, with no sharp edges • they are equipped with an integral safe stabilising device that presents no hazard to players or spectators, or they are secured using chains or anchor weights, when in use or stored, outside or inside • the anchor systems are appropriate to the ground conditions, and do not present any tripping hazard • they are regularly checked for wear and tear and, where practical, any damage made good by a suitably qualified person • they are not 'home-made' or altered from their original specification – such equipment should not be used • staff or students with responsibility for moving and positioning the posts apply safe lifting and carrying techniques; use an appropriate number of people who are strong enough and trained in manual handling techniques, and pull or push the posts backwards according to the design • **staff and students are very aware of the danger of serious injury or death resulting from unstable goalposts falling on to them; climbing or swinging on the uprights and crossbars should be strictly forbidden** (for additional information, see 'Harrod UK Goalpost Safety Information Pack', www.harrod.uk.com)

(continued)

Games Equipment (continued)	Check that:
Unfixed posts (eg netball posts)	<ul><li>posts are slotted into holes in the ground; where this is not possible, free-standing posts need to be safely weighted</li><li>posts are padded along the entire length of post where required by the governing body of sport, in accordance with specifications, particularly at competitive level</li><li>posts are adjustable for different age groups, if applicable</li><li>when not in use, unfixed posts that cannot be stored inside a building are secured at all times to prevent unauthorised use</li><li>unfixed posts are carried out by staff or students who have been shown safe lifting techniques from the work area to storage</li><li>students are supervised if they are moving unfixed posts</li><li>metal posts are free from corrosion and sharp edges</li></ul>
Playing area markers	<ul><li>cricket stumps or sharp-ended items are not used as markers or posts – a fall on to a sharp point could cause serious injury</li><li>corner flags are flexible and sufficiently high so as not to constitute a hazard to falling players</li><li>throw-down discs and lines, cones and skittles are not used in fast-moving activities, where a fall is foreseeable</li><li>bean bags and hoops are not used as markers for indoor work if the floor surface is shiny as they can present a slipping hazard when stepped on.</li></ul>
Athletics Equipment	**Check that:**
	<ul><li>items are carried correctly</li><li>all staff and students are familiar with the required procedures for carrying and retrieving discus, shot and javelin</li><li>all staff and students are familiar with the correct use and purpose of rakes and spades in sand jumping pits</li><li>hurdles are positioned correctly with stabilisers facing the approach and not the other way round</li><li>all staff and students know about storage of equipment that is appropriate for safe retrieval (eg javelins should be stored horizontally on a rack or, where one is not available, on the floor).</li></ul>

Case law

2.12.13 **Steed versus Cheltenham Borough Council (2000):**

*The crossbar of some rugby posts collapsed and fell on to a boy. It was judged that the posts were **rusty and deteriorating,** and that the council did not carry out sufficiently frequent inspections of the condition of the posts.*

2.12.14 **Hall versus Holker Estate Co Ltd (2008):**

*An adult was injured during a game of football when he caught his foot in the **net of a portable goalpost that should have been pegged into the ground.** The goalposts collapsed and hit him, causing facial damage. He claimed the owner of the site should have checked the pegs regularly to ensure the facility and equipment were safe. At appeal, it was held that there was no evidence of a suitable inspection system, and negligence was evident. This illustrates the importance of ensuring **equipment is regularly inspected.** This is particularly important where it is clear the equipment needs to be regularly maintained and properly assembled for safe use, and where it is likely that parts of the equipment are occasionally misplaced or removed, rendering it unsafe.*

Mats

2.12.15 It is essential that both staff and students understand the structure, function, capabilities and limitations of mats when used within the PESSPA programme.

2.12.16 Mats are primarily designed to **absorb impact** when landing on the feet. Their construction dissipates force, thereby reducing reaction to what would otherwise constitute a hard and unyielding surface.

2.12.17 Over the years, considerable improvements have been made to the design and specification of mats to enhance safety. However, it is important to recognise that mats, whatever their construction and size, should **never be seen as fail-safe protection** systems that supersede effective technique. Students need to be aware that a correctly performed landing contributes significantly to preventing injury. **Correct landing technique** needs to be taught and re-emphasised regularly.

2.12.18 When **buying new mats,** care should be taken that they meet any current standard, where available, and that they fully comply with **fire regulations**. Assurance should be sought from manufacturers on both these requirements. (Currently, these specifications are set out in BS 1892-3:2003, reconfirmed in 2011.)

2.12.19 The following guidance relates to the **maintenance of mats.** In order to promote safe practice, mats should be:

- covered with material that is **easy to clean**; in order to minimise slippage, the underside will need to be cleaned from time to time, and the top surface periodically, according to the extent of use; they should be checked regularly for any embedded objects, such as stones or pins

- **stable and lie flat** to the floor; wherever practical, mats should be **stored in a horizontal** position to prevent warping of closed-cell polyethylene foam and disintegration of foam padding

- free from holes and tears, and display no rucking in the cover or foam infill

- **light enough for students to handle easily**, preferably in pairs if the mats are lightweight; four students may need to carry mats according to their size and strength in relation to the size and weight of the mat

- subject to regular inspection; damaged mats should immediately be taken out of service until repaired by a specialist maintenance firm, or replaced.

2.12.20 In gymnastics, mats should never be **indiscriminately placed** around the working area. Each mat should be placed with a **specific purpose** in mind.

2.12.21 **Examples of safe use of mats would be where they are used to**:

- provide a comfortable, cushioned area for aspects of floor work (eg developing rolling activities)

- identify suitable landing areas to students as they work around equipment

- provide confidence in feet-first landings from apparatus such as beams and equipment used for vaulting and balancing (though it is the efficiency of technique in landing from a height that minimises injury, not dependence on a mat absorbing the momentum)

- extend sequence work by providing choice for changes of direction, level and mode of travel.

2.12.22 General-purpose mats (approximately 25mm thick) are generally suitable for curriculum work in gymnastics. Thicker mats (eg 200mm) may be necessary for more specialised, advanced gymnastic activity in which the performer generates high levels of momentum.

2.12.23 Staff need to exercise **caution** when using thick weight-absorbing mattresses ('crash mats' or 'safety mats') as landing areas. Too much absorption may compromise safe dismounts on to feet by creating rotation on landing. In such situations, it is advised that the landing surface is 'firmed up' by overlaying the mattress with general gymnastic mats where necessary.

2.12.24 If more than one weight-absorbing safety mat is used to create a longer area (eg for landing from a vaulting horse), the mats should be secured together by placing a longer agility mat roll on the surface of the safety mats. This will lessen the risks associated with a student landing on the line where two mats meet, and offers protection from the safety mat 'bottoming out'.

2.12.25 Where mats for landing areas are placed together or overlaid, regular checks should be made to ensure that no gaps appear. Procedures to ensure this is carried out should be introduced.

2.12.26 **Mats should never be used to protect against the foreseeable outcomes of poorly developed skill**, such as anticipating that students will fall while suspended from a horizontal ladder or similar apparatus. In such situations, it is better that equipment and task are modified to reflect student need and capability accurately, thereby **minimising the risk of falling** and of poorly controlled dismounts.

2.12.27   **Athletics landing modules** are necessary for the safe performance of high-jump technique in which the transference of weight moves from feet to some other body part (eg as in the 'Fosbury flop' technique and its related progressions). It is strongly recommended that staff using specialised high-jump facilities have undergone **appropriate training** through the governing body of sport (UK Athletics) or as part of a specialist physical education training programme.

2.12.28   When using landing modules, staff should ensure that:

- multiple modules, where used, are firmly locked together, and a coverall pad used to prevent slippage

- the landing area is sufficiently large and deep to accommodate the abilities of the students involved and probable variations in landing position, extending beyond both uprights

- the density of the landing module is sufficient to avoid any 'bottoming out'. Compliance with BS EN 12503-2:2016 will aid this.

2.12.29   Mats used in **martial arts** activities need to be specific to the activity to minimise the risk of injury from high-impact falls and throws. Mats should comply with BS EN 12503-3 in order to provide adequate shock-absorbing properties, with a strong base to prevent sliding during activity. General-purpose gymnastics mats should not be used as their density is inadequate for martial arts purposes.

2.12.30   Canvas covers should not be used to cover or secure martial arts arenas. Frames can be constructed to secure mat areas permanently. Frames are usually purchased upholstered and cushioned with fabric or carpet to prevent injury or hazard.

Gymnastics equipment

2.12.31   **Primary school gymnastics equipment** includes fixed and portable apparatus, such as climbing frames, ropes, benches, movement platforms, nesting tables, boxes, low level beams, planks, trestles and springboards.

2.12.32   **Secondary school gymnastics equipment** includes fixed and portable apparatus, such as wall bars, ropes, benches, movement platforms, nesting tables, boxes, planks and trestles, and might also include equipment associated with competitive gymnastics (including that for vaulting and agility activities such as trampettes).

2.12.33   Whatever the function of gymnastics equipment, staff should ensure that:

- only equipment that has been officially provided, approved and/or Kitemarked is used

- improvisation beyond the design specification of the equipment is avoided

- equipment is assembled and dismantled systematically and that students are taught to do this, wherever possible

- equipment is checked by staff to ensure correct assembly before activity commences, and that students are encouraged to remain alert to, and report, any unintended adjustment to equipment as work proceeds

- sufficient space is left between equipment to allow safe movement around it

- dismount points and planned landing areas are free from obstruction and always well away from walls – mats may be used to designate intended direction of dismount

- equipment is returned to its designated storage space and left in a stable position after use

- equipment is regularly inspected and repaired, where necessary, by qualified maintenance engineers on at least an annual basis

- between inspections, the condition of the equipment is constantly monitored by staff, on a day-to-day and lesson-by-lesson basis, and students are encouraged and equipped to do the same

- equipment deemed unsafe but reparable is moved well away from the working area and clearly labelled as unsafe until made good

- equipment 'condemned' following an inspection is completely removed from the facility and disposed of

- staff familiarise themselves with key safety points to check on gymnastics equipment

- equipment is age-appropriate such that students are able to manage **lifting, carrying** and placing in a safe manner

- students learn how to lift, carry and place equipment safely:
    - keep back straight
    - keep close to the load
    - feet apart with one foot in front of the other
    - lift with knees bent, using the legs as the lifting power
    - have a good grip on the load before lifting
    - do not change grip when carrying a load
    - do not allow the load to obstruct fields of view.
    - face towards the intended direction of travel without excessive twisting
    - set the load down gently with a straight back and knees bent.

For information about students learning about safe exercise practice, see Chapter 3, Section 5, page 320, and safe lifting and carrying, see Section 8, page 341.

FAQ

2.12.34   **At what height it is safe to allow my year four students to work on the climbing equipment?**

The type of climbing equipment most commonly found in primary schools ranges in height from two to three metres (six feet, six inches to 10 feet). This presents a range of options with regard to how high students climb. There will be a number of factors to be considered in making this decision:

- Prior learning – have the students regularly worked on the equipment since the start of Key Stage 1?

- Quality of teaching – have the students been progressively taught correct climbing technique in order to ascend and descend safely?

- Competence of the member of staff – is the staff member sufficiently confident and competent to supervise and manage students on the climbing equipment effectively?

Where the answer to any of these questions is 'no', the member of staff may feel a need to restrict the height at which the students work. A lack of training in correct climbing technique means that some staff members are reluctant to use the equipment with students, and this needs to be addressed so that it is not used as a reason to restrict students' learning.

Setting restrictive heights is not recommended, and a risk assessment approach is preferred, using questions such as those suggested above. Staff are encouraged to pursue additional training where required so that they can enable students to fully develop these skills. As with all practice, any employer's guidance concerning this should be followed.

2.12.35   **Should I place mats at the base of the gymnastics climbing equipment?**

Students should understand the purpose and limitation of gymnastics mats (see page 196), and appreciate that it is safe practice and good technique that will prevent them from falling. Although it is common practice to see mats at the base of climbing equipment, these mats may have limited potential to reduce the impact of a low-level accidental fall, and cannot be considered adequate in preventing head injury and/or concussion. Their primary purpose is to provide an area to extend a sequence on to the floor, or to indicate the planned area for dismount from the climbing arrangement. Care should be taken to ensure that mats do not present a tripping hazard in other areas of the activity space.

Staff working in gymnastics need to feel competent that they can teach safely. Where this is not the case, they should make this clear to their line manager, and until sufficient training has been completed, should only use low-level equipment in the lesson.

Play equipment

2.12.36   Soft play shapes should offer firm and predictable support, with replacement as wear and tear takes place. The surfaces of soft play equipment should be cleaned periodically.

2.12.37   **Wheeled equipment**, such as tricycles, should be confined to designated areas.

2.12.38   The use of **bats and balls** can prove hazardous in confined areas. Careful planning using **zoned areas** of the playground can help reduce any risk of injury.

2.12.39   Where lunchtime supervisory staff are involved in setting up activities or distributing equipment, they should be trained to do so. Care should be taken to ensure that equipment appropriate for different age groups is **not mixed up**. This avoids students inadvertently using equipment not designed for them in subsequent sessions.

2.12.40   Any **'young leaders'** leading activities using play equipment should be supervised at all times.

Playground climbing equipment

2.12.41   All climbing equipment should be appropriate for the age and developmental needs of the students who will use it. It is advisable to provide separate use of climbing frames for younger and older students, and for more timid students and more adventurous individuals.

2.12.42   Professional judgement should be used to decide whether inclement weather restricts the use of outdoor climbing frames. Considerations would include type of footwear worn, age and experience of the users, and materials used in the construction.

2.12.43   Safety surfaces require regular maintenance.

See **PESSPA equipment inspection and maintenance** in this section, page 206, and **Safety surfaces for playground climbing areas** in Chapter 2, Section 13, page 219.

Trampolines and trampettes

2.12.44   It is recommended that assembling, positioning and folding of trampolines is carried out under the supervision of a person who has received training from a qualified tutor.

2.12.45   In schools, this could mean that older students, sufficiently mature and strong enough, may carry out the folding and unfolding of trampolines, with training, under the **close supervision of qualified staff** who are ready to give immediate hands-on assistance if needed.

2.12.46   There have been several accidents where younger students, lacking the necessary strength and physique, have been left to carry out this task without direct staff involvement. It is important that, in circumstances with such students, qualified staff are directly physically involved as part of the process.

2.12.47   Clear communication, awareness and a responsible attitude are essential, particularly in the phase where the end of a trampoline has been opened, to ensure it is held with sufficient force to counter the tension of the springs. Injury most commonly occurs when elbows and forearms get trapped in the trampoline, and for this reason, they should be kept clear of the gap between the folding ends and frame while lowering under control.

2.12.48   Trampolines need to be **positioned** well away from any overhead obstruction such as hanging beams or lights. Governing body of sport recommendations state that an overhead clearance of at least **five metres** from the floor to the lowest hanging object is required for non-somersault trampolining, ie low-level shaped jumps and body landings, and **eight metres** where somersaults or other rotational skills are being taught.

For further guidance from British Gymnastics, see https://goo.gl/Mxculx

For more information about choosing the correct size of trampoline, see Chapter 4, Section 6, page 417.

2.12.49   Hydraulically assisted trampoline roller stands are now available to assist with the setting up and putting away of trampolines. Where these and fixed-height roller stands are used, they should be safely stored away from the working area when not in use. Care must be taken when operating the hydraulic system depending on the mechanism it uses. Contact the manufacturer for any additional guidance or instruction.

2.12.50   When unfolding a trampoline, staff should ensure that:

- training shoes are worn, and feet kept well away from the wheels

- the trampoline is angled and lowered carefully, and that the lower leg section is held firmly so it does not crash to the floor

- the frame sections are opened with a firm, continuous movement, and with steady force applied and maintained to prevent them from springing back

- fingers, forearms and wrists are kept clear of all hinges.

2.12.51   The space under and around trampolines should be clear and free from obstructions.

2.12.52   **Before** allowing a trampoline or trampette to be used, staff should check that:

- all leg braces have been properly fitted, and hinge units securely housed

- all adjustments are tight

- the hooks of the springs/rubber cables are properly attached, with the hooks pointing down

- the springs/cables are all in good condition

- the safety pads are fitted and entirely cover the springs/cables

- Allen screws are tight (if present)

- the bed is clean and free from damage of any kind

- all coverall pads are in good condition and in place covering the frame surround.

2.12.53   For trampolines, also check that:

- the wheeling devices are operating smoothly, and the pivotal housing on the frame holds the hub of the wheeling mechanism at right angles without any movement of the hub and the housing

- the floor surround has 25mm non-slip **matting two metres wide along the sides of the trampoline**

- each end of the trampoline has safety mats, supported where possible at trampoline level, of a sufficient size and weight absorbency to meet the requirements of body impact in the event of unwanted travel forwards or backwards; to achieve this, 'spotting deck platforms' or **'end deck platforms'** may be purchased, either with or separately from the mattress

- safety matting is placed on the floor behind the end mats

- where trampolines are positioned in a line, weight-absorbing mattresses are placed on the frame and springs between each trampoline; specific 'middle mats' can be purchased for this purpose or standard large safety mats used.

2.12.54   When folding a trampoline, staff should ensure that:

- training shoes are worn

- the wheels are securely housed

- adult support and supervision are directly at hand to step in if needed

- the frame sections are closed using a firm, continuous movement, and with steady force applied and maintained to resist the tension of the springs or cables

- fingers, forearms and wrists are kept clear of all hinges

- feet are kept well away from the wheels

- the lower frame and leg sections are positioned inside the upper frame and leg sections as the trampoline is rotated from the horizontal to the vertical.

2.12.55   **Once folded**, trampolines should be **locked** to prevent unauthorised use. This can be achieved by locking together two links of one of the leg chains.

2.12.56   **Trampettes** should be disabled in some way when not in use or kept in secure storage.

2.12.57   Damaged trampolines and trampettes should never be used until repaired or replaced.

2.12.58   When provided, overhead support rigs should be supplied and fitted by recognised specialist manufacturers and engineers. On no account should improvised rigs be used. An overhead support rig may be used to help students to learn movements involving rotations or twists on the trampoline. The supporter (usually an adult) needs to be competent in the use of the rig, and capable of holding the weight to control the descent of the student. The positioning of the trampoline and rig needs to be checked to ensure the centre of the rig is vertically aligned to the centre of the trampoline

2.12.59   Training for staff in the correct use of rigs is essential. British Gymnastics offers specific training for the use of an overhead rig within the Teachers' Trampoline Awards or as an add-on module.

For more on the Teachers' Trampoline Awards, see https://goo.gl/E9uZ97

Trampoline and trampette activities in primary schools

2.12.60 It is not common practice to find trampolining taught within the curriculum in primary schools. The use of trampettes as a piece of gymnastics equipment is not recommended within primary curriculum lessons. Both items require very specialised knowledge, and **staff are expected to be appropriately qualified** to teach trampolining (ie hold a Teachers' Trampoline Award, and to have received training in the use of trampettes, before using them with students).

2.12.61 Where coaches or specialist staff are brought in to deliver these activities in after-school clubs, care should be taken to secure the equipment during the day, to prevent it being accessed by students, or used by staff who are not sufficiently trained.

2.12.62 Mini trampettes for rebounding classes (on the spot, low-level bouncing) have been introduced into some schools as a fun activity with beneficial health outcomes, but safe storage of sufficient numbers of rebounders for a class prevents many schools from pursuing this. Staff leading this activity need to be suitably trained.

2.12.63 The use of trampolines as a **therapeutic activity** is considered to be beneficial for some students with SEND, both primary and secondary.

 For more information about trampoline qualifications, see Chapter 4, Section 6, page 416.

Case law

2.12.64 **Clarke versus Derby City Council (2015):**

A 15-year-old student was injured while helping to put away a trampoline at a local authority (LA) school.

The LA denied liability against a failure to supervise the task properly, failure to implement a safe system for it, and causing or permitting too many students to engage in the task. It contended that the trampoline was put away under the teacher's direct supervision and in accordance with the national guidelines – Safe Practice in Physical Education and Sport – issued by afPE.

The LA countered that the teacher was only made aware of the student's injury after the first part of the procedure, which the teacher claimed was carried out without any incident. The LA also claimed that there was no history of any previous similar incidents, and that the trampoline was inspected annually and, at the previous inspection, was found to have been in good working order.

It was further argued that the student's accident was caused by her own negligence in failing to follow the teacher's instructions and to take proper care for her own safety.

At trial, the student alleged that the teacher had been called outside to attend to noisy students waiting for the next lesson. However, there was no lesson after the one in which the student was injured, and the teacher could not therefore have been called outside for the reason claimed. The judge also found significant changes between the student's initial allegations and those made later in court.

The judge said that a failure to supervise was such an obvious complaint that it would have been made at the outset, but that allegation was not initially made. The claim was dismissed.

This case stresses the importance of supervising tasks involving equipment where a foreseeable risk of injury is recognised, following established systems and procedures, and the importance of equipment inspections. In addition, the teacher's comprehensive record of the incident at the time was shown to be of great value.

2.12.65 **Greenwood versus Dorset County Council (2008):**

*A group of students were involved in folding away a trampoline. One student's arm was fractured when the folding end trapped it. The teacher was judged to have **complied with the established code of practice** in that she had:*

- *supervised adequately*
- *taught the correct process*
- *regularly reminded the students of the correct process*
- *provided step-by-step monitoring of the process*
- *involved sufficient students in the folding process.*

Storage of PESSPA equipment

2.12.66   Storage of equipment should be discussed by staff so that all are aware of what equipment is stored where and why.

2.12.67   All storage areas should be **kept tidy** in order to minimise the potential for tripping, and to allow safe accessibility for students to pick up, transport and site the equipment they are using.

2.12.68   Storage areas need to be of **sufficient size** so as not to create hazards. Access should be as **wide** as possible to prevent 'bottlenecks'. Where a separate fire-rated mat store is provided, it should be used. Most schools store mats with other equipment, and when this applies, the mats should be stored well away from heating sources and electrical circuits to minimise the possibility of fire causing toxic fumes.

2.12.69   Where equipment is stored around the perimeter of an indoor facility, it should be stored in a safe manner so as to encroach minimally on the work area, and placed, where possible, close to where it is generally used, to minimise carrying distances.

2.12.70   The Work at Height Regulations 2005 address situations where anyone could fall a distance likely to cause personal injury. Where equipment is **stored above reach height**, appropriate steps, ladders or platforms should be used in order to comply with the regulations. Heavy items are best stored at waist height to minimise the likelihood of back injury through lifting heavy weight from the floor or being dropped on to feet if over-reaching above.

For more information on the Work at Height Regulations 2005, see http://goo.gl/cbJMRI

2.12.71   Storage located outdoors should be secured, to **prevent unauthorised access** to potentially dangerous items.

PESSPA equipment inspection and maintenance

2.12.72   Maintaining PESSPA equipment prolongs its life and use, and helps to ensure that safe standards are met.

2.12.73   The Health and Safety at Work etc Act 1974 (http://goo.gl/JjdaTM) requires employers to provide safe plant and equipment for employees and other visitors (eg students, community use, lettings), and the Provision and Use of Work Equipment Regulations 1998 (PUWER) (http://goo.gl/Oy1nmL) require that all equipment should be subject to **systematic and regular inspection** to identify any signs of damage or wear and tear that may cause injury.

2.12.74   The British Standards Institute (BSI) (http://shop.bsigroup.com) states that 'it is important that all physical education apparatus is maintained in a first class, fully safe condition. General maintenance should take place **regularly**. An inspection should be carried out **at least once a year**.'

2.12.75   The regular maintenance of sports hall, gymnastics, fixed play, fitness and sports equipment is essential for safety. **'Regular'** is not time defined by the BSI. However, it typically means annually, with more frequent inspection where use is higher than normal for a school (such as where community use adds significantly to equipment usage). Where a school chooses not to undertake annual inspections, presentation of a clear rationale for this is strongly advised.

2.12.76   **BS EN 1176** recommends a more rigorous approach for outdoor fixed play equipment, recommending recorded visual, periodic and annual engineering inspections by a competent person.

2.12.77   **BS EN 1177** covers safety surfaces around fixed play equipment that should be checked as part of the inspection of the fixed play equipment.

2.12.78   An annual inspection of school PESSPA equipment should include, as appropriate:

- gymnastics equipment

- trampolines and trampettes

- fitness equipment – multi-gyms and free weights

- indoor and outdoor adventure play equipment

- indoor and outdoor sports posts, nets, goals and tables

- indoor and outdoor cricket nets

- high-jump landing modules

- parkour equipment

- adventure activities facilities – climbing towers, climbing walls

- fixed play equipment and safety surfaces

- ball courts.

2.12.79   An **'inspection'** – contractors check the equipment and produce a report indicating all the minor and major work that is identified as being needed.

2.12.80   A **'maintenance inspection'** – contractors will check and carry out minor repairs at the time of the inspection, plus provide a report on more extensive and expensive repairs that are advised. 'Same day' minor works to bring slightly faulty equipment up to an acceptable standard may be negotiated within the basic contract or costed separately.

2.12.81   Many schools combine inspection arrangements with maintenance provision into one contract for convenience. Others may require separate inspection from maintenance provision as a quality-assurance factor.

Planning a PESSPA equipment inspection

2.12.82   Academies, free schools and other non-LA schools are responsible for making their own contractual arrangements for PESSPA equipment inspections, and are advised to put in place procedures for ensuring that it is organised annually, or in accordance with the arrangements expected by their employers and insurers. Where the LA is the employer, it generally makes central contractual arrangements for its schools' annual PESSPA equipment inspection. Action based on the report is the responsibility and decision of the head teacher (HT) and governing body.

2.12.83   In order to achieve appropriate safe-practice standards for PESSPA equipment and facility maintenance, inspection contracts should include reference to the scope of the work, the quality and standards of work, the identification of hazards and risks to be managed, and the maintenance tasks to be carried out. The school leadership team has a responsibility to ensure agreed maintenance requirements are achieved.

2.12.84   The inspection schedule should include all necessary timber repairs, cleaning and re-covering of plastic and leather surfaces, checking metal items for wear, lubrication of moving parts, inspection of wall and roof fittings, replacement of worn parts and items including those on trampolines, multi-gyms, and sports and play equipment.

2.12.85   The contract content needs to be sufficiently detailed to ensure that all PESSPA equipment requested is checked and repaired/reported on. It should not be assumed that any equipment outside the agreement will be checked without extra cost.

2.12.86   The 'employer' should read thoroughly the contract and promotional information that is provided by any equipment inspection company, and clarify any uncertainties before committing to the contract.

2.12.87   Employers should check that the work will be carried out in compliance with BSI 1892 (1986) with some period of guarantee.

2.12.88   In addition, employers should check the following:

- The equipment inspection company has a known **reputation** for competent inspection and maintenance using fully trained personnel that can be checked through references. Any company should be audited to the ISO 9001:2008 level of quality assurance.

- Appropriate **insurance** is held by the contractor and made available for scrutiny if necessary – typically, public and product liability insurance and employer's liability insurance for £10million for each.

- The company has sufficient workers, tools and materials to fulfil the agreed schedule of work (eg there might be a need for at least two operatives where heavy trampolines need to be erected for inspection; appropriate access equipment might need to be carried if the contract requires that high-level apparatus, such as ropes, is inspected at the installation points rather than visually from the floor).

- All company personnel carry suitable **ID cards** and, where required, have a valid Disclosure and Barring Service (DBS) check. This will be necessary to gain access to some schools and may be required where the workforce comes into contact with students.

2.12.89   The maintenance and inspection work should seek to disrupt teaching as little as possible but be open to observation and monitoring.

2.12.90   Agreeing the time and date for an inspection will ensure access to the facilities and items involved, which, in turn, should prevent complicated arrangements and wasted time caused by inspection team visits outside school hours. In some areas, LAs have arranged for these inspections to take place in the school holiday period. This is not good practice as it reduces the possibility of staff being present during the inspection, and the subsequent benefits of this.

2.12.91   An appropriate school representative should be involved in the overall inspection process. In addition, an opportunity should be given to school staff to identify any equipment or apparatus concerns prior to the inspection/maintenance work commencing, and where feasible, a member of the physical education department should be present during the PESSPA equipment inspection.

After the inspection

2.12.92   The PESSPA equipment inspection company should provide a dated, written report, describing the condition of equipment checked, the separate costs of all recommended repairs and any recommendations for prioritising any repairs.

2.12.93   Signed authorisation should be given and a receipt obtained for any equipment needing to be removed for workshop repair before being returned to school. A return time for equipment should be agreed, and checks made that the cost of return is included in the overall repair cost.

2.12.94   Any item judged to be unsafe and beyond economic repair needs to be clearly identified as **condemned** and **must be taken out of service immediately**. It is unlikely the inspecting company will physically remove condemned items. A system for attending to this needs to be clear, and removal or decommissioning of the items from use guaranteed.

2.12.95   Condemned items should not continue to be used even for limited (eg 'only sitting on') or non-physical education purposes. All condemned items need to be removed so that they cannot come back into use 'inadvertently'. Condemned equipment needs to be made readily identifiable by the inspecting company in order that teachers do not continue to use it in ignorance of the unsafe situation.

2.12.96   Agreement is needed between the employer and the inspecting company that any PESSPA equipment needing repair is shown to a nominated member of the school staff and the situation explained. Clarification as to whether any such equipment can continue in use until it can be repaired needs to be agreed before the inspection concludes.

2.12.97   Any report subsequent to an equipment inspection is like an 'MOT' in that it comments on the state of the equipment at the time of the inspection and does not guarantee condition and safe use at a later date.

2.12.98   A specialist PESSPA equipment inspection does not negate the obligation on teachers to inspect all equipment visually prior to each use.

         (Guidance regarding PESSPA inspection and maintenance uses information provided by Continental Sports Ltd, and developed by Peter Whitlam.)

 ## Case law

2.12.99   **Beaumont versus Surrey County Council (1968)**:

         *This ruling held the LA responsible for the teacher **not disposing** of old trampette elastics **adequately**. A student picked the elastics out of a waste bin and, while playing with them, caused another student to lose an eye.*

      More information on the inspection of fixed play equipment can be found at http://goo.gl/L3c2MM

Electrical equipment

2.12.100   **Portable appliance testing (PAT) helps** to protect staff and students against the increased likelihood of harm caused by electrical equipment in a variety of PESSPA environments and during the movement of such items. In addition, PAT testing assists the identification of safe and tested electrical equipment, eases the tracing of such equipment and provides an audit trail.

2.12.101   Someone in school should have the responsibility for ensuring that regular PAT tests are carried out by an authorised person who is usually external to school.

2.12.102   All portable electrical appliances, such as computer equipment, musical equipment, timers, whiteboards or kettles, must be inspected for safety at regular, appropriate intervals, and a small PAT sticker attached to each individual item, identifying the date of their last test. Frequency of tests varies depending on the item.

    Information regarding this can be found on the Health and Safety Executive (HSE) website: http://goo.gl/mU9S7x

2.12.103   Staff providing their **own items** of electrical equipment need to have them PAT certified by the school before using them in their work.

2.12.104   PAT testing is a whole-school responsibility, and it is important that the leadership team is kept informed of all portable appliances that need to be PAT registered for use in PESSPA.

2.12.105   Any portable electrical appliance lacking a current PAT certificate should not be used.

© yauhenka/Shutterstock.com

Chapter 2/Section 13: Facilities

Work spaces

2.13.1   Facility provision has moved towards **flexible learning spaces** to meet learning outcomes. Schools will no longer have common provision. However, generic aspects of health and safety in relation to facilities will remain the same as before. Whatever physical education, school sport and physical activity (PESSPA) facilities are available for use, risk assessments will need to be specific to those, and to the particular school's use of the facilities.

2.13.2   Adaptable facilities require a risk assessment that considers the variable use of the facility, the implications of converting the facility (particularly where students may be involved), the particular usage the school intends and any guidelines manufacturers provide.

2.13.3   Where schools **share facilities** with other groups within a network, it is good practice to establish an understanding that the host school will decide **normal operating procedures (NOPs)** and **emergency action plans (EAPs)**. These should be made available to other user groups, who should accommodate them within their risk assessments for travelling to and using a shared a facility.

2.13.4   **Before and during all lessons**, and wherever facilities are used by a **new group** for the first time, the work area needs to be checked to ensure that:

- the **floor, poolside** or **outdoor** work surface provides secure footing to prevent tripping, slipping or other injury

- **obstructions** are identified and removed, where possible, or the students made aware of any immovable obstructions, and the member of staff takes these into account throughout the session

- there is sufficient space for the planned activity; activities that involve freedom of movement (eg dance, games) require more space than those that involve restricted movement (eg performing exercises/movements on a personal mat)

- there is **safe and appropriate access**, including for people with disabilities

- transport implications have been addressed, such as the provision of a safe embarkation/disembarkation area

- the use of additional equipment and the level of noise do not impact on the safety of the other facility sharers

- safe and appropriate storage and management of movement of equipment in and around **storage areas** have been carefully considered

- there are **sources of liquid** to maintain hydration, where necessary.

2.13.5 **Fixed equipment** within a facility, such as dance barres or folding gymnastics frames, should be stable, substantial in design and able to accommodate participants of different ages and abilities. Where mirrors are installed, they should be of strengthened glass.

2.13.6 There should be sufficient space for the safe use of equipment and **adequate electrical points and Internet connections** so that trailing wires or ill-placed or unstable items do not present a hazard.

Floors, courts, playing surfaces and pitches

2.13.7 **Indoor floors** should be kept clean and swept regularly. Economies in floor-cleaning arrangements can make planning a safe PESSPA programme difficult as significant levels of dust increase the likelihood of slipping. Whenever possible, school staff should be involved in decisions about cleaning schedules, highlighting concerns that affect PESSPA situations that may not normally have been considered.

2.13.8 Any cleaning and/or polishing of floors should not leave a slippery finish. Loose boards, splintering, cracking and lifting edges sometimes occur with heavy use, and floor sockets and screws can become proud, creating an irregular surface that can affect the likelihood of harm and the security of footing. Dampness caused by condensation or residual wet mopping after school meals should be dried thoroughly before activity begins.

 Case law

2.13.9 **Bassie versus Merseyside Fire and Civil Defence Authority (2005):**

*This determined that it was foreseeable that, where a floor was not kept clean, it could lead to **slipping injuries**.*

2.13.10 **Sprung or semi-sprung floors** are most beneficial to certain activities within PESSPA programmes, such as dance, gymnastics and some health and fitness type activity, in that they offer bones and joints protection from damage that can arise from the absorption of impact energy. Where floors are not sprung, care should be taken with high-impact landings during such activities.

 For more information about safe management of impact for safe exercise practice, see Chapter 2, Section 9, page 160.

2.13.11 Where facilities are used for other purposes, such as dining, examinations and assemblies, safe use of the floor in PESSPA lessons may become compromised, and schools should seek to avoid this practice wherever possible by:

- raising the concern with employers who may not appreciate the detrimental effects this practice has in PESSPA situations

- investigating the use of alternative areas to accommodate these other activities

- developing strategies and procedures for dealing with hazards posed by alternative use.

2.13.12 **All outdoor playing surfaces** need to be suitable for activity and in sound condition. They should be checked routinely to ensure security of footing, and where concerns exist, an effective reporting system needs to be in place.

2.13.13 Safety on **playing fields, sports pitches and athletics areas** can be adversely affected by the aftermath of trespass. Broken glass, cans and other rubbish generally deposited on these sites create serious risks to students.

2.13.14 Deposits of dog faeces infected by toxocara (roundworm) can cause toxocariasis in humans, with symptoms that include blindness, asthma, epilepsy and general aches and pains. All practical measures should be taken to keep **animals** off the playing surfaces and encourage owners to remove any offending deposits immediately. In some schools, this poses a significant problem, and staff need to be guided by the leadership team and governors as to what is a safe standard for participation and how this safe standard is to be maintained.

2.13.15 **Remote pitches, courts and fields** require additional consideration. Staff who are working away from the main building on fields, courts or other play areas should be equipped with mobile phones, radios or alternative reliable communication devices in order to make immediate contact with colleagues if necessary. Some emergencies necessitate immediate support, often including access to first aid, including a defibrillator where installed.

 For more information, see Chapter 2, Section 15, 2.15.51, page 257.

2.13.16 **Pitches** should be **marked out** safely in order that playing surfaces are, and remain, level. Corrosive marking substances should not be used. Regular maintenance is essential. Holes (including rabbit scrapes) should be filled as soon as possible after identification.

2.13.17 Under the rules of The Football Association (FA), effective in England from the 2014–2015 season, any **3G artificial pitch** that is used for affiliated football is required to be tested, following which it will appear on the 3G Football Turf Pitch Register. Schools league match football is affiliated, therefore will need a test to be performed.

 To see whether your 3G artifical pitch is registered, visit http://3g.thefa.me.uk

2.13.18 Where such pitches are only used for lessons and friendly matches, the inspection requirement would not necessarily be applied. However, for regular and correct maintenance of what is a costly investment, it would be seen to be good practice to follow this procedure. Schools should check the FA website to find a list of companies recommended by The FA to carry out this work.

2.13.19 Guidance on the design and specifications for artificial surfaces can be sought through the Sport England facilities department.

 To access the Sport England guidance on artificial surfaces, go to https://goo.gl/en0JEI

2.13.20 Where playing fields are used as **multi-purpose play areas**, litter may be a problem that needs to be controlled. Gang mowers can shred plastic and metal containers into sharp shards that create significant risk.

2.13.21 **Sand landing areas** for athletics need to be **dug** before and during the activity, and also regularly raked.

 For more information, see Chapter 4, Section 2, page 373.

 ## Case law

2.13.22 **Sutton versus Syston Rugby Football Club Ltd (2011):**

A 16–year-old rugby player was injured during a tag rugby game at his local club, resulting in a knee injury caused by colliding with a partially buried object.

He claimed compensation for the club's negligence in failing to inspect the pitch. The club argued that while a pitch inspection had not taken place before the match, had it done so, it would only have identified obvious obstacles such a broken glass, not the item that had caused the injury (a partially buried cricket marker stub that did not extend up above the level of the grass).

*The initial trial (based on inspecting certain areas of the pitch more rigorously than others) granted compensation, but the Appeal Court disagreed and applied the standard that, before a game or training session, a pitch should be **walked over at a reasonable walking*** *pace* and that the standard of the inspection should be the same whether the activity was a training session or match, and that all areas of the pitch should be treated with the same attention, particularly given that the danger to be avoided (ie falling on to or into foreign objects) could happen on any part of the pitch.

Given this standard, the court concluded that a reasonable walkover inspection of the pitch would not have revealed the stub, and therefore the appeal was allowed.

2.13.23 **Jones versus Monmouthshire County Council (2011)**:

*Compensation for injury was awarded when a student tripped over a kerb while retrieving a ball from the area surrounding an AstroTurf pitch. The difference in the height of the kerb and pitch was described as being 'borderline' as a tripping hazard. The judge determined that if it was recognised as a **tripping hazard**, something should have been done to manage the hazard. A common sense solution would have been to remind participants about the difference in height, and monitor that they were paying attention to the task of retrieving the ball sensibly by looking where they were going.*

2.13.24 **Douch versus Reading Borough Council (2000)**:

*A player stumbled and injured himself while running to retrieve a ball during a cricket match, blaming grass-covered humps in the outfield. The judge dismissed the claim on the basis that they were 'minor undulations', with only a remote likelihood of someone falling because of them. However, it was stated that playing areas need to be checked regularly to ensure they are safe to use. This suggests **minor undulations** can be expected on playing fields.*

2.13.25 **Taylor versus Corby Borough Council (2000)**:

*While playing a ball game on a grassed recreation area, an adult was injured because his foot went down a 10cm hole. No regular inspection of the playing surface was carried out, with the repair of defects being reactive, rather than based on risk assessment and regular checks. It was judged that some system of regularly checking playing surfaces is necessary, and it is foreseeable that **holes** in playing surfaces are likely to cause serious injury.*

2.13.26 **Futcher versus Hertfordshire Local Authority (LA) (1997)**:

*A long-jump participant was awarded damages when injured by landing on **compacted sand**. The area had been raked, but not dug over before or during the competition.*

2.13.27 **Jones versus Northampton Borough Council (1990)**:

*A man hired a sports centre for a game of football and was told the floor was wet due to a leak in the roof, but failed to tell the other players the floor was unsafe. One player slipped on a wet patch and was injured. The person hiring the facility was held to be negligent for **failing to inform** the other players of the risk even though he was aware of it.*

Floor areas and pitch sizes

2.13.28   Staff need to consider how a specific PESSPA activity can be presented in order to allow safe movement of all students in the working area.

2.13.29   The amount of **floor area** required for safe practical work indoors depends on the number of participants taking part, their age and mobility, and the type of activity planned. The National Dance Teachers Association (NDTA) (now part of One Dance UK) recommends a minimum of three square metres per student for primary **dance** and five square metres per student for secondary dance. Some styles/types of dance require limited movement, while others require significant freedom to move. Without sufficient space, variation in choreography or style may be necessary.

 For information about dance floor space, see http://goo.gl/8MDooq

2.13.30   **Gymnastics** generally requires more space per student than dance in order to allow for safe movement and the use of apparatus. Historically, approximately eight square metres per student was the standard for a then-typical class size of 30 in a typical secondary school gymnasium where a range of activities would be taught. Gymnastics activities and apparatus arrangements will need to be planned and adapted carefully if less space is available.

2.13.31   In **sports halls**, the space required for games depends on the standard of play – the higher the standard, the larger the space needed due to greater run-off areas and clearance heights. Where halls are divided into sections using partitions or netting, thought needs to be given to appropriate shared use. Netting should not foul footing at any time.

2.13.32   Pitches and courts should be suitable in size **for the ages and abilities** of those using them.

2.13.33   There should be a suitable distance between the playing area and the perimeter of the working space in which it is located, particularly if other students are working in adjacent areas. The distance between the playing surface and features such as boundary fences, roads and windows must be sufficient to avoid accident or injury, and the directions of play should account for this. Proximity to hazardous fixtures and fittings should be avoided.

2.13.34   There needs to be a sufficiently clear space to **run off** the pitch or court without danger of collision with objects or people (typically a minimum of two metres). Reference should be made to Sport England (2015) 'Comparative sizes of sports pitches and courts' (outdoors and indoor), https://goo.gl/en0JEI

2.13.35   On occasions, it might be necessary to 'condition' the rules or organisation of games activities to make safe use of restricted space or the space available.

Case law

2.13.36   **Morrell versus Owen (1993):**

*The court determined that the organisers of an indoor athletics event failed to exercise the degree of **organisational care** necessary when the netting in a sports hall was used for discus throwing. Someone the other side of the netting was hurt because the netting billowed out into the adjacent space and failed to absorb the momentum of the discus.*

Playground areas for recreational use

2.13.37   Playground activity occurring at break and lunchtime, preschool or at the end of the school day is varied and involves students of all ages. Playground activity may be student-regulated, with minimum levels of adult supervision, or directly controlled and supervised by a member of staff. It may consist of highly creative activity or be based on traditional sports and games.

2.13.38   **Zoned play areas** should be known and respected, and activities restricted to their particular designation. 'Quiet areas' should not be intruded on.

2.13.39   Sufficient safe space should be allocated for specific activities. Careful planning of playground areas should help with this by:

- avoiding car park areas, and areas where there is any likelihood of traffic entering or leaving the school premises

- assigning activities involving rapid movement, the use of balls and sudden changes of direction to areas that are away from sloping ground or areas with sudden drops

- assigning individual activities such as skipping and circus skills to areas with appropriate vegetation or shrubs (that won't affect the activity)

- avoiding areas with poor drainage known to frequently retain lying water.

2.13.40   Activity areas should be supervised during playtimes, particularly where hazards are unavoidable (eg windows opening outwards, the exposed corners of buildings).

2.13.41   Schools should have procedures in place to ensure that the items in Table 21 are regularly monitored, and strategies implemented to minimise the risk of injury.

Table 21: Potential hazards relating to playground areas

Play-area Surface	Surrounding Vegetation
• Uneven or cracked • Loose grit • Slippery in wet weather • Frost damage • Vegetation growing on or through surface • Litter, including broken glass • Patches of silt from poor drainage • Covers missing from post sockets	• Possibility of students overrunning into plants/shrubs • Type of plants/shrubs (eg shrubs with large thorns, stinging nettles) • Possibility of poisonous berries adjacent to play area • Seasonal coverage of wet fallen leaves
Play-area Drainage	**Access to Play Area**
• Standing water after rain • Drain grids below or above surface level • Drain grids with oversized spaces • Drain grids broken or missing	• Possibility of unauthorised student access • Possibility of vehicular access • Vehicular deposits on play area if used as a car park outside school hours • Use as public right of way • Possibility of access by unauthorised adults
Play Area Built on Sloping Ground	**Fixed Climbing Equipment**
• Steep steps • Lack of secure handrail • Condition of steps • Presence of rubbish or vegetation on steps • Possibility of students overrunning play area • Possibility of stones, gravel or dirt rolling on to play area	• Lack of inspection and repair schedule • Peeling paint and rust • Inappropriate or lack of safety surfaces (see page 219) • Proximity to other hazards (eg windows, projections) • Excessive fall height (see page 219)
Buildings Around Play Area	
• Exposed external corners adjacent to play areas • Projections below head height (adult)	• Outward-opening windows • Outward-opening doors • Non-toughened glass

Safety surfaces for playground climbing areas

2.13.42   Safety surfaces must be provided indoors or out, where the fall height is greater than 600mm (BS EN 1177). However, a school-specific risk assessment may deem it safe practice to install a safety surface at fall heights below this requirement.

2.13.43   Appropriate impact-absorbing surfaces, such as rubber-based materials, have been shown to reduce injuries. Dependent on the fall height, regular gymnastics matting (25mm) may be sufficient indoors, and suitable safety surfaces, such as rubber combinations or natural bark, should be sourced for outdoor use, where required, to a depth between 300 and 400mm depending on the critical fall height. It should be free of entrapments, sharp edges or projections that could cause injury.

2.13.44   Recommended sizes of impact-absorbing surfaces increase in line with the critical fall height, typically:

Critical Fall Height	Free Fall Space Needed
1.5m	1.5m diameter
2.0m	1.85m diameter
2.5m	2.15m diameter
3.0m	2.5m diameter

 For information regarding safe supervision of outdoor play and activity areas, see Chapter 2, Section 8, page 154.

Climbing, traverse and bouldering walls

2.13.45   The construction of bouldering and climbing walls should meet the requirements of the standards EN 12572:1 and 2.

2.13.46   Where climbing walls are installed in school, staff operating the facility need to be adequately trained, or suitably qualified external staff should be used. Most accidents have occurred in schools where staff are not sufficiently competent, or where support staff have been used to prepare and 'set up' equipment without having received training.

2.13.47   When climbing walls built within sports halls or gymnasiums are not in use, two-metre high wall matting is available to purchase to prevent access to the wall, and to use as a protection against the uneven surface of the wall. Access to climbing walls inside and outside needs to be carefully managed and supervised. Procedures might include:

• educating students about rules regarding use of the facilities

• roping off the area, and using appropriate signage to clearly indicate when the area is out of bounds

• removing or tying up and securing all ropes and other equipment

• keeping facilities that house indoor climbing walls locked when they are not being supervised.

2.13.48   Many websites offer guidance on the design and maintenance of climbing walls, as well as information regarding appropriate staff training. Schools considering installing climbing walls will find the guidance offered in the British Mountaineering Council (BMC) *Climbing Wall Manual* useful.

 For more information on the BMC *Climbing Wall Manual*, see https://goo.gl/uxjXTi

Safety surfaces for climbing and bouldering walls

2.13.49   Injury from falls is increased where inadequate safety surfaces are installed, or technique is poor. Both rubber crumb and dense foam products are available to reduce the severity of the injury from such falls.

 For more information about safe surfaces for playground climbing frames, see 2.13.43.

2.13.50   For low traverse walls outside, where the fall height is less than 600mm, a safety surface may not be required. However, some schools identify a need for such a surface in their risk assessment even where the fall height is below this level.

2.13.51   For bouldering walls, a minimum 300mm depth of matting should be installed where a maximum climbing height of 4.5 metres is possible.

2.13.52   Climbing and bouldering walls located outdoors need to consider slip-resistant flooring protection, and a surface that is frost-proof and water permeable to prevent surface water presenting a hazard.

2.13.53   All walls built to the specification of the standards EN 12572:1 and 2 must have appropriate impact flooring that is fit for purpose, but beyond this, set depths are not specified.

 ## A case in point

2.13.54   **Managing the climbing wall, February 2014**:

A Bradford grammar school paid £12,500 in fines after the physical education equipment manager fell nine metres from a climbing wall. In his position at the school, he had become more involved in the lessons and 'learnt the basics'. He was working his way up the wall to rig it for a lesson by threading the rope through anchor points. A colleague on the ground was belaying to provide added rope when needed, but minimising the amount of loose rope, which meant a slip would only result in a drop of a short distance for the climber. However, the technique failed, and the climber fell, hitting the gym floor below. There were no mats or padding, and he was not wearing a helmet. The school was found to be in breach of Section 2(1) of the Health and Safety at Work etc Act 1974. The Health and Safety Executive (HSE) inspector reported:

It is essential that those who provide climbing instructions should themselves be properly trained and certificated. The training and development of staff using the climbing wall at this school was not adequate, and they were allowed to undertake tasks on it that they had not been trained for.

Fitness rooms

2.13.55　Care should be taken when planning the layout of fitness rooms. Staff should check that:

- items of equipment are located at a safe distance away from any obstructions such as doors, windows and other equipment, to enable safe access, circulation and use of each piece

- sufficient space is available between and behind items of equipment to enable a group of students working on one machine to position themselves correctly

- the layout allows clear visual supervision across the room

- working surfaces are firm and stable

- free weights, weight stations and multi-gyms are positioned appropriately, preferably in separate areas so that they can be clearly signed as 'not for use' in some lessons

- emergency exits are accessible and clear of equipment

- regular inspection and repair programmes are organised and that these are carried out by recognised specialists

- clear instructions (diagrams and words) for safe weight-training procedures and technique are available in the fitness room

- floor areas are protected with mats in areas where free weights are used – these should not cause a tripping hazard

- free weights are stored on purpose-built stands, with heavier weights near the top for ease of lifting

- locking collars are used on free weights when in use

- the room is at a consistent temperature (Sport England recommends an air temperature of 12–18°C with adequate ventilation where heat gains are likely).

Swimming pools

2.13.56　Swimming pools are high-risk environments. Owners of public swimming facilities are expected to provide a safe working environment for users under the terms of the Occupiers' Liability Acts 1957 (http://goo.gl/xwyABX) and 1984 (http://goo.gl/FwyN5a). However, school staff accompanying students, together with specialist swimming staff, should ensure that they know and implement the NOPs and EAPs for the facility being used.

2.13.57   **Clarity of water** is essential in swimming, such that staff can see the bottom of the pool at all times, being aware of **glare and shadow**. Staff should frequently **scan** the bottom of the pool during lessons to ensure that no student has inadvertently slipped below the surface of the water. Pools should not be used where the water clarity is such that the bottom of the pool cannot be seen at all depths.

2.13.58   **Glare** across the water surface, from natural or artificial lighting, may restrict vision of the bottom of the pool across large areas. In such circumstances, frequent movement by staff (both supervisory and teaching) is necessary to maintain maximum visual awareness. Glare may also trigger an adverse reaction in students with identified special needs or medical conditions.

2.13.59   The **depth** and extent of shallow- or deep-water areas should be clearly marked and noted by those responsible for safety. A pool divider, usually a rope, should normally be positioned to delineate shallow from deep water whenever non-swimmers are present. However, this is not always feasible during mixed sessions. It is particularly important that any sudden changes in pool depth via a slope are highlighted. This can be achieved using brightly coloured painted lines down the sides and along the floor of the pool.

2.13.60   **Signs** should identify potential risks and be positioned in order that pool users can see them clearly and interpret them easily. Staff should explain their significance, especially to beginners. All signs should conform to the appropriate British Standards/British Standard European Norm, and the Health and Safety (Safety Signs and Signals) Regulations 1996, where they apply.

    For more information on regulations about signs and signals, see http://goo.gl/Rp2ahg and http://goo.gl/XB67qz

2.13.61   **Entry** from the changing rooms on to the poolside is safest where the water is shallow. Where pool design precludes this precaution, students should be made aware of the hazard, both verbally and by the use of signs and barriers or cones. Care should be taken when entering on to the poolside, and strict behaviour standards applied.

2.13.62   The design of **steps and rails** should be such as to prevent any part of the body becoming trapped. Where this risk exists, warning signs and regular verbal reminders to pool users should be provided.

2.13.63   The Amateur Swimming Association (ASA) recommends that the **temperature of the water** should be about 29°C to enable young people to be comfortable and not become unduly cold during the period of time allocated to swimming. Water temperatures for disabled swimmers may be set much higher (as high as 32°C; for hydrotherapy pools, this may increase to 35°C). The ambient air temperature should be slightly above that of the water, to avoid condensation, typically 1–4°C greater.

2.13.64   Those responsible for the management of pools should ensure **outlet pipes** at the bottom of pools have grilles in place that are securely fastened. Holes in grilles should not be large enough for fingers to become trapped.

2.13.65   Leisure pools, many with special water features and irregular shapes, may cause potential supervisory **blind spots** that need to be checked regularly.

2.13.66   Pool surround, pool depth, the implications of any protruding ladders or steps, and the use of electrical equipment are key considerations when determining whether the facility is suitable for other aquatic sporting activities, such as competitive swimming, water polo or synchronised swimming.

2.13.67   All pools need to operate swimming **pool cleaning systems** that meet acceptable hygiene standards.

2.13.68   **Chemical levels** should be monitored at the beginning of the day and at regular times throughout the day. At no time should chemicals be added to water when swimmers are present.

2.13.69   Swimming **pool surrounds** should be kept clear at all times. Pool equipment (eg flotation aids, emergency equipment, lane markers) should be stored appropriately, taking into account the need for safe access to and from the pool. Particular care should be taken on poolside surrounds where **wet surfaces** may contribute to slipping injuries.

2.13.70   Adequate, well-maintained **lifesaving equipment** must be readily available in known locations and staff (and students as appropriate) must be trained in its use.

Further information can be found in HSE (2003) *Managing Health and Safety in Swimming Pools.* **London: HSE. ISBN: 978-0-717626-86-1. Available from http://goo.gl/Mife4z**

The revision of this guidance by a number of industry stakeholders has recently been completed. Following HSE agreement, the six documents that make up the revised publication will be available online. See www.hse.org.uk for details of updates.

Changing areas

2.13.71   This principle is about ensuring **dignity, decency and privacy** where needed, be it for reasons of physical development or other individual needs.

2.13.72   The changing space should be **checked** regularly, before and during use, to ensure that:

- pegs, where installed, are not broken or exposing sharp edges
- adequate space is available for the number of students changing, including space to store their clothes neatly
- additional accessible space is provided, where required, for students with special educational needs and disabilities (SEND) (eg wheelchairs users, those requiring help with changing)
- benching and other furniture is fixed to prevent it toppling over during use
- there are no sharp edges to tiling or heaters that could cause injury
- floor surfaces are not slippery when wet
- personal items and clothing do not litter the floor to cause potential tripping hazards
- where showers are provided, water mixer valves are regulated by one control key, positioned out of reach of students to reduce any risk of scalding.

2.13.73   Where **safety standards** are compromised, alternative arrangements need to be made and faults reported to the school leadership team.

2.13.74   Many **primary schools** lack purpose-built changing rooms but find spaces where the sexes, individuals or small groups can change separately. Preference expressed for separate sex areas regularly extends to students as young as the start of Key Stage 2. Schools should begin to consider how they can accommodate this safely by:

- using screens in a classroom to separate the room
- allowing one sex to change during a break time, if this occurs directly before the lesson

- using two different areas, such as a cloakroom and a classroom if supervision is available
- considering how appropriate changing areas might be provided in their long-term planning.

2.13.75   When changing, there is no statutory requirement for students to be **supervised** at all times. However, case law provides a clear indication that the incidence of injury is much higher when students are not supervised than when they are.

2.13.76   The degree and method of supervision will vary according to the particular circumstances, but age, behaviour, potential bullying, and safety aspects of the space itself will contribute to deciding whether constant direct supervision is necessary or intermittent direct supervision is safe. The location of the staff responsible for the group is of particular importance. It must be considered whether they can provide the level of supervision required while they are fulfilling their usual pre-lesson organisational tasks. Some schools use changing time as a positive part of the learning experience.

2.13.77   **Remote supervision** refers to a situation in which a member of staff responsible for a group of students is not directly present. This type of supervision may be implemented in appropriate circumstances where only one member of staff is available for changing-room supervision (eg in situations such as teaching mixed-gender groups). Remote supervision might involve tasking a reliable student with reporting any concerns in the changing area to the member of staff who is outside the changing area.

2.13.78   The suitability of remote supervision would be dependent on the location of the changing areas, student behaviour, age and ability. This method is only satisfactory when the member of staff remains on hand in the immediate vicinity outside the changing area to respond to any alert.

2.13.79   **Direct supervision** of students enables the member of staff to intervene at any time. Decisions to supervise less directly should not be taken lightly.

2.13.80   At **swimming pools**, separate school **changing areas** should be made available. Where this is not possible, and 'village style' changing areas are used, attendance at the pool at different times to the public may be requested. Failing this, schools should request that students are provided with a section of the changing area specifically for their use, away from that being used by the public.

2.13.81   Whatever the circumstances, changing rooms should be **adequately supervised**. Ideally, a male and female member of staff should accompany each mixed-gender class in order to fully supervise the changing areas. Staffing pressures may mean a known adult volunteer of the opposite gender is used. If this adult is unsupervised, disclosure and barring clearance would be required for this role with children in this situation. Where this level of staffing is not available, it may be possible to enlist the cooperation of pool staff to supervise the other changing room. This arrangement with the pool management needs to be assured and consistent. If only one suitable adult is available, they would need to establish procedures to deal with any emergency in the other changing room.

2.13.82   If these arrangements are not to the school's satisfaction, it may be necessary to combine classes and take single-gender groups, where appropriate staffing allows this. Adults supervising students need to be familiar with, and adhere to, the relevant safeguarding policies.

Heating, lighting and structural considerations

2.13.83   **Walls** should be smooth to avoid friction injury if body contact occurs, with rounded corners where the possibility of impact is likely, and to facilitate safe ball-rebound activities. Background colours and the need for the safe sighting of accelerating projectiles (such as balls) should be considered. Essential features other than physical education apparatus should be positioned, wherever possible, well above working height, or recessed where this requirement cannot be met.

2.13.84   **Ceiling height** needs to be sufficient so as not to restrict movements such as lifts in dance, vaults in gymnastics, throws in combat sports and clearance for trampolining at school or higher competitive levels.

For more information about safe positioning of trampolines, see Chapter 2, Section 12, 2.12.48, page 202.

2.13.85   **Doors and door frames** should be flush wherever possible. Main access doors should open outwards and have some system of closure control. This is especially important on exposed or windy sites, to minimise the risk of doors opening or slamming unexpectedly.

2.13.86   **Glass doors** can be hazardous. Where they are necessary, the glass should be smoked or coloured for visibility, reinforced and resistant to impact fracture. If a pane is cracked, it should be replaced as soon as possible. Door glazing should be at a height to accommodate wheelchair users. Where doors are glazed around hand-pushing height, there should be push battens across the door on both sides. While recommended, it should not be assumed that all glass in a school is toughened in case someone falls into it or seeks to push off from it. This needs to be confirmed, and systems put in place to minimise the likelihood of injury occurring.

2.13.87   **Lighting** should be uniform wherever possible, and adequate for safe participation.

2.13.88   In the indoor environment, the effectiveness of artificial lighting needs to be taken into account. It would be hazardous to ask students to undertake any activity where their safety was compromised due to inadequate or overly bright lighting. Artificial lighting should be made from unbreakable materials or set in protective cages. Strip lighting that produces a flickering or stroboscopic effect should be avoided as this could impair visual focus, induce disorientation and trigger seizures.

2.13.89   Any risk of being dazzled by sunlight coming through windows or directly into students' eyes, or glare reflected from water needs to be managed by the considered placement of apparatus, direction of play or movement, frequent changing of teaching position or a more permanent resolution, such as tinting the glass or the use of blinds.

2.13.90   **Heating systems** should provide an adequate working temperature, adjustable to accommodate varying conditions, and be designed so that there is no danger of any student being adversely affected by burns, fumes or other hazards to health.

2.13.91   Where old models of radiators are still in place, exposed spindles with caps removed or lost can present a danger to students if they fall on to them. A regular inspection and maintenance programme of all heating systems should be established.

2.13.92   The **temperature** needs to be adequate for safe activity, and maintained evenly throughout the facility. The minimum temperature for **indoor** PESSPA activities is technically 15°C. Where this temperature is not met, the warm-up and preparation might be extended, and the pace increased, if the lesson can continue with reasonable safety. Alternatively, the lesson may be shortened or abandoned completely.

2.13.93   There is no upper limit of temperature for activity or statutory maximum working temperature. Staff will need to be sensitive to the impact of significantly high temperatures on active sessions and plan accordingly. If outside, sun protection and regular hydration should be encouraged.

 For more information about weather conditions, see Chapter 2, Section 5, page 124.

Fire safety and emergency evacuation

2.13.94   Schools are **now responsible** for determining their own assessment of fire safety. It is the responsibility of the leadership team to ensure specific fire safety regulations are applied in the school. This should form part of a school's risk assessment or be a separate risk assessment.

2.13.95   Fire precaution procedures must be known and applied by all school staff. In the **PESSPA context**, this would typically involve staff visually checking:

- emergency evacuation signs are in place and illuminated where required
- emergency exits are operative
- emergency exits are not locked or blocked when a facility is in use, such as where trampolines or other equipment are placed across them
- fire safety equipment is in place and not misused.

2.13.96   It must be possible for both staff and students to open fire doors from the inside of the facility.

2.13.97   Where possible, fire exit doors should have flush-mounted push pads to minimise the likelihood of injury.

2.13.98   Mats should be stored in a specific mat store, where provided, or stored away from electrical circuits to minimise the possibility of fire causing toxic fumes.

2.13.99   Staff must know how many and which students they are responsible for, be familiar with the emergency evacuation procedures, and know the quickest routes to safety.

2.13.100   Staff should plan for the possibility of **emergency evacuation** taking place in cold or inclement weather, and any implications for potential hypothermia when students may need to leave an indoor facility for an extended period of time while wearing minimal clothing or in bare feet. These procedures should enable evacuation without students needing to delay in order to put on clothing and footwear. Schools might consider providing a set of emergency (foil) blankets that are taken out by one of the appointed fire officers during every evacuation.

2.13.101   The implications for the evacuation of students and staff with reduced mobility, and wheelchair users, need to be considered and planned. Discussion with students will inform them of their role in an emergency evacuation.

2.13.102   The **head teacher** is the 'senior manager on site' directly responsible for fire safety in law. If they are not on site, then the next most senior person on site temporarily becomes the responsible person.

Security

2.13.103   Security of working areas is essential. Facilities that offer unauthorised access to high-risk environments (such as a pool or climbing wall) or equipment (such as trampolines) need to be made **secure** when not in use.

Further guidance about facility design

2.13.104   Technical guidance about the design and use of all sports facilities is available from governing bodies of sport, commercial companies, such as Continental Sports (www.continentalsports.co.uk) and national sport associations, particularly the Sport England website: https://goo.gl/3EFF1M

Hire of facilities

 FAQ

2.13.105   **A community gymnastics club has approached us and asked if they can hire the school sports hall to run public gym sessions. We are happy to do this, but what is the best way to arrange it?**

Community use of school facilities is something that is very much encouraged. Many school facilities are unused in the evening and at weekends, while clubs and organisations struggle to find a suitable venue.

As the host for the venue, the school should draw up a contract of hire, the conditions of which need to be agreed with the users. This contract should contain information outlining that the school will 'hand over' the facility in a safe condition and fit for purpose to the community user. The community user will need to check the facility on arrival and report any concerns about the condition of the facility to the host, ideally before the session starts.

Terms of use may include the host stipulating items/equipment within the facility that should not be used by the club (eg the school trampoline) and also areas of the facility that should not be accessed (eg the school storage cupboard). The community club would be responsible for ensuring that its members and spectators respect these conditions.

The school will also need to check that the organisers of the club hold the necessary insurances, such as their own public liability insurance. The school's own public liability insurance should only be required where a person linked with the club is injured as a result of a fault with the facility itself (eg a tripping hazard on the stairs or a wet floor) where the school is seen to be at fault. The school would not be liable for claims made by those associated with the club concerning the activities of the club.

The school employer should be agreeable with any such arrangements, and professional advice sought with regard to the contract.

Chapter 2/Section 14: Special educational needs and disabilities, and medical conditions

Student entitlement

2.14.1   There is widespread agreement that physical activity brings benefits to all who participate, including significant and long-lasting gains to psychomotor and sensory development, physical health, emotional well-being, and social integration for students with special educational needs and disabilities (SEND).

2.14.2   The **Equality Act 2010** makes clear that schools must make **reasonable adjustments** for students with disabilities, or for an aspect of their disability, that enable them to access as full a programme of education, including physical education, as possible. Examples might be:

- supplying auxiliary aids and services

- providing additional support staff

- ensuring that changing facilities are suitable.

2.14.3   In addition, for those with SEND, organisations must have regard for the latest Department for Education (DfE) code of practice.

   To access the SEND code of practice, see https://goo.gl/DhDcS7

2.14.4   The Equality Act 2010 defines a disability as 'a physical or mental impairment which has a long-term and substantial adverse effect on their (the person's) ability to carry out normal day-to-day activities'. Many students who have SEND may have a disability according to this definition. 'Long-term' is 'a year or more', and 'substantial' is 'more than minor or trivial'.

2.14.5   Sensory impairments such as those that affect sight or hearing, and long-term health conditions such as asthma, diabetes, epilepsy and cancer are all included in this definition. Students with these conditions do not necessarily have SEND, but the overlap between disabled students and those with SEND is significant. Where a disabled student requires special educational provision, they will be covered by the SEND definition.

(Summarised from DfE/Department of Health (2015) 'Special educational needs and disability code of practice: 0 to 25 years', https://goo.gl/DhDcS7)

Education, health and care plan

2.14.6 **Table 22, pages 234–244,** details a number of specific conditions that students might present, and is designed to support **safe inclusive practice** within a physical education, school sport and physical activity (PESSPA) programme. There are, however, a number of generic safety considerations that apply regardless of the specific disability or special educational need. This information should be shared with, and understood by, all who contribute to the PESSPA programme.

2.14.7 In all cases and for all conditions, specialist advice, guidance and support should be sought to help plan and develop an individual **education, health and care plan**. Such plans were introduced in April 2015 as an additional part of the Children and Families Act (http://goo.gl/1iaKQm), and replace the former special education statements. The plan should consider what would help the individual to access PESSPA within the curriculum and as part of an extracurricular programme, and might cover issues such as:

- personal health care equipment (eg inhalers, syringes, incontinence pads)
- body splints and aids
- valves and shunts
- administration of drugs and treatments
- mobility aids
- daily living aids
- frequency and duration of professional input
- contraindicated activity for the condition.

2.14.8 The **student** and their parents are key in developing such a plan alongside teachers, support staff, physiotherapists and medical staff. The outcomes of the plan should focus on ability, ie what the student **can do**, and would like to be enabled to do, rather than the disability/medical condition. An important part of an education, health and care plan is ensuring that it can be actioned safely. This involves carrying out appropriate **risk assessments** that consider the extent to which the activity in question is safe, appropriate and accessible for the individual student. A PESSPA risk assessment should consider whether:

- the activity needs to be modified or adapted (eg in terms of space or equipment) to meet the specific needs/medical condition of the student
- the facility or environment where the activity will take place is suitable (eg if the acoustics and lighting are suitable for the student, the surfaces are sufficiently stable and even, there is suitable access for wheelchair users, there are sufficient accessible emergency exits, the environment is too 'busy' and noisy' and likely to cause stress)
- the safety of other participants can be maintained
- the support person is a specialist in the PESSPA activity, understands their role and is able to fulfil it (eg if they are supporting a student for swimming, they can swim)
- external staff brought in to deliver on the PESSPA programme (eg sports coaches) are suitable to supervise the student in question, have been made fully aware of the needs of the student, and have the competences required to work with this student.

2.14.9 **In the case of wheelchair users,** it will need to be considered whether it is possible and safe for the individual to take a full part in PESSPA situations that involve mixed groups of non-disabled and disabled students. The **student should be consulted** about how safe they feel. A risk assessment should be carried out to establish the normal routines for the class to ensure the safety of both the wheelchair users and the ambulant students. This would include consideration about the stability of wheelchairs in activities, who should push a wheelchair, and particular conditions during activities (eg placement of equipment used). Where an activity is obviously not suited to, or safe for, participation in a wheelchair (eg rugby on the field), discuss with the student what alternative activity they might want to do.

Enabling safe participation and inclusion

2.14.10 While students may share the same disability or condition, their abilities will vary, as will their needs. To enable suitable and safe participation, and to demonstrate optimum inclusion as appropriate, staff should:

- **establish the students' aspirations within PESSPA**
- have some knowledge of the specific learning difficulty, disability, medical condition, or emotional or behavioural disorder
- fully understand how the individual's condition affects them
- be aware of any constraints on physical activities as a result of the learning difficulty, disability, medical condition, or emotional or behavioural disorder, or as a result of any medication/treatment the student might be taking
- be able to provide the emergency treatment/action necessary if physical activities exacerbate the learning difficulty, disability, medical condition, or emotional or behavioural disorder
- be aware of any personal and family background knowledge about the student that might be significant
- be confident in their approach to teaching students with SEND
- have the knowledge, techniques and strategies necessary for safe teaching
- notice when a student's condition deteriorates by being alert to changes in their ability, attitude, levels of stamina, or how quickly they fatigue
- be able to adapt tasks, or know when to suggest that the student rests, or requires additional support or medical input.

2.14.11 Failure to properly address a student's needs may lead to their not being able to complete tasks, a perception of failure, frustration and despondency, and in some cases, disruptive behaviour, which may present risks to the student and others.

 Case law

2.14.12 **Faithful versus Kent County Council (2015):**

A 12-year-old student with autism fell and was injured during a physical education task involving pupils jumping between two tyres. It was alleged that, with the school's knowledge of her disability, she was allowed to participate in a lesson likely to cause injury to her, that the activity was unsuitable for her condition, and that the school generally failed to take adequate care of her.

The judge dismissed the claim on the basis that:

- *it would have been unfair to exclude the student from the physical education lesson because she had striven to overcome her disability*
- *her parents would not have wished her to have been excluded*

- *the parents had not informed the school about certain of the student's health issues relevant to her participating in physical education*
- *if third parties, such as occupational therapists, considered that the student required particular adjustments, they would have contacted the school direct, but had not done so.*

2.14.13　As far as possible, and if appropriate, details of the SEND and medical conditions should be shared with other class members so that they understand and respect the individual's needs, and are aware of any measures they can take to promote a safe environment for the student and themselves (eg to be aware of how to respond if a student experiences a seizure, to make eye contact before speaking to a person with a hearing impairment).

2.14.14　In some activities, it is helpful to operate a **'buddy system'**, in which a student 'looks out' for a partner with a SEND/medical condition in terms of their requirements for any additional help. A buddy can also be used to inform/alert staff about any concerns associated with the student's condition during activity. This often operates in swimming activities, but can be used as a useful safety measure in other PESSPA activities.

2.14.15　**Teaching styles** and tasks should be varied according to need, and staff should be able to adapt as required, using a range of inclusive methods, as well as recognising when specific students may need to be set separate activities, or when the task set is not suitable or safe (eg wheelchair users may find it difficult to take part in activities on a muddy games field).

2.14.16　For some students with poor mobility, or conditions where bones are brittle or limbs prone to injury, certain activities, particularly team sports involving contact, are not suitable. Staff should discuss with these students safer alternatives that they would like to develop, and build steady **progression, challenge and appropriate supervision** of these alternative activities into their planning.

2.14.17　**Ad hoc provision** from week to week does not constitute satisfactory provision, and does not allow adequate time to consider all aspects of safety. Wherever possible and practical, such alternative activities might link with those being undertaken by the student outside the school setting.

2.14.18　In many cases, safety can be improved by providing a range of adapted equipment (eg yellow balls with bells or buzzers for visually impaired students; balls of different textures, sizes, and pace for those with motor skills difficulties; sticks, bats and rackets with shorter handles to aid control).

2.14.19　Ongoing positive feedback and reward will be necessary to keep students on task. Developing confidence is fundamental to helping students achieve success, especially if they may become frustrated with some of the challenges they experience, or where they feel overwhelmed by what is expected of them. Frustrations and challenges can lead to disruptive behaviour in specific students. However, as self-esteem increases through increased success, disruptive behaviour generally reduces, and this is an important safe management consideration.

2.14.20　It is not always possible to pre-empt what external experiences students bring to a lesson. Historical life traumas, or simply a problem that has arisen in a previous session that day, can have a bearing on the state of mind of a student and on their ability/willingness to adopt a safe approach to learning. Staff need to be aware of, and sensitive to, the different situations students face and, as far as possible, take these into account in their efforts to create a calm and encouraging environment.

2.14.21   Some students develop **coping strategies**. An example could be time spent watching other students before starting the activity or being last 'in the queue', thereby allowing them time to assess what is required of them. Such strategies should be recognised and tolerated by staff, rather than putting pressure on the student to become involved at a pace that is not suitable for them.

2.14.22   More apparent physical concerns may cause a student to be reluctant to take part. For example, the presence of a skin condition such as psoriasis or eczema may result in a lack of confidence and/or unwillingness to change for activity in front of others, students who are overweight or obese may feel self-conscious and embarrassed with their peers. Consistency in approach, which recognises and adapts to individuals' concerns, will help to maintain an appropriate and positive climate to support full participation in PESSPA activities.

 FAQ

2.14.23   **Who can push a wheelchair?**

There is no legal age limit for being able to push a wheelchair. Where appropriate, students can be taken through basic safety points to enable them to push their peers safely in wheelchairs. Employees who have completed manual handling training will have covered pushing and pulling wheelchairs to enable them to carry this out, and can be asked to share this knowledge with students.

A risk assessment to decide who should push a wheelchair should be completed considering all of the following:

The Wheelchair User	The Person Pushing the Wheelchair	The Environment
Their: • ability to communicate • weight • ability to bear weight • ability to cooperate and follow instructions • physical conditions affecting their mobility (eg spasms and muscle tone) • behaviour.	Their: • sensitivity in speaking to the wheelchair user, encouraging them to voice any concerns, and not speaking for them unless required • individual capability and strength • condition that might affect this such as pregnancy or injury • training needs • level of competence.	The: • constraints of space • floor quality • how the layout restricts movement.

Case law

2.14.24   **Sloan versus the Governors of Rastrick High School (2014):**

A learning support assistant's role developed to include pushing students in wheelchairs. She attended two days of training and shadowed another assistant for three days, then worked on her own. Eleven days later, she allegedly sustained an injury when pushing a student in his wheelchair.

She claimed damages, alleging she sustained soft-tissue injury to her spine and shoulder, caused by pushing students in wheelchairs. She claimed that, in breach of the Manual Handling Operations Regulations 1992, the employer failed to:

- *avoid the need for her to undertake a manual handling operation that risked injury to her*
- *carry out a suitable risk assessment*
- *take steps to reduce, to the lowest level reasonably practicable, the risk of her being injured while carrying out the task. She said the employer could, for example, have provided power-assisted wheelchairs.*

At trial, the judge held that she had suffered a strain, but any other symptoms were constitutional. Also, she had not proven that the employer had breached its duty to her. Her claim was dismissed. She appealed. The Appeal Court also dismissed the case, and held the employer had taken the requisite appropriate steps and had carried out a proper risk assessment of the task.

Supporting students with SEND and medical conditions in PESSPA

2.14.25   The points discussed above should be considered when working with any student with SEND or a specific medical condition. Table 22, pages 234–244, provides more specific information and guidance for PESSPA staff about a number of SENDs and medical conditions. The information provided in the table should be used in conjunction with the recommended websites.

Table 22: Supporting students with SEND and medical conditions in PESSPA

Condition	What Do Staff Need to Know?	Advice for Staff Teaching and Supporting PESSPA
Asthma www.asthma.org.uk	• Very common condition affecting many children, caused by a combination of genetic and environmental factors. • Can be triggered by viral infections, allergens (eg dust mites), irritants (eg air pollutants), and the onset of exercise in some instances. • Symptoms include coughing, wheezing, shortness of breath, tight chest. • Mild attack: the student should sit, try to relax, breathe out, and use an inhaler if required. • Severe attack: access prompt medical support. • Exercise is generally beneficial for children with asthma, leading to improved cardiorespiratory fitness and reduced breathlessness at a given exercise intensity.	• Ensure that their inhaler (and spacer) is available when exercising. • Encourage them to use their inhaler (reliever) approximately five minutes prior to warm-up if exercise usually triggers asthma. • Ensure that they warm up and cool down thoroughly, this should last at least 10 minutes. • Increase intensity of physical activity gradually. • Discourage participation in physical activity when the air is affected by known trigger elements (eg grass cutting pollens, dust, pollutants such as cigarette smoke, car exhaust fumes, changes in temperature). • Allow the child to stop exercising if symptoms occur, and use the reliever inhaler to relieve the symptoms until they are ready to resume.
Attention deficit hyperactivity disorder (ADHD) www.addiss.co.uk	• Children with ADHD find it difficult to concentrate and remember instructions. • In some cases, medication is used to help students focus.	• Provide and repeat clear, easy-to-follow instructions. • Reward and encourage achievement to retain focus. • Be consistent in approach. • Risk assess activities to ensure that they can be safely managed by the staff and students.

(continued)

Condition	What Do Staff Need to Know?	Advice for Staff Teaching and Supporting PESSPA
Autism/autistic spectrum disorder (ASD)/Asperger's syndrome www.autism.org.uk www.autismeducationtrust.org.uk www.afpe.org.uk for hyposensitivity	• Students display a range of symptoms dependent on where their condition sits within the spectrum. • Those with very mild conditions may not be diagnosed. • Many have difficulty processing everyday sensory information such as sounds, sights, and smells, and will display either an oversensitive (hyper) or under-sensitive (hypo) reaction to these. • Some may find interaction and conversation with others difficult, interpreting jokes or sarcasm literally (eg if they were told to 'pull their socks up' as an instruction to work harder, they would interpret this in its literal sense). • They like routine and order, and find change unsettling. • Noise and crowded conditions make them anxious.	• Speak clearly, and allow time for instructions and expectations to be understood. • Prepare students if manual support is required in PESSPA activities – some students are intolerant to touch. • Encourage, and give both verbal and visual prompts. • Prepare students thoroughly for the activity they will be doing by showing photographs, video and demonstrations, and sharing plans. • Be mindful that they might react adversely to noise and multiple activity (eg if sharing a sports hall space, in a busy swimming pool environment or using loud music, they might find it difficult to filter out noise that others would be able to ignore). • Be prepared to provide support with spatial awareness if this is needed.

(continued)

Condition	What Do Staff Need to Know?	Advice for Staff Teaching and Supporting PESSPA
Brittle bones www.brittlebone.org	• A condition brought on by lack of collagen – a protein within parts of the body, including the bones, that provides structure and strength. • Bones are prone to fractures.	• Make staff and other students aware of the situation. • Develop a clear understanding of the extent of the condition. • Plan activities that reduce the risk of injury while still enabling activity (eg individual activities rather than activities in large groups).
Cerebral palsy www.scope.org.uk	• Caused by damage to. or failure in the development of, the motor areas of the brain before or during birth, or in the first few years of life. • May be affected in one or a combination of ways: **Spastic:** – Increased muscle tone, resulting in restricted movement. – Sudden movements extending the back and neck. – Swallowing and speech difficulties. – In some cases, cognitive development is affected. **Athetoid:** – Involuntary movements and uncontrolled motion. – Speech, hearing and sight may be impaired. **Ataxic:** – Movements are slow and awkward. – There is a lack of directional control and balance, which may result in falls.	• Develop a clear understanding of the range of conditions. • Check for understanding of instructions, use demonstration where helpful. • Work with specialists to assess the specific needs of each student, and plan activity accordingly. • Ensure other students are mindful of space required for wheelchairs or other mobility aids where used. • Allow sufficient time for movement about the area.

(continued)

Condition	What Do Staff Need to Know?	Advice for Staff Teaching and Supporting PESSPA
Congenital heart conditions www.chfed.org.uk www.bhf.org.uk/heart-health/yheart	• These are conditions that some children are born with. • There are a range of different conditions. Some never require treatment, others have no cure. • A range of symptoms might be seen, including unexplained breathlessness, tiredness, palpitations, dizziness, fainting or collapsing. • Common medications include diuretics (to reduce excess fluid), anticoagulants (to prevent the blood clotting) and anti-arrhythmic medicine (to control the rhythm of the heart). • Regular physical activity can improve the function of the heart and circulation.	• PESSPA lessons should be adapted to allow students to take part at their own level and pace (eg lower intensity, longer rests). • Students should be encouraged to work to a level where they can feel warm and slightly 'out of puff', but can still talk. If they become too breathless to talk, they need to slow down or stop and rest. • The warm-up and cool-down are very important and should last at least 10 minutes to allow for a gradual increase in heart rate and breathing. • Appropriate intensity of dynamic activity (eg walking, running, swimming, dancing) is more suitable than static (isometric) activity – where the pressure is loaded on the heart, and there is a sudden rise in systolic blood pressure, which can be difficult to control. For this reason, static exercises and stretching should also be avoided.
Cystic fibrosis (CF) www.cysticfibrosis.org.uk	• An inherited condition where glands in the body (primarily the pancreas) secrete excessive mucus, leading to blockages, which can prevent food being broken down and absorbed. • Sweating can produce additional mucus in hot weather and after exercise. • Lungs needs to be kept clear and physical activity monitored. • Participation in physical activity is very important for students with CF because it helps clear mucus from the lungs, and improves physical bulk and strength.	• Encourage students with CF to take part in as much physical activity as possible, ideally types of exercise that leave them out of breath, like running, swimming, football or tennis. • Recognise when a student with CF feels unusually tired and lacks energy after a cold or chest infection, to which they are prone.

(continued)

Condition	What Do Staff Need to Know?	Advice for Staff Teaching and Supporting PESSPA
Diabetes www.diabetes.org.uk	• A condition where the amount of glucose (sugar) in the blood is too high because the body cannot use it properly due to either no insulin being produced (type 1 diabetes) or insufficient insulin produced (type 2 diabetes).	• Encourage physical activity as part of a planned and managed programme as it stimulates the action of the insulin by lowering blood sugar through the use of the sugar in the muscles.
	• In children under the age of 18, type 1 is the most common form, although the number of children affected by type 2 is increasing.	• Know how to react to the onset of **hypo**glycaemia (when the brain is starved of glucose energy), and how to look for and identify early symptoms such as tiredness, loss of alertness, muscle strength, and coordination.
	• Children are encouraged to check their blood glucose level before taking part in physical activity. Where it is lower than recommended, they should have a snack before starting the activity.	• Recognise signs of **hyper**glycaemia – students will feel ill if blood sugars are too high, and if they have type 1 diabetes, will need to test their blood sugars and, if required, their ketones to determine if they need to correct their sugars with insulin.
		• Be aware of those students who have an insulin pump, and never insist that it is removed.
		• Check that the student has the items they may need close at hand (eg blood glucose testing kit, food, glucose tablets, drinks), and allow them to use these at any time. Physical education departments are advised to keep some sugared energy drinks available in preference to snacks in case they are required, following recent advice.
		• Inform students well in advance about how long and how intense the physical activity session will be so that they can prepare by eating sufficient snacks.
		• Check that the student has carried out a blood glucose check before starting activity.
		• Build up physical activity programmes gradually.

(continued)

Condition	What Do Staff Need to Know?	Advice for Staff Teaching and Supporting PESSPA
Down's syndrome (DS) www.downs-syndrome.org.uk	• Sometimes referred to as trisomy-21, due to the failure in cell division of chromosome 21, leading to the development of 47 rather than 46 chromosomes. • Every student with DS will have different needs and conditions. • Students with DS may have reduced muscle tone, heart conditions, hearing and vision difficulties, respiratory difficulties, and learning difficulties. • Students with DS may suffer from instability and acute dislocation of the atlanto-axial joint. They may experience pain behind the ear or in the neck. There may be a deterioration of posture, manipulative skills, or bowel and bladder control – these symptoms require specialist advice.	• Break down instructions or tasks into short, manageable chunks, and speak directly to the student to check that they have understood. • Use demonstrations, signs and gestures. • Collisions should be avoided. • Jumping or diving into water is not advised. • Proceed with extreme caution when using trampolines – this activity may be high risk due to risk of damage to the atlanto-axial joint. • Offer frequent praise and encouragement. • Allow students who may have associated heart conditions to rest if they complain of tiredness.
Dyspraxia www.dyspraxiafoundation.org.uk	• The condition presents an immaturity in movement, displaying 'clumsy' action. • Poor balance and coordination of body parts. • Difficulty with gross and fine motor skills.	• Give clear instructions, allowing the student to position him/herself safely at each stage. They may require help with placing their hands and feet correctly. • Use cones, marker lines and spots to direct the student back to their work area. • Have a variety of equipment, such as larger bats and slower balls, available to accommodate coordination challenges. • Encourage the development of skills as an individual, rather than incorporating them into team activities. • Think about the activity surface – running on a track may be acceptable, but a rough cross-country course would be difficult.

(continued)

Condition	What Do Staff Need to Know?	Advice for Staff Teaching and Supporting PESSPA
Epilepsy www.epilepsynse.org.uk www.epilepsyresearch.org.uk www.epilepsy.org.uk	• The effects of epilepsy vary from person to person. • The condition is characterised by seizures originating in the brain as a result of excessive or disordered discharge of brain cells. • Some children may never have a seizure at school. • Participation in physical activity is dependent on each individual's condition.	• Organise a support system, such as a 'buddy system'. • Be aware that prolonged periods underwater, and environments with strobe or flickering lighting may cause seizures. • Be vigilant when students are working at height (eg in gymnastics or on a climbing wall). • Know how to respond if a seizure occurs.
Foetal alcohol spectrum disorder (FASD) www.fasdtrust.co.uk www.fasdnetwork.org www.nofas-uk.org www.afpe.org.uk for hyposensitivity	• This condition occurs as a result of the mother consuming high levels of alcohol during pregnancy, which results in the development of the foetus being affected. • Physical signs around the face include low nasal bridge, short nose, thin upper lips, and minor ear abnormalities. • Symptoms are similar to those on the autistic spectrum – fine and gross motor skills tend to be poor, students find it difficult to sit still and concentrate. • Motivation is low, there may be the appearance of 'daydreaming' or laziness. • Spatial awareness is poor. • Either hypo (under) or hyper (over) sensitivity (see Autism) is experienced in relation to touch, smell, pain and noise. • Students can master a task one day, and forget how to do it the next day. • Physical activity can be very beneficial for students with FASD.	• Explain tasks simply and thoroughly. • Use simple and brief language, providing key safety points. • Repeat instructions. • Provide practical demonstrations for clarification. • Allow students to work at their own pace.

(continued)

Condition	What Do Staff Need to Know?	Advice for Staff Teaching and Supporting PESSPA
Haemophilia www.haemophilia.org/inhibitors	• A hereditary condition that mainly affects boys. • The blood-clotting mechanism is affected, and bleeding following a minor incident may be life-threatening, although levels vary. • By secondary school age, students generally treat themselves with a blood-clotting factor that is injected, usually into existing cannula in their veins. • Participation in PESSPA activities is encouraged as it strengthens joints and muscles, which helps to improve stability and coordination.	• Ensure that the severity of the condition is known and implications understood. • Make provision for participation in individual and small-sided or individual PESSPA activities (eg swimming, badminton). • Ensure that activities such as basketball, netball and athletics are well controlled. • Avoid involving these students in contact sports such as rugby, martial arts or boxing. • Ensure that students carry out a thorough warm-up before activity and that they have had their blood-clotting factor infusion prior to taking part in any physical activity. • Ensure that full PPE and, in some cases, additional protective equipment such as knee pads and wristbands are worn, when appropriate.
Hearing impairment www.actiononhearingloss.org.uk www.ndcs.org.uk www.mid.org.uk	• Conductive hearing loss is a condition often caused by a build-up of fluid, such as in glue ear, in which sounds cannot pass through the outer or middle ear. • This condition is generally temporary, and can clear up or may require surgery. • Sensorineural deafness is a condition caused by a problem in the inner ear or auditory nerve that may affect a person's speech and balance, and is likely to be permanent.	• Ensure that the student can clearly see the member of staff when instructions are given or demonstrations carried out. • Establish eye contact before starting to give instructions. • Be mindful of activities that require good balance, particularly in gymnastics and dance. • Use gestures and visual alternatives to auditory prompts, particularly in relation to a 'stop' command when there is danger. • Check understanding regularly.

(continued)

Condition	What Do Staff Need to Know?	Advice for Staff Teaching and Supporting PESSPA
Hydrocephalus www.headway.org.uk/ hydrocephalus.aspx	• Caused by an obstruction in the circulation of the cerebro-spinal fluid around the spinal cord and brain. • The accumulation of this fluid in the brain can lead to a variation in the severity of damage caused by pressure on the brain cells. • In most cases, to relieve this pressure, a valve or shunt is inserted behind the ear just below the skin. • Students struggle to store information.	• Break down tasks/instructions into small stages for safety. • Talk through tasks, in addition to providing practical demonstrations. • Support students, and be prepared to adapt activities that require judging distance and direction. • Encourage all activities, including contact sports. There is very little problem with shunts being damaged during activity or minor falls. Advice to avoid contact sports is very much in the minority.
Multiple sclerosis www.nationalmssociety.org	• This condition disintegrates the nerve fibres over time in a random way so that progress of the disease can vary and be at different paces. • Those affected may experience spasticity, difficulties with attention and balance, blurred or loss of vision, incontinence, loss of memory, and speech problems. • It is more common in adults, but some students are diagnosed while still at school. • Swimming is a particularly beneficial and safe activity when supported correctly.	• Be vigilant to the changes in symptoms, which may vary from week to week. • Provide clear, brief instructions. • Repeat instructions. • Check regularly with the student about the clarity of their vision, and notice signs that vision has deteriorated. • Ensure that students work on even surfaces and are made aware of surface issues that might make them lose their balance.

(continued)

Condition	What Do Staff Need to Know?	Advice for Staff Teaching and Supporting PESSPA
Muscular dystrophy www.muscular-dystrophy.org	• Relates to a group of conditions characterised by a breakdown of muscle fibres, leading to weak and wasted muscles. • The condition exists on a continuum from severely disabled to only a mild disability. • The condition is progressive, but at variable pace. • The most prevalent type, Duchenne, sees symptoms appear usually before the age of five. • Early signs include difficulty when running, standing and climbing stairs. • Swimming provides appropriate and safe activity.	• Clarify manual handling issues with wheelchair users, and provide guidance on whether the student can get out of the chair for activity. • Be aware of frequent changes in the student's physical condition.
Spina bifida www.spinabifidaassociation.org	• A congenital condition through which a deformity in the spine causes damage to the nerves that communicate movement and feeling. • At its most severe, there will be a complete loss of motor and sensory function below the area of damage. • The extent of the disability is dependent on the position and severity of the damaged area. • Symptoms are generally paraplegia and a wasting of the lower limbs. • Students with this condition may also have hydrocephalus (see above). • Students tend to have little feeling in their lower limbs and are not aware of the pain when they bang into objects or walls (while in their wheelchair).	• Adapt activities to make them safe for students who are using wheelchairs or other mobility equipment. • Provide clear instruction, and repeat regularly. • Use modified equipment when students are in wheelchairs (eg shorter sticks, slower-paced balls). • Avoid 'tagging' the wall as a 'safe' zone.

(continued)

Condition	What Do Staff Need to Know?	Advice for Staff Teaching and Supporting PESSPA
Social, emotional and behavioural difficulties www.sebda.org	• A range of responses are required to different needs. • Many students with social, emotional and behavioural difficulties will lack confidence, and may develop a perceived sense of failure that can lead to refusal to participate in physical activity. This may in turn lead to disruptive behaviour. • Some students prefer to avoid large-group and team games, where they might be overwhelmed or intimidated, whereas others are motivated by these situations.	• Gauge the 'mood' of students. Be aware that they may have been affected by incidents prior to the lesson. • Be prepared to be flexible in making adaptations as necessary to accommodate the 'mood' of the students. • Set achievable targets for each student. • Vary activities frequently to keep students on task and interested. • Encourage an ethos of praise for themselves and each other. • Discuss safety with the students, and encourage them to understand how they can contribute to safe practice. • Allow time for students to cool down and relax at the end of a lesson.
Visual impairment www.rnib.org.uk	• This impairment exists along a continuum, from being able to manage with or without support to those who are registered blind and will need specialist support. • Those students who have a degree of sight may still struggle with moving objects and people moving quickly in a PESSPA environment. • Students are usually encouraged to be independent with regard to mobility and movement around the facility. • Eye conditions, such as a history of retinal detachment, mean that activities such as trampolining, diving and contact sports should be avoided.	• Be prepared to modify tasks as necessary. • Use modified equipment such as balls with bells, and buzzers attached to goals or targets. • Use brightly coloured tape on walls, and brightly coloured equipment. • Provide clear and precise instructions. • Give accurate spatial instructions (eg size of area of pitch or hall, fixed objects within that space). • Remove obvious hazards from the working area. • Provide opportunities to take part in individual personal fitness activities. • Allow the use of glasses or peaked caps if bright light is a problem. • Position the student in the optimum place for vision, taking account of sunlight and glare.

For more information regarding SEND and medical conditions:

The National Co-ordinating Committee – Swimming for People with Disabilities (no date) 'Let's All Swim'

British Heart Foundation National Centre (2015) 'Physical activity for all – Physical activity for children and young people with medical conditions', http://goo.gl/qZTRnl

Managing medical information, needs and conditions

2.14.26   *Governing bodies should ensure that their arrangements are clear and unambiguous about the need to support actively pupils with medical conditions to participate in school trips and visits, or in sporting activities, and not prevent them from doing so.*

       DfE (2015) 'Supporting pupils at school with medical conditions', https://goo.gl/ud1Jjg

2.14.27   It is standard practice for schools to request student medical information from parents and to update this information regularly. The onus is on the **parents** to provide adequate information and to inform the school when any medical conditions change.

2.14.28   DfE (2015) 'Supporting pupils at school with medical conditions', https://goo.gl/fDwuHv details how:

       The governing body must ensure that arrangements are in place to support pupils with medical conditions. In doing so it should ensure that such children can access and enjoy the same opportunities at school as any other child.

       The governing body should ensure that its arrangements give parents and pupils confidence in the school's ability to provide effective support for medical conditions in school... They should ensure that staff are properly trained to provide the support that pupils need.

2.14.29   Some students who have medical needs may also be disabled. More information about SEND can be found in Table 22, pages 234–244 in this section. Where a child has SEND but does not have an education, health and care plan, their special educational needs should be mentioned in their **individual healthcare plan.**

2.14.30   Schools should have a secure system to inform and **regularly update staff** about student medical conditions and associated triggers, signs, symptoms, treatments and risks in order for them to take account of such information when planning and delivering a PESSPA session or lesson. Staff should understand how a student's medical condition will impact on their participation, and on maintaining a safe learning environment. This may involve adjusting particular tasks for particular students, such as not asking a student who has epileptic seizures to work at a height in case a seizure occurs with little or no notice. There should be enough flexibility for all students to participate safely according to their own abilities.

2.14.31   The staff member responsible for the students (eg the class teacher) must also **inform any support staff,** whether on or off site, on a need-to-know basis of any medical conditions existing in the groups they will teach during their visit. This will enable the student's needs to be accommodated within the lesson. Communicating this information to external staff coming into school is not always as effective and reliable as it needs to be. Procedures should be in place to enforce this.

Case law

2.14.32   **R versus Taverham High School, 2013:**

A 12-year-old girl died after catching her foot on a pommel horse and falling during a physical education lesson. The cause of death was a hyperextension injury to the neck.

A choice was given towards the end of the lesson to use any equipment. The student chose the horse and ran up well, but when jumping, her foot caught the front end of the horse, and she tumbled forward, landing face down on the mat.

The student had a pre-existing neck condition that could have limited her ability to take part in some sports, including gymnastics. The school knew about the condition, but due to an administrative oversight, they had failed to inform all staff. The pathologist's report, however, determined that the injuries suffered in the fall could have killed somebody with an 'anatomically normal' neck.

Given the conclusion that the pre-existing neck condition was not the cause of death, the inquiry found no evidence of any failings at the school, and concluded that the death was accidental. This case, however, demonstrates how easily such important information can be overlooked.

2.14.33   Schools should consider any reasonable adjustments they might need to make to enable students with medical needs to participate fully and safely on **trips and visits**. This usually includes carrying out a risk assessment in consultation with the student, their parents and any additional medical staff to establish safe inclusion.

2.14.34   The **school's medical policy** should set out clear guidelines regarding the administration of medicines, and staff should follow this policy. It should help to clarify decisions regarding:

- whether students should be allowed to carry their own medicines and devices, or procedures for accessing them quickly and easily for self-medication – students who can take medicines or manage procedures themselves may still require a level of supervision

- the role of the staff – staff are not compelled to **administer medicines** to students nor to supervise the administration of medicines. They must not give out prescription medicines or undertake health care procedures without appropriate training. A first aid certificate does not constitute appropriate training in supporting students with specific medical conditions.

2.14.35   Where there are variations to this, or individual needs differ, the outcomes of discussions with all those involved should be recorded within a student's individual health care plan in order to guide staff. Arrangements will vary in practice from one school to another.

2.14.36   There are now many students in schools recognised as having asthma, epilepsy, diabetes or conditions that may cause anaphylactic shock. These conditions can be severe and long-lasting, and can therefore become **disabilities**. Within equality legislation, schools are required to take this into account. Governing bodies should ensure that sufficient staff have received suitable training to support children with specific medical conditions, that they are competent to take on the responsibility, and that they can access information and further support as needed.

FAQ

2.14.37 **I have been told that it is compulsory for me to undertake training in the use of EpiPens. Is this correct?**

In the past, it was a requirement that in order to use an EpiPen, the user had to have undergone training. Under the revision of the Medicines Act 2012, this is no longer the case, and any layperson can administer adrenalin through the use of an EpiPen. If you know that you are working with students for whom this may be required, it makes sense to be trained, but it is no longer compulsory.

Case law

2.14.38 **Hippolyte versus Bexley London Borough (1994):**

An established asthmatic student in a secondary school suffered a degree of brain damage subsequent to an attack developing during a lesson. She refused the teacher's request to report to the first-aider until the teacher's concern was so great that she then took the student to the school office for attention and expert support. The Court of Appeal dismissed the claim for negligence because the school had **clear and detailed procedures, and the teacher followed the procedures fully**. *It was also determined that the 16-year-old student, as an established asthmatic, would be fully aware of the implications of her refusal to follow the teacher's request for her to visit the first-aider and had therefore contributed to the tragic outcome.*

HIV and AIDS

2.14.39 The human immunodeficiency virus (HIV) is a non-notifiable disease, which means that parents of students affected or infected, or the students themselves, may choose not to inform the school. This is because the infected student presents no risk of onward transmission in everyday contact.

2.14.40 There are no known reported cases of HIV transmission occurring in a UK school either from a student or a member of staff.

2.14.41 Students may take part in PESSPA and outdoor and adventurous activities, providing they do not have any other medical condition that prevents them from participating.

2.14.42 No cases have been recorded of HIV transmission from child to child by biting, fighting, playing or any other normal childhood interaction. Small cuts or grazes do not pose any concern.

2.14.43   Bleeding resulting from accidents should be dealt with immediately. First-aiders should wear disposable waterproof gloves following normal first aid procedures and standard hygiene practices. This will be effective in preventing transmission of all blood-borne infections, including HIV.

2.14.44   The Children's HIV Association (CHIVA) has written clear guidance for schools, explaining how students known to have a diagnosis of HIV should be supported. This can be used to raise awareness about HIV among staff, and to inform them about procedures to take should a student disclose their condition. This information may already be contained within existing school policies. Where it is not, it can be accessed on the CHIVA website.

 Further guidance is available on the CHIVA website at http://goo.gl/ANNOI9

© Alan Edwards

Chapter 2/Section 15: First aid

Health and safety regulations for first aid

2.15.1   A range of individuals in schools can suffer injuries or be taken ill. It does not matter whether the injury or illness happens in school or elsewhere, it is important to give immediate attention and call an ambulance in serious cases.

2.15.2   In schools, it is the responsibility of the employer to make sure that the Health and Safety (First-Aid) Regulations 1981 are met. These require employers to provide:

- a sufficient number of trained first-aiders (where 25 or more people are employed, one such person should be provided)

- appropriate first aid equipment, kits and facilities

- a system for incident and accident reporting.

 For more information on these regulations, see http://goo.gl/gf5DYA

2.15.3   The regulations do not commit employers to provide first aid for anyone other than their own staff, but employers do have health and safety responsibilities towards non-employees. The Health and Safety Commission (HSC) guidance recommends that organisations, such as schools, that provide a service for others should include them in their risk assessments and provide for them.

Providing a sufficient number of trained first-aiders

2.15.4   Head teachers (HTs) are required to assess the first aid needs of their school. What is 'adequate and appropriate' will depend on the outcome of this needs assessment and the circumstances of each school. In such an assessment, they may consider:

- the size and design of the school (eg on different levels or split sites)
- school location and accessibility for the emergency services

- any hazards or dangerous substances on site
- consideration of the number of pupils with special educational needs and disabilities (SEND)
- number of first-aiders required, giving particular attention to how this might have an impact for physical education, school sport and physical activity (PESSPA) staff taking students to fixtures and sports event.

 For more information, see Department for Education (DfE) (2014) 'First aid in schools', https://goo.gl/znQuyY

2.15.5   The findings of a first aid needs assessment will identify the type of training that is appropriate:

- first aid at work (FAW)
- emergency first aid at work (EFAW)
- appointed person (AP)
- other appropriate training, such as the British Red Cross 'First Aid for Sports' training (http://goo.gl/M88MKd)
- paediatric first aid or emergency paediatric first aid certificate.

2.15.6   All schools, as a minimum requirement, must have an **'appointed person'** to take charge of first aid arrangements, including looking after first aid equipment and facilities, and calling the emergency services when required. In practice, most schools would have several 'appointed people', in order to be available at all times. Appointed people are not necessarily first-aiders, and should not undertake treatment for which they are not trained. However, it is good practice for them to have some emergency first aid training, and to be able take control of all first aid arrangements at all times when required.

Appropriate first aid training

2.15.7   EFAW training enables a first-aider to give emergency first aid to someone who is injured or becomes ill while at work. FAW training includes the same content as EFAW and also equips the first-aider to apply first aid to a range of specific injuries and illnesses.

EFAW Training Specification	FAW Training Specification

• Understand the role and responsibilities of a first-aider.
• Be able to assess an incident.
• Be able to manage an unresponsive casualty who is breathing normally.
• Be able to manage an unresponsive casualty who is not breathing normally.
• Be able to recognise and assist a casualty who is choking.
• Be able to manage a casualty with external bleeding.
• Be able to manage a casualty who is in shock.
• Be able to manage a casualty with a minor injury.
	The specification includes **all** components of the EFAW training plus the following:
	• Be able to conduct a secondary survey.
	• Be able to administer first aid to a casualty with:
	  – injuries to bones, muscles and joints
	  – suspected head and spinal injuries
	  – suspected chest injuries
	  – burns and scalds
	  – an eye injury
	  – sudden poisoning
	  – anaphylaxis
	  – a suspected major illness.

From 31 December 2016, the EFAW and the FAW will include training in the use of an automated external defibrillator (AED) as the Resuscitation Council UK guidelines now state that the management of a casualty requiring CPR is to request an AED.

2.15.8   Where standard FAW training courses do not include content pertinent to children (such as resuscitation procedures for children), the employer should request that they are tailored to meet the needs of the employees being trained.

2.15.9   FAW certificates are only valid for three years, and need to be refreshed before expiry to avoid having to undertake another full course. Employers can arrange for a refresher course up to three months before the expiry date, and for this reason, schools should keep a record of first-aiders and their certification dates.

2.15.10   Since 1 October 2013, the Health and Safety Executive (HSE) no longer approves training and qualifications for the purposes of first aid at work. The flexibility arising from the changes in the regulations gives employers more choice in the first aid training they provide for their employees and who they choose to provide it. An employer will need to undertake varying levels of due diligence (reasonable enquiry or investigation) in order to make their selection. For schools, the updated guidance from the DfE is that they should select what is in their opinion the 'best provider'. *(Information provided in response to a question to the DfE, February 2016.)*

2.15.11   Following a review in 2016, the HSE changed its rules regarding blended learning. It now accepts that some elements of workplace first aid training (FAW, EFAW or other) can be delivered remotely via distance-based online methods. Employers are expected to conduct the necessary checks to decide if a blended approach is sufficiently effective and suitable for their staff as exclusively face-to-face learning. They should make sure that sufficient time is allocated to classroom-based learning and assessment of the practical elements of the syllabus.

Appropriate first aid equipment

First aid kits

2.15.12   First aid kits are a legal requirement for every workplace. All staff should be made aware of where the nearest first aid container is located. Each first aid container must be clearly marked in a green box with a white cross on it.

2.15.13   They should be:

- made of suitable material, designed to protect the contents from damp and dust

- easily accessible to staff

- checked regularly to make sure all contents are in stock and in date.

2.15.14   British Standard (BS) 8599 is the standard that the manufacturers of first aid kits have been granted. A risk assessment should be carried out to determine the contents of every workplace first aid kit and the number of kits needed. This should consider split sites, distant sports fields or playgrounds, and any other additional high-risk areas.

2.15.15   The HSE does not issue a definitive list for what a first aid kit contains. However, it offers a guide to the **minimum provision** in a low-risk environment. (See Table 23, page 253.) Sufficient quantities of each item should always be available in every first aid kit, with no additional equipment included.

2.15.16   The school should identify in their first aid procedures the **person responsible** for ensuring that the contents of the first aid kits are in date, discarded if expired, and replaced after use. Extra stock should be kept available for this purpose.

2.15.17   Sterile first aid dressings should be packaged in such a way as to allow the user to apply the dressing to a wound without touching the part of the dressing that is to come into direct contact with the wound.

2.15.18   When mains tap water is not readily available for eye irrigation, at least 900ml of sterile water or sterile normal saline (0.9%) should be provided in sealed disposable containers. Each container should hold at least 300ml and should not be reused once the sterile seal is broken. Eye baths, eye cups or refillable containers should not be used for eye irrigation.

2.15.19   Soap and water, and disposable drying materials, should be provided for first aid purposes. Siting first aid kits near to hand-washing facilities is recommended where possible. Alternatively, wrapped, moist cleaning wipes, which are not impregnated with alcohol, may be used.

2.15.20   Staff should exercise special care to **avoid infection** through the use of disposable gloves and effective hand washing when dealing with blood or other bodily fluids, or disposing of soiled equipment and dressings.

2.15.21   If an employee has received additional training in the treatment of specific hazards that require the use of special antidotes or equipment, these may be stored near the hazard area or kept in the first aid kit.

Supplementary equipment

2.15.22   In addition to the minimum provision of first aid items, there may be a need to have additional products available and stored alongside first aid kits. (See the list in Table 23, page 253.)

Travelling first aid kits

2.15.23   The contents of travelling first aid kits should be appropriate for the circumstances in which they are to be used. Before undertaking any off-site PESSPA visits, the level of first aid provision needs to be assessed. First aid kits should be taken to all PESSPA events and be easily accessible where the activity is taking place. The minimum recommended items (where no special risk is identified) are listed in Table 23, page 253.

2.15.24   Transport regulations require a first aid kit to be carried in the school minibus when transporting students to fixtures and events. Items required to be kept on-board are listed in Table 23, page 253.

2.15.25   School staff undertaking specialised outdoor and adventure activities with students should consider attending the relevant first aid course to equip them with the specific knowledge required, such as the mountain first aid course, which includes practice in the use of inflatable splints.

Table 23: First aid kit contents

Standard First Aid Kit (minimum provision)*	Supplementary First Aid Equipment (can be stored with or alongside the standard first aid kit)
• leaflet giving general advice on first aid • 20 individually wrapped sterile plasters (hypoallergenic if necessary) in assorted sizes • two sterile eye pads • four individually wrapped triangular bandages, preferably sterile • six safety pins • two large, sterile, individually wrapped un-medicated wound dressings (approximately 13cm x 9cm) • six medium-sized, sterile, individually wrapped, un-medicated wound dressings (approximately 10cm x 8cm) • pair of plastic, sterile disposable gloves	• blunt-ended stainless steel scissors (minimum length 12.7cm) – when used, consideration should be given to avoiding cross-contamination • disposable plastic gloves and aprons, suitable protective equipment and appropriate protection against hypothermia – these should be properly stored and regularly checked to ensure they remain in good condition • plastic disposable bags for soiled or used first aid dressings – employers should ensure systems are in place for the safe disposal of items such as used dressings • blankets – it is recommended that these are stored in such a way as to keep them free from dust and damp • suitable carrying equipment for transporting casualties – this is recommended if a school covers a large area or is divided into a number of separate and self-contained working areas
Travelling First Aid Kit (based on assessment of needs)	Public Service Vehicles (including Minibuses) First Aid Kit (based on transport regulations 1981) and for Minibuses Used not for Reward (based on Road Vehicles [Construction and Use] regulations 1986 [as amended])
As a minimum: • leaflet giving general advice on first aid • six individually wrapped, sterile adhesive dressings • one large, sterile, un-medicated dressing (approximately 18cm x 18cm) • two triangular bandages • two safety pins • individually wrapped, moist cleaning wipes • pair of disposable gloves	• leaflet giving general advice on first aid • 10 antiseptic wipes, foil wrapped • one conforming disposable bandage (not less than 7.5cm wide) • two triangular bandages • one packet of 24 assorted adhesive dressings • three large, sterile, un-medicated ambulance dressings (not less than 15cm x 20cm) • two sterile eye pads with attachments • 12 assorted safety pins • pair of rust-free stainless steel blunt-ended scissors • disposable gloves • mouth mask for resuscitation

* DfE (2014) 'First aid in schools', https://goo.gl/znQuyY

First aid accommodation

2.15.26   The Education (School Premises) Regulations 1996 require every school to have a suitable room (with washbasin and near to a toilet) that can be used to administer medical or dental treatment as required, and for the care of students during school hours. This facility can be used as a 'first aid room', although first aid provision may be required in various locations at different times.

Defibrillators

2.15.27   An automated external defibrillator (AED) is a machine used to give an electric shock to a person who is in cardiac arrest. Cardiac arrest can affect people of all ages without warning. In the event of a cardiac arrest, swift action in the form of early cardiopulmonary resuscitation (CPR) and prompt defibrillation can help save lives. The British Heart Foundation suggests that after a cardiac arrest, every minute without CPR and defibrillation reduces an individual's chance of survival by 10%. It is important to understand that defibrillators are not intended for use with heart attack patients.

2.15.28   The recommended procedure for dealing with cardiac arrest is referred to as the 'Chain of Survival'. Defibrillation forms a key part of this chain. The four recognised links of the chain are:

- early recognition to prevent cardiac arrest – at this stage, a 999 call to the emergency services is made; the operator can stay on the line and advise on giving CPR and using an AED

- early CPR to buy time – either through mouth-to-mouth resuscitation or compression-only CPR

- early defibrillation to attempt to restore the heart to a healthy rhythm, and blood and oxygen circulation

- post-resuscitation care to stabilise the patient and restore quality of life.

2.15.29   While defibrillation is the third link in the chain, for maximum effect, the two preceding links must have been achieved.

2.15.30   It is becoming increasingly common to see defibrillators available for emergency use in a wide range of public places. The DfE publication 'Supporting pupils at schools with medical conditions: statutory guidance for governing bodies of maintained schools and proprietors of academies in England' (2014) advises schools to consider purchasing an AED as part of their first aid equipment.

To access 'Supporting pupils at schools with medical conditions: statutory guidance for governing bodies of maintained schools and proprietors of academies in England', go to https://goo.gl/fDwuHv

2.15.31   DfE (2016) 'Automated external defibrillators (AEDs): A guide for maintained schools and academies' highlights the part that AEDs can play in ensuring the health and safety of pupils, staff and others, and encourages all schools to consider purchasing AEDs as part of their first aid equipment. However, it is also makes clear that the decision to purchase and install AEDs is one for each school to determine.

To access the DfE guidance on AEDs, see https://goo.gl/JZVEpE

Deciding whether a defibrillator is required in school

2.15.32   In order to establish the need for an AED, a risk assessment should be undertaken by the school. If it is thought prudent to go ahead with the purchase, the risk assessment can also be used to decide how many machines are required.

2.15.33   The Northern Ireland Education Authority (EA) and DfE both provide guidance for deciding the number of AEDs needed.

2.15.34   Schools in England can receive assistance with purchasing AEDs that meet a certain minimum specification, through the DfE's arrangement with the National Health Service Supply Chain.

Further details about schools purchasing AEDs can be found on page 11 of the DfE guidance: https://goo.gl/JZVEpE

2.15.35   The Northern Ireland Education and Library Boards (NEELB) and Council for Catholic Maintained Schools (CCMS) 'AED guidelines for schools (2014) also recommends models, sourced centrally through ongoing procurement procedures that are available to schools.

To view Northern Ireland AED guidelines for schools, access http://goo.gl/DXPNIZ

Locating defibrillators

2.15.36   To ensure optimum coverage and swift access from anywhere on the premises, schools may decide to have a number of AED machines. The DfE suggests that they should be situated no further than a maximum of two minutes' walk from the areas where they are most likely to be needed. The distance of school playing fields from the main school buildings might be an important consideration in this respect. Locating a machine in the vicinity of the sports facilities and play areas would seem sensible. Schools may also wish to consider using portable machines taken out to sports fields, especially where they are away from the main school site.

2.15.37   AEDs mounted outside require heaters to keep them at the optimum temperature. There are also a number of different options for installing AED cabinets so that they are anti-theft and tamper-proof while still being sufficiently accessible in an emergency.

2.15.38   Both the DfE (2015) and NEELB (2014) documents provide suggestions regarding sites that might be used by both the school and the community, and the best way to enable access to the AED by all parties during and out of school hours.

Defibrillator training

2.15.39   AEDs are work equipment and, as such, are covered by the HSE (1998) 'Safe use of work equipment: Provision and use of work equipment regulations (PUWER) (1998) approved code of practice and guidance'. As such, training in the use of AEDs should be provided by the employer.

To access the PUWER 'Safe use of work equipment' code of practice, see http://goo.gl/EupbiP

2.15.40 Staff need a sound understanding of when it is appropriate to use an AED, ie in the case of cardiac arrest when the heart stops beating, and not following a heart attack, when oxygen is prevented from getting to the heart. Where appropriate, staff should also understand about the difference between treating adults and those children under eight years old, and that AEDs are perfectly acceptable to use on pregnant mothers when required.

2.15.41 In light of these requirements, staff who have undergone a process of structured and organised training are more likely to feel confident and be better equipped to use an AED appropriately and safely in an emergency situation.

2.15.42 The guidance from NEELB (2014) requires that all AED operatives in schools undertake their approved training course and, in line with the Resuscitation Council UK's recommendations, do not accept a demonstration by the AED manufacturer as being adequate training. Attendance at AED training and subsequent refresher sessions must be suitably recorded.

2.15.43 In all cases, schools that purchase AEDs should inform their local ambulance service of their existence and location, and develop a relationship with the service that can support ongoing training in the use of the defibrillator, potential funding available to purchase them, and additional advice and guidance around their location. Schools should also inform them when the device has been used.

Managing and maintaining defibrillator units

2.15.44 It will be necessary to appoint at least two individuals to take responsibility for the ongoing (daily, weekly and other) operating checks on the units. It is essential that the device is always in working order ready for when it may be required. Modern AEDs are set up to carry out regular self-checks, with problems being flagged up to the user. These must be noticed as promptly as possible, hence the need for daily checks. Northern Ireland guidance provides a number of templates for use in setting up checking routines.

2.15.45 Action plans should be developed, setting out the resuscitation procedures, assigning responsibilities, and clarifying the order of response. This should also initiate records of incidents and follow-up action taken.

2.15.46 Appointed staff should understand the need to update the software used in the machine. This is in response to new UK and European resuscitation guidelines, which are issued every five years. Suppliers appointed under the arrangements put in place by the DfE (2015) must agree to provide such updates to schools free of charge. The various components of the device (eg pads, batteries) have an anticipated service life. This needs to be noted and the units replaced when necessary.

2.15.47 A very comprehensive table of the maintenance responsibilities and checking requirements is presented in the NEELB (2014) guidance.

Use of defibrillators and the law

2.15.48   Schools may have concerns regarding the legal risks of trying to resuscitate a casualty. Information from the Resuscitation Council (UK) states:

> *at the present time there are no statutory laws in the UK designed to protect rescuers who attempt to help others. It can be seen, however, that there remains a good deal of protection in the common law principles that are described in this guide.*
>
> *It is, in practice, extremely difficult to envisage (and no precedent has yet been set) how a victim could successfully sue an individual who rendered him aid in an emergency situation. If anyone were to bring a successful claim, it is likely that the rescuer would have to have acted in a grossly negligent fashion and, if this was the case, it would probably not be desirable to introduce legislation to protect him.*
>
> Resuscitation Council (UK) (2015) 'The legal status of those who attempt resuscitation', https://goo.gl/eZZHnq

Accident and emergency procedures

2.15.49   As part of general risk management processes, all schools should have arrangements in place for dealing with accidents and emergencies. **School policy should set out what should happen in an emergency situation**.

2.15.50   Staff should know, and be able to apply, the **school's procedures** for dealing with injuries and other emergencies. Where concerns exist about not knowing the whole-school procedures or how to apply them, staff should consult the HT.

2.15.51   Particular forethought should be given to dealing with accidents and emergencies that may occur at the **extremities of the school site** and also during off-site activities that extend beyond the normal school day. In such circumstances, effective and efficient communication through the school's accident report point (ARP), which is usually the school office, or with the school leadership team is essential.

2.15.52   Staff need not be qualified in **first aid** (see page 249 for details), but all need to have a working knowledge of dealing with accident and emergency situations to the extent that they can **manage** an initial injury effectively and summon an appointed person or first-aider to take over management of the situation.

2.15.53   First aid organisations advise that, in the event of an accident, a responsible person should **manage** the situation typically by:

- keeping calm

- assessing the situation – making any danger safe and not moving any casualty unless they are in immediate danger

- reassuring any casualties

- ensuring the rest of group is safe – stopping all activity

- sending for help – preferably by mobile, walkie-talkie or sending students to the ARP (usually the school office)

- monitoring, treating and managing situations where there is more than one casualty in the order of those:
  - who are unconscious
  - have severe bleeding
  - have broken bones
  - have other injuries

- regularly checking consciousness and informing the paramedic if consciousness is lost (also informing them of any relevant medical issues)

- not trying to do too much

- getting others to help

- asking the students (according to age and ability) what happened if the full incident was not seen

- recording the details as soon as possible after the incident.

2.15.54   If a student needs to be taken to hospital, a staff member or responsible adult should be prepared to accompany them in the ambulance. In all cases, where required, the ambulance should be called immediately and the parents informed. The member of staff or responsible adult should stay with the student. If the parent arrives in time, they may accompany the student in the ambulance. Failing this, the staff member or responsible adult should do so.

2.15.55   Where injury occurs to a student visiting another school, such as during a fixture, if the visiting school has only one member of staff accompanying them, they will hopefully have previously entered into a **reciprocal arrangement** with the host school. Within the scope of such an arrangement, the host school agrees to supervise the remaining students until arrangements can be made for another staff member from the visiting school to arrive. This then enables the staff member to accompany the injured student in the ambulance.

2.15.56   Where possible, staff should not take students to hospital in their own cars. If this becomes necessary, in the case of an emergency, or where a student needs medical attention away from the school, and the parents are not available, an additional staff member or responsible adult should accompany them. Where the immediacy and seriousness of the injury does not allow time to arrange this, the teacher should proceed independently to hospital with the student (Children Act 1989, Section 3, Subsection 5). Schools need to ensure that they understand the local emergency services' cover arrangements and that the correct information is provided for navigation systems.

2.15.57   Where a student has an education, health and care plan or individual health care plan, this should clearly define what constitutes an emergency, and explain what to do, ensuring that all relevant staff are aware of emergency symptoms and procedures. Other students in the school should know what to do, such as informing a teacher immediately if they think help is needed.

2.15.58   On the very rare occasions a major crisis or **critical incident** occurs, staff need to be aware of, and apply, the school's plan for dealing with such instances. School policy should make staff aware of the relevant aspects of such a plan, and PESSPA staff should familiarise themselves with how they would respond, to what would be a small section of the plan, should they ever become involved in a major incident while taking teams to fixtures, festivals or on sports tours.

2.15.59   It is essential that where schools have adopted **standard accident procedures (SAPs)**, school staff and students are aware of them. This will help to ensure they all respond to an emergency in the same way, thus minimising the time spent between the accident occurring and the injured student(s) receiving first aid.

2.15.60   A suggested format for SAPs is illustrated in the three procedure flow charts in Figures 6–8 on pages 260–262.

2.15.61   Please note that these examples do not attempt to constitute an authoritative legal interpretation of the provisions of any enactment, regulations or common law. That interpretation is exclusively a matter for the courts.

1   **Suggested red procedure:** for serious accidents that require immediate hospitalisation

2   **Suggested yellow procedure:** for an accident that can be referred to a doctor, clinic or hospital using transport by parent, staff or responsible adult

3   **Suggested green procedure:** for accidents that can be dealt with at the school, by school personnel.

The **red** procedure should always be used when:

• there is any doubt about the level or nature of the injury

• concussion is suspected.

© RTimages/Shutterstock.com

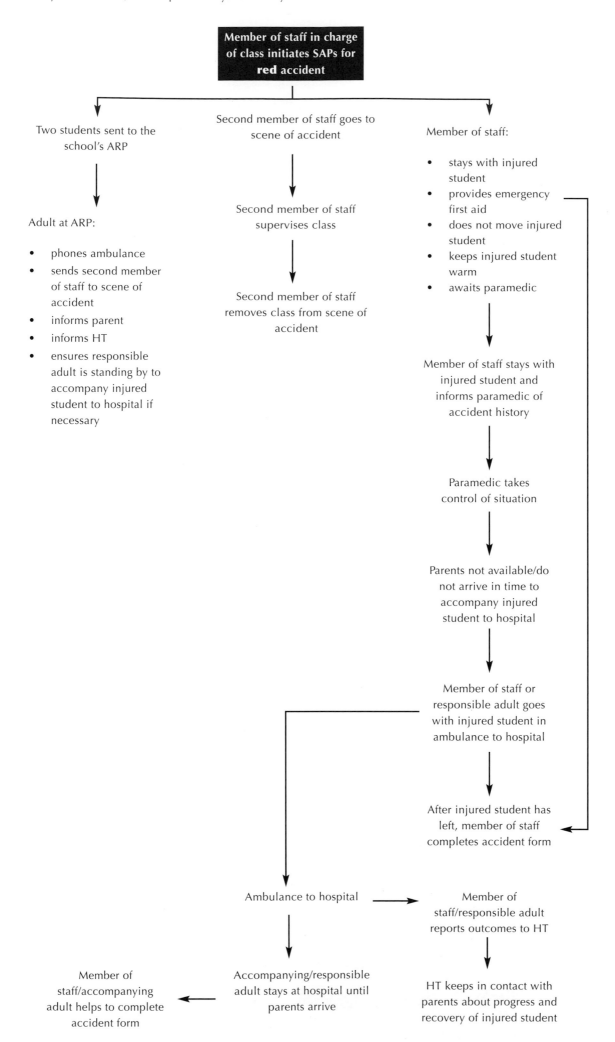

Member of staff in charge of class initiates SAPs for red accident

Two students sent to the school's ARP

Adult at ARP:

- phones ambulance
- sends second member of staff to scene of accident
- informs parent
- informs HT
- ensures responsible adult is standing by to accompany injured student to hospital if necessary

Second member of staff goes to scene of accident

Second member of staff supervises class

Second member of staff removes class from scene of accident

Member of staff:

- stays with injured student
- provides emergency first aid
- does not move injured student
- keeps injured student warm
- awaits paramedic

Member of staff stays with injured student and informs paramedic of accident history

Paramedic takes control of situation

Parents not available/do not arrive in time to accompany injured student to hospital

Member of staff or responsible adult goes with injured student in ambulance to hospital

After injured student has left, member of staff completes accident form

Ambulance to hospital

Member of staff/responsible adult reports outcomes to HT

Member of staff/accompanying adult helps to complete accident form

Accompanying/responsible adult stays at hospital until parents arrive

HT keeps in contact with parents about progress and recovery of injured student

Figure 6: Suggested red accident procedures

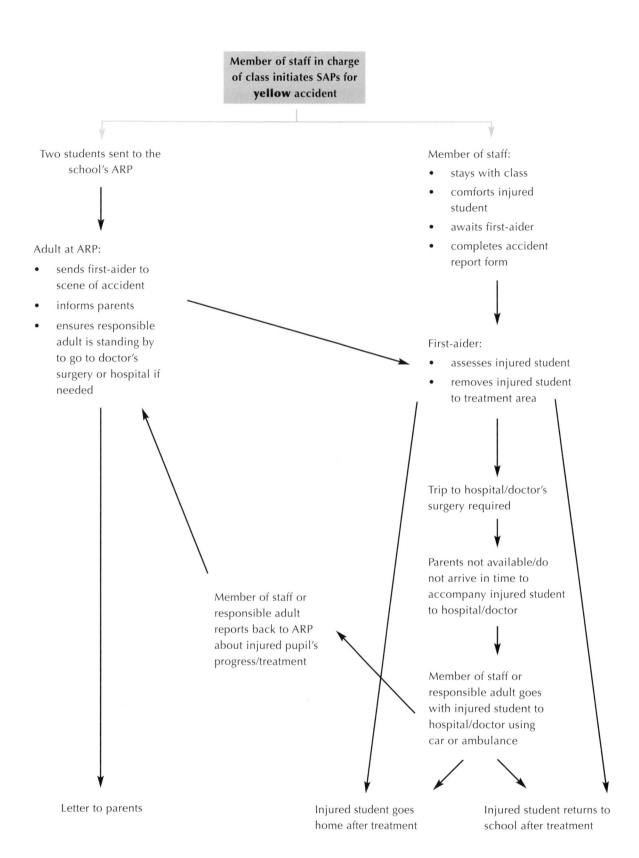

Member of staff in charge of class initiates SAPs for yellow accident

Two students sent to the school's ARP

Adult at ARP:
- sends first-aider to scene of accident
- informs parents
- ensures responsible adult is standing by to go to doctor's surgery or hospital if needed

Member of staff:
- stays with class
- comforts injured student
- awaits first-aider
- completes accident report form

First-aider:
- assesses injured student
- removes injured student to treatment area

Trip to hospital/doctor's surgery required

Parents not available/do not arrive in time to accompany injured student to hospital/doctor

Member of staff or responsible adult goes with injured student to hospital/doctor using car or ambulance

Member of staff or responsible adult reports back to ARP about injured pupil's progress/treatment

Letter to parents

Injured student goes home after treatment

Injured student returns to school after treatment

Figure 7: Suggested yellow accident procedures

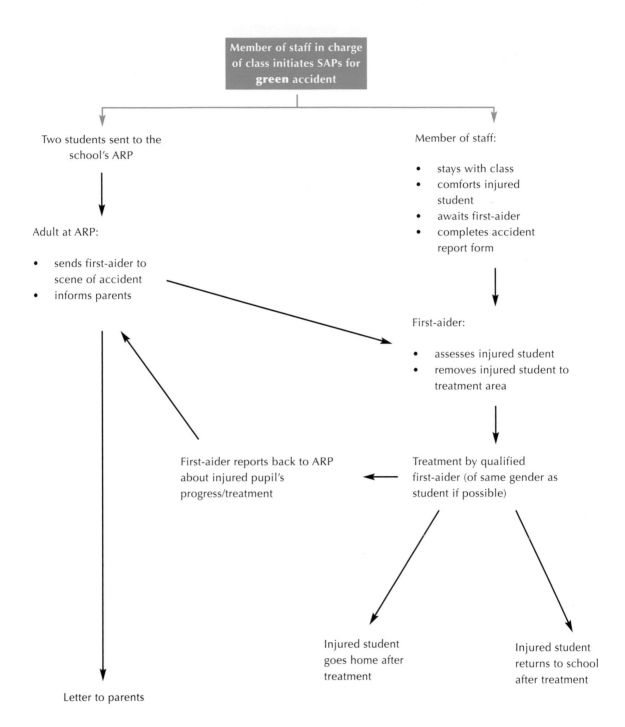

Member of staff in charge of class initiates SAPs for green accident

Two students sent to the school's ARP

Adult at ARP:

• sends first-aider to scene of accident
• informs parents

Member of staff:

• stays with class
• comforts injured student
• awaits first-aider
• completes accident report form

First-aider:

• assesses injured student
• removes injured student to treatment area

First-aider reports back to ARP about injured pupil's progress/treatment

Treatment by qualified first-aider (of same gender as student if possible)

Letter to parents

Injured student goes home after treatment

Injured student returns to school after treatment

Figure 8: Suggested green accident procedures

Case law

2.15.62   **Felgate versus Middlesex County Council (1994):**

While sitting on the lower of two horizontal bars in a gymnastics apparatus arrangement, a six-year-old girl lost her balance and fell off on to the mats located below, breaking her arm. The bar was set at a height of one metre. The parent alleged inadequate supervision. The teacher had been close by, attending to a boy who had climbed up a ladder on the same apparatus arrangement. In addition, the parent criticised the post-accident procedures at the school. The child had been sent to hospital before her parents were informed. The claim was dismissed. It was held that neither the teacher nor the method of supervision was negligent. The teacher had adopted a 'well recognised practice'.

With regard to the post-accident procedures, the judge stressed the importance of calling the ambulance immediately where skilled treatment is deemed necessary. He suggested: 'Children are happier if they have their mothers with them, but I think the presence of the mother before the ambulance is summoned is not nearly so important as the summoning of the ambulance.'

While this case recognises the action taken as necessary and correct, school procedures in respect of contacting parents, where possible, should still be adhered to as set out in this section.

© Tim Large/Shutterstock.com

Accident and incident reporting system

2.15.63   Most accidents that happen in schools or on school trips do not need to be formally reported under the Reporting of Injuries, Diseases and Dangerous Occurrences Regulations (RIDDOR) 2013 set out below. The school health and safety policy should explain its own required reporting procedures and responsibilities.

2.15.64   However, under RIDDOR, some must be reported to the HSE.

2.15.65   Those that come into this category for **employees** are work-related accidents (including those caused by physical violence) that result in:

- death or a specified injury (these include some fractures, injury leading to loss or reduction of sight, serious burns, any loss of consciousness caused by head injury or asphyxia)

- accidents that prevent the injured person from working or performing their normal work duties for more than seven consecutive days.

2.15.66   In addition, any work-related disease (specified under RIDDOR) that affects an employee and is confirmed by a doctor must be reported.

2.15.67   For **students and visitors**, accidents at school or on activity organised by the school are reportable if the accident results in:

- the death of a person, and arose out of or **in connection with a work activity**

or

- an injury that arose out of or in connection with a work activity where the person is taken directly to hospital for treatment.

2.15.68   **An accident would be deemed to be 'in connection with a work activity'** if caused by:

- a failure in the way a work activity was organised (eg poor or inadequate supervision)

- the way equipment or substances were used (eg the incorrect use of fitness room equipment, or use of swimming pool chemicals)

- the condition of the premises (eg potholes on a football pitch).

2.15.69   If the accident was attributed to one or more of these criteria, it would be reportable. Consequently, many common incidents in school playgrounds and during PESSPA lessons are not formally reportable.

 For more information about RIDDOR, see http://goo.gl/GCEw0y

Case law

2.15.70 **CMG (a minor) versus Rhondda Cynon Taf County Borough Council (2014):**

A primary school student injured her finger In a classroom lesson for which the local authority (LA) was responsible.

It was alleged that the teacher had told the group to sit on the floor behind a swivel chair on which another student was sitting. The student on the chair leaned over to pass some information to the other student seated behind him, and when he was doing this, the chair fell over, injuring the student sitting behind him.

It was alleged that the injured student had complained to the teacher that the student on the chair was deliberately making the chair collide with her. Negligence was alleged on the basis that the teacher was not paying sufficient attention to the student in the chair behaving mischievously, that the class was inadequately supervised, and that the teacher should have known there was a foreseeable risk of injury to students sitting on the floor behind a student on a swivel chair.

The LA denied liability, contending that the floor and chair were fit for their intended purpose, the class was sufficiently supervised, with one teacher for the 11 students in the class, and there was no record of any similar incident in the preceding 12 months before the accident. It was also claimed that the injured student had not complained of any injury at the end of the class or during the rest of the day, and the teacher had regarded the accident as so minor, it did not need to be recorded in the school's accident record book.

*The judge determined that the chair accidentally fell over when the student in it leaned over. The staff:student ratio was sufficient, and the teacher could not be criticised for deciding not to complete the accident record book as 'no real harm' had occurred. The judge also decided that the floor behind the chair was not a dangerous area for students to sit and that the **accident** had not been reasonably foreseeable. The judge held this was a pure accident with no one to blame. The claim was dismissed.*

2.15.71 The above case illustrates that completing an accident record log for a trivial incident is not always a requirement. The injured student not complaining about any injury during the rest of the day nor leaving school early reinforced that the injury was insignificant and therefore required no further action than the teacher had taken – **'trust your professional judgement'.**

Further guidance for schools on what, how, where and when to report is explained in HSE (2013) 'Incident reporting in schools (accidents, diseases and dangerous occurrences): Guidance for employers', http://goo.gl/OKPwYv

2.15.72 The school reporting procedures will also set out policies in relation to additional requirements that contribute to maintaining records of:

- accidents that result in the person being incapacitated **for more than three consecutive days;** these do not require reporting to the HSE, but do need recording

- other minor incidents, that do not fall into the other categories, but where reports and witness statements might help in any future complaint or claim; it is a requirement to keep statutory accident records for a minimum of three years, but it is recommended that schools store their records for a longer period as there are some cases when this information may be requested several years later

- first aid treatment given to students and staff, including details of treatment and after-care monitoring.

Case law

2.15.73 **Liddell versus City of York Council (2015):**

A 13-year-old student attending an extracurricular trampoline lesson alleged that, at the end of the lesson, while she was helping to dismantle the trampoline, she sustained a fractured arm after her arm became caught in the dismantled bars. She blamed the teacher supervising the dismantling of the trampoline, stating that some pupils, who were to catch the trampoline bars when it was dismantled, failed to catch them, and that other students, who did catch them, let them go. Her key allegation was that the teacher had instructed her to take the weight of the trampoline alone. In her witness statement, she said she knew she alone was to receive the end section of the trampoline during its dismantling. At trial, she changed this and claimed that she only became aware after her accident that she alone was to receive the end section. The teacher said she gave proper instructions and warnings to the pupils as to the correct dismantling of the trampoline.

The court dismissed the claim, finding the teacher to be 'conscientious and careful' regarding health and safety matters, and that the dismantling procedure would have been safe if the students had followed it according to training and instructions. The court said that the student would have been able to understand and follow those instructions.

2.15.74 The above case illustrates the importance of retaining records of accidents to students at school and of recording as much contemporaneous evidence as possible at the time of the accident. Where no particular complaint is made by or on behalf of the injured pupil at the time, as here, this does not necessarily indicate that a future claim is not possible. Here, the claim was made seven years after the accident due to C claiming she continued to suffer ongoing symptoms from the original accident.

2.15.75 It is also useful to record **'near misses'**, where an incident occurred, but injury was avoided. These, along with the incident report forms, can be analysed to establish whether any pattern exists to the causes of injury. This is a valuable exercise to carry out within department or staff meetings, and can help to inform future safe practice.

 An exemplar template for a school accident report form is included in Table 24, page 267.

 This exemplar template – which can be downloaded from www.pesafepractice.com – can supplement the employer's accident report form.

Table 24: Exemplar school accident report form

1 Accident Details		Date:	
Student's name:	Age: yrs mths	Sex:	Height in cm:
Student's home address:		Tel no.:	
Date and time of accident:		Class:	No. in class:
Member of staff in charge:		Other adults present in lesson:	
Type of lesson:		Unit no.:	Lesson no.:
Nature of injury:			
Location:			

In the space above, draw a plan of the location of the accident showing the position of:

- any apparatus, equipment or other people
- the student involved in the accident
- any adults present
- two witnesses.

Give approximate measurements to show the relative relationship of the people to the apparatus and to each other.

Other persons involved Names of any school staff sent to assist at the scene of the accident:	
Name of person who carried out emergency aid:	
Names of witnesses – indicate both **adults** and **students:**	
Statements obtained from witnesses: *(Circle appropriate response)*	Yes No
Name of person who contacted: • ambulance service: • student's parents:	

(continued)

2 Post-accident Procedures	Date:

Assessment of the nature of the injury determined that the student should be treated by:
(Circle appropriate response)

school only   hospital A&E department   student's doctor

Treatment at school

• Name of person who carried out treatment:

• Treatment details (brief):

Treatment at A&E department

• Approximate time between accident and arrival of ambulance:

• Name of paramedic (if possible):

• Who accompanied student to hospital?   Parent   Staff member   Responsible
  (Circle appropriate response)   adult

• If school staff, state name:

  – Did hospital ask member of staff to sanction   Yes   No
    any action or form of treatment prior to arrival
    of parents? *(Circle appropriate response)*

(The Children's Act places a duty on school staff to take the emergency action necessary to ensure the health, safety and well-being of children in their care).

  – If **Yes**, specify action or treatment:

• Approximate time parents arrived at hospital:

• Was student admitted to hospital following   Yes   No
  treatment in A&E? *(Circle appropriate response)*

• Did the student receive treatment for   Yes   No
  identified injuries at hospital?

(continued)

3 Follow-up Procedures	Date:

Completion of employer's accident report form

- Form completed by:

- Date forwarded to employer:

Compliance with the **Reporting of Injuries, Diseases and Dangerous Occurrences Regulations 2013 (RIDDOR)** requires that, for students and visitors in schools, only certain accidents need to be reported to the **HSE**. They are those accidents that result in:

- the death of a person, where the accident arose out of or **in connection with a work activity**

- an injury that arose out of or in connection with a work activity where the person was taken directly to hospital for treatment.

(For further information, see 2.15.63.)

Risk assessment

- Risk assessment of the lesson/session reviewed by:

- Date carried out:

- Was a change to procedures recommended?   Yes   No
  (Circle appropriate response)

- What was the nature of the change(s)?

- When and how were these changes implemented?

Contact with parents

- Who contacted parents to ascertain student's progress?

- How soon after the accident was contact made?

- Brief details of information received:

Student's return to school

- Date of return to school:

- Date of restart of physical education:

Any restrictions on student's involvement in physical education laid down by medical profession:

Form completed by:

Signed: Date:

Note: Schools may choose to attach additional information to this form (eg employer's accident report form, witness statements, risk assessment form covering activity, photocopy of register covering the four weeks prior to the accident).

Administering medication at school

2.15.76   School staff are not legally required to administer medication as part of their professional duties – this is a voluntary duty. Those who agree to do so should:

- have a clear understanding of their legal responsibilities

- be protected by an effective system of medication management

- be adequately trained to ensure they have the understanding, expertise and confidence required

- be familiar with normal precautions for avoiding infections

- be issued with written confirmation of insurance cover to provide specific medical support.

2.15.77   In an emergency situation, staff need to be prepared to fulfil their duty of care, but need do no more than is obviously necessary to relieve immediate distress or prevent further harm.

Supporting students with medical conditions

2.15.78   Employers should ensure that policies set out clearly how staff will be supported in carrying out their role to support students with medical conditions, and how this will be reviewed. This should specify how training needs are assessed, and how and by whom training will be provided.

 For information about supporting students with SEND and medical conditions, see Chapter 2, Section 14, page 233.

The use of Entonox in schools

2.15.79   Entonox is a medical analgesic gas that is a mixture of **50% nitrous oxide and 50% oxygen**. Its pain-relieving effect is strong, and it is very fast acting. However, it wears off very quickly. It is most commonly used in pre-hospital care, childbirth and emergency medicine by medical professionals such as doctors, nurses, midwives and paramedics. Entonox is known colloquially as 'gas and air'.

2.15.80   Schools that wish to make Entonox available for use by staff who have medical, nursing or first aid responsibilities should seek suitable training from the local ambulance trust, hospital anaesthetic department or resuscitation training officer, as well as from the manufacturer. However, most common uses of Entonox in school situations (eg moving injured casualties to an ambulance and changing large, painful dressings) are more suited to trained medical or nursing staff, and generally outside the capabilities, knowledge and duties of a trained first-aider.

2.15.81   Entonox should not be used for individuals with a range of conditions (eg bowel obstruction, pneumothorax [collapsed lung], middle ear or sinus disease) and those with reduced levels of consciousness, such as in sporting injuries.

2.15.82   The final decision about whether or not to administer Entonox in schools needs to be made by the employer. A risk assessment considering the benefits and risks of administering pain management in the scope of your school's typical PESSPA injuries would be an appropriate process in making this decision.

Concussion

2.15.83 Concussion is a minor traumatic brain injury that involves a sudden but short-lived loss of mental function. Concussion can occur after a blow or other injury to the head that involves the brain being shaken against the inside of the skull. Symptoms are often immediate but can be delayed for up to 48 hours. Concussion is known to have potential dangers both at the time of injury and in later life.

2.15.84 **All concussions need to be taken seriously** to safeguard the health and welfare of children and young people. Failing to do so can have serious consequences including, in extremely rare cases, death (Sport and Recreation Alliance [2015] 'Concussion guidelines for the education sector', http://goo.gl/07Grlo).

2.15.85 All staff should be aware that concussion could affect anyone, anywhere at any time. Play and PESSPA activities, and travelling to or from school may be occasions when staff may be more aware of such incidents.

2.15.86 Special attention should be paid to children who may have:

- experienced a fall in the playground

- fallen from heights on to hard surfaces or while cycling

- been involved in road traffic collisions either recently or in the past

- been or are involved in contact sports.

Second impact syndrome

2.15.87 Second impact syndrome (SIS) is a very rare condition in which a second concussion occurs before the first concussion has properly healed. SIS can result from even a very mild concussion that occurs minutes, hours, days or weeks after the initial concussion. SIS can cause rapid and severe brain swelling and is often fatal, even if the second injury was far less intense. Survivors of SIS are frequently left with disabling conditions.

2.15.88 Most cases of SIS have occurred in young people, who are thought to be particularly vulnerable. In order to prevent SIS, guidelines have been written (see references listed on page 274) to ensure that all young people who have sustained a concussion, either in PESSPA activities or other contexts, make a full recovery before returning to any activities in which a second concussion is likely to occur.

A case in point

2.15.89 **School rugby, 2011:**

A schoolboy died after suffering concussion during a school rugby match in County Antrim in January 2011. He was reported to have been involved in a number of 'heavy tackles' during the game before collapsing afterwards. The coroner explained that the death was as a result of 'second impact syndrome' arising from a blow causing swelling to the brain before it had fully recovered from an earlier injury.

Recognising, treating and managing concussion

2.15.90   Guidelines highlight the importance of **removing** the individual with suspected concussion from participation and ensuring that they **recover** fully and appropriately (eg over a period of weeks) and **return** to academic studies before taking part in PESSPA activities again. (See Table 25 below.)

Table 25: A summary of guidance on recognising, managing and treating concussion in PESSPA

Where any of the indicators in **bold type** are observed or reported:

*   obtain immediate qualified professional medical opinion (where available)

     or

*   transport by ambulance for urgent medical attention.

Signs to Look for	Symptoms to Ask about, and Older Students to Self-express Feelings about
• **Knocked out/loss of consciousness**	• Headache/**severe or increasing headache**
• **Seizure or convulsion**	• **Neck pain**
• General confusion/**increasing confusion or irritability**	• **Double vision or blurred vision**
• Vomiting/**repeated vomiting**	• **Weakness or tingling/burning in arms or legs**
• **Strange or inappropriate behaviour** (laughing, crying, getting angry easily)	• Dizziness
• **Deteriorating level of consciousness**	• Feels dazed/slowed down
• Slow to get up/lying motionless	• Feels 'dinged', 'stung', 'having my bell rung', 'in a fog'
• Poor coordination or balance/unsteady on feet	• Sees stars or flashing lights
• Grabbing or clutching head	• Feels pressure in head
• Does not know time, date, place, period of game, score, what the lesson is	• Ringing in ears
• Cannot remember things that happened before or after the injury	• Sleepiness
• Blank stare or glassy eyed	• Loss of vision
• Slurred speech	• Sensitivity to light
• Slow to answer questions or follow direction	• Sensitivity to noise
• Easily distracted	• Difficulty concentrating
• Poor concentration	• Stomach ache or stomach pain
• Not playing or participating as well as before the incident	• Nausea or sickness
	• Fatigue or low energy

(continued)

Protocols to be Followed in the Case of Concussion	Additional School Procedures
• **Recognise** the signs, symptoms and danger signs of potentially more serious brain injury • **Remove** immediately from further participation in the lesson, activity or match • Do not leave alone • Have them seen by a doctor/medical professional as soon as possible • If knocked out, immediately call an ambulance to take them to hospital • **Recover** – give time – avoid sports activity, running, cycling, swimming, fitness; minimum of 14 days' rest is advised unless cleared to return earlier by a doctor (parental responsibility to obtain this) • **Return** – student should return to academic studies before returning to physical activity; sometimes, symptoms may be prolonged • **Gradual return to participation** – if symptom-free following the recommended 14-day recovery phase a gradual return to activity should be implemented; for example: – short session of light walking or stationary cycling – activity-specific non-contact (including no heading in football) work – contact activities (once cleared by a doctor) – full activity/game participation Each phase should take a minimum of one day; if symptoms recur, then stop all activity for 1–2 days, recommencing at previous phase according to individual needs of student • **'When in doubt, sit them out'**	• Review and include in school policy/procedures • All staff to be aware of signs and symptoms • Consider school procedures for dealing with possible concussion in lessons, club activities and matches where a medical professional is not likely to be present • Keep parents informed: – of policy and procedures – any occurrences with their child It is a parental responsibility to obtain confirmation from a medical source that a student is fit to return to physical activity – verbal confirmation will suffice if a fee for a medical letter is involved • Teach students about the symptoms of concussion, and action to follow if feeling concussed or dazed • Make all relevant staff in other subjects or classes aware when a student has concussion so that this is taken into consideration in lessons, and any impact on studies noted and referred if necessary

Adapted from a collation produced by Peter Whitlam (2014) for use on afPE risk management courses. Sources:

- Concussion in Sport Group (2013) 'Pocket concussion recognition tool', http://goo.gl/U51yKm

- Department of Education Northern Ireland (DENI) (2014) 'Concussion', https://goo.gl/pL9Er8

- Forum on Concussion in Sport (England) (2014) 'Concussion guidelines for schools'

- McCrory, P. et al (2013) 'Consensus statement on concussion in sport', *British Journal of Sports Medicine*, 47: 250–258

- Parachute Canada (2014) 'Concussion toolkit', http://goo.gl/lRF1CJ

- Rugby Football Union (2013) 'Concussion – headcase', http://goo.gl/1CNZPx

- Scottish Government (2014) 'Sports concussion: If in doubt, sit them out', http://goo.gl/1BheaS

More guidance on concussion is available online for each home country:

England

Sport and Recreation Alliance (2015) 'Concussion guidelines for the education sector', http://goo.gl/07Grlo

Northern Ireland

DENI (2015) 'Concussion – Informing the school: Advice for parents', http://goo.gl/radn0o

Scotland

Scottish Government (2014) 'Sports concussion: If in doubt, sit them out', http://goo.gl/1BheaS

Wales

Welsh Government (2014) 'Concussion is dangerous: Welsh Government guidance on concussion for school and community sport up to age 19', http://goo.gl/v70cec

Students learning about concussion

2.15.91 Helping students to learn about the potential dangers of concussion, how to recognise the signs and how to take immediate and appropriate action if they suspect concussion is highly important.

For information about promoting student learning about concussion, see Chapter 3, Section 4, page 319.

Professional learning about concussion

2.15.92 Training is available through afPE (cpd@afPE.org.uk). Table 25, pages 272–273 is an integral part of this learning and collates information from a range of existing publications on the topic with additional information specific to school policy.

FAQ

2.15.93   **Do schools need to have a specific policy about concussion?**

If schools already have protocols and procedures **for head injuries** as part of their whole school first aid and emergency treatment policy, including guidance regarding concussion, a separate policy is not required. Subject leaders should check that this policy covers specific guidelines about concussion in PESSPA contexts. Where this is not the case, they can develop these as part of PESSPA policy and procedures using the information already provided in this section, and the suggestions listed below:

- ensure that the well-being and safety of students are paramount above all else
- understand that symptoms can be delayed for up to 48 hours, and recognise the need for monitoring anyone with possible concussion over that period
- apply the whole school policy at all times
- know how to recognise, assess and treat possible concussion injuries (a copy of the pocket concussion recognition tool for all staff would be helpful)
- understand what SIS is and how critical it is that such situations are avoided
- have their own knowledge and understanding about concussion assessed when they first enter school
- risk assess where such injuries may arise within their individual teaching, supervision or management contexts
- record any and all possible concussion occurrences within a whole school register of incidents
- ensure parents are made aware of any such situation their child has experienced
- be in a position to advise parents that recreational activities such as prolonged reading, television, computers, video games, smartphones, exercise and sport should be avoided until a gradual return to full health is achieved
- follow up post-incident, within established whole school procedures
- ensure that parents are aware that it is a parental responsibility to obtain confirmation from a recognised medical source that their child is fit to participate in a gradual return to full learning and activity sessions
- develop students' understanding about concussion, how it may occur, how it may be recognised, and what safe practice outcomes are essential to mitigate such an injury
- communicate with other staff who teach a student who has been diagnosed as being concussed so that this is taken into consideration in lessons, with any impact on studies noted and referred if necessary
- be aware that concussion will impact on academic learning and that adjustments need to be made during convalescence and a gradual return to full involvement in school activities, such as by applying a 'no homework' rule.

2.15.94   **Select from this list – and add to it where appropriate – according to the organisation of school and structure of your policies.**

2.15.95   **Adding the home country version of the concussion pamphlets is advised.**

Whitlam, P. (2014), created for use on afPE concussion awareness courses

Chapter 2/Section 16: Digital technology

Digital imagery

2.16.1   Schools should be clear about when and who can **photograph students** in school, and how images might be used to promote physical education, school sport and physical activity (PESSPA) using various online media.

2.16.2   The interpretation of the Data Protection Act 1998 by the Information Commissioner's Office clarifies that parents **can take photos or video** at schools events, as this personal data, processed by an individual and only for the purposes of that individual's personal, family or household's use, is exempt from the Act.

2.16.3   Similarly, events where there will be large groups of participants and/or spectators are deemed to take place in public areas, and as such, the permission of those in shot is not required. For example, a parent photographs or videos their child and some friends taking part in a school sports day for the family photo album or video archives. These images are for personal use, and the Data Protection Act does not apply: https://goo.gl/Zpht0L

2.16.4   However, due to safeguarding concerns and inappropriate use of child imagery, schools should have clear guidance for the filming and photographing of students, and for keeping parents informed regarding this.

2.16.5   Photographs taken for official schools use are generally covered by the Data Protection Act 1998, and for this reason, parents and students should be advised of why these pictures are being taken, and appropriate consent should be sought.

For more information on the Data Protection Act 1998, see http://goo.gl/L9JSiF

2.16.6   It is good practice to include relevant details on school admission forms, websites and the school prospectus to inform parents that digital imagery is used in education to support learning, and to reassure them that it will only be used in specific circumstances about which they will be advised. While implied consent can be assumed through such notification, many schools also seek to obtain such consent in written form. This written consent could be obtained on one occasion to cover the whole time the student is at the school, or could be obtained more regularly, such as annually. Even with such consent, it is still good practice to keep parents and students informed of events where photographs may be taken or videos made. Where an objection is raised, the school should do everything in its power to respect the instruction where possible.

2.16.7   A list of students who are not permitted to have their photo taken or be filmed should be made available to all staff for reference purposes.

 For further information see the Information Commissioner's Office (2016) 'Data sharing code of practice', https://goo.gl/5baJRG

2.16.8   The development of digital technology (eg digital cameras, electronic tablets, portable gaming devices with inbuilt cameras, mobile phones and analysis software programmes) has opened up an exciting and highly effective way of **enhancing learning in schools**. A great deal of visual learning currently takes place in PESSPA.

2.16.9   Digital photographs and video clips can provide students with clear images of performances and specific techniques, as well as immediate visual feedback about their own progress. New software enables this process to be managed easily during physical education lessons, school sport and off-site activities. The availability of specific sport, physical activity, fitness and exercise applications ('apps') can add to the variety of tools that staff and students can access on different devices within and outside a lesson.

2.16.10   Procedural and protocol issues (as set out above) need to be addressed to ensure that the producers of digital (and non-digital) images manage them effectively and securely. This is particularly important since images can now be transmitted and manipulated easily.

2.16.11   Great care should be taken to safeguard students when storing and using digital images in an educational context. An image policy should set out how this is to be achieved. Schools are free to produce their own policy, and the member of staff with responsibility as safeguarding officer would generally undertake this as part of their role, controlling the way images are used and stored at all times. Any member of staff using images in PESSPA must have them freely available for scrutiny and must store them securely in accordance with school policy.

2.16.12   Whenever new devices are introduced into schools, a risk assessment should take place in relation to their use. For example, where schools decide to issue electronic tablets to students, the foreseeable risks would need to be considered and mitigated as far as possible, including making decisions about whether the tablets can go home with students and what Internet sites the students can access.

2.16.13   All devices and equipment should be security marked and should be signed out and in when used by staff and students. This provides a record of who has been using each device.

2.16.14   Access to the images should be controlled by **authentication mechanisms** (eg password protection, with passwords being changed on a regular basis, and the use of encryption and access permissions).

Guidelines for filming

2.16.15   When filming or taking photographs in PESSPA sessions, it is recommended that:

- students know the purpose of the filming and have agreed to it

- parental consent is sought, if appropriate

- clutter-free backgrounds are used to focus students' attention on the specific performance issues

- care is taken over the angles chosen for filming, particularly in sensitive sporting situations (ie swimming, gymnastics, trampolining, some athletics events)

- profile shots of students (side on) are used – these are generally more informative and less prone to risk of misuse

- where possible, action shots rather than static pictures of individuals are used

- filming students on poolside is avoided (profile shots or in water are more appropriate)

- care is taken to ensure images cannot be misinterpreted – some specialist sports clothing (eg swimming costumes, close-fitting running wear) can create added risk.

2.16.16   Schools should consider whether staff and students may use mobile phones to video within lessons. Best practice would suggest that where this does happen, a policy regarding deleting the images is enforced. Measures to reduce concerns, such as a student only being videoed on their own phone, could be considered. Many schools now issue electronic tablets to students for this purpose. Where this is the case, similar codes of conduct should be established regarding removal or storage of the images when they have been used. All content used by students on their own phones should be monitored and checked by the relevant member of staff wherever possible.

2.16.17   **The publishing** of images refers to when they are distributed beyond a defined group via DVD, a website or other social media sites such as Facebook, Twitter, Instagram, Snapchat and many others. Publishing images has obvious associated risks, particularly for students in PESSPA environments. Many schools have websites for the physical education department, and use their sites to promote their activities. Staff responsible for operating these sites should receive relevant and regular training, and understand how to maintain safe operating procedures.

Guidelines for publishing

2.16.18   When publishing PESSPA images, it is recommended that:

- permission is obtained from the students (and parents where required) to use the image(s) as intended

- general-view shots are used to establish the theme

- shots held for a maximum of three seconds are used – this makes the clip very difficult to manipulate and reduces risks

- no individual names of students are attached to images; generic team names such as 'the under-15 football team' are acceptable alongside a whole or part team photograph as long as no individual names are included

- images show students suitably dressed, including wearing personal protective equipment (if appropriate)

- filmed interviews only show the head and shoulders of the students involved; students should not be identified by name (this includes voice-overs and text-overs)

- group shots are in wide vision.

2.16.19 It is not recommended for staff or students to publish video content to YouTube or other free Internet video-sharing sites. Although effective and far-reaching, these sites generally allow anyone to view them and can be difficult to monitor. It is best practice to upload content to secure sites that restrict viewers and operate an 'invite to view' only policy, such as DropBox.

2.16.20 Staff and students should be aware of the dangers of distributing any images via email or the large range of social media sites. This leads to a **loss of control** of the images by the user group.

 Further guidance on photographing and videoing children in sport is available from the Child Protection in Sport Unit at https://goo.gl/vm0D5P

 FAQ

2.16.21 **We are running a large school PESSPA event and want to adopt a correct and manageable approach to photography. What should we consider?**

In most cases, schools will already hold permissions or rejections for their students to be photographed or filmed, and should be able to inform the organisers of the event, which will avoid the need for the organisers to request duplicate information. As set out in the Data Protection Act 1998, parents attending the event are able to take photographs or video of their child when it is for personal use. Where official photographers are used for the event, a procedure should be agreed with the organisers. This could include issuing coloured bands or stickers to students without consent to be filmed, and ensuring that the photographer respects these. Both schools and organisers, however, will need to clarify to parents that at such large events, the possibility of a student being photographed without consent can, at times, be unavoidable. Where this happens, every step should be taken to prevent the picture being printed. Where pictures are printed, they should not include individual names, as set out above.

2.16.22 **At some sporting events, parents and other spectators are asked to register their intention to take photographs. Is this necessary/good practice?**

As outlined above, parents and spectators should be clear about the organiser's expectations regarding photography at events. It is seen as good practice for a register to be signed by those wishing to use photographic equipment, and for the organiser to issue stickers or badges so that others are aware of who has registered and may be prepared to question those who have not. Details concerning photography and video should be clearly printed in any pre-event information and event programmes, and could also be reinforced during pre-event briefings.

Storing material

2.16.23   Master photographic materials and digital photographs used in PESSPA should be stored in a secure environment since these are more readily manipulated if they fall into the wrong hands. Videos and still photographs are less of a risk since manipulation is more difficult.

2.16.24   In addition to having a manager to oversee the storage of digital images across the whole school, it is good practice to appoint a staff member from each department to regularly check and delete digital files that are no longer required.

2.16.25   A number of **examination boards** require DVD/digital evidence to be sent to them, labelled with the individual candidate's name and number. This is more difficult to monitor as each board will have its own safety protocols, outside the control of the school and the student concerned. In these circumstances, both the school and the examination board must ensure that all hard copies are returned within a set period of time, and that no duplicate copies are made. Examination boards have strict policies for dealing with this material, and schools must adhere to these.

2.16.26   Libraries of photographic materials should be managed with care. Unnecessary storage of material should be avoided. Materials should be stored in a locked cabinet and saved for a maximum of five years.

2.16.27   The reuse of DVDs that have not been erased can increase the risk of unwanted images being used inappropriately.

Mobile telephones

2.16.28   Staff using mobile telephones during lessons, training sessions or at competitions, for the purposes of either making or receiving calls, is not good practice. The primary responsibility of staff is the supervision and safety of students. Anything that compromises the staff member's ability to maintain a safe environment and give their full attention to the supervision and coaching of the students should be actively discouraged.

2.16.29   There are situations, however, where access to a mobile phone will make a positive contribution to the safety and welfare of students and staff, particularly when an emergency occurs. Using a mobile phone at sporting fixtures would be an example of this, where an emergency may require a rapid response. Schools should consider **providing mobile phones to all staff** taking part in extracurricular activity both on and off site. These phones should be kept topped up with credit and used as required for matters of safety or security, or for contacting parents. This practice removes the need for staff to feel that they must use a personal phone. Staff using their own phones to contact parents or pupils expose themselves to their personal mobile number and details being stored and shared without their consent.

2.16.30   Commercial systems are available for mobile phones whereby staff can contact parents collectively in the event of an emergency or change in published arrangements. While some cost is involved, such systems contribute to good practice in keeping parents informed about events, training, delays and other relevant information.

Email

2.16.31   There are occasions when a member of staff may email a student or reply to an email from a student for educational reasons, regarding homework or coursework, for example. This is acceptable as long as parents are aware of this practice, and a senior member of staff is always copied in to all communications as evidence of the correspondence. It is important that the school email is always used for this purpose, never a personal email.

2.16.32   Email communication may also be used as part of a disclosed list (having received prior permission from parents to disclose in a group email) where information in relation to training or competitions is disseminated. Sports clubs may also wish to use disclosed lists for sending club information via a designated and suitably trained adult. This person should also have been subject to appropriate selection and vetting processes.

2.16.33   Individuals should be given the opportunity to have their contact details removed from a group email list. This can be achieved by adding a statement at the end of every group email, such as: 'If you wish to be removed from this email list, please contact the administrator.'

The Internet

2.16.34   Students' use of the Internet is common in education and can be extremely beneficial to learning, whether accessed via mobile phones or other devices. There is debate about whether students should be self-regulated in their use of the Internet in schools. Many schools 'filter' access on school equipment. It is also possible to monitor Internet use.

2.16.35   Filtering and monitoring are carried out to ensure that students' use of the Internet remains relevant to the learning environment. However, such monitoring could be seen as an infringement of an individual's privacy. For this reason, schools should share with parents the intention, reasons and process whereby such monitoring might be carried out.

2.16.36   Use of the Internet in PESSPA for researching examination material should be carefully managed. Students should be advised to adhere to strict plagiarism policies, which, if compromised, could lead to copyright infringement. At the same time, staff who recommend specific applications or websites should always check their security certificates and safety, and ensure that students are not exposed to malware or viruses through their use.

2.16.37   Staff need to be fully aware of the school policy and protocols, and ensure requirements are followed in PESSPA situations. 'Acceptable use' policies for staff and students, and 'eSafety policies' should form part of the safeguarding suite of information provided, and positive eSafety messages should be promoted at all times. The latest DFE 'Keeping Children Safe in Education' 2016 document includes the directive that students must be safeguarded from potentially harmful and inappropriate online material (https://goo.gl/127V8n).

2.16.38   Where students use classroom-based **computers** in physical education, they should learn about, and take increasing responsibility for, implementing the standard health, safety and welfare protocols, such as:

- ensuring an adjustable sitting position, setting the eye level at mid-screen height

- taking regular short breaks to rest the eyes and loosen the body

- ensuring the keyboard is positioned appropriately in relation to the screen

- checking for loose wiring that could cause tripping incidents

- ensuring that bags and other items are placed away from the work area to prevent tripping incidents.

Social networking

2.16.39 Social networking sites are popular and commonly used by students, as well as adults. An approach needs to be taken by schools to balance their popularity with the possible adverse consequences, such as the potential for instantaneous circulation of mobile phone video clips taken in changing rooms while students are in a state of undress, or the tweeting of messages, often automatically, into the public domain. Several local safeguarding children boards (LSCBs) and governing bodies of sport provide advice on good practice.

2.16.40 Schools need to impose **strict protocols** about the use of social networking sites in any school context and include reference to this in the school's required code of conduct for staff and students. Staff must report any concerns within the school's safeguarding procedures.

2.16.41 Other than within the school's published protocols, staff should not communicate with students via social networking sites and, where such communication occurs, should include a third person (a member of staff) for monitoring and evidential purposes.

2.16.42 It is highly recommended that staff avoid allowing any student to be a 'named friend' unless the school protocols allow this via limited contexts, strict guidelines and parental approvals. In addition, staff should refrain from adding past students to their friends network. Past students will often be siblings of current students, and be connected to other students via different accounts. This can compromise both staff and students.

2.16.43 Staff should be aware of the increasing practice of **cyber-bullying**, which includes posting upsetting or defamatory remarks about an individual online, and name-calling or harassment using mobile phones. These may be general insults or prejudice-based bullying.

2.16.44 Cyber-bullies use their mobile phones and social network platforms to send sexist, homophobic or racist messages, or they attack other kinds of differences, such as physical or mental disability, cultural or religious background, appearance or socio-economic circumstances. In some cases, bullies may physically assault other students, post images of the bullying or fights online, or send recorded messages to other people.

2.16.45 **Fraping** has developed as another form of this practice, in which the perpetrator accesses another person's social media profile and sends messages as if from the owner.

2.16.46 In a PESSPA context, comments can be made in the changing areas and other sporting environments. Staff need to be alert to these types of incidents and be prepared to act quickly if they suspect any acts of cyber-bullying.

2.16.47 In some environments, these practices appear to be so commonplace that they have become 'normalised' and not viewed as bullying at all. Schools may wish to take opportunities to discuss these issues with students, such as during assemblies or student council meetings so that students recognise that such practices will not be tolerated and that sanctions are in place to deal with the perpetrators. Staff should be mindful of the signs that students are victims of these practices, looking out especially for isolated students or noticeable changes in behaviour. All types of cyber-bullying are wholly unacceptable, and where staff become aware of any aspect of them, they must inform the school leadership team immediately.

Closed-circuit television

2.16.48   The use of closed-circuit television (CCTV) for security has become fairly common in facilities that have shared community use. There is a statutory requirement for schools to inform the Information Commissioner (www.ico.gov.uk) if they wish to install CCTV, setting out clearly the purposes for which is it being used. Such notification has to take place on an annual basis, stating any changes in use.

2.16.49   Schools need to plan carefully whether and where these cameras should run during the school day. In areas where privacy would be expected, such as changing rooms, they should only be used in extreme circumstances, such as identifying reported bullying or vandalism. Good practice would include informing staff and students where this occurs, and clear signage should be used wherever CCTV is in operation. Under no circumstances should CCTV be placed where it could capture images of pupils changing.

2.16.50   It is important that images are viewed in a restricted area and only by staff authorised to do so. The member of staff responsible for this operation should be fully trained in the school's policy, and the Data Protection Act and code of practice.

2.16.51   Recordings should be retained and stored for as short a period as possible, dependent in some cases on the purpose of the filming. School policy should cover how this will be organised and reviewed, as well as being clear about allowing access to recordings by external agencies.

Biometric information

2.16.52   Schools must notify both parents of students under 18 if they wish to process students' **biometric information** to use as part of a biometric recognition system (eg fingerprint traits for authentication purposes when paying in the school canteen). As long as the student or parents do not object, the written consent of only one parent is required. Objections from students can be verbal; from parents, they must be written. Where neither parent can be notified (so consent cannot be obtained from either), Section 27 of the Protection of Freedoms Act 2012 sets out who should be notified and who can give consent: http://goo.gl/R0flSP

Electronic signatures

2.16.53   Some schools choose to communicate with parents by email and text to avoid postage and paper costs, and accept electronic signatures as consent for students to take part in fixtures, trips or events.

2.16.54   Schools considering or using this method of communication may make use of the following options:

- sending electronic notes out, and requesting handwritten letters with signatures back

- offering another level of security by responding to an electronic consent with a confirmation of receipt

- collecting parental consent once a year or once a term for all activities with the 'original' being handwritten; once this is obtained, any additional consent required could be accepted electronically.

2.16.55   Whatever policy and procedure is in place, it needs to be agreed by the school senior management and governors, and communicated clearly to all parties concerned.

Staff use of digital equipment

2.16.56   Staff using school equipment at home should remain vigilant to the guidelines and policies provided, to avoid compromising themselves and their school.

2.16.57   All schools should ensure laptops/tablets have security logins that are regularly changed, and that staff do not store personal data and images on their school laptop, tablet or phone. It is strongly recommended that staff do not allow their families or friends to access their school equipment in case this leads to inappropriate use.

2.16.58   Staff and students should 'lock-screen' their laptops or tablets when not in use and ensure their digital hardware is security code enabled to prevent 'Fraping' and other such 'non-consent'-based incidents from occurring.

2.16.59   The use of digital cameras/camcorders for filming and taking photographs by staff at home is particularly sensitive. If digital files are not deleted, images of a personal nature, including family trips and activities, can be viewed by students when they come to use the same equipment. For this reason, it is not recommended that staff use school equipment for any reason other than educational purposes for their school.

Sample consent form for the use of digital imagery in school

2.16.60   Digital imagery may be used in a number of school activities. The sample letter opposite does not specifically refer to PESSPA activities/situations and should be seen as a means of obtaining parental consent for the use of digital imagery in all school-related activities.

Further information for schools

CEOP Command

The National Crime Agency's CEOP Command (formerly the Child Exploitation and Online Protection Centre) works with child protection partners across the UK and overseas to identify the main threats to children both on and offline: http://goo.gl/O5Nqr7

E-Safety Mark

https://goo.gl/S2tukJ

South West Grid for Learning Online safety services

http://goo.gl/YhU8j4

Student Help Advice Reporting Page System

The Student Help Advice Reporting Page (SHARP) System, personalised to each school, is a web-based system that allows young people to report any incidents that occur within the school and local community anonymously: www.thesharpsystem.com

UK Safer Internet Centre

www.saferinternet.org.uk

Dear Parent

Digital imagery, both still photographs and video, are useful mediums within schools, which can motivate and inspire students. Although the associated risks are minimal, schools have a duty of care towards students.

The Data Protection Act 1998 does not prevent the taking of photographs for family purposes by parents and carers, nor the taking of photographs in public places. Within the meaning of this Act, the school does not prevent parents from taking photographs of their children in school events even though other children may be included within the scope of a photograph. However, we do expect parents to demonstrate sensitivity in the taking and use of such photographs.

We use digital imagery as a learning tool within school, such as in physical education or GCSE courses <amend as appropriate>. For this, the permission is required of you, as parent, and of the student(s) involved.

<school name> recognises the need to ensure the welfare and safety of all young people. In accordance with our safeguarding (child protection) policy, we will not permit photographs, videos or other images of students to be taken where the Data Protection Act applies without the consent of the parents and students involved.

<school name> has policies relating to the use of photographs and videos. Copies can be obtained from <named person>.

<school name> will take all necessary steps to ensure any images produced are used solely for the purposes for which they are intended. Photographs may be used in our printed publications for display around the school, as teaching resources within the curriculum and on the internal school website. Video clips may also be used as learning aids within the curriculum, and for staff training and educational purposes at both local and national level.

Student names will never be published alongside their photograph outside of the education setting. Names may be used internally on displays and award boards.

At no time will the images be sold or made available for wider publication without further parental approval.

Please complete, sign and return this form to <named person> at <school name>. The information on this form will be valid from the date of signing until <the school can choose to make this for the lifetime of the child in that setting or, for example, annually. However, it may be possible that images used for publicity purposes may remain in circulation beyond the student's time at the setting>.

This consent may be withdrawn at any time in writing to the school, although we cannot guarantee that images already in circulation can be removed.

Name of child: ....

Name of parent: ....

Address: ....

....

I consent to <school name> photographing and videoing my child as described above, and the associated terms.

Signature: ....

Date: ....

Queries regarding this form should be addressed to <school name and address>.

Figure 9: Sample consent form for the use of digital imagery in school

Chapter 2/Section 17: Transport

Preparation when considering transporting students

2.17.1   Staff taking groups off site should be **competent** in discipline, control, organisation and dealing with any crisis that may arise. They should ensure there is an effective **emergency contact system**, such as via a mobile phone or an alternative arrangement if a mobile phone is not available.

2.17.2   **Effective management** and control, particularly with younger students, are more easily achieved where large groups are subdivided into smaller groups with a designated adult responsible for each subgroup.

2.17.3   In readiness for transporting students, staff need to have considered plans for:

- deciding safe embarkation points

- deciding where staff will sit in the mode of transport in order to maintain adequate supervision and control

- deciding where students will sit, leaving the rearmost seats empty if possible in case a vehicle runs into the back of the bus, coach or minibus

- knowing the number of students on the vehicle and for counting them out of, and back on to, the vehicle after any break in the journey

- taking the emergency contact information of all students in the transport, and ensuring access at any time to information held back at school

- organising dismissal and dispersal of the group after the event, ie students should be dropped at the location the teacher has informed the parents of prior to the event; parents need to be made aware of arrangements for any additional drop-off points that may be requested and agreed

- the number of staff required for the journey – this is determined by the type of transport, group-management implications at the event, behaviour, discipline, disability, length of journey or driving requirements.

2.17.4   A **risk assessment** including transport arrangements to cover all regular activities (such as away fixtures, swimming lessons at external pools) should be carried out, as well as additional specific assessments for each special event involving travel.

2.17.5   Consideration of the school's **crisis management plan** (sometimes referred to as a critical incident plan or disaster plan) should be built into the risk assessment. In the very unlikely event of the transport in question being involved in a major road traffic accident, this will support individual members of staff unable to deal with the situation alone.

Parental consent in relation to transporting students

2.17.6   Parental **consent forms** are not required when students are transported off site for curriculum experiences during the school day. Schools are expected, however, to keep parents informed of where their child will be. Should a parent wish to contact the student in an emergency, the school would have details of how to reach them.

2.17.7   Written consent is usually only requested where:

- an activity during or outside school hours is considered to involve a higher level of risk, such as a long journey or an adventure activity

- the activity starts in curriculum time but extends beyond this

- the entire activity takes place outside of school hours.

 The DfE 'one-off' consent form is intended to cover all school trips and other off-site activities where parental consent is required: http://goo.gl/G5l3re

2.17.8   Where such forms are used, schools should still provide parents with comprehensive information about the nature of the visit, the activities to be undertaken and the transport arrangements.

2.17.9   Where it is the intention that students are transported in a vehicle belonging to another adult or in a taxi, it is recommended that parental consent is obtained. Such consent may also be sought for students being transported in a vehicle belonging to another student of adult age (this could be applied from age 17 and above, given the legal driving age). Parents should be asked to give consent in the knowledge that the adults providing the car have satisfied the conditions set by the school, such as that they:

- confirm they are willing to use their own vehicle for transporting students to and from inter-school fixtures and other sporting events

- accept responsibility for maintaining appropriate insurance cover, and have checked with their insurance company that students carried voluntarily are insured

- have a current clean, valid driving licence

- shall ensure the vehicle is roadworthy in all respects

- shall ensure that all passengers wear correctly fastened seat belts, and comply with the use of child seats and booster seats where required

- shall at no time transport a single student, other than their own child, as part of any journey (this does not apply to any 17/18/19-year-old student transporting their peers)

- agree to the terms and conditions outlined in this declaration and will operate within them

- have never been interviewed, cautioned or convicted of any offence that would render them unsuitable to work with young people

- shall at no time transport a student or students while the driver is under the influence of alcohol or drugs.

 For further information, see Parental consent – Chapter 2, Section 7, page 143.

Walking routes

2.17.10   Wherever possible, if movement off site involves walking, staff should check the route personally before embarking on the excursion so that it is **familiar** to them. Potentially hazardous points should be identified, and precautionary strategies known by all staff and, in an appropriate way, shared with the students.

2.17.11   **Ratios** of accompanying adults need to be calculated according to the students' age, safety awareness, behaviour, and familiarity with the route, and staff competence in relation to group management, knowledge of the group, familiarity with the route, and the distance and safety demands of the route.

2.17.12   Immediate **communication** with the school base should form part of the planning and organisation of the trip. Schools will also need to check with their employing authority in respect of any further requirements that would need to be adhered to.

2.17.13   If at any time staff judge that the route is unsafe for any reason, or has become unsafe over time (eg through shrub growth, weather conditions or increase in vehicles parking), they should consult the leadership team.

Pushing wheelchairs

2.17.14   There is **no legal age limit** for pushing a wheelchair. Employees who are trained in manual handling would cover pushing/pulling wheelchairs within this training. When transporting students in wheelchairs within and beyond the school, a risk assessment would need to be undertaken, taking the individual's circumstances into account.

 For more further information about who can push a wheelchair, see Chapter 2, Section 14, page 232.

Seat belts and child restraints

2.17.15   On school trips, the staff should consider their duty of care in taking all measures necessary to ensure that students are transported safely, that transport is in good condition, and that selected outside transport companies use fit and competent drivers. Where a **school arranges the transport**, it remains responsible for ensuring that the correct child restraints and seat belts are available.

2.17.16   While some vehicles may still not have seat belts fitted, schools have a responsibility, when sourcing transport for student use, to use reputable companies whose vehicles are fitted with seat belts.

2.17.17   By law, a **seat belt must be worn** in all vehicles where one is fitted. There are very few exceptions to this. The driver is legally responsible if a passenger under the age of 14 does not use a seat belt provided. Anyone 14 or over must wear a seat belt, but is responsible for doing so themselves. It is, however, expected that in accordance with their duty of care, staff will remind all students (including those over 14) of this requirement.

2.17.18   Children aged up to three years old must use a **'child restraint'** when travelling in the front or back seat of any **car** or van. At this age, this should take the form of a child seat. This also applies in a licensed **taxi or private hire vehicle** where child restraints are available. Where they are not available in a taxi, the child may travel in the rear seat unrestrained. Care should be taken to ensure that diagonal fitting seat belts, when used, do not present a danger to the head or neck of a small child.

2.17.19   Children aged 3–11 years and under 135cm tall must use an appropriate child restraint if available, and if not available, wear a seat belt. On reaching 135cm tall or their 12th birthday (whichever comes first), the student must wear a seat belt where fitted.

2.17.20   Schools using **staff and parents' cars** to transport students to matches and events will need to apply these requirements on the use of child restraints. It is the school's responsibility, on behalf of parents, to check that booster seats are provided and used. Seat belts must be worn.

2.17.21   Students must use an adult seat belt if the correct child restraint is not available:

• in a licensed taxi or private hire vehicle

• in a minibus

• for a short distance in an unexpected emergency

• where two occupied child restraints prevent the fitting of a third.

2.17.22   **Minibuses and coaches** used to carry three or more students on an organised school trip where the transport of children is central to the journey must have seat belts fitted.

2.17.23   The minimum requirement is for all children and young people between the ages of three and 16 years (but not including 16-year-olds) to be provided with a forward-facing seat with seat belt in minibuses or coaches used to take them on organised trips, including journeys to and from school or college.

2.17.24   The driver is responsible for ensuring that seat belts are worn by all passengers under 14 years during journeys. Passengers over the age of 14 are legally responsible for wearing a seat belt themselves, but staff are responsible for ensuring all students wear seat belts.

2.17.25   **Buses** are not required to have seat belts. (See 2.17.78 in this section.)

Additional information can also be found at:

• **Royal Society for the Prevention of Accidents (RoSPA): http://goo.gl/DCSX3i**

• **Outdoor Education Advisers' Panel (OEAP) National Guidance: http://goo.gl/YxOMzw**

Using private cars to transport students

2.17.26 **The employer's policy** should be checked in relation to the use of private cars to transport students. Local requirements vary considerably. Some employers do not allow it.

2.17.27 If using private cars to transport students, a clean driving licence is usually expected. Definitions of a **clean licence** may vary from one employer to another. Having some penalty points may be accepted as a clean licence, and staff need to check with their employer.

2.17.28 The car must be **roadworthy** and have a valid MOT if relevant.

2.17.29 Enquiries should be made about the **insurance procedures** required to use private cars for school business. School staff are advised to check whether the school's insurance covers the use of their personal car for school business, within and beyond the school day. In addition, they should contact their own insurers to let them know what they intend to do. In most cases, staff will be advised to add **business use** cover to their policies.

2.17.30 Staff working at academies, free schools and other eligible schools that are signed up to the government's risk protection arrangement (see Insurance, Chapter 2, Section 3, page 86) will find that this scheme does not cover staff intending to use their own or others' private cars on occasional 'business use.' Parents and volunteers must have fully comprehensive insurance and may add a business use clause in line with their insurer's requirements.

2.17.31 **Charging** is not allowed for the use of a private car to transport students.

2.17.32 Agreed procedures should ensure **no adult is ever alone** in a car with any child, other than their own in the case of parents transporting. Where a 'responsible adult' transports a student in an emergency, it is advised that, where possible, a second adult is in the car. This may not always be possible in emergency situations. (See Chapter 2, Section 15, page 258.) Appropriate **disclosure certification** should be obtained if applicable. This would usually arise if the driver is in **regulated activity**, ie is used to transport children on four or more days in any period of 30 days.

For more information about vetting and barring, see Chapter 2, Section 4, page 105.

2.17.33 The driver of the car **cannot drive and supervise** student passengers at the same time. For this reason, the behaviour of the students being transported should be taken into account. Where this is a concern, an adult in a supervisory role should also be in the car. All drivers should be equipped with a mobile phone for emergency contact, and be familiar with any emergency plans and procedures.

2.17.34 Staff, parents and volunteer drivers must be responsible for themselves and their passengers complying with all seat belt and car child restraint legislation. (See pages 288–289 in this section.)

2.17.35 Travelling **in convoy** is not recommended as it can divert a driver's attention. Drivers should know the route to their destination and not rely on following others.

2.17.36 It is recommended that parents give consent for their child to travel in **another adult's car**. (See Parental consent in relation to transporting students, page 287 in this section.)

2.17.37   Local requirements will apply as to whether **senior students** may use their own cars to transport their peers.

Using taxis to transport students

2.17.38   Taxis are increasingly used to transport small groups as a more cost-effective means than hiring coaches.

2.17.39   Staff should check the **employer's policy** to ensure that the use of taxis is allowed.

2.17.40   Checks to establish whether or not the taxi firm is **accredited** by the employer should be carried out. Some local authorities (LAs) maintain lists of approved firms that employ Disclosure and Barring Service (DBS)-checked drivers. If using a firm not on an approved list, schools will need to make their own arrangements with the firm in relation to DBS clearance.

2.17.41   Discussions with the taxi firm with regard to timings of arrivals and departures of taxis will help to inform decisions about how staff will supervise disembarkation and check student numbers.

2.17.42   The **risk assessment** should determine whether each taxi should have an adult supervisor or whether a student may be designated to carry a list of names, base contact details and details of procedures to be implemented in case of an accident or emergency during the journey.

2.17.43   **Seat belts**, where provided, must be worn. Taxi firms used regularly for transporting students may also provide child restraints. These should be used where required.

2.17.44   Parents should be informed and their **consent obtained** prior to children being transported by taxi.

Using minibuses to transport students

The minimum statutory requirements for operating minibuses

2.17.45   School minibuses are usually operated with what is called a **Section 19 or 'Standard' Permit** (a section 10b permit in Northern Ireland).

2.17.46   It is the school governors' responsibility, as the **operator** of the minibus, to apply for a Section 19 Standard Permit. To obtain such a permit, the minibus cannot be run with a view to making a profit. In other words, the minibus is used for voluntary purposes only, but a charge can be made to cover running costs, directly as a fare or indirectly as a general contribution to school.

2.17.47   Section 19 of the Transport Act 1985 allows non-profit-making organisations, such as schools, to make a charge to passengers for providing transport. Without this permit, the school would need to have a public service vehicle (PSV) operator's licence, and drivers would need a passenger-carrying vehicle (PCV) entitlement on their driving licence (a full category D addition).

2.17.48   If **no charge** is made for the use of the bus at all, then no permit is required. However, any payment that gives a person a right to be carried on a vehicle (the legal term for this is 'for hire or reward') would require the operator to hold either a Section 19 Standard Permit or PSV operator's licence.

2.17.49   Maintained schools, free schools and academies are considered non-commercial bodies, as are independent schools holding charitable status. They are considered to be using the minibus for social purposes, ie non-commercial activities. This includes school trips and travel to sporting fixtures within the school day or as an extracurricular activity.

2.17.50   Fee-paying schools that do not have charitable status may not be viewed as non-commercial bodies with automatic exemption from the need to hold a PSV operator's licence. They should take legal advice about their status regarding hire or reward and eligibility for permits.

2.17.51   The Section 19 Standard Permit must be **displayed** in the windscreen of the minibus.

 FAQ

2.17.52   **Who can drive the minibus?**

Drivers who passed their car test **before 1 January 1997** were automatically granted additional entitlement to drive minibuses with 9–16 passenger seats (**category D1**) not used for hire or reward. For as long as they hold a D1 (not for hire or reward) entitlement, these drivers may drive a 9–16-seater minibus of any weight used under a permit and may receive remuneration for this. Drivers with a D1 + E (not for hire or reward) entitlement can also tow a trailer over 750kg (0.75 tonnes).

Drivers who passed their test on or after 1 January 1997 are no longer granted a D1 (not for hire or reward) entitlement. However, they may still drive a 9–16-seat minibus under a standard permit, provided the conditions set out below are met.

Drivers of a minibus with a Section 19 Standard Permit must:

• be aged 21 or over

• have held a category B licence for at least two years

• be driving the minibus for a non-commercial body for social purposes

• receive no payment or consideration for driving the vehicle, other than out-of-pocket expenses.

For a driver without a **D1 licence**, the minibus weight **must not exceed 3500kg (3.5 tonnes)** or 4250kg (4.25) tonnes when including any specialised equipment for the carriage of disabled passengers. A trailer cannot be towed.

Thus, where the school offers the minibus to students for a charge, but on a non-profit basis under a Section 19 Standard Permit, the driver is exempt from the D1 requirement. This is because the Section 19 Standard Permit exempts the employer from holding a PSV operator's licence and exempts the driver from the D1 requirement, providing they receive no payment for driving the minibus, and they meet the criteria listed.

Additional conditions for driving a minibus

2.17.53 There is no national standard other than that set out in the Transport Act 1985. However, employers may make whatever additional conditions they wish as to who drives a minibus. Some employers choose to demand a D1 addition; others do not, but, as recommended by the Driver and Vehicle Standards Agency (DVSA), they may require some additional training, such as the Minibus Driver Awareness Scheme (MiDAS), RoSPA or local driving course/test (hence schools having their own minibus driving tests) for what is a 'small bus'.

2.17.54 Anyone who has obtained a **driving licence abroad** is not usually entitled to drive a vehicle with more than eight seats.

2.17.55 **Drivers applying for their first licence or to renew their licence on or after 19 January 2013**, where it includes category D1 (minibus) or D1E (minibus with a trailer), the licence issued will be valid for a **maximum of five years**.

2.17.56 Having been issued with a five-year licence, it must be renewed when it expires. For people who have already passed a driving test in one of the above categories, the new rules will apply when they next renew their driving licence.

Driving a minibus abroad

2.17.57 Driving a minibus under a Section 19 Standard Permit is acceptable **only within the UK**.

2.17.58 The governing body, as the operator of the minibus, should ensure that staff driving a minibus abroad meet the requirements set out in the latest **European Directive** (EU3D) (2006/126/EC) – which came into force on 19 January 2013.

2.17.59 The requirements of this regulation include the following:

- A specific **PCV licence** is required. Section 19 Standard Permits are not recognised abroad. The PCV licence will provide a D1 category on a licence obtained since 1 January 1997.

- Higher **medical criteria** are applied. For example, insulin-dependent diabetics cannot drive a minibus.

- The **tachograph** is to be completed and used. This is not a requirement in the UK. However, when the journey starts in the UK, the tachograph must be initiated in the UK – see Table 27, page 296.

- Familiarity with the driving requirements and regulations in the countries to be visited is required, including carrying the **safety equipment** specified by the countries to be visited (eg French law requires drivers to be able to produce an unused and in date approved breathalyser kit).

- Maximum **driving hours** and minimum rest requirements are imposed, which are more stringent than in the UK – see Table 27, page 296.

- Vehicle **documentation** must be carried at all times. For example, passenger lists are to be carried with the vehicle.

Management of the minibus

2.17.60   The Public Passenger Vehicles Act 1981 identifies **the operator** as the person for whom the driver drives the vehicle. If the driver is driving the minibus on authorised school business, then the operator who is responsible for the lawful use of the vehicle is the governing body, trustee, proprietor or LA, according to the type of school.

2.17.61   Best practice is where someone on the school staff has responsibility for ensuring maintenance, confirmation of roadworthiness, scheduling, record keeping and driver management are organised effectively.

2.17.62   The manager must ensure that regulations and responsibilities regarding positioning of seats, seat belts and child restraints are understood and applied by staff and students. (See page 289.)

2.17.63   Adequate **wheelchair passenger restraints** must be provided to enable wheelchair users to take advantage of, and travel safely on, minibuses. An occupied wheelchair must itself be held securely in position using a recognised wheelchair-securing system.

2.17.64   A driver cannot drive and supervise at the same time. It is **not a legal requirement that more than one adult accompanies a group on a minibus**, but the driver should not be distracted except on safety grounds. Where a risk assessment identifies that student needs or behaviour warrant additional supervision, a second adult (or more if required) should be present to fulfil the supervisory duty.

2.17.65   **Trailers** should not be used unless unobstructed access is provided at all times to at least two doors – one on the nearside and one on the offside. This is in case any incident causes the trailer load to slide forward and block the rear exit.

2.17.66   The yellow and black **'school bus' sign**, compulsory for home to school transport, is not a requirement for minibus use on other types of journey, but many schools choose to have it on display in the rear window as a warning notice to other traffic.

Minibus driver responsibilities

2.17.67   The driver is responsible for:
- the roadworthiness of the vehicle when it is on the road
- ensuring that the minibus is not overloaded and not carrying more passengers than allowed
- doing a risk assessment for the journey
- ensuring that all seat belts and child restraint regulations are adhered to (see 2.17.24)
- knowing how to adjust seat belts
- ensuring all passengers have their own seat – three children sharing two seats is not allowed, neither are standing passengers
- satisfying him/herself that passenger supervision is adequate
- ensuring luggage is securely stored with no obstructions on the floor between the seats or in front of any exit
- notifying the employer of any changes in their driving circumstances
- observing speed limits and other traffic controls – buses carrying eight passengers or more are now restricted to a maximum stabilised speed of 100kph (62mph), with lower speeds according to the type of road being travelled
- knowing the locations and use of the fire extinguisher and first aid kit
- driving with the doors unlocked and good visibility through all windows.

2.17.68   **Safe embarkation and disembarkation** are important. The location should be away from the roadside where possible. It is advisable for passenger loading to be allowed only by the side doors, and not the back doors where passenger safety may be compromised by passing traffic.

Safe driving hours

2.17.69   Driving is defined as being at the controls of a vehicle for the purposes of controlling its movement, whether it is moving or stationary with the engine running, even for a short period of time. Vehicle operators and drivers must assess the likely risk of suffering from fatigue, particularly on long journeys or **working days extended by additional activities**.

2.17.70   If a driver is going to drive for more than four hours in any one day, then they must comply with British domestic **rules for driver hours** if operating solely within the UK, and with EU rules if operating in any other EU country.

2.17.71   If they drive for more than **four hours** for up to **two days in any week**, they are exempt from the British domestic rules, **but** on these two days:

- all working duties must start and finish within a 24-hour period

- a 10-hour period of rest must be taken immediately before the first duty and immediately after the last duty

- rules on driving times and length of working day must be obeyed.

2.17.72   If any working day overlaps into a week in which drivers are not exempt from the rules, the limits on driving time and length of working day must be obeyed on that day.

2.17.73   An exemption from the rules on driving time and rest applies during any time spent dealing with an emergency.

Table 26: Domestic driving limits

Daily driving	10 hours on any working day.
Cumulative or continuous driving	5½ hours – after this, a break of at least 30 minutes must be taken in which the driver is able to obtain rest and refreshment; or 8½ hours' driving, as long as breaks from driving totalling at least 45 minutes are taken during the driving period so that the driver does not drive for more than seven hours and 45 minutes. In addition, the driver must have a break of at least 30 minutes to obtain rest and refreshment.
Length of working day	No more than 16 hours between the time of work starting and finishing work (including work other than driving and off-duty periods during the working day).
Daily rest periods	10 hours continuously must be taken between two working days; this can be reduced to 8½ hours up to three times a week.
Fortnightly rest periods	In any two weeks in a row (Monday–Sunday), there must be at least one period of 24 hours off.

European travel and tachographs

2.17.74   In the EU as a whole, the requirement to fit a tachograph applies to all vehicles with 10 or more seats, including the driver. However, the UK has made use of a national derogation from these regulations so that minibuses with 17 seats and under (including the driver) are exempt from the requirement to fit and use a tachograph within the UK.

2.17.75   When taking a minibus with 10 or more seats abroad, the EU driver hours and tachograph rules will apply from the start of the journey in the UK until the final destination.

2.17.76   Under EU rules, any tour that starts or finishes in an EU member state is subject to EU regulations. Other tours between UK and non-EU countries are subject to EU or European Agreement Concerning the Work of Crew of Vehicles Engaged in International Road Transport (AETR) rules. If travelling to a non-EU country, check which rules apply. A record of hours driven must be kept, and all vehicles with nine or more seats (excluding the driver) must have a tachograph, as explained in leaflet PSV 375.

Table 27: EU drivers' hours

Maximum daily driving	Nine hours, extendable to 10 hours on two days in the driving week.
Maximum weekly driving	Maximum of 56 hours.
Maximum fortnightly driving	90 hours.
Maximum driving before a break	4½ hours.
Minimum breaks after driving	45 minutes or other breaks of at least 15 minutes each.
Minimum daily rest	11 hours, reducible to nine hours three times a week; compensation must be given before the end of the following week; alternatively, 12 hours if split into two or three periods (one of which must provide at least nine hours of continuous rest).

Adapted from DVSA (2015) 'Drivers' hours and tachograph rules: buses and coaches (PSV375)', https://goo.gl/bs8ySS

Further information regarding operating a minibus:

HM Government (2015) 'Driving a minibus', https://goo.gl/eAf94Q

HM Government (2013) 'Driving school minibuses: Advice for schools and local authorities', https://goo.gl/bo7vMz

OEAP (2014) 'Transport in minibuses', http://goo.gl/iTZrJJ

Minibus Website: http://goo.gl/rzGYXX

Using buses and coaches to transport students

2.17.77   Where schools use buses or coaches, it is good practice to use a **reputable transport company**. Many schools and LAs maintain an approved list of companies.

2.17.78 **Coaches** are fitted with seat belts, and staff must ensure that students of all ages use them on all journeys. **Buses** are not required to have seat belts, and staff should therefore seriously consider whether buses should be used to transport students involved in physical education, school sport and physical activity (PESSPA) activities.

2.17.79 **Supervision levels** need to be considered according to the students involved, the journey, and any breaks in the journey. The adults should be positioned through the coach so that they can observe all students.

2.17.80 **Evacuation procedures** need to be known by all before departure. When disembarking, it is good practice for the adults to disembark first to direct students to an assembly point away from the roadside or in the car-park area.

Case law

2.17.81 **R versus Unwin (2011):**

*A coach driver was late to collect a school group from an outdoor activities centre. To make up time on the return journey, he took a short cut that was wholly unsuitable. The teachers complained, and one student received whiplash injuries. The driver had 12 points on his licence already for speeding and driving while using a mobile phone but had been spared a ban. He was found guilty of dangerous driving and given a 12-month 'alternative to custody' order and banned from driving for 14 months. He was sacked from the coach company the day after the incident. There was no reported indication that the coach company was disreputable, but this case emphasises the importance of **checking the standards of coach companies**. It would usually be sufficient to use a coach company with which the school is familiar and one that has a good timekeeping record, along with evidence of good, considerate drivers and well-maintained coaches.*

Using public transport to transport students

2.17.82 Schools should establish a **code of conduct** for students who use public transport for PESSPA events, to ensure group interaction with the public is of an acceptable standard.

See Codes of conduct, Chapter 2, Section 7, page 146.

2.17.83 Some schools choose not to provide transport to off-site events and leave students' transport arrangements to parents. Where the event is within school time, the school, under its duty of care, may still be seen as responsible for any accident that occurs if the parent contests that the school failed to provide transport, and as a result, the parent had to make alternative arrangements to allow the student to take part.

2.17.84 This position could also be taken where parents are asked to arrange transport to an event outside school time, when it is felt that the student had little option not to attend. These scenarios have not yet been contested in law, but schools should be mindful of their position, and maintain clear and informative communication with parents regarding their ability to transport students, and about when responsibility is understood and agreed to have been transferred.

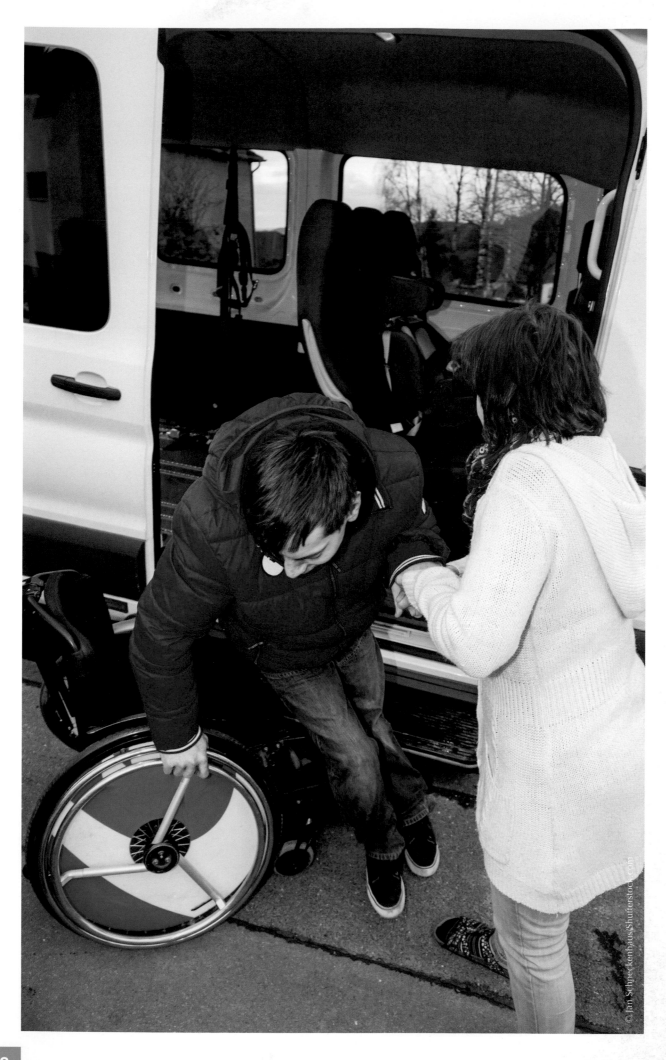

3 Teaching safety – promoting effective learning

What is this chapter about?

This chapter focuses on the importance of promoting relevant and effective student learning about risk management and keeping safe in and through the context of physical education, school sport and physical activity (PESSPA). Examples of objectives, outcomes and tasks are provided to support students' learning in the areas listed here:

Section 1: Introduction – promoting effective learning about safety
Section 2: Learning about Safeguarding
Section 3: Learning about Assessing and managing risk
Section 4: Learning about First aid
Section 5: Learning about Exercise safe practice
Section 6: Learning about safe practice in relation to Space
Section 7: Learning about safe practice in relation to Tasks
Section 8: Learning about safe practice in relation to Equipment
Section 9: Learning about safe practice in relation to People

How can you make effective use of this chapter?

This chapter supports the strategic planning of 'teaching safety' within schools. The sections highlight aspects of learning that are relevant to PESSPA. Teachers can select and prioritise learning objectives and outcomes that are most relevant to the needs and stages of development of their students, and that complement and build on similar learning embedded in other parts of their curriculum. The learning tasks and links with other sources of information and resources provide examples of how this learning can be made explicit, well informed, progressive, inclusive, relevant, interesting, fun and, wherever possible, practical.

Chapter 3/Section 1: Introduction – promoting effective learning about safety

The importance of learning about safety

3.1.1   Accidents account for a large number of preventable deaths and serious injuries to children and young people. This may be partly due to their lack of experience in managing risk. However, it is also being increasingly attributed to low impulse control, particularly in their teens, which is thought to be caused by the continuing development of the frontal cortex of the brain associated with decision making, insight, judgement and inhibitory control – Packard, A. (2007) 'That teenage feeling', *Monitor Staff*, 38 (4): 20.

3.1.2   It follows that learning about safety is important for all students because their appreciation of risk is not fully developed, which might contribute to their vulnerability in terms of accidents.

3.1.3   In addition, there is a need for students to develop the necessary skill and competence to assess and manage risks associated with their personal participation in physical education, school sport and physical activity (PESSPA) activities as part of a healthy active lifestyle.

3.1.4   There is strong agreement among prominent organisations about the importance of promoting effective learning about safety in schools – Institute of Health Promotion and Education (IHPE); Royal Society for the Prevention of Accidents (RoSPA); Personal, Social and Health Education (PSHE) Association; and Ofsted. Furthermore, many of these organisations largely agree that all schools have a responsibility to make **'teaching safety'** a central part of the whole-school agenda.

Guidance for learning about safety

3.1.5   National curriculum statutory requirements would seem a likely source of guidance for informing how schools plan for learning about safety. Indeed, learning about safety is a strong feature of:

- the **Northern Ireland Curriculum** – Council for the Curriculum, Examinations and Assessment (CCEA) (2016) 'Curriculum', http://goo.gl/xRhlGm – as a statutory component of the area of learning: Personal Development and Mutual Understanding from Foundation to Key Stage 4

- Scotland's Curriculum for Excellence – Education Scotland (2016) 'Health and wellbeing', http://goo.gl/l7sGsH

- the National Curriculum for Wales – Department for Children, Education and Life-long Learning Skills (2008) 'Personal and social education framework for 7 to 19-year-olds in Wales', http://goo.gl/tZXt1N

3.1.6   The National Curriculum for England (2014) refers only to the importance of 'water **safety**' and 'using technology **safely**'. However, the importance of learning about safety is implied in other parts of the statutory framework, which states that the school curriculum should prepare students for the opportunities, responsibilities and experiences of later life. The requirement is that all schools should make provision for PSHE. Learning about safety is an important element of PSHE. In the absence of national guidance, the PSHE Association has compiled its own programme of study (PoS), which outlines what students should learn about:

- managing risks to physical and emotional health and well-being

- keeping physically and emotionally safe

- responding appropriately in an emergency.

3.1.7   The documentation and reports of the schools inspectorate also provides useful guidance:

*The vast majority of children are developing a very good understanding of how to keep themselves safe and manage risks. They **demonstrate exceptionally positive behaviour and high levels of self-control, cooperation and respect for others.***

*Pupils are safe and feel safe at all times. They **understand how to keep themselves and others safe in different situations and settings.***

Ofsted (2015) 'School inspection handbook: Handbook for inspecting schools in England under section 5 of the Education Act 2005', https://goo.gl/NYPspV

Keeping children safe and providing learners with appropriate knowledge and personal resilience skills to cope with risks in the real and virtual worlds remains a key priority for the departments and the education and training organisations.

Education and Training Inspectorate (2014) 'Chief Inspector's report 2012–14', http://goo.gl/ur1AlG

3.1.8   afPE's poster **'The Difference PE & School Sport Makes to Whole School Improvement'** reinforces the importance of personal development, behaviour and welfare as factors that contribute to high achievement in schools: http://goo.gl/7aij5V

Planning effective learning about safety

3.1.9   The general consensus is that learning about safety should take place through active involvement in risk assessment and risk management situations that are appropriate for the developmental capacity of the students. This is considered to be key to independent involvement in lifelong physical activity.

It is important that children learn to understand and manage the risks that are a normal part of life.

Department for Education (DfE) (2014) 'Health and safety: advice on legal duties and powers – For local authorities, school leaders, school staff and governing bodies', https://goo.gl/cH1ewj

3.1.10   In an appropriate way and from the earliest age in school, the youngest students should:

- be encouraged to look around them to identify whether they perceive anything that could harm them

- consider whether specific situations are safe and what considerations need to be made to make them safer

- play a role in organising learning contexts, albeit closely monitored by the teacher, to ensure that the necessary safety considerations have been addressed.

3.1.11   Ultimately, older students should be able to plan and manage their own physical activities in safe contexts. In a school situation, these would be at least remotely supervised rather than truly independent because of the continuing duty of care.

3.1.12   All students should learn about safety across the school curriculum and beyond. In addition to physical education, the sciences, food technology and PSHE can also contribute to students' understanding of this important area of learning. Wherever learning is promoted, effectiveness is increased when the member of staff, as facilitator, adopts enabling, learner-centred strategies that make thinking important and explicit.

3.1. 13   'Active learning environments' should be used, providing opportunities for students to take ownership of the learning process and learn through doing in order to work towards increasing independence.

3.1.14   Learning about safety should have a clear learning goal (see Figure 10) that focuses on students 'feeling empowered' to make informed and positive decisions about keeping themselves and others safe. Figure 10 summarises how promoting effective learning about safety is about engaging with 'appropriate content' in an 'appropriate context' and through 'empowering pedagogy'.

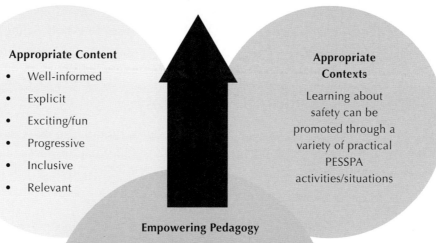

Goal for learning about safety in PESSPA:

Students feeling **empowered** to make well-informed, responsible and timely decisions to ensure their own and others' safety in the context of PESSPA activities and situations

Appropriate Content
- Well-informed
- Explicit
- Exciting/fun
- Progressive
- Inclusive
- Relevant

Appropriate Contexts

Learning about safety can be promoted through a variety of practical PESSPA activities/situations

Empowering Pedagogy
- Personalised, enabling, collaborative
- Facilitates informed decision making
- Enables and promotes the development of intrapersonal skills
- Uses active learning strategies (eg makes thinking important and explicit, promotes independent learning, encourages making connections, uses effective questioning, promotes collaborative learning)

Figure 10: Planning for learning about safety in PESSPA

3.1.15   It is essential that learning about safety is made **explicit**. In other words, learning needs to be planned, progressed and assessed in the same way as other aspects of curriculum learning. This chapter includes a range of examples of clear and specific learning objectives ('students are learning to:') and learning outcomes ('students will be able to:') to support effective learning about safety in PESSPA in schools. (See Tables 28–35, pages 305–350.)

3.1.16   The outcomes are organised to suggest how learning might **progress** in relation to each learning objective. Staff can decide which objectives and outcomes are the most relevant and appropriate for their students, and how to integrate and progress this learning within and beyond PESSPA. Students' prior learning about safety across the curriculum should be taken into consideration.

3.1.17   It follows that promoting effective learning about safety will involve helping students not only to understand why this learning is important but also how it can directly and personally benefit their lives.

3.1.18   It has been suggested that 'needing to' and 'wanting to' are essential factors underpinning successful learning (Race, P. [2014] *Making Learning Happen*. 3rd edition. London: Sage. ISBN: 978-1-446285-96-1). Ensuring that all students 'want to learn' about safety is challenging and complex, and will involve making the learning really **relevant** to each student so that they:

- understand why learning about safety is important and essential for their health and well-being

- develop the intrapersonal skills (eg decision-making skills, resilience, communication skills) to feel empowered to make decisions about their own and others' safety.

3.1.19   Learning about safety needs to be **well informed**, and expose students to consistent messages about risk assessment and risk management that are based on high quality health and safety guidance.

3.1.20   It can be helpful for PESSPA staff and students to have an easily remembered acronym as a reminder of important principles. **SAFE STEP** has been developed to embrace the important areas of learning about safety in the context of PESSPA:

- **S**afeguarding

- **A**ssessing and managing risk

- **F**irst aid and accident procedures

- **E**xercise safe practice

- **S**pace

- **T**asks

- **E**quipment

- **P**eople.

3.1.21   Tables 28–35 suggest examples of learning objectives, learning outcomes and learning tasks associated with each heading.

Chapter 3/Section 2 Learning about Safeguarding

3.2.1   In the context of **safeguarding**, students should learn about both **being safe** and **feeling safe** in physical education, school sport and physical activity(PESSPA) sessions and situations. In this section, the focus will be on students learning about **feeling safe**. Learning associated with **being safe** is predominantly covered in other sections of this chapter. Examples of learning objectives associated with **being safe** include students learning to:

- conduct their own risk assessments prior to participating in PESSPA sessions and situations (assessing and managing risk – **Chapter 3, Section 2, page 305**, and **Chapter 3, Section 3, page 311**)

- develop and maintain correct alignment of joints in their own and others' exercise technique (exercise safe practice – **Chapter 3, Section 5, page 320**)

- be vigilant and alert to what is going on around them when in a PESSPA session/situation (space – **Chapter 3, Section 6, page 331**)

- make safe and effective progress when learning new skills and techniques (task – **Chapter 3, Section 7, page 333**)

- lift, move and place equipment safely and effectively (equipment – **Chapter 3, Section 8, page 341**)

- take increasing responsibility for others' safety by responding appropriately to their peers (people – **Chapter 3, Section 9, page 347**).

Table 28: Learning about Safeguarding

Examples of Learning Objectives	Examples of Learning Tasks	Examples of Learning Outcomes
Students are learning to: • understand what it means to 'feel safe' in PESSPA and about the role that they and staff can play in achieving this • develop a proactive and responsible approach to 'feeling safe' in PESSPA situations.	Students can participate in a range of practical PESSPA activities/situations, after which they link their experiences to positive words/vocabulary associated with 'feeling safe in PESSPA' (eg happy, comfortable, warm, protected, included, important, being with others). PESSPA staff can help students to understand that they all have the right to 'feel safe' in all PESSPA sessions/situations (eg physical education lessons, at playtime, in clubs). Students select one or more 'feeling safe in PESSPA' words (eg happy, comfortable, warm, protected, included, important) and monitor how they feel during PESSPA lessons, clubs and/or playtime (eg using a simple scale or RAG rating as a monitoring tool). Students explain their findings (eg 'What made me feel really safe? What made me feel less safe? What might have made me feel safer? What do I need to do if I do not "feel safe in PESSPA"?'). Students decide sensible rules to help a wide range of age groups feel safe at playtime (eg be aware of others, keep to designated areas, listen to play leaders, try to include others apart from your friends). Students discuss the following scenarios in relation to the questions 'Would you feel safe if: • you were playing tag in the same area as much younger/older students	Students will be able to: • identify words associated with 'feeling safe in PESSPA' sessions/situations • explain what 'feeling safe in PESSPA' means • explain why it is good to 'feel safe' and why it is not good to feel 'unsafe' in PESSPA • give simple examples of what helps them to feel safe in PESSPA sessions/situations • explain how they can help younger students to feel safe in a play situation • give simple examples of what might make them feel less safe in PESSPA sessions/situations • recognise and name the adults and play leaders who keep them safe in PESSPA sessions/situations and at playtime • explain when and who they should ask for help if they feel unsafe in PESSPA or at playtime • demonstrate that they can find and ask for help quickly from adults whose job it is to keep them safe in PESSPA or at playtime • explain ways in which the adults working with them in PESSPA can make them feel safe • suggest appropriate role expectations of adults working with them in relation to helping them to 'feel safe in PESSPA' • explain in what situations it is inappropriate for staff to participate fully with students in PESSPA • describe what would be considered violent or reckless play in PESSPA

(continued)

Examples of Learning Objectives	Examples of Learning Tasks	Examples of Learning Outcomes
See previous page.	• there was nowhere to play quieter/less active games at playtime • the playground was very crowded?' Students meet and take part in some practical activities with the adults whose job it is to keep them safe in PESSPA (eg in the playground, in physical education lessons, in a club). Ask students: • How do the adults make sure that you 'feel safe' in PESSPA? • What can you do if you do not 'feel safe'? Students discuss why it is inappropriate for staff to compete with students in specific sports (eg a staff versus students netball or football match). Discuss: • what is meant by violent or reckless play in PESSPA • how violent or reckless play might impact on safety • possible reasons why violent or reckless play might arise in PESSPA sessions/situations • how rules and officials might prevent and/or stop violent or reckless play • how to respond positively in PESSPA sessions/situations where violent or reckless play occurs.	• explain positive ways of responding to situations where violent or reckless play occurs • explain how, when and to whom they should report any situations/examples in which they feel threatened or intimidated as a result of violent or reckless play in PESSPA.

(continued)

SAFE STEP

Examples of Learning Objectives	Examples of Learning Tasks	Examples of Learning Outcomes
Students are learning to feel safe and make others feel safe in relation to the use of manual support and 'spotting' in PESSPA activities.	Students develop a practical understanding of: • the positive outcomes of manual support in specific PESSPA activities (ie feeling safe while learning more challenging skills) • appropriate and safe ways to give and receive manual support in specific PESSPA activities (eg in gymnastic balances/vaults, in lifting and weight-bearing activities in dance). Students discuss how 'safe' and 'comfortable' they might feel in PESSPA if: • the teacher explains and demonstrates exactly how and why manual correction will be given • students can choose whether to accept or refuse manual correction either from the teacher or their peers • manual support is given without explanation or permission • students agree to manual support but do not feel comfortable when it is given. Students develop a practical understanding of: • the positive outcomes of 'spotting' in specific PESSPA situations (ie feeling safe while learning more challenging skills) • appropriate and safe ways to take on spotting roles in specific PESSPA activities (eg in trampolining, weight training and vaulting).	Students will be able to: • describe PESSPA situations in which they might need manual support (eg learning difficult balances, jumping from a height) • describe accurately how PESSPA staff should explain manual support before it is used • explain why it is important for PESSPA staff to explain, demonstrate and ask permission before giving manual support • explain the benefits of receiving manual support in specific PESSPA activities • explain what action they should take if they do not feel comfortable with receiving any manual support in PESSPA • provide effective manual support to their peers under the guidance of PESSPA staff • explain the benefits of 'spotting' in specific PESSPA activities • show that they can be reliable and effective in fulfilling a spotting role under the guidance of PESSPA staff.

(continued)

Examples of Learning Objectives	Examples of Learning Tasks	Examples of Learning Outcomes
Students are learning to:	Students rehearse saying 'yes' or 'no' at appropriate times through play-based learning or practical PESSPA-related scenarios.	Students will be able to:
• develop strategies to resist pressure in PESSPA situations to do something dangerous, that makes them uncomfortable or that they believe to be wrong	Students discuss why people sometimes do things that their friends have persuaded them to do, even if they know they are wrong.	• describe simple ways to resist pressure from their friends to do unsafe things or things that they feel are wrong (eg say 'no', say why it is unsafe or wrong, tell an adult)
• understand the dangers of specific situations and behaviours in PESSPA	Students evaluate the extent to which specific PESSPA situations are dangerous, unhealthy or would make them or others feel uncomfortable or vulnerable because they believe them to be wrong.	• accurately identify PESSPA activities/situations that are dangerous, unhealthy, or would make them or others feel uncomfortable or vulnerable because they believe them to be wrong
• decide appropriate action to take to avoid or remove themselves if PESSPA situations/activities make them uncomfortable or vulnerable.	Students discuss the procedure for disclosing information to another adult in the context of PESSPA, and the process that will follow after disclosing information to an adult.	• distinguish between negative and positive peer pressure
	Students discuss the following scenarios in relation to the questions '**Should** you feel safe if:	• suggest a range of strategies for resisting pressure in PESSPA sessions to do something dangerous, unhealthy, that makes them uncomfortable or anxious, or that they believe to be wrong
	• you are asked to travel alone to a PESSPA event with an adult other than your own family	
	• staff do not allow you to wear sufficient warm clothing for outside PESSPA activities in very cold conditions	
	• you do not feel comfortable about receiving manual support from a member of PESSPA staff (eg in gymnastics)	
	• you are being bullied in a PESSPA situation (eg players "ganging up" on you on the pitch)?'	

(continued)

Examples of Learning Objectives	Examples of Learning Tasks	Examples of Learning Outcomes
See previous page.	Students discuss the possible sources of pressure to behave in an unacceptable, unhealthy or risky way (eg from peers and the media).	See previous page.
	Students discuss strategies for ensuring that peer approval does not lead to them adopting behaviours that may impact negatively on their safety (eg overtraining, being sedentary).	
	Students research the dangers of:	
	• taking performance-enhancing drugs and supplements	
	• overtraining.	
	Students discuss their thoughts and opinions about what motivates young people in PESSPA to adopt these behaviours.	
	Students devise strategies to deter others from:	
	• taking performance-enhancing drugs and supplements	
	• overtraining.	

(continued)

Examples of Learning Objectives	Examples of Learning Tasks	Examples of Learning Outcomes
Students are learning to ensure that digital technology is used safely in PESSPA.	Students discuss how it feels to have a picture of themselves posted on social media without their agreement.	Students will be able to explain:
	Students produce a code of conduct in relation to the use of videoing on personal mobile phones in PESSPA.	• how to use digital technology responsibly in PESSPA situations
	Students research the legal implications of sending and posting PESSPA material online without people's consent.	• why, in some cases, it would be inappropriate for staff to contact students by phone, email or text
	Students discuss appropriate and inappropriate ways for staff to contact students with information about PESSPA using digital technology.	• the legal implications of sending and posting material online without people's consent.

Chapter 3/Section 3: Learning about Assessing and managing risk

Table 29: Learning about Assessing and managing risk

Examples of Learning Objectives	Examples of Learning Tasks	Examples of Learning Outcomes
Students are learning to take increasing responsibility for following advice, rules and procedures (written or verbal) relating to safe practice.	Students learn to respond appropriately to safety commands when involved in physical education, school sport and physical activity (PESSPA) activities (eg 'listen', 'lock', 'stop' and 'go' – red and green 'traffic light' symbols, written words, gestures, signals or verbal commands can be used).	Students will be able to: • recognise and respond appropriately to very simple verbal instructions, written words, signs and/or symbols associated with their safety in PESSPA
	Students gain a practical understanding of safety words associated with specific PESSPA activities/situations.	• listen carefully when receiving information/instructions about safety advice, rules and procedures in PESSPA activities/situations
	Students consider the following question in practical PESSPA activities/situations: 'What might happen if you do not listen to or follow safety advice, rules and procedures?'	• recall simple safety rules that PESSPA staff have communicated
	Students monitor and evaluate, in practical, low-risk PESSPA tasks, the extent to which they and others can successfully follow safety advice, signs, rules and procedures.	• accurately and consistently follow simple safety rules, signs and procedures in PESSPA activities/situations
	Students compare and discuss the challenges of following written or verbal instructions in PESSPA activities/situations.	• accurately follow simple safety rules and procedures relevant to taking on different roles in familiar PESSPA activities/situations (eg coach, official)
		• accurately interpret the meaning of more complex advice, rules and procedures about safe practice in PESSPA

(continued)

Examples of Learning Objectives	Examples of Learning Tasks	Examples of Learning Outcomes
See previous page.	Students consider appropriate action they should take if they have not understood or listened carefully to safety information and advice about PESSPA activities/situations. Students design 'safety rules' posters for specific PESSPA activities/situations.	• accurately follow safety rules and procedures relevant to personal participation in new or unfamiliar PESSPA activities/situations • evaluate how successfully they and others are able to follow safety advice, rules and procedures in PESSPA activities/situations • suggest helpful strategies to ensure that safety advice, rules and procedures are followed accurately in PESSPA activities/situations • offer suggestions for rules to ensure safety for a variety of PESSPA activities/situations • explain the possible consequences of not following safety advice, rules and procedures relating to personal participation in PESSPA.

(continued)

Examples of Learning Objectives	Examples of Learning Tasks	Examples of Learning Outcomes
Students are learning to take increasing responsibility for conducting their own risk assessments prior to participating in PESSPA activities/situations.	Students complete the following sentences: • 'Being hurt or injured makes me feel:' • 'Being hurt or injured stops me doing:' Students compile (with the help of PESSPA staff) a very simple list to check to prevent injury or harm in PESSPA activities/sessions, for example: • safe kit (eg 'Am I wearing safe footwear, the correct top and shorts/trousers? Is my hair tied back? Have I taken my jewellery off or made it safe?') • safe equipment (eg 'Have PESSPA staff checked the equipment before I use it? Is the equipment broken?') • safe space (eg 'Is there anything I might bump into or trip over?'). Students consider the following questions at appropriate times during practical PESSPA activities/sessions: 'How does safe kit, safe equipment and/or safe space help to prevent you and/or others from being hurt or injured?'	Students will be able to: • explain what it means to get hurt or injured in PESSPA • describe what might cause them to get hurt in a PESSPA activity/situation or the playground • make accurate safety checks (under the guidance of PESSPA staff) of their own kit, the equipment they are using and the working area • explain what they should do if their safety check finds something that is not safe about any aspect of their kit, the PESSPA equipment or the working area • make very simple judgements about what is 'safe' and what is not 'safe' in terms of familiar PESSPA facilities, equipment, activities and procedures • identify and describe advice, rules and procedures that keep them and others safe when taking part in PESSPA activities/situations • explain what is meant by harm (eg injury or damage) • accurately identify what might cause harm in the context of familiar PESSPA facilities, equipment, activities and procedures

(continued)

Examples of Learning Objectives	Examples of Learning Tasks	Examples of Learning Outcomes
See previous page.	Students identify in practical PESSPA sessions/situations (with the help of PESSPA staff) what: • might cause someone to get hurt (eg bumping into one another, falling over, collapsing equipment) • has been done to reduce the chance of this happening (eg teacher instructions to look up and watch out for others when running, teacher instructions to check that the floor is clear before playing, teacher checking that the equipment is safe before use). Students choose very simple safety rules from those provided by PESSPA staff that are important for PESSPA activities/situations in which they are participating (the safety rules can be communicated on posters through written words and pictures). Students decide very simple safety 'rules' for familiar PESSPA facilities and activities.	• explain what is meant by a hazard (ie something that might cause harm) • describe what is meant by a risk (ie the likelihood that an identified hazard will cause harm to them and others) • evaluate the likelihood that an identified hazard in PESSPA will present a risk to them and others • describe the benefits of taking part in a range of familiar PESSPA activities/situations • describe the risks involved in a range of familiar PESSPA activities/situations • offer suggestions for specific PESSPA activities/situations of how likely it is that a risk might result in harm • make simple judgements about whether the risks outweigh the benefits for a range of familiar PESSPA activities/situations • offer suggestions for what should be done if the risk in PESSPA activities/situations is greater than the benefit • explain the purpose of risk assessment in PESSPA and how it can be achieved effectively

(continued)

Examples of Learning Objectives	Examples of Learning Tasks	Examples of Learning Outcomes
See previous page.	Students make independent decisions in practical PESSPA learning activities/situations about what: • harm might happen in this situation, and what might cause this harm • can be done to reduce the likelihood that this harm will happen. Students plan posters of safety advice, signs, rules and procedures to manage the risks identified in specific PESSPA activities/situations. Students discuss the importance for safety of conducting risk assessments ahead of participation in PESSPA activities/situations. Students work in small groups to: • conduct their own risk assessments prior to participation in familiar/unfamiliar PESSPA activities/situations • evaluate their own and others' risk assessments • discuss their risk assessments with an appropriate adult • make any necessary changes before putting their risk assessment into operation.	• explain the purpose of the steps involved in the risk assessment process • conduct a thorough and accurate risk-benefit analysis for a new or unfamiliar PESSPA activity/situation or facility • explain their risk-benefit analysis with appropriately qualified/competent PESSPA staff and make any necessary changes • explain the importance for their own and others' safety of planning ahead before taking part in PESSPA activities/situations • explain the significance of being able to conduct effective risk assessments for lifelong participation in physical activity.

(continued)

Examples of Learning Objectives	Examples of Learning Tasks	Examples of Learning Outcomes
Students are learning to take increasing responsibility for conducting ongoing risk assessment (ie dynamic risk assessment) while an activity or event is taking place.	Students look for specific and very simple hazards during a PESSPA session (eg is the floor clear of any equipment that might make you trip?). Students take on the role of 'safety officers' in a PESSPA session or at playtime, with a special responsibility for identifying safety issues. (These issues can be more specific and simple with younger students.) Students design posters, Twitter updates or Facebook ads to highlight tips for keeping vigilant about safety while participating in PESSPA activities.	Students will be able to: • describe a range of common hazards that might occur during any PESSPA activity/situation • accurately recognise when there are safety issues, using simple criteria identified by PESSPA staff • accurately recognise when there are any safety issues, using complex criteria identified by PESSPA staff • explain why 'ongoing' dynamic risk assessment in PESSPA is necessary.

Chapter 3/Section 4: Learning about First aid

Table 30: Learning about First aid

Examples of Learning Objectives	Examples of Learning Tasks	Examples of Learning Outcomes
Students are learning to take increasing responsibility for keeping themselves safe from danger.	**British Red Cross** **Life. Live It. First aid education for children (appropriate for primary students):** A combination of interactive activities, film scenarios, information sheets and quizzes that build lifesavers by increasing students' ability, confidence and willingness to give first aid. Students will learn the importance of giving first aid without risk to themselves. http://goo.gl/sQYYs7	Students will be able to do the following in the context of physical education, school sport and physical activity (PESSPA) activities/situations: • look and listen carefully for dangers • accurately spot dangers • know what to do if they spot dangers • suggest how to make an area safe • explain what is meant by risk • identify school rules about safety • explain the purpose of having school rules about safety
Students are learning to take increasing responsibility for keeping themselves safe from danger when giving help to others.	**British Red Cross** **First aid learning for young people (appropriate for secondary students):** The resource has a range of interactive content, including films, written case studies, photos, animations, role plays and activities. Students can use the website independently or engage with first aid learning through activities that the teacher facilitates. This flexible approach can be adapted for a range of different ways of learning, settings and abilities. http://goo.gl/LYsmNM	• explain what could happen if safety rules are not followed • explain where and how to get help if they feel a situation is unsafe. Students will be able to do the following in the context of PESSPA activities/situations: • accurately identify circumstances in which it would be dangerous for someone giving first aid help • suggest how to make an area safe for a first-aider.
Students are learning to take increasing responsibility for giving first aid in different situations.	**St John's Ambulance** **First Aid for Children:** School first aid resources and lesson plans cover a range of first aid scenarios and treatments for 7–16-year-olds to learn. The resources include presentation, customisable lesson plans, worksheets and videos. http://goo.gl/oWhdl1	Students will be able to: • explain what is meant by first aid • explain and demonstrate appropriate action in a range of common first aid situations (eg nosebleed, bad bleed, choking, burn, broken bone, allergic reaction)

(continued)

Examples of Learning Objectives	Examples of Learning Tasks	Examples of Learning Outcomes
See previous page.		• give appropriate help to an unconscious person who is breathing • explain in what circumstances it is not appropriate to move an injured person • show how to keep an injured person safe • explain simple strategies to prevent a situation becoming more serious.
Students are learning to take increasing responsibility for acting efficiently and appropriately in an emergency situation.		Students will be able to: • explain what an emergency is in the context of first aid • describe appropriate examples of emergency situations in PESSPA • explain why getting help in an emergency is an important part of first aid • accurately distinguish between PESSPA situations that are and are not 'emergencies' • show appropriate awareness of who it is safe for them to offer help to in PESSPA situations (ie if they are not with an adult and they don't know the person who is seriously ill or injured) • check if someone is breathing • explain when to get adult help • show appropriate awareness of which adults it would be appropriate to ask for help in an emergency PESSPA situation • explain when and how to call 999 • explain what will happen when they call 999 and what information they need to give the operator

(continued)

Examples of Learning Objectives	Examples of Learning Tasks	Examples of Learning Outcomes
See previous page.		• explain the importance of keeping calm in an emergency PESSPA situation • explain simple strategies for keeping themselves and others calm in an emergency PESSPA situation.
Students are learning to take increasing responsibility for recognising the symptoms of concussion and acting appropriately if they recognise these in themselves and others.	**Northern Ireland Council for the Curriculum, Examinations and Assessment (CCEA) concussion website** This focuses on recognising and removing concussion and aims to teach about concussion. Activities are appropriate for primary and post-primary students. http://goo.gl/euCFoY **Without Your Brain, You Have No Game** Young Social Innovators from Cashel Community School and LIT Limerick School of Art and Design produced this concussion awareness animation. http://goo.gl/dU7MaU	Students will be able to: • describe what concussion means • describe how a person might get a concussion • describe possible causes of concussion • explain why concussion is so serious • describe and know how to spot the main symptoms and signs of concussion • suggest appropriate action they would take if they suspect that they or another person has concussion (ie inform a member of staff quickly, 'if in doubt, sit it out') • explain how they can provide appropriate support to a friend who is recovering from concussion (eg help them to be patient about getting back to physical activity, make sure they don't get involved in situations where they might get bumped or knocked while they are recovering, encourage them to be honest about whether the symptoms are going).

Chapter 3/Section 5: Learning about Exercise safe practice

Table 31: Learning about Exercise safe practice

Examples of Learning Objectives	Examples of Learning Tasks	Examples of Learning Outcomes

Students are learning to take increasing responsibility for developing and maintaining correct joint alignment in their own and others' exercise technique.
 	
(See Chapter 2, Section 9, page 163.)
	Students take part in a simple movement tasks to help them to name joints and decide how they move; for example:
	
	• 'Show me how your elbows move.'
	• 'Show me how your knees move.'
	• 'Show me how your shoulders move.'
	• 'Show me how your spine moves.'
	
	Students make and cut out pictures of joints. They take part in a 'team relay race' to pin them in the correct place on a poster of the 'body'. Alternatively, students can write the names of joints on sticky paper and take part in a 'team relay race' to attach these in the correct place to one of their team members.
	
	Students develop a practical understanding of how to demonstrate the teaching points associated with correct joint alignment (eg knees over toes/ankles, tummy pulled through to backbone, keep back tall).
	
	Students discuss how correct joint alignment keeps them safe (ie reduces the stress on ligaments – frequent/long-term stress on ligaments can lead to joint problems).
	
	Students conduct simple risk assessments of specific exercises or activities in terms of whether they can be performed with correct joint alignment.
	
	Students observe, evaluate and give feedback about correct joint alignment in their own and others' technique.
		Students will be able to:
		
		• describe which joints are being used in simple physical education, school sport and physical activity (PESSPA) activities
		• identify correct joint alignment using teaching points such as:
		  – knee alignment (knee over ankle, knee no less than 90 degrees, knees straight but not locked out)
		  – spine alignment (pull tummy through to backbone, stand/sit tall, slightly squeeze between shoulders)
		• explain what joint alignment means (ie moving joints in ways in which they are supposed to move – anatomically correct ways)
		• show how the major joints (eg knee and spine) can be moved with correct alignment
		• explain the importance for their health and safety of correct joint alignment
		• recognise when joints are being hyperextended (locked out) or hyperflexed (fully bent)
		• explain the possible risks of hyperextending or hyperflexing joints, particularly when weight bearing or working against resistance (ie stress on ligaments, which can lead to joint problems or poor alignment in other joints)
		• make increasingly accurate judgements about the extent to which correct joint alignment is demonstrated in their own and others' technique.

(continued)

Examples of Learning Objectives	Examples of Learning Tasks	Examples of Learning Outcomes
Students are learning to take increasing responsibility for developing and maintaining appropriate use of control in their own and others' exercise technique. (See Chapter 2, Section 9, page 161.)	Students take part in simple movement tasks to help them to understand what 'control' means: • 'Draw big circles with your arms and freeze when I shout stop!' • 'Run fast in the space, and freeze when I shout stop!' Students travel from a starting line towards a person some distance away whose back is turned to them. Whenever this person turns around, all students must freeze. If the person sees a student move or wobble, they must return to the starting line. Is it possible to travel fast and still be able to stop with control? Students develop a practical understanding of teaching points associated with appropriate use of control (eg the movement is easily stoppable and does not involve flinging). Students discuss how appropriate use of control keeps them safe (ie reduces the stress on ligaments and tendons – frequent/long-term stress on these can result in muscle tears and/or lead to joint problems). Students conduct simple risk assessments of specific PESSPA exercises/activities in terms of whether they can be performed with appropriate use of control. Students observe, evaluate and give feedback about appropriate use of control in their own and others' technique.	Students will be able to: • show increasing 'control' when copying and performing simple PESSPA activities/exercises • identify correct control through the following teaching points: movement is stoppable, no flinging • explain what 'control' means (ie movements that are stoppable, not flinging) • show how a range of simple exercises/activities can be performed with control • make increasingly accurate judgements about the extent to which control is demonstrated in their own and others' exercise technique • explain the importance for their health and safety of performing exercises/activities with control • explain the possible risks associated with performing exercises/activities without appropriate use of control • make increasingly accurate judgements about the extent to which appropriate use of control is demonstrated in their own and others' technique.

(continued)

Examples of Learning Objectives	Examples of Learning Tasks	Examples of Learning Outcomes
Students are learning to take increasing responsibility for maximising the benefits and minimising the risks of high-impact activities in their own and others' practice. (See Chapter 2, Section 9, page 162.)	Students copy very simple exercises/activities demonstrated by PESSPA staff and decide whether they involve jumping or not. Students take part in simple movement tasks to help them to understand what 'high impact' means: • 'Skip, march, walk, jumping jacks – in which of these activities is your whole body leaving the floor?' Students develop a practical understanding of teaching points associated with correct jumping and landing technique (ie bend knees, keep knees in line with toes, use arms to balance, ball/heel action with feet). Students discuss how correct jumping and landing technique can keep them safe (ie reduces the stress on joints). Students conduct simple risk assessments of specific high-impact PESSPA activities in terms of whether the risks associated with high impact can be minimised. Students design simple 'circuits' of exercises and PESSPA activities that alternate high and low impact at each station.	Students will be able to: • distinguish between activities in which the whole body leaves the floor and activities in which the whole body does not leave the floor (eg jumping and non-jumping activities) • show correct jumping and landing technique in a range of increasingly complex PESSPA exercises/activities • describe the benefits of high-impact (jumping) activities (eg strengthen bones and heart) • explain the possible risks associated with high-impact (jumping) activities (eg may cause damage to joints and bones) • offer suggestions for reducing the risks associated with performing high-impact activities (eg jump and land with correct technique, wear training shoes, mix jumping with non-jumping activities, avoid frequent and long duration jumping activities on hard surfaces) • offer suggestions for people who might need to avoid high-impact PESSPA activities (eg elderly people, pregnant women, people with joint problems, people who are severely overweight)

322

(continued)

Examples of Learning Objectives	Examples of Learning Tasks	Examples of Learning Outcomes
See previous page.	Students practise, apply and improve safe and effective take-off and landing technique in a range of PESSPA activities and situations.	• offer suggestions for alternatives to high-impact PESSPA activities (eg walking instead of jogging).
	Students explore and discuss the health benefits and safety risks associated with high-impact activities.	• make increasingly accurate judgements about the extent to which correct jumping and landing technique is demonstrated in their own and others' performance
	Students conduct a risk assessment of a facility/PESSPA activity, focusing on safe and effective use of impact.	• make increasingly accurate judgements about the extent to which the risks associated with high-impact activities have been minimised in PESSPA activities/exercises.
	Students observe, evaluate and give feedback about their own and others' technique when performing high-impact activities.	

(continued)

Examples of Learning Objectives	Examples of Learning Tasks	Examples of Learning Outcomes
Students are learning to take increasing responsibility for performing warm-up and cool-down exercises with safe and effective technique. (See Chapter 2, Section 9, page 170.)	Students copy very simple warm-up and cool-down activities demonstrated by PESSPA staff. Students copy practical demonstrations of warm-up and cool-down exercises, paying attention to correct joint alignment, appropriate control and appropriate use of high impact. Students make simple judgements about their own performance of warm-up and cool-down activities in terms of correct joint alignment, appropriate control and appropriate use of high impact. Students observe, evaluate and give feedback about others' technique when performing warm-up/cool-down exercises. Students evaluate a range of commonly used warm-up and cool-down exercises/activities in terms of whether they can be performed with correct joint alignment, appropriate control and appropriate use of high impact. Students conduct risk assessments of complex and/or new/unfamiliar warm-up and cool-down exercises/activities in terms of whether they can be performed with correct joint alignment, appropriate control and appropriate use of high impact.	Students will be able to: • copy simple warm-up/cool-down actions and whole-body stretches • show correct joint alignment, appropriate control and appropriate use of high impact when copying simple and familiar warm-up/cool-down activities • show correct joint alignment, appropriate control and appropriate use of high impact when performing increasingly complex and/or unfamiliar warm-up/cool-down activities • make increasingly accurate judgements about their own and others' exercise technique when performing warm-up and cool-down exercises/activities.

(continued)

Examples of Learning Objectives	Examples of Learning Tasks	Examples of Learning Outcomes
Students are learning to take increasing responsibility for understanding the purpose of warm-ups and cool-downs. (See Chapter 2, Section 9, page 170.)	Students copy simple warm-up/cool-down exercises/activities. PESSPA staff describe: 'This activity: • moves our joints/keeps us moving gently • makes us feel warm • makes us breathe faster/slower • makes our hearts beat faster/slower • stretches our muscles • wakes up our brain/calms us down.'	Students will be able to: • describe when a warm-up/cool-down should be performed • recognise simple warm-up activities that move their joints, make them warm, make them breathe faster and their heart beat faster, stretch their muscles, wake up their brain • recognise simple cool-down activities that make them cooler, keep them moving gently, slow down their breathing and heart rate, stretch their muscles, calm them down. Students describe the effects of warming up and cooling down on their breathing, temperature and how they feel (using Figure 11: Chart for monitoring how physical activity feels – see page 330).

(continued)

Examples of Learning Objectives	Examples of Learning Tasks	Examples of Learning Outcomes
See previous page.	Students monitor the effects of warming up and cooling down on their breathing, temperature and how they feel (using Figure 11: Chart for monitoring how physical activity feels – see page 330).	Students will be able to:
		• explain simple reasons for warming up and cooling down
	Students discuss the purpose of warming up before PESSPA (ie prevent injury, prepare the body safely and gradually for activity, 'wake up' the brain) and cooling down afterwards (ie prevent muscle tightness and soreness, help the body recover from energetic activity, and help the person feel calmer).	• explain why it is important for a warm-up to include exercises/activities to:
		– move joints – moving joints makes the joint release more fluid, which 'oils' the joint and makes it move more freely
		– get warm – muscles become more stretchy or pliable, which allows the joints to move more freely and over a bigger range; moving joints also helps us to get warm
		– increase the breathing and heart rate to carry more oxygen more quickly to the muscles in order to give the energy required to do energetic activities
	Students discuss what might happen if a warm-up or cool-down was not performed.	– stretch muscles to prepare them for tightening and lengthening quickly when we do energetic and fast activities
	Students distinguish between static and dynamic stretches, and consider the appropriate use of dynamic and static stretches in warm-ups and cool-downs.	• explain why it is important for a cool-down to include exercises/activities to:
		– keep moving gently to keep blood pumping to the heart and brain (otherwise, we might feel dizzy or sick)
		– decrease the breathing and heart rate to allow the body to recover
		– stretch muscles to help prevent them feeling tight and sore after exercise
		– calm us down (eg to prepare to go back to the classroom or to go home)
		• explain the difference between dynamic and static stretching and the appropriate place of each in warm-ups and cool-downs. (See Chapter 2, Section 9, pages 171 and 173.)

(continued)

Examples of Learning Objectives	Examples of Learning Tasks	Examples of Learning Outcomes
Students are learning to take increasing responsbility for designing effective warm-ups and cool-downs. (See Chapter 2, Section 9, page 170.)	Students plan (independently or with others) exercises and components of/a whole warm-up/ cool-down for familiar activities.	Students will be able to:
		• select simple warm-up activities that move their joints, make them warm, make them breathe faster and their heart beat faster, stretch their muscles, wake up their brain
	Students plan components of/a whole warm-up/ cool-down for new/unfamiliar activities.	• select simple cool-down activities that make them cooler, keep them moving gently, slow down their breathing and heart rate, stretch their muscles, calm them down
	Students plan warm-ups for different purposes (eg personal health-related exercise programmes, preparation for participation in specific sports).	• design components of warm-ups/cool-downs for specific and familiar PESSPA activities (eg ball games, gymnastics)
	Students plan independent warm-ups and cool-downs that are specific to a personal exercise/training programme.	• justify their selection of activities/exercises for warm-ups/cool-downs for specific and familiar PESSPA activities
		• analyse and identify the warm-up requirements of a range of new/unfamiliar activities
		• analyse and identify the requirements of a warm-up/cool-down for a personal exercise/training programme with a specific purpose
		• distinguish between requirements of health-related and performance-related warm-ups and cool-downs.

(continued)

Examples of Learning Objectives	Examples of Learning Tasks	Examples of Learning Outcomes
Students are learning to take increasing responsibility for evaluating the effectiveness of warm-ups and cool-downs.	Students decide simple criteria to evaluate the effectiveness of warm-ups and cool-downs (eg by using Figure 11: Chart for monitoring how physical activity feels – see page 330). Students lead their peers through components of/a whole warm-up/cool-down that they have planned (independently or with others) for familiar or unfamiliar PESSPA activities. Students work in groups to evaluate the effectiveness of the warm-up or cool-down.	Students will be able to: • describe how a warm-up should make them feel (ie warm, loose, ready for action, alert) • describe how a cool-down should make them feel (ie cooler, calm, relaxed, recovered) • decide simple criteria to evaluate the effectiveness of warm-ups and cool-downs • apply appropriate and simple criteria to evaluate the effectiveness of warm-ups and cool-downs • make appropriate adaptations to warm-ups and cool-downs to increase their safety and effectiveness • explain how warm-ups and cool-downs can be adapted for specific situations (eg adverse weather conditions).
Students are learning to take increasing responsibility for assessing and reducing risk associated with a range of other factors that can impact on their safe participation in PESSPA activities. (See Chapter 2, Section 5, page 114.)	Students explore safety issues associated with tiredness, dehydration, being unwell and extreme weather conditions through play-based learning (eg PESSPA staff tell a story involving these issues, and children act out the story to show how each might affect their safe participation).	Students will be able to: • describe what might make PESSPA activities less safe for them (eg being really thirsty, carrying on when they are very tired, playing in the sun with no hat or suncream on)

(continued)

Examples of Learning Objectives	Examples of Learning Tasks	Examples of Learning Outcomes
See previous page.	Students discuss how the following can impact on their safety and performance when taking part in PES activities/sessions: • tiredness • dehydration • common medical conditions (eg asthma, diabetes, coughs, colds, tummy bugs) • extreme weather conditions. Students design a poster, Twitter update or Facebook ad that: • explains how to exercise safely in summer and/or winter • gives advice to those with different medical conditions • gives advice about whether to exercise with common minor illnesses • gives advice about exercising in extreme weather conditions.	• describe the signs and symptoms of physical and mental tiredness and explain how tiredness might impact on their safety in PESSPA situations • suggest appropriate action they can take to keep safe in PESSPA situations if they are suffering from mental or physical tiredness • describe the signs and symptoms of dehydration, and explain how this might impact on their safety in PESSPA situations • explain how to hydrate appropriately before, during and after participation in PESSPA activities/sessions • explain how common medical conditions might impact on the safety of individuals in PESSPA situations (eg asthma, diabetes) • describe the signs and symptoms of common illnesses such as coughs, colds and tummy bugs • suggest appropriate advice about participating in PESSPA activities/sessions with coughs, colds and tummy bugs • describe the risks of extreme weather conditions (eg heat, cold, dampness) when taking part in PESSPA activities/sessions (eg heatstroke, sunburn, dehydration, hypothermia) • suggest appropriate advice for avoiding the risks of heatstroke, sunburn, dehydration, hypothermia • suggest appropriate action for managing heatstroke, sunburn, dehydration, hypothermia.

Rating of How Activity Feels	Breathing	Temperature	Heartbeat	How Physical Activity Feels
1	Very quiet and very slow Very easy to talk	Cool	Slow, gentle	Easy
2	Quiet and slow Easy to talk	Warm		Comfortable
3	'Huff and puff' sound, brisk Can still hold conversation	Very warm		Energetic
4	Panting, loud and fast Difficult to hold conversation	Hot		Very energetic
5	Gasping, noisy and rapid Impossible to hold conversation	Very hot	Fast, thumping	Exhausting

Figure 11: Chart for monitoring how physical activity feels

Chapter 3/Section 6: Learning about safe practice in relation to Space

Table 32: Learning about safe practice in relation to Space

Examples of Learning Objectives	Examples of Learning Tasks	Examples of Learning Outcomes
Students are learning to take increasing responsibility for checking that their personal space is safe for activity.	Students familiarise themselves with the space they are working in by marking the perimeter with marker spots, lines or cones.	Students will be able to:
	Students are led through a series of activities that require them to travel and/or place themselves around the edges, inside and outside of their activity space.	• find an appropriate space to sit or stand in when requested
		• show that they know the boundaries of their activity space
	Students make simple safety checks of their activity space (eg is the floor/ground slippery? Are there any sharp or gritty objects on the ground, especially if working in bare feet? Is there anything that might cause tripping, falling or collisions? Are there too many people to work safely in the space?).	• describe what hazards might make their activity space unsafe
		• explain appropriate action they would take if they spot hazards in their activity space
	Students make and share posters to promote taking responsibility for checking that their activity space is safe in physical education, school sport and physical activity (PESSPA).	• recognise and respond appropriately to potential hazards within and around their activity space
	Students are given increasing responsibility (with appropriate supervision) for checking that the areas to be used for specific PESSPA activities/sessions have been checked for hazards.	• make appropriate and effective safety checks on their activity space for a range of unfamiliar PESSPA facilities, venues and activities.

(continued)

Examples of Learning Objectives	Examples of Learning Tasks	Examples of Learning Outcomes
Students are learning to take increasing responsibility for being vigilant and alert to what is going on around them when in a PESSPA environment/situation.	Students take part in practical 'games' and activities that require them to look up and show good awareness of their environment and others when running, skipping or walking (eg 'tag games', dance/gymnastics warm-ups, keeping possession/control of a ball).	Students will be able to: • describe appropriate precautions for a range of familiar PESSPA activities/situations (eg looking before throwing, kicking or hitting in an activity space) • make appropriate judgements about when it is safe to throw, kick or hit in specific PESSPA environments/situations
	Students discuss and suggest safety rules for using specific PESSPA equipment (eg rackets, bats, balls) when working with others in a specific PESSPA environment/situation.	
	Students discuss and suggest safety advice associated with participant vigilance for new and unfamiliar PESSPA environments/situations.	• explain how to check for safety before moving into an activity space. • suggest appropriate safety advice for using the space safely in a new or unfamiliar PESSPA environment/situation.
Students are learning to take increasing responsibility for making adaptations to enable safe use of restricted space.	Students solve problems about how to adapt activities and equipment to work safely in a restricted space. Students design PESSPA activities that will be safe to perform in a given space.	Students will be able to make: • accurate judgements about whether their working space is large enough to accommodate the requirements of the PESSPA activity and/or the skill level of themselves and their peers • appropriate suggestions about modifying PESSPA activities and/or the equipment used to enable safe use of restricted space.

(continued)

Chapter 3/Section 7: Learning about safe practice in relation to Tasks

Table 33: Learning about safe practice in relation to Tasks

Examples of Learning Objectives	Examples of Learning Tasks	Examples of Learning Outcomes
Students are learning to take increasing responsibility for seeking and acting on help and guidance about physical education, school sport and physical activity (PESSPA) tasks when appropriate.	Students receive and act on verbal instructions/teaching points (TPs) given to them by PESSPA staff (eg 'Run this way. Stay inside the blue cones. When I shout "stop", get off the apparatus carefully and s t on the floor.'). Students consider what might happen if they: • do not listen carefully to instructions • cannot remember all the instructions • do not know what the instructions mean. Students position apparatus/equipment (under the supervision of PESSPA staff) using simple diagrams to help them, and evaluate the impact of diagrams on safe positioning of the apparatus/equipment. Students build their understanding of technical language (eg through practical demonstrations/pictures/diagrams that show the words 'in action'). Students decide on questions to ask before starting a PESSPA task. They ask PESSPA staff their questions, and evaluate how the answers make the task safer.	Students will be able to: • act appropriately when given very simple verbal instructions/TPs • accurately recall simple verbal instructions/TPs (eg 'Which way will you run? Which cones must you stay inside? What should you do if I shout "stop"? Where should you be looking – ahead or down at the ground?'). • describe what might happen if they do not listen to or cannot remember instructions, or do not know what instructions mean • describe appropriate action to take if they need instructions to be explained again or made clearer (ie ask the member of staff leading the session) • accurately explain the purpose of simple verbal instructions/TPs (eg why it is important to look up whenever possible when dribbling, why it is important to know and keep inside the boundaries of their working area for a task) • give examples of how listening to, remembering and understanding instructions can make PESSPA tasks safer

(continued)

Examples of Learning Objectives	Examples of Learning Tasks	Examples of Learning Outcomes
See previous page.	Students design guidance (eg TPs, instructions, diagrams) to help younger students complete simple PESSPA tasks. They evaluate the appropriateness of these with PESSPA staff before trying them out. They use the tasks with some younger students, and evaluate the impact on safety. Students are involved in practical problem-solving tasks that require them to decide whether they can make their own decisions about how to tackle specific PESSPA tasks or whether they need to ask an appropriate adult for advice and help. For example, work cards to support learning partner balances in gymnastics (with TPs, diagrams, written instructions) – students decide whether it is safe to start the task – this example will require the teacher to give much more detailed help and advice about issues such as safe communication required, safer parts of body for supporting a partner's weight, only using balance skills that are already developed – before the commencement of the task.	• show or explain their understanding of specific technical vocabulary involved in learning a new PESSPA skill/technique • follow diagrams accurately and independently when positioning apparatus and equipment • accurately identify elements of PESSPA tasks that require clarification to enable safe participation • demonstrate a mature understanding of what type of help and guidance can impact on safety in specific PESSPA tasks • make appropriate decisions about when to act independently on their own decisions, and when to seek adult help/approval before starting PESSPA tasks.

(continued)

Examples of Learning Objectives	Examples of Learning Tasks	Examples of Learning Outcomes
Students are learning to take increasing responsibility for making safe and effective progress when learning new skills and techniques.	Students participate in tasks of different degrees of difficulty (eg designed by applying the STEP framework to simple PESSPA tasks). Younger students decide which tasks were easy and which were hard. Older students can rank the tasks (using a simple continuum) according to how hard or easy each task felt.	Students will be able to:
		• describe which PESSPA tasks they find easy and which they find hard to do
		• explain which tasks feel easier or harder to do
	Students consider answers to the following questions in relevant practical contexts:	• suggest why we all feel different about how hard or easy the same PESSPA task feels
	• What would happen to your safety and progress if you:	• describe what can impact on how hard or easy PESSPA tasks feel
	– only perform PESSPA skills that you find easy to learn (eg 'This would be safe, but I would not make any progress')	• explain how a person's capabilities and prior experience impact on how easy or hard they find it to learn new PESSPA skills and techniques
	– try to perform PESSPA skills that are much too hard for you (eg 'This might not be safe as I might hurt myself or others, I might not make any progress')?	• explain why it is important, when learning new PESSPA skills/techniques, to be honest and accurate when giving information to PESSPA staff about personal capabilities and prior experience
	• What advice would you give to someone about making safe and effective progress when learning new PESSPA skills/techniques (eg be patient and progress sensibly, make sure you can do easier versions well before you move on to harder versions of the skill/technique, listen to the teacher's advice about when it is appropriate for you to move on to harder versions)?	• explain what action they should take if the level of challenge of a task is not appropriate for them
		• explain what procedures or information help PESSPA staff to ensure that the challenge of tasks is appropriate for every student
		• describe the effect of repeating practices on PESSPA skills/techniques

(continued)

Examples of Learning Objectives	Examples of Learning Tasks	Examples of Learning Outcomes
See previous page.	Students take part in physical education lessons that have an explicit focus on learning how concentration is linked to progress (eg 'Today, we are going to learn what concentration means, how we can learn to concentrate and how concentration can help us to improve our batting/balancing/dribbling skills'). Learning can focus on helping students to develop skills associated with listening carefully, sticking to a task, staying 'on task' and focusing only on what they are learning. Students can evaluate the impact of developing these skills on helping them to perform more challenging PESSPA tasks safely. Students repeat skill/technique practices and monitor their impact in terms of making the skill stronger (eg more accurate, technically precise, controlled and/or consistent, as appropriate). For example, with younger students, simple throw/bounce/catch challenges can be used – 'How many can you do without losing the ball?' With older students – 'How fast can you slalom dribble without touching a cone?' Students explore though simple practical tasks how changes in space, task, equipment or people (STEP) make PESSPA activities feel harder or easier. Students apply (with the help of PESSPA staff) STEP to simple PESSPA skills, and monitor the effect on how challenging the skill feels to learn/perform.	• explain how repeating practices to make skills stronger, more accurate and more consistent is important in achieving safe progression • show that they understand and can apply the TPs needed to learn new or harder PESSPA skills • explain how concentration can help them to learn increasingly complex PESSPA skills and techniques • suggest simple and appropriate advice about how to make safe and effective progress when learning new PESSPA skills and techniques • make accurate choices about which versions of PESSPA activities are appropriately challenging for them • adapt a range of exercises (eg cardiovascular, resistance) to make them appropriately challenging for them

(continued)

Examples of Learning Objectives	Examples of Learning Tasks	Examples of Learning Outcomes
See previous page.	Students discuss what makes a PESSPA skill feel easier or harder for them to learn – for example, their current: • level of skill and coordination • physical fitness • ability to perform the skill under pressure • level of familiarity with the PESSPA skill/technique • ability to work at the level of independence required/expected • ability to meet the level of cooperation required. Students design a series of progressive tasks to enable young students to make safe and effective progress when learning a new PESSPA skill or technique, evaluate the appropriateness of tasks with PESSPA staff before trying them out, use the tasks with some younger students, and evaluate the impact on helping make safe and effective progress. Students make choices (with guidance from PESSPA staff) about which version of a practice/task (presented on a task card or via practical demonstration) provides the most appropriate starting point for them when learning a new PESSPA skill or technique.	• make appropriate decisions about when it is safe to try to perform a new PESSPA skill/technique straight away, and when it is appropriate to start with simple practices • decide safe and effective plans for progressing appropriate PESSPA skills/technique according to their individual ability, experience and confidence • decide an appropriate starting point for themselves when learning new PESSPA skills and techniques • suggest appropriate advice or strategies for ensuring safe and effective progress when learning new skills and techniques

(continued)

Examples of Learning Objectives	Examples of Learning Tasks	Examples of Learning Outcomes
See previous page.	Students evaluate how sensible and appropriate progression impacts on safety when learning new skills and techniques. Students make a progress chart to illustrate the necessary steps in the safe development of PESSPA skills (eg observing demonstrations, listening to safety points, trying out parts of the skill, putting the skill under more pressure). They use the chart to discuss why repetition and consolidation are a necessary part of this skill-learning process. Students design and use a simple scale to monitor and judge the challenge involved in practical PESSPA tasks (eg 0 = in my comfort zone, 5 = in my challenge zone, 10 = in my panic zone). Students can use the chart to monitor how they feel about a range of PESSPA tasks. Students can consider what happens to progress and safety if PESSPA tasks: • are within their comfort zone • are within their challenge zone • take them into their panic zone.	• suggest why individuals might try to put their peers under pressure to perform PESSPA skills/techniques beyond their current capability • suggest strategies for resisting peer pressure to attempt PESSPA skills/techniques that they do not feel ready to try • explain the impact on safety of putting peers under pressure to attempt PESSPA skills/techniques that they do not feel ready to try • suggest appropriate action they would take if they felt that an individual was being persuaded to perform PESSPA skills/techniques that they do not feel ready to try.

(continued)

Examples of Learning Objectives	Examples of Learning Tasks	Examples of Learning Outcomes
See previous page.	Students discuss how the level of challenge might impact on behaviour, which might in turn impact on safety (eg too little challenge can lead to boredom, which can cause individuals to go 'off task' and may result in them trying activities that are beyond their capabilities or prior learning). Students make and check personal decisions about which of a choice of PESSPA tasks is the most appropriate for them (eg tasks could be described on colour-coded, progressive task cards). Students offer suggestions for what they need to know, understand and be able to do before taking part in specific PESSPA tasks. Students engage in role play to explore strategies for resisting peer pressure that encourages individuals to attempt tasks beyond their capability. Students discuss how judgements about when and how to progress in PESSPA activities are linked to their personal safety.	See previous page.

(continued)

Examples of Learning Objectives	Examples of Learning Tasks	Examples of Learning Outcomes
Students are learning to take increasing responsibility for following and adhering to the rules of PESSPA activities.	Students participate in PESSPA activities with very simple rules that directly impact on safety (eg throw/catch games in which contact is not allowed, not crossing someone's path in fast running races).	Students will be able to:
	Students discuss with the teacher how the rules of familiar PESSPA activities keep them and others safe.	• recall and describe rules in familiar PESSPA activities that help to keep them safe
	Students consider the safety implications of the rules of more complex PESSPA activities (eg rules associated with tackling in rugby, rules associated with performing routines in trampolining).	• explain how rules keep them safe and reduce the likelihood of harm
	Students suggest rules for keeping participants safe in new or unfamiliar activities. They compare their suggestions to the official rules of the specific PESSPA activity in question.	• explain what might happen if the rules of specific PESSPA activities are not followed or adhered to
	Students explore sanctions within the rules of games that penalise individuals or a team who do not adhere to rules associated with safety.	• identify and explain the purpose of rules that reduce risk in increasingly complex PESSPA activities
	Students evaluate the effectiveness, in terms of minimising risk, of ways in which non-adherence to rules is penalised in a range of PESSPA activities (eg does sending players off in football prevent harm? Does the 'sin bin' in rugby prevent harm? Does a penalty shot in netball prevent harm?).	• explain how the rules of specific games include sanctions for those who do not adhere to them
		• explain how sanctions within specific PESSPA activities are designed to prevent harm.

Chapter 3/Section 8: Learning about safe practice in relation to Equipment

Table 34: Learning about safe practice in relation to Equipment

Examples of Learning Objectives	Examples of Learning Tasks	Examples of Learning Outcomes
Students are learning to take increasing responsibility for lifting, moving and placing physical education, school sport and physical activity (PESSPA) equipment safely and effectively.	Students copy practical demonstrations of safe and effective lifting and carrying technique provided by the PESSPA staff.	Students will be able to:
	Students lift, move and place a variety of PESSPA equipment under the supervision of PESSPA staff.	• accurately copy simple, safe and effective technique when lifting, carrying and lowering PESSPA equipment on their own and with others
	Students discuss the short- and long-term risks associated with lifting, carrying and lowering with poor technique (eg lower-back pain, knee injuries).	• make appropriate decisions about when to seek help or advice with lifting, carrying and placing PESSPA equipment
	Students play an active role (under appropriate supervision) in deciding how specific PESSPA equipment is moved and placed.	• work cooperatively with others to lift, carry and place PESSPA equipment
	Students take part (under appropriate supervision) in problem-solving tasks that challenge them to plan how to lift, move and place specific PESSPA equipment safely and effectively.	• follow instructions/maps/plans carefully and accurately to set out small pieces of PESSPA equipment
	Students sit on the floor and alternate 'slumping' with 'sitting tall'. Students identify the postural muscles that need to be squeezed/contracted to achieve correct alignment of the spine (eg abdominals, erector spinae [long back muscles], glutes [backside], trapezius [between shoulders]).	• demonstrate correct alignment of the knees and spine when lifting, lowering and carrying
	Students learn to perform simple resistance exercises to strengthen the postural muscles.	• identify and show principles of safe and effective technique when lifting (eg keep weight close to body, lift with the legs, keep spine and knees in correct alignment)
		• make accurate judgements about the lifting, carrying and placing technique of themselves and others

(continued)

Examples of Learning Objectives	Examples of Learning Tasks	Examples of Learning Outcomes
See previous page.	See previous page.	• make accurate suggestions for safe placement of equipment in a range of familiar PESSPA activities/situations • apply their knowledge of safe lifting, carrying and placing technique to a range of unfamiliar PESSPA apparatus/situations • carry and set out PESSPA equipment independently, showing good safety awareness, and safe and effective lifting, carrying and placing technique • accurately identify the location of the postural muscles • perform with safe and effective technique appropriate resistance exercises to strengthen their postural muscles (eg curl up – abdominals, shoulder squeeze – trapezius, back raises – erector spinae and prone alternate leg raises – glutes) • explain how strong postural muscles make lifting, carrying and placing safer • identify and select appropriate resistance exercises to strengthen the postural muscles used in lifting.

(continued)

Examples of Learning Objectives	Examples of Learning Tasks	Examples of Learning Outcomes
Students are learning to take increasing responsibility for checking PESSPA equipment before and during use.	Students copy simple equipment checks demonstrated by PESSPA staff, and learn how to report any faulty equipment. Students work in groups to suggest, for specific PESSPA equipment, what needs to be checked before and during use. Students take on the role of 'safety officers' in PESSPA sessions or at playtime, with a special responsibility for identifying safety issues regarding equipment. Students design a poster, Twitter update or Facebook ad to highlight tips for keeping vigilant about safety while participating in PESSPA activities.	Students will be able to: • accurately identify equipment that is faulty or 'broken' • effectively check a range of familiar PESSPA equipment for signs of wear and tear • explain why it is necessary to report faulty equipment promptly to an appropriate person • explain why PESSPA equipment checks need to be made, how to make the checks, and the possible consequences of not doing so. • identify appropriate adults to whom they should report faulty equipment in a range of PESSPA situations (eg sports coach, physical education teacher, supervising adult) • show that they can consistently follow appropriate procedures for ensuring that PESSPA equipment is checked prior to use • make similar observations as PESSPA staff, when conducting their own equipment safety checks • explain why it is important to ask PESSPA staff to check equipment before they start to use it • describe a range of common hazards relating to equipment that might occur during any PESSPA activity/session, which participants need to be able to spot • recognise with increasing accuracy safety issues associated with the equipment to be used in specific PESSPA activities/sessions.

(continued)

Examples of Learning Objectives	Examples of Learning Tasks	Examples of Learning Outcomes
Students are learning to take increasing responsibility for using PESSPA equipment in a safe and responsible manner.	Students discuss the safety implications of inappropriately adapting the use of PESSPA equipment. Students discuss what the word 'responsible' means in the context of use of PESSPA equipment (ie making independent decisions about PESSPA equipment that benefit their own and others' safety). Students discuss and decide appropriate action they should take if they see PESSPA equipment being used inappropriately. Students design a code of conduct/posters focusing on using specific PESSPA equipment in a safe and responsible manner.	Students will be able to: • describe how to use specific PESSPA equipment safely • give examples of how adapting the use of equipment might make the PESSPA activity/situation less safe • explain how rules and procedures for using specific PESSPA equipment keep themselves and others safe • accurately identify when specific PESSPA equipment is not being used appropriately • explain why it is important to report inappropriate use of PESSPA equipment promptly to PESSPA staff • explain how concentrating and adhering to instructions, rules and procedures in relation to safe use of equipment can keep them and others safe • make accurate judgements about the extent to which they and others use PESSPA equipment in a responsible manner.

(continued)

Examples of Learning Objectives	Examples of Learning Tasks	Examples of Learning Outcomes
Students are learning to take increasing responsibility for ensuring behaviour, kit, footwear and personal effects (jewellery, hair, adornments) meet the health and safety expectations of the PESSPA activity/situation.	'Stick the kit on the poster' – students make and cut out pictures of important items of PESSPA kit. They take part in a relay race activity to pin them in the correct place or a figure drawn on a flip chart poster. (Different posters might depict different PESSPA activities.)	Students will be able to:
		• suggest kit, footwear and personal effects that are appropriate for reducing risk in familiar/unfamiliar PESSPA activities
	Students make accurate, simple checks (under the guidance of PESSPA staff) of their own kit, footwear and personal effects for specific PESSPA activities.	• demonstrate and explain how to check and maintain PESSPA footwear effectively
	Students design posters, a Twitter update or Facebook advert to encourage/remind their peers to check their kit, footwear and personal effects.	• explain why it is important to tie laces of PESSPA footwear
	Students learn how to check that their footwear and kit are appropriate, safe and fit for purpose.	• explain the importance of removing jewellery and other adornments before active participation
	Students discuss the risks of wearing jewellery and adornments, chewing gum and not tying long hair back when taking part in PESSPA activities.	• explain why any exception to the 'no jewellery or adornments' rule must always be sanctioned by PESSPA staff.
	Students discuss why any exception to the 'no jewellery or adornments' rule always needs to be sanctioned by a member of staff.	

(continued)

Examples of Learning Objectives	Examples of Learning Tasks	Examples of Learning Outcomes
Students are learning to take increasing responsibility for ensuring that personal protective equipment (PPE) meets the health and safety expectations of the PESSPA activity/situation.	Students make accurate, simple checks (under the guidance of PESSPA staff) of their PPE for specific PESSPA activities/situation. Students design posters, Twitter updates or Facebook adverts to encourage their peers to check their PPE. Students make their own judgements about whether an item of PPE offers protection and fits appropriately and check their decisions with PESSPA staff. Students discuss the risks of not using appropriate PPE for specific PESSPA activities. Students discuss why it is important to know that appropriate PPE reduces, but cannot eliminate, the possibility of injury in PESSPA activities/situations.	Students will be able to: • make accurate judgements about whether items of PPE offer protection and fit appropriately • explain the hygiene implications of sharing PPE, and identify when sharing is not advisable • make accurate suggestions about what PPE is appropriate for a particular PESSPA activity/situation and when it should be used • explain why it is important it is to replace PPE after damage or normal wear and tear.

Chapter 3/Section 9: Learning about safe practice in relation to People

Table 35: Learning about safe practice in relation to People

Examples of Learning Objectives	Examples of Learning Tasks	Examples of Learning Outcomes
Students are learning to take increasing responsibility for others' safety by acting responsibly towards their peers.	Students learn how to share equipment and take turns when participating in simple physical education, school sport and physical activity (PESSPA) activities. Students participate in very simple PESSPA activities that help them, for example, learn how to: • collect equipment in an orderly manner and only when asked to do so • stop promptly when asked • keep inside the boundaries set • be aware of what is happening around them • avoid collisions with others • avoid unnecessary 'rough' behaviour • listen to and carry out instructions carefully. Students discuss why the above are examples of 'good'/positive behaviour and how this behaviour can benefit their own and others' safety. Students discuss what 'acting responsibly' toward others means in PESSPA situations (ie making independent decisions that benefit their own and others' safety).	Students will be able to: • describe/identify simple ways in which they can show 'good' or 'positive' behaviour towards their peers in PESSPA activities • distinguish between positive and negative behaviour towards their peers in PESSPA situations • describe PESSPA situations in which it is particularly important to respond positively and responsibly to their peers • provide appropriate examples of how good or positive behaviour towards others in PESSPA activities/situations can keep them safe • explain what is meant by 'acting responsibly' towards others • demonstrate that they can effectively take some responsibility for others' safety in appropriate PESSPA situations • suggest appropriate teaching points (TPs) for PESSPA activities in which they are taking some responsibility for others' safety

(continued)

Examples of Learning Objectives	Examples of Learning Tasks	Examples of Learning Outcomes
See previous page.	Students participate in practical PESSPA activities/situations that involve them learning how to take 'real' responsibility for others' safety under appropriate supervision of PESSPA staff (eg performing pairs balances in gymnastics, performing contact lifts in dance, learning to perform a scrummage in rugby, 'spotting' in trampolining and supporting in gymnastics).	• explain why responding positively and responsibly to their peers can minimise risk in PESSPA activities/situations
	Students participate in and/or consider a range of PESSPA activities/situations, and rank them in terms of the extent to which they feel sufficiently confident to take part (eg 0 = not confident at all, 10 = extremely confident). They discuss why people's confidence about the same PESSPA activity/situation differs.	• explain why it is important to respect that some peers may feel less confident about the same PESSPA task
	Students discuss why it is important not to put peers under pressure to attempt tasks that they do not feel sufficiently confident to try.	• suggest appropriate ways of supporting peers who feel less confident about the same PESSPA task
	Students role-play case studies (simple and more complex) that consider appropriate and positive responses they might make to others in PESSPA situations.	• explain the safety implications of putting peers under pressure to attempt tasks that they do not feel sufficiently confident to try.
	Students design a poster/code of conduct focusing on how to respond appropriately to peers to minimise risk in PESSPA.	

(continued)

Examples of Learning Objectives	Examples of Learning Tasks	Examples of Learning Outcomes
Students are learning to take increasing responsibility for their own behaviour in terms of how it impacts on safety.	Students select words or phrases (from those that describe behaviour) that are associated with keeping them safe in PESSPA situations, and explain and discuss the reasons for their choices (eg concentrating, listening, being responsible, being sensible, being considerate, being positive, being patient, being careful).	Students will be able to:
		• describe what it means to 'behave well' in PESSPA situations (eg concentrating, listening, being responsible, being sensible, being considerate, being positive, being patient, being careful)
	Students design a poster, Twitter update or Facebook ad to promote the role of concentration in keeping people safe in PESSPA (additional learning tasks on page 336).	• suggest clear reasons why PESSPA situations might be less safe if they do not 'behave well'
		• make eye contact when listening to instructions
	Students design a 'safe behaviour' code of conduct for a range of different activities/situations.	• listen carefully when receiving instructions, and accurately recall what has been said
		• ask relevant questions to clarify understanding
		• describe what it means to concentrate
		• explain what helps them to concentrate well
		• explain what might cause them to lack concentration, and make suggestions for how this can be avoided
		• explain how their own behaviour can impact positively and negatively on the concentration of others
		• identify PESSPA activities/situations that require concentration in order to maintain safety
		• explain how appropriate standards of behaviour associated with familiar PESSPA activities/situations affect their own and others' safety
		• suggest appropriate standards of behaviour for new and unfamiliar PESSPA activities/situations.

(continued)

Examples of Learning Objectives	Examples of Learning Tasks	Examples of Learning Outcomes
Students are learning to take increasing responsibility for giving high quality and supportive feedback to their peers.	Students develop their observational and communication skills when working with others in practical PESSPA activities/situations.	Students will be able to: • communicate safety instructions effectively: – explain what effective communication means and why it is important – speak audibly and clearly when giving instructions – make eye contact when giving instructions
	Students observe a partner's practical performance of a PESSPA task and look for simple teaching points relating to safe practice.	• observe and identify safe technique in others' performances: – adopt appropriate positions to observe others' performances – accurately identify teaching points associated with joint alignment and control in others' performances
	Students describe the teaching points they see using the following statement: *Well done. I could see the following safety points in your performance:* · *It would make your performance even safer if you could do the following next time:* ·	– explain the role of video clips/pictures/practical demonstrations to support identification of TPs – explain the value of being able to identify TPs in others' performances
		• give supportive feedback: – explain the meaning and purpose of feedback – distinguish between positive and negative feedback – start feedback with a positive comment about what is going well – explain what needs improving in a positive manner – evaluate the limitations of negative feedback and the strengths of positive feedback – explain the importance of being honest when giving feedback – evaluate their ability to give supportive feedback – give advice to someone about how to give supportive feedback
	Students video each other's and their own performances, and decide feedback relating to safe practice.	• show respect and empathy in feedback situations: – describe what 'respect' and 'empathy' mean in the context of giving feedback – explain the importance of respect and empathy in feedback situations – suggest and demonstrate strategies for showing respect and empathy in feedback situations.

4 Teaching safely – activity-specific information

What is this chapter about?

This chapter provides additional information about safe practice that is relevant to specific physical education, school sport and physical activity (PESSPA) activities. Information complies with the fundamental principles of safe practice (Chapter 1) and the principles of safe organisation and management (Chapter 2). It is presented in the following sections:

Section 1: Aquatic activities
Section 2: Athletics activities
Section 3: Combat and martial arts activities
Section 4: Dance activities
Section 5: Games activities
Section 6: Gymnastics activities
Section 7: Health-related physical activities
Section 8: Outdoor and adventure activities

How can you make effective use of this chapter?

This chapter supports PESSPA staff who are planning to promote learning in and through specific practical contexts. The information in this chapter is most effectively applied when combined with a sound understanding of the fundamental principles of safe practice (Chapter 1) and the principles of safe organisation and management (Chapter 2).

Reference to this chapter alone is unlikely to ensure good standards of safe practice.

Chapter 4/Section 1: Aquatic activities

The aquatic activities context

4.1.1 Swimming is a very inclusive, health-promoting activity that can be continued for life. Learning to swim and be confident in water not only saves lives, but can also provide the essential foundation for individuals to access many water-based recreational activities. Aquatic activities include swimming, water safety activities, lifesaving, diving and open-water swimming.

General safe-practice issues

4.1.2 Fundamental principles of safe practice (**Chapter 1**) and principles of safe organisation and management (Chapter 2) should be understood and applied to all school provision of aquatic activities. A helpful summary of these is provided in Table 6, Chapter 2, pages 64–67. More specific guidance and information about aquatic activities is provided in this section, and staff should familiarise themselves with this and apply it to their unique set of circumstances. The rules of the governing bodies of sport may not always be appropriate to schools, and schools should adjust their practice where necessary. (See **Chapter 1, Section 2, 1.2.10–1.2.14,** and Chapter 2, Section 5, 2.5.60–2.5.61.) Links to websites can be followed to access additional information relating to safe provision of aquatic activities.

Provision

4.1.3 Due to the evident hazard of drowning, learning to swim and develop water safety skills continues to be an entitlement and a statutory element of the national curriculum (eg in England [2014] and Northern Ireland [2015]).

For more information on these curricula, see:
- **England – https://goo.gl/9OmSDx**
- **Northern Ireland – http://goo.gl/s5AGnX**

4.1.4   Where this is not the case or where schools do not choose to follow a national curriculum, it is wise to consider how provision is made to enable all students to learn this important life skill.

Structure of aquatic sessions

4.1.5   **Programmed aquatic activities** refer to those with formal structure, supervision, control and continuous monitoring from the poolside. School swimming lessons are programmed sessions where the risk is reduced due to the nature of the activity and degree of control exercised.

4.1.6   **Un-programmed aquatic activities** refer to sessions without a formal structure but with supervision and continuous monitoring, in most cases from the poolside. 'Free swimming' time at the end of a school swimming lesson, or public session in a community pool are examples of un-programmed aquatic activities.

4.1.7   The Health and Safety Executive (HSE) has clearly identified a reduced level of risk to the safety of swimmers when participating in programmed aquatic activities, compared to **un-programmed** public sessions. It is therefore recommended that school swimming lessons avoid any periods of **'free swimming'** and maintain a structured, programmed approach.

Qualifications and competence

4.1.8   Aquatics teachers and school staff who have **responsibility for the water safety** of students in **programmed activities** should hold, as a minimum, either of the following awards:

- National Rescue Award for Swimming Teachers and Coaches (NRASTC)

- Swimming Teachers' Association (STA) Level 2 Safety Award for Teachers.

4.1.9   Aquatics teachers and school staff who have **responsibility for the water safety** of students taking part in **un-programmed activities**, or for a shared space where programmed and un-programmed activities are taking place should hold a current **swimming pool lifeguard** award such as:

- Royal Life Saving Society (RLSS) National Pool Lifeguard qualification

- STA Level 2 Award for Pool Lifeguard.

 See Table 36, pages 355–357, for details of water safety awards and swimming teaching qualifications.

4.1.10   All lifeguards, lifesavers and supporting staff need to:

- update their lifesaving and water safety skills regularly, relevant to their role

- practise their lifesaving skills and, where appropriate, lifeguarding skills regularly

- remain diligent, alert and effectively organised throughout an aquatic session

- be aware of the standard operating procedures for the pool that they are using

- be appropriately dressed in order that they can fulfil the requirements of their role promptly, effectively and without restriction.

4.1.11   **School staff** may also contribute to **swimming teaching**. They should:

- be clear about what their qualifications enable them to do

- ensure that their qualifications are kept up to date and/or refreshed when required

- make it clear what standard of swimmer they are confident to teach

- demonstrate good knowledge and be able to communicate this clearly to the students

- adapt their approach to suit the needs of different students

- ensure that they maintain a good teaching position at all times – this often means having to move frequently to overcome anything that makes visibility difficult (eg glare, shadow, sunlight)

- not enter the water without leaving a supervising adult on the poolside

- not exceed the recommended student:teacher ratios arrived at through a risk assessment of the particular group, or provided by the employer

- maintain a good relationship with the pool operators and aquatics teachers, ensuring that communication is effective in ways that benefit the students, and that roles and responsibilities regarding water safety cover remain clear and understood.

Aquatics teachers

4.1.12   These specialist staff may be employed at the pool where the lessons take place, bought in by the pool provider, or bought in to a school to deliver at the school pool. They should:

- demonstrate good swimming and curriculum knowledge, and hold the appropriate qualifications

- have high expectations that appropriately inspire, motivate and safely challenge students

- plan and teach well-structured lessons developed in conjunction with the school

- be able to organise a number of other staff (pool staff or school swimming staff) so that the teaching groups are a 'best fit' for the standards and ability stages of the students

- be familiar with the emergency action plan (EAP), and understand their role and responsibility in the case of an emergency.

Table 36: Water safety awards and swimming teaching qualifications

Name of Qualification or Award	Awarding Body	About this Award	How Long is the Award Valid?
RLSS UK National Pool Lifeguard Qualification (NPLQ)	RLSS	• Minimum of 36 hours' training followed by a practical assessment on **pool lifeguard** theory, pool rescue, first aid and cardiopulmonary resuscitation (CPR).	Two years.
Level 2 Award for Pool Lifeguard	STA	• Holders can take responsibility for the safety of swimmers: – in un-programmed activities (free or public swimming) – where an un-programmed session shares the space with a programmed session (ie a structured session such as a school lesson that is monitored and supervised from the poolside) – in deep water (over 1.5 metres if tested beyond that depth).	
National Rescue Award for Swimming Teachers and Coaches (NRASTC) http://goo.gl/XvjDm3	RLSS	• This (or the STA Level 2 Safety Award for Teachers outlined below) comprises approximately 16 learning hours and is the minimum award that should be held by any swimming teacher or school swimming teacher who has responsibility for the water safety of a class in a programmed session, whether or not they are teaching swimming. • It is good practice for as many as possible of the school teaching staff and assistant school staff involved in a school swimming programme to undertake this award.	Recommended to refresh every two years. This may be dependent on employer/ insurer's requirements. The refresher course is eight hours' teaching time.
Aquatic Therapy Shallow Pool Rescue Award (ATSPRA)	RLSS	• This is a supervision and rescue qualification for therapists, teachers and support staff working on the poolside or in the water during activities such as aquatic therapy or therapeutic exercise/play. • The qualification is suitable for use in shallow pools where the rescuer will not be required to swim to perform a rescue, with water no deeper than the rescuer's chest depth. • Comprises approximately seven guided learning hours.	Same as NRASTC (above).

(continued)

Name of Qualification or Award	Awarding Body	About this Award	How Long is the Award Valid?
Level 2 Safety Award for Teachers https://goo.gl/JYz7AX	STA	• Equivalent award to NRASTC above and a minimum requirement for water safety responsibility in a programmed session. • Comprises six guided learning hours.	Two years.
Level 2 Award in Swimming Teaching	STA	• Comprises 49 guided learning hours to enable teachers to teach up to 10 beginners, and deliver STA children's courses. • A holder of this qualification can assist in larger groups under the direct supervision of a qualified swimming teacher.	Does not expire – the prerequisite lifesaving qualification must remain in date.
Level 2 Award in Aquatic Teaching – People with Disabilities	STA	• Comprises 48 guided learning hours, and trains candidates to teach aquatic activities to individuals and groups with most types of disabilities. • The Safety Award for Teachers must be held in order to access this award.	Does not expire – the prerequisite lifesaving qualification must remain in date.
Level 1 Award in Teaching Aquatics	Amateur Swimming Association (ASA) United Kingdom Coaching Certificate (UKCC)	• Comprises 73 learning hours, and enables the holder to **assist** a more highly qualified swimming teacher to deliver a swimming session. • It is a requirement to hold this award before undertaking the Level 2 Certificate in Teaching Aquatics. • Recently, opportunities for a blended learning approach have been introduced. Information can be found at http://goo.gl/cBTeGH	This award does not expire. However, the holder would be expected to keep their knowledge and practice up to date through additional professional learning and online training.

(continued)

Name of Qualification or Award	Awarding Body	About this Award	How Long is the Award Valid?
Level 2 Certificate for Teaching Aquatics	ASA UKCC	• Comprises 60 additional guided learning hours, and enables the holder to lead the teaching of a swimming session. • This is the level of qualified swimming teacher that schools should be looking to employ if buying in specialist swimming teachers.	This award does not expire. However, the holder would be expected to keep their knowledge and practice up to date through additional professional learning and online training.

National Curriculum Training Programme
 	
http://goo.gl/t93m9G
	ASA	• Comprises two training programmes, which use a combination of theory and practical sessions:
		
		  – Fundamentals of School Swimming – enables the holder to assist and support a more qualified teacher.
		
		  The holder can then progress on to:
		
		  – Aquatic Skills of School Swimming – following which they will be qualified to plan and evaluate session plans, and teach independently within a school swimming programme.
		
		• **It does not provide a water safety qualification** (such as the NRASTC and Level 2 Safety Award for Teachers above).
		
		• Those who have completed these modules are not qualified to lead programmed swimming sessions alone.	

4.1.13   **Adults accompanying students to aquatics lessons** should:

- be given a clear role

- understand the limits of their role

- be confident on the poolside

- communicate effectively and appropriately with the other adults on safety issues

- have the necessary discipline and control standards

- regularly carry out head counts during, as well as at the beginning and end of, sessions

- know, understand and be able to apply the pool normal operating procedures (NOPs) and EAP

- be suitably dressed for the role they are to play in the lesson.

4.1.14   Staff should not be deployed in a poolside role if they:

- **lack confidence** in the role

- cannot swim

- are reticent about being on the poolside.

4.1.15   Staff should have the opportunity to express a lack of confidence or ability before being deployed in a poolside role.

Supervision

4.1.16   Whenever students are in water, and for all aquatic activities, a **suitably qualified adult** should be present at the poolside who is able to effect a rescue from the water and carry out CPR. (See Chapter 2, Section 2, page 68, for more information about suitable qualifications and competence.) The total number of adults required in relation to student numbers should be decided through risk assessment.

For more information about risk assessment, see Chapter 1, Section 6, page 29.

4.1.17   A minimum of **two** people on the poolside is common, and good practice to cover eventualities in the teaching and safety aspects of aquatic activities. Where only one adult is present, the risk assessment needs to indicate clearly why this ratio is acceptable and should highlight alternative emergency arrangements.

4.1.18   Where specialist aquatics teachers are employed to lead a lesson, it is strongly recommended that **school staff remain on poolside** to provide an assisting role.

4.1.19   Specialist aquatics staff may also provide essential **lifesaving cover**. Another responsible adult should be available to supervise the students in any situation where the specialist aquatics teacher has to enter the water to carry out a rescue.

4.1.20   **Ratios** of adults to students will be different for each class. A risk assessment to decide an appropriate ratio should consider:

- numbers of 'qualified' staff

- numbers of 'non-qualified' adult helpers who are on poolside in a supervisory role

- student ability

- the facility, including water depth and un-programmed activities taking place at the same time

- student behaviour

- students with special educational needs and disabilities (SEND).

4.1.21   While a minimum number of staff may satisfy ratio requirements, schools should consider whether the safety of the session and quality of teaching would be enhanced by assigning additional staff, to teach smaller groups or carry out monitoring roles such as head counts or watching for signs of student fatigue.

4.1.22   In some cases, employers will set **local requirements**, and these must be followed. Ratios should allow for all students to be managed safely.

4.1.23   Some governing bodies of sport and other professional bodies may also set maximum generic adult:participant ratios. While these should be considered, they may not take into account the specific or varied circumstances that need addressing by staff leading school swimming sessions.

4.1.24   **Un-programmed** sessions, such as leisure and play sessions, or where the pool space is shared between un-programmed and programmed activities may require **higher levels of supervision** and lifeguard expertise because of their less controlled nature.

4.1.25   The supervision of activities such as canoeing or scuba diving in pools requires **specialist knowledge** in both teaching and lifesaving, which needs to be identified in the appropriate risk assessment.

 For information about supervision of changing areas, see Chapter 2, Section 13, pages 223–224.

Management of aquatic sessions

4.1.26   A nominated school staff member should be responsible for ensuring risk assessments are carried out, and for monitoring:

- student progress

- accompanying staff confidence and competence

- the application of policies and procedures

- informing other staff of procedures and standards.

4.1.27   Whoever is responsible for the water safety of the group should be told the **number in the group** by school staff so that regular scanning and accurate head counts can be carried out during the session.

4.1.28   Where an adult has responsibility for teaching more than two students, the recommended **teaching position** is from the side of the pool as this provides the best position to oversee the whole group and respond quickly to any teaching or emergency situation.

4.1.29   All school staff and specialist aquatics staff should be able to see all students throughout the lesson. The bottom of the pool should be **clearly visible**, and any problems of glare, light reflected from the water surface, or shadow caused by hoists or similar apparatus should be satisfactorily overcome. Where this cannot be achieved, staff should regularly change their teaching position and/or request additional help in monitoring 'blind spots' from accompanying adults available on the poolside.

4.1.30   **It is imperative that staff count the students out of the pool and off the poolside. Staff should walk around the pool at the end of each aquatics session to ensure that all areas are clear of students.**

4.1.31   **Additional adults** may be in the water to assist individual students or small groups according to their age, ability and confidence. Where manual support is provided, care needs to be taken to:

- avoid embarrassment to student or adult

- ensure support is provided in an appropriate form

- promote student learning about feeling safe in relation to the use of manual support in physical education, school sport and physical activity (PESSPA) activities. (See **Chapter 2, Section 8, page 157,** and **Chapter 3, Section 2, page 307.**)

4.1.32   Students with **medical problems** may need clearance provided through the written permission of parents before they are allowed to participate in school aquatics programmes. Additional advice may also be necessary from relevant organisations with regard to specific risk factors relating to aquatic activity that may affect the student.

4.1.33   The requirements of students with **epilepsy** may vary depending on whether an effective medication regime is in place. They may need to:

- be observed from the poolside by a staff member assigned specifically to that role

- work alongside a responsible person in the water when out of their depth

- if appropriate, work within a 'buddy' system with a student or helper in the water to provide an **unobtrusive** paired supervision that avoids embarrassment.

4.1.34   The extent of their participation will need to be informed by the effectiveness of their medication to control the onset of epilepsy, and whether the student has a history of episodes in swimming.

For further information about education, health and care plans, see Chapter 2, Section 14, page 229, **and about epilepsy, see** page 240.

4.1.35   Pool lifeguard staff should be trained in the use of **spinal boards/special recovery stretchers**, where these are available at pools. Spinal boards more easily meet the need of recovering patients, especially where they may have suffered head and neck injury. School staff and those on poolside duty should know how to assemble and use such equipment, where it is available and where their role may include responsibility for water rescues.

4.1.36   All students should be made aware of the necessary procedures, and learn the importance of taking increasing responsibility, for personal **safety routines**, including:

- removing, or making safe, all jewellery

- not chewing sweets or gum

- carrying out appropriate hygiene procedures

- reporting any illness

- walking (not running) on the pool surround

- remaining away from the pool edge until told to approach the water

- knowing and responding appropriately to the emergency procedures for stopping activity and evacuating the pool

- reporting unseemly or unacceptable behaviour that may compromise safety

- responding immediately to all instructions.

The ASA guidance 'Safe supervision for teaching and coaching swimming' is currently under review and will be published as 'Safe management and supervision of programmed swimming lessons and training sessions'.

See http://goo.gl/DjYqwU or contact the ASA for further details.

The STA 'Swimming Teaching Code of Practice' is available from www.sta.co.uk

Swimwear and equipment

4.1.37   **Swimwear** should be suitable for purpose. For reasons of safety, it should be sufficiently tight-fitting to allow freedom of body and limb movement without causing unsafe water resistance. Cultural or religious sensitivity needs to be demonstrated, but staff should ensure the correct balance between safety, cultural requirements and the need to be able to see the limb movements of students to ensure appropriate learning and safe practice.

For information about clothing, footwear and personal effects, see Chapter 2, Section 10, page 174.

4.1.38   Students with **long hair** should wear caps to prevent vision being affected. (This can also reduce the amount of hair that becomes trapped in the grilles and filters.)

4.1.39   **Swimming goggles** – see Chapter 2, Section 11, 2.11.34–2.11.44, pages 187–188.

4.1.40   **Safety equipment,** such as poles, throwing ropes or throw bags, first aid provision and emergency alarms, needs to be:

- fit for purpose

- sufficient in quantity

- regularly checked

- positioned so as to be readily available when needed without creating additional hazards to pool users.

4.1.41   A variety of teaching and **flotation aids** should be available. Equipment should:

- conform to any BS EN standard, where available

- be checked before the session to ensure it is safe to use

- be close at hand for easy access and use during the session

- be placed tidily on the poolside to minimise tripping or other safety hazards

- be used appropriately to avoid over-reliance

- be appropriate and safe for the needs of the students

- be correctly fitted or held according to the design and purpose of the aid.

4.1.42   **Leisure or play** equipment may adversely affect supervision by restricting the supervisor's view. When in use, leisure or play equipment should be:

- observed from all sides

- removed from use if additional lifeguarding provision is not available.

4.1.43   Any **electrical equipment** on the poolside needs to be:

- designed to be used in an aquatic environment

- of low voltage or battery operated

- located so as not to create an additional hazard

- have current circuit breakers attached

- be PAT tested annually

- be checked regularly.

4.1.44   No one in the water should handle any electrical equipment.

The swimming facility

4.1.45   Schools will often use swimming or hydrotherapy pools on **premises other than their own**. By law, the manager of the facility must ensure that it is safe and presents no risk to health for visiting groups. This applies equally when schools use pools belonging to other schools.

4.1.46   A swimming or hydrotherapy pool on a school site is regarded in law as part of a place of work and, as such, is under the responsibility of the host school. However, visiting staff with duty of care for aquatic sessions should always ensure that, before allowing students to use the facility at another school, they make whatever checks they can, both prior to setting up the programme and as part of each visit.

4.1.47   As with all facilities, where the user hires out a pool, once they have accepted that the facility has been handed over, fit for purpose and in a safe condition, the user then becomes responsible for overseeing the safety of that facility.

For further information about swimming pool facilities, see Chapter 2, Section 13, page 221.

Pool safety operating procedures

4.1.48   **Pool safety operating procedures (PSOPs)**, consisting of NOPs and an EAP, should be known, applied and practised, as relevant, by all staff (school and pool) working in the lesson.

Table 37: Pool safety operating procedures

NOPs (Normal operating procedures)	EAP (Emergency action plan)

These are the day-to-day organisational systems based on risk assessment, and would typically include information relating to:
 	
• pool design and depth
• potential areas of risk
• arrangements for lessons
• responsibility for safety
• staffing levels and qualifications
• supervision and student conduct
• arrangements for students with particular needs (eg very young children, or those with SEND or medical conditions)
• pool safety and equipment
• clothing and personal equipment
• maximum numbers
• first aid provision
• water quality.
	This should establish who assumes leadership in managing emergencies and the action to be taken in relation to such issues as:
	
	• serious injury to a bather
	• dealing with casualties in the water
	• sudden overcrowding in a public pool
	• sudden lack of water clarity
	• disorderly behaviour
	• faecal fouling
	• vomit
	• blood contamination
	• emergency evacuation due to:
	  – fire alarm
	  – bomb threat
	  – power failure
	  – structural failure
	  – toxic-gas emission.

4.1.49   **Safety notices** should be highly visible and located in positions relevant to the issue. For example, signs indicating 'shallow water, no diving' should be placed at the sides of the pool where they are clearly visible from the shallow end, and not behind the person entering the shallow water. Safety signs should be brought to the attention of all students, and should be clear and understandable, including for those who are visually impaired or have difficulties with reading, or for those for whom English is not their first language.

4.1.50   Consideration needs to be given to the fact that, during an **emergency evacuation**, students will have bare feet, be wearing little clothing and may be outside for an extended period of time. Pool operators should make provision for these factors in their EAPs. Some pool management systems provide, for example, space (foil) blankets and, in some instances, rubberoid surfaces near the emergency exits.

4.1.51   Access to a **telephone** giving direct contact from the pool to the emergency services is essential. The system for providing this access should be guaranteed during all hours when the pool is in use.

Further information can be found in HSE (2003) *Managing Health and Safety in Swimming Pools*. London: HSE. ISBN: 978-0-717626-86-1. (Available from http://goo.gl/QYavjH)

The revision of this guidance by a number of industry stakeholders with HSE support has recently been completed. Following HSE agreement, the six documents that make up the revised publication will be available online. See www.hse.org.uk for details of updates.

Guidance on specific aquatic activities

Diving

4.1.52   **Prior** to any dives being taught, students should have developed an appropriate level of confidence and competence in aquatic practices, progressing to the execution of safe feet-first and head-first entries from the poolside. Typical progression from this is for students to learn to perform the plunge dive. As well as being taught technique, the students should also learn when it is appropriate to use the dive.

4.1.53   **Where diving forms part or all of a swimming lesson**, the pool **freeboard** (the distance from the poolside to the water surface) should be less than 0.3 metres with a sufficient **forward clearance** (the horizontal distance at which the minimum depth of water is maintained) typically in excess of 7.5 metres.

4.1.54   The depth of a dive is affected by:

- the height from which the dive is made – more height can lead to a deeper dive

- the angle of entry – a steeper entry can lead to a deeper dive

- flight distance – a short flight can lead to a deeper dive

- the strength and drive from the diver's legs – a strong drive can result in a deeper dive.

4.1.55   The water **depth for diving**, other than racing starts, should ideally be standing height plus arms and fingers fully extended. However, this advice is exemplary as some pools do not provide sufficient depth to meet this requirement for tall students. Where this is not practicable, the deepest water available, with a minimum depth of 1.8 metres, should be used with the exercise of additional caution.

4.1.56   Staff should ensure dives are executed into the deeper end of the swimming pool as a matter of routine safety. Where plain header dives are taught, the water should be a minimum of three metres in depth. Generally, entry into water less than 1.5 metres in depth may best be effected from a sitting position on the side of the pool.

4.1.57   Diving blocks should always be fitted at the deepest end of the swimming pool.

4.1.58   Where diving provision is made in a main pool rather than a diving pit, the designated diving area should be **clearly defined**, and other swimmers discouraged or prohibited from entering that area. Students should check the diving area is clear before commencing any dive.

4.1.59   Good class organisation and discipline are paramount in diving activities. Staff and students need to be fully aware of the additional safety implications for diving, over and above those for general aquatic activities to ensure safe practice. These include the following:

- Divers should not wear goggles.

- Toes should be curled over the pool edge for each dive.

- Dives should be performed from a stationary position.

- Arms should be extended beyond the head, with the hands clasped for a safe entry.

- Prolonged underwater swimming after a dive should be discouraged.

4.1.60   Students should be thoroughly familiar with the water space and environment in which they learn to dive. Diving should never take place in **unknown waters**.

4.1.61   To avoid the risk of collisions during simultaneous dives, there should be:

- sufficient pool space

- sufficient forward clearance

- no underwater obstructions

- clearly understood exit routes from the entry area on resurfacing from a dive.

4.1.62   Care should be taken with a feet-first entry from a jump as this can cause damage to the ankles, arches of the feet or lower spine if the pool bottom is struck with force when water is shallow. Safe feet-first entry can be achieved by considering the:

- extent of knee bend

- water depth

- freeboard height

- size and weight of the student.

4.1.63   Competitive shallow-entry dives should be taught in water of no less than 1.8 metres in depth. When students have achieved the standard of the ASA Competitive Start Awards and can execute a competitive shallow dive consistently, they may progress to performing such a dive in water of no less than 0.9 metres in depth.

 For more information on the ASA Competitive Start Awards, see http://goo.gl/BgyE51

4.1.64   Any student commencing a swimming race with a plunge-dive entry should be checked for their competence to do so safely, especially when the entry is from a starting block. It is not recommended that raised blocks are used for school swimming instruction, unless the school has a very highly developed programme taught by suitably qualified instructors.

4.1.65   **Vertical poolside dives and diving from a board should not form part of mainstream school swimming unless delivered by a qualified diving teacher in an environment where the following safety factors have been applied:**

- Diving boards should be checked before use to ensure that security of footing will not be affected by damage or slipperiness.

- Only one student should be allowed on any part of the board at any time.

- Both the student and the teacher should check that the water is clear of other swimmers or obstruction before each dive is performed.

- Progression should be achieved gradually and appropriately from low level to greater heights.

- Dives of three metres or more require the water surface to be disturbed by a specialist facility or hosepipe with a spray nozzle played across the surface. This helps the diver to identify the water level, and avoids them mistiming their entry, which might possibly cause injury.

Water safety sessions

4.1.66 It is important that personal survival and water safety skills are taught. Students should understand the **effects and dangers of cold water**, their ability to assess a water safety situation and the application of the principles of personal survival.

4.1.67 **Swimming in clothes** is common practice in water safety sessions as it helps to simulate real situations. These sessions should teach students how to conserve energy and body heat while staying afloat, through the use of gentle swimming movements and holding specific body positions. Swimming teachers should take account of the fact that wearing clothes presents different challenges for swimmers in that they offer more resistance, which can result in swimmers tiring more easily and swimming more slowly.

Lifesaving sessions

4.1.68 When teaching lifesaving, children below eight years of age should only learn to reach with a pole or similar item, and to perform throwing rescues.

4.1.69 **Contact rescues** should not be taught to children under 13 years of age.

4.1.70 Information about teaching resources and lifesaving awards for primary and secondary students are available from the RLSS, STA and ASA.

Open-water swimming

4.1.71 Where open-water swimming opportunities are offered to students, either as part of a residential experience during curriculum time or outside of normal school hours, parents should be fully informed.

4.1.72 A thorough **risk assessment** in consultation with agencies that have local knowledge of the venue should be undertaken and reliable weather information included. Plans should be continually reviewed, to inform decisions regarding whether to continue at any given time.

4.1.73 Swimming in open water needs to be closely supervised by **competent staff** who are able to effect rescue and resuscitation procedures. Depending on the nature of the event, this may involve the need for lifeguards with an **open-water endorsement**. Consideration should also be given to the benefit of safety boats, rescue equipment, provision of facilities to treat hypothermia, the presence of emergency services and changing accommodation.

4.1.74 Before allowing anyone to enter the water, precautions should be taken to check:

- for easy entry and exit points

- for underwater obstructions

- the depth of the water

- the extent of weed

- the composition of the bottom

- the likelihood of hazardous rubbish

- for any possible effects of current, tidal flow, wave height or wind-chill factor

- that water traffic is not impinging on safety.

4.1.75   While the extent of pollution is difficult to establish, a professional judgement may need to be made on the **quality of water** and its suitability for recreational or competitive swimming.

4.1.76   One of the most prevalent diseases found in urban rivers and canals as well as lakes is **leptospirosis**, more commonly referred to as **Weil's disease**. This is a bacterial infection spread by animal urine, especially rats', that can be caught either through swallowing water or by it getting into the bloodstream through a cut or graze.

4.1.77   Symptoms of the disease can develop from between two and 30 days after exposure, and include:

- a high temperature

- chills

- headaches

- loss of appetite

- muscle pain

- irritation of the eyes

- a rash.

4.1.78   If untreated, the symptoms of a severe infection can develop 1–3 days after the more mild symptoms have passed. The disease can become life-threatening, through organ failure.

4.1.79   Any cuts or grazes should be covered with a waterproof plaster before swimming, and swallowing water should be avoided. Swimming in urban canals is not recommended.

For more information about leptospirosis, see:
www.nhs.uk/Conditions/Leptospirosis/Pages/Introduction.aspx

4.1.80   Appropriate **footwear** is advisable when swimming in open water in order to avoid the likelihood of foot injuries.

4.1.81   Swimmers are recommended to wear **wetsuits** when swimming or diving in open water, to reduce any risk of hypothermia. **Adequate clothing** needs to be available for swimmers to change into when they leave the water.

4.1.82   **Students should be briefed** thoroughly and made aware:

- that the temperature of open water is often lower than temperatures in a swimming pool

- that they should proceed with caution when entering the water

- of set boundaries that should be clearly visible and over a manageably contained area

- that they should not venture outside the set boundaries

- that weaker swimmers should keep to areas where it is easier to stand up.

4.1.83   Supervising staff positioned around the boundaries should make regular **head counts**, and **monitor** swimmers in relation to:

- their ability to cope with the conditions

- signs that they are cold

- signs of fatigue

- signs of discomfort

- signs of fear

- staying within the set boundaries

- signs of adverse effects caused by sun, wind, tide, sea state, current or weather.

4.1.84   Additional information may be obtained from the ASA, STA, and RLSS.

Hydrotherapy pool sessions

4.1.85   Hydrotherapy pools, sometimes located in special schools, provide the opportunity for students to exercise in warm water. This is of particular benefit to students with complex physical difficulties.

4.1.86   The adult:student ratio should not be determined in accordance with any swimming-specific written guidelines that may exist. A safe ratio can only be determined by carefully examining individual students' medical profiles and health-care plans in conjunction with relevant medical staff.

4.1.87   Hydrotherapy pool activity programmes usually involve **team teaching** by the class teacher, learning support/care assistants and a physiotherapist.

4.1.88   As hydrotherapy pools tend to be shallow in depth and small in size, it is not usual to require a lifeguard to be present. Depending on the particular circumstances of the students, a specialist swimming teacher may be used.

4.1.89   All staff involved in the hydrotherapy sessions need to be confident and competent to complete any water-based rescue that may become necessary, and should access regular training to ensure this.

4.1.90   A **pool watcher** should be present on the poolside, whose sole duty is to observe all pool activities and draw attention to any problems developing in the water.

4.1.91   As the pool will be used by students with complex physical difficulties, particular attention should be given to the development of risk-management schemes for:

- lifting and carrying students

- transporting students between the changing rooms and the pool

- dressing/undressing areas and support staff

- emergency equipment and procedures.

4.1.92   Due to the temperature, it is recommended that **regular maintenance** of the plant and filtration and sterilisation systems, and a comprehensive programme of water testing are carried out to ensure the safe use of hydrotherapy pools.

For more information about working with students with SEND in hydrotherapy pools and swimming pools, see:

National Co-ordinating Committee – Swimming for People with Disabilities (no date) *Let's All Swim*. **Billericay: National Co-ordinating Committee – Swimming for People with Disabilities.**

National Co-ordinating Committee – Swimming for People with Disabilities (in press) *Safe at the Pool*. **Billericay: National Co-ordinating Committee – Swimming for People with Disabilities.**

Website links

Amateur Swimming Association (ASA):	http://goo.gl/wPU5rH
ASA school swimming and water safety:	http://goo.gl/G4fuz3
Chartered Institute for the Management of Sport and Physical Activity (CIMSPA):	www.cimspa.co.uk
Government safety advice on water sports and coastal activities:	https://goo.gl/Uj54oF
	https://goo.gl/vrdIQm
Marine and Coastguard Agency (MCA):	https://goo.gl/mM7oPC
National guidance document 7x swimming pools (swimming on visits):	http://goo.gl/JOFVqu
Royal Life Saving Society (RLSS) UK:	www.rlss.org.uk
Sport England advice and guidance on swimming pool design:	http://goo.gl/ZcMWDL
Scottish Swimming:	www.scottishswimming.com
Swim Ireland:	www.swimireland.ie
Swim Wales:	www.swimwales.org
Swimming Teachers' Association (STA):	www.sta.co.uk

Chapter 4/Section 2: Athletics activities

The athletics context

4.2.1   Curriculum provision of athletics can play a key role in developing physical literacy. It provides an introduction to, and progression in, running, jumping and throwing, and can establish firm foundations for confident and competent participation in other physical education, school sport and physical activity (PESSPA) activities. Primary school is a key environment in which to develop the fundamental principles associated with these skills in their purest forms.

General safe-practice issues

4.2.2   Fundamental principles of safe practice (**Chapter 1**) and principles of safe organisation and management (Chapter 2) should be understood and applied to all school provision of athletics activities. A helpful summary of these is provided in Table 6, Chapter 2, pages 64–67. More specific guidance and information about athletics activities are provided in this section, and staff should familiarise themselves with these and apply them to their unique set of circumstances. The rules of the governing bodies of sport may not always be appropriate to schools, and schools should adjust their practice where necessary. (See **Chapter 1, Section 2, 1.2.10–1.2.14,** and Chapter 2, Section 5, 2.5.60–2.5.61.) Links to websites can be followed to access additional information relating to safe provision of athletics activities.

Guidance on specific athletics events/activities

4.2.3 **It is recommended that any multi-event athletics session within a PESSPA programme should comprise a maximum of four activities at any one time, with only one of these to be a throwing event, which should be closely supervised.**

Throwing activities

4.2.4 Staff should be clear about which throwing activities/events are developmentally appropriate for their students. The schools athletics websites listed at the end of this section provide the necessary recommendations.

4.2.5 Basic standing throws should be taught before adding turns or run-ups.

4.2.6 Competitive throwing events (eg javelin, shot, discus, hammer) are **higher risk activities**. Staff and officials teaching, supervising and/or officiating competitive throwing events need to be competent to do so. This may require them to undertake additional professional learning.

Throwing equipment

4.2.7 Students should be provided with the appropriate **age- and stage-related** type, weight and dimensions of throwing implement. For further information, see schools athletics websites at the end of this section.

4.2.8 The approved safety procedures associated with throwing activities (see 4.2.12–4.2.24) should still be enforced when child-friendly equipment such as foam javelins, quoits and balls are used to teach throwing techniques (eg in primary or special schools).

4.2.9 Students should be reminded to check that the grip on a throwing implement is dry.

4.2.10 Purpose-made hammers with a free spindle and wire in good condition should be used.

4.2.11 Slightly shorter 'training' javelins are now available. They have a blunt end, and a solid flexible body with plastic tips and tails. Due to the shorter length, they are considered to be easier to control and are designed to develop correct technique.

Transporting, handling and storing throwing equipment

4.2.12 Staff should supervise the carrying of throwing implements **in transit** to the lesson as well as during the lesson. All throwing implements should be carried and retrieved singly using two hands to prevent students attempting 'mock' throwing actions. Javelins should be carried upright, and the ends protected if possible. Multiple shots, discuses and hammers may be carried in baskets provided the overall weight is not excessive.

4.2.13 All throwing implements should be carried and retrieved at **walking pace**. They should always be **carried** back to the throwing line (**never** thrown), and placed on the ground (**never** dropped).

4.2.14 Javelins, when not in use, should be placed vertically in a storage rack or, when a rack is not available, laid flat on the ground.

Throwing areas

4.2.15 Risk assessments should consider whether throwing activities should be adapted, limited or abandoned if the **grass surface** of a work area is wet.

4.2.16   Work areas for approach and release for throwing events should be checked to see that they are stable, level, smooth and non-slip, with sufficient space between participants.

4.2.17   Staff should ensure that **throwing lines and zones** for lessons and competition are clearly identified and demarcated, and that procedures for **entering throwing zones** are known and reinforced.

4.2.18   Wide margins of error should be allowed for the release and direction of throws. Staff and students need to check that all possible lines of flight are clear before staff allow throws to commence.

4.2.19   **Left-handed** discus throwers should be positioned at the left side of a throwing group to minimise the likelihood of injury in the event of an early release.

4.2.20   **Safety nets and cages** that meet British Athletics standards should be used whenever students employ a turn technique for appropriate throwing events (ie in practice, training or competition).

Throwing procedures

4.2.21   Staff should use auditory and visual **'ready and response signals'** to indicate when students are to throw and to retrieve throwing implements. Staff should check that these signals are clearly understood by all students and that they know how to respond appropriately.

4.2.22   Throwers in group situations should throw **sequentially** and in a predetermined order. Students waiting to perform need to **stand well behind** the throwing line or circle, and focus on the thrower until told by staff to move forward. To ensure a safe waiting distance is maintained, staff may use cones or mark a line.

4.2.23   Throwers need to remain **behind** the throwing line until told by staff to retrieve their implement.

4.2.24   Staff and/or officials should always be **appropriately positioned** before and during throwing activities/events, and should regularly remind students of required safety procedures and correct technical points, and encourage them to contribute to checking safety and demonstrating safe practice.

Jumping activities

4.2.25   Staff should be clear about which jumping activities/events and equipment are developmentally appropriate for their students. The schools athletics websites listed at the end of this section provide the necessary recommendations.

4.2.26   Students should understand and be competent in basic **feet-to-feet** jumping before progressing to more advanced techniques.

4.2.27   Competitive jumping events such as pole vault and high jump using Fosbury-flop technique are **higher risk activities**. Staff and officials teaching, supervising and officiating competitive jumping events need to be competent to do so. This may require them to undertake additional professional learning.

High jump

4.2.28   Take-off markers or zones should be used to indicate take-off positions in the early stages of learning **high jump** to ensure that the bar is negotiated at the midpoint and that landing occurs in the centre of the sand pit or landing module.

4.2.29   Round bars are recommended for feet-to-body high-jump styles (eg Fosbury flop). Triangular bars should no longer be used.

4.2.30   The uprights for flexi-bars need to be secured so that they do not collapse on jumpers.

Long jump

4.2.31   Brightly coloured boards placed on a long-jump runway can help to indicate when jumping is not allowed. Take-off boards should be flush with the runway to prevent tripping injuries.

Pole vault

4.2.32   Fibre-glass vaulting poles need to be checked regularly for damage and:

- discarded if cracked or spiked

- stored suitably to prevent bending

- used only in planting boxes with a sloping back plate (not vertical).

4.2.33   Only suitably qualified staff should teach students how to bend a vaulting pole.

Landing areas

4.2.34   Landing areas need to be sufficiently large to accommodate all abilities of performer.

4.2.35   **Sand areas** in **high jump** are only suitable for horizontal and low-level jumping for height, involving feet-to-feet landing. In these cases, wooden or concrete surrounds should not present a danger. Where a sand area is not available, schools should consider using a **standing jump** technique.

4.2.36   Indoor jumping requires the correct landing modules (or sufficient depth of matting and cover) that are not normally considered primary PESSPA equipment. Loose 'crash mats' without a cover should never be used as landing areas.

4.2.37   Multi-unit high-jump **landing beds** should:

- be large enough to extend beyond the uprights (at least five metres by 2.5 metres)

- be deep and dense enough to prevent bottoming out (refer to BS EN 12503-2:2016)

- be fitted with a coverall to hold them together and prevent athletes falling between the modules

- be inspected regularly

- conform to British Athletics standards when used for competition.

4.2.38   In **long jump**, multiple take-off boards (ie set at different distances from the sand) are helpful to ensure that jumpers of different abilities can land safely in the sand area.

4.2.39   Sand levels should be to the top of the long-jump pit, and level with the runway, and need to be regularly checked for fouling (see Chapter 2, Section 13, 2.13.14, page 213) and dangerous objects (2.13.13).

4.2.40   Non-caking sharp sand should be used and should be **at least 30cm deep** to prevent jarring on landing. A sand landing area should be **regularly dug and raked during practical sessions** to avoid compacted sections.

4.2.41   Digging and raking implements should be left stored at least three metres from the landing pit and with prongs and sharp edges into the ground.

4.2.42 Students should be taught how to rake the pits effectively, and to do so before the sand becomes compacted, which might cause impact injuries.

4.2.43 Approach and take-off areas for jumping events should be checked to see that they are stable, level, smooth and non-slip, with sufficient space between participants to avoid collisions.

4.2.44 Primary schools wishing to introduce jumping activities should only consider doing so if they have a sand area that meets the requirements set out above.

Jumping procedures

4.2.45 Staff should use auditory and visual **'ready and response signals'** to ensure that students are aware of when the area is clear to begin a run-up in a jumping activity. Staff should check that the signals are clearly understood by all students and they know how to respond appropriately.

4.2.46 Staff and/or officials should always be **appropriately positioned** before and during jumping activities/events, and should regularly remind students of required safety procedures and correct technical points, and encourage them to contribute to checking safety and demonstrating safe practice.

Running activities

4.2.47 Staff should be clear about which running events and distances are developmentally appropriate for their students. The schools athletics websites listed at the end of this section provide the necessary recommendations.

Running surfaces

4.2.48 Work areas for all running activities should be checked to see that they are level, free of potholes and litter, and non-slip, with sufficient space between participants to avoid collisions.

4.2.49 Risk assessments should consider whether running activities should be adapted, limited or abandoned if the **grass surface** of a work area is wet.

Running equipment

4.2.50 **Spiked shoes** should be stored and placed with the spikes facing down.

4.2.51 **Finishing tapes**, historically used to indicate winners, should be avoided wherever possible.

4.2.52 **Hurdles** for competition need to conform to British Athletics standards and be positioned appropriately so as to **topple over** if struck. Hurdles should never be jumped in the wrong direction, ie with the struts on the far side of the hurdle.

Cross-country running

4.2.53 Courses should be planned in order to ensure:

- ease of supervision

- maximum visibility of participants by staff

- suitability for the age and capability of the runners

- the slowest runners can be easily tracked

- a wide start and long clear approach before any constrictions (eg narrow gateways)

- ease of counting runners out and in.

Running procedures

4.2.54   Staff should use auditory and visual **'ready and response signals'** to ensure that students are aware of when an area is clear to begin a running activity. Staff should check that the signals are clearly understood by all students and they know how to respond appropriately.

4.2.55   Staff and/or officials should always be **appropriately positioned** before and during running activities/events, and should regularly remind students of required safety procedures and correct technical points, and encourage them to contribute to checking safety and demonstrating safe practice.

Sportshall athletics

4.2.56   It is common practice for schools to pursue athletics activities indoors through the provision of Sportshall athletics, which is a fully inclusive activity, with suggested adaptations for the range of events.

4.2.57   Staff should be clear about and check which Sportshall athletics events are developmentally appropriate and recommended for the age of students with whom they are working.

4.2.58   The recommended Sportshall **equipment** is designed to be safe and appropriate for the age group and for safe indoor use (ie made of plastic, vinyl and foam).

4.2.59   The layout required for each activity is explained in the Sportshall rules and should be followed. Tracks should be clearly designated and clear of obstructions, with dry surfaces. Adequate 'run–off' areas should be allowed.

4.2.60   Ideally, walls should have no indentations or projections, but where these exist, they should either be protected or care should be taken that activities with likely collisions or tripping hazards are conducted at a safe distance. For example, the landing areas for jumps should be well away from walls.

4.2.61   **Reversaboards** for turning should be set at a safe angle against a firm wall. Students should be taught the correct technique for using the boards.

4.2.62   It is recommended that, during **relay races**, all students waiting should be seated at the end of the activity space until their turn.

4.2.63   Students' footwear should always be clean and dry.

4.2.64   Spectators should sit well away from the activity. Officials supervising competitive running events need to be appropriately positioned before and during an activity.

Sports days

4.2.65   A sports day programme of events should reflect curricular provision. Students should be suitably prepared to participate at a level that reflects their ability.

4.2.66   All officials should receive appropriate **induction** in safe procedures, with rules and safety reminders appended to the recording sheet or clipboard.

4.2.67   Strict rules should be enforced for the safe movement around event areas for participants and spectators. Throwing areas should be roped off at some distance from the throwing zone lines. Clear signage should aid safe movement. Spectators and athletes need to be marshalled to specific safe zones effectively.

4.2.68   Throwing implements need to be stored safely and supervised at all times.

4.2.69   First aid arrangements should be known by all.

4.2.70   Water stations should be easily available.

4.2.71   Appropriate precautions need to be taken to protect spectators and athletes from the harmful effects of the sun.

4.2.72   **Firearms** are not acceptable as starting devices in schools, with the exception of very small-calibre cap-firing pistols. Clapperboards or similar implements are preferred.

4.2.73   The Olympic 380 BBM imitation handgun, the model most commonly used by lower-graded starters, clubs and schools, was reclassified as a prohibited weapon and withdrawn from usage. However, following development work by the manufacturer, the item is now legally available in the UK as the barrel is ceramic and meets all the testing requirements. It is still classified as an imitation firearm and must be in an **orange colour** to be legal. Where starting pistols are used in competition, British Athletics risk assessment guidelines should be fully complied with.

 For more information regarding planning and risk assessing sports events, see Chapter 2, Section 6, page 128.

Website links

British Athletics:	www.britishathletics.org.uk
British Athletics safe practice video clips:	https://goo.gl/CCuieB
English Schools' Athletic Association:	www.esaa.net
Scottish Schools' Athletic Association:	www.ssaa.co.uk
Sportshall athletics:	www.sportshall.org
Wales Schools' Athletic Association:	http://goo.gl/XoEi5V
uCoach (teaching courses and coach qualifications):	http://ucoach.com
Ulster Secondary Schools Athletics Association:	www.ussaa.co.uk

Chapter 4/Section 3: Combat and martial arts activities

The combat and martial arts activities context

4.3.1   **Combat activities** are competitive contact sports that are characterised by one-on-one combat in which a winner is determined against a set of rules. In many combat sports, a contestant wins by scoring more points than their opponent (eg boxing, fencing, self-defence and wrestling). Some combat activities are regulated by **recognised governing bodies of sport**, and others are not. This does not necessarily imply unsafe practice.

4.3.2   **Martial arts** are traditions of combat techniques practised for a variety of reasons, such as self-defence, competition, physical health and fitness, entertainment, as well as mental, physical and spiritual development. Martial arts include the activities aikido, judo, karate, kendo, ju-jitsu, kung fu and taekwondo. The activity known as **'mixed martial arts'** (MMA) takes place within a caged arena for safety. This is currently not an activity that afPE condones in schools.

4.3.3   **Mixed combat activities** lessons are becoming common, providing a 'taster' of several different sports. Where schools offer more than one combat activity in any one session, staff should be appropriately qualified in **each of the activities** involved. The term 'mixed combat activities' should not be confused with the activity of 'mixed martial arts' as detailed above.

General safe-practice issues

4.3.4   Fundamental principles of safe practice (**Chapter 1**) and principles of safe organisation and management (Chapter 2) should be understood and applied to all school provision of combat activities. A helpful summary of these is provided in Table 6, Chapter 2, pages 64–67. More specific guidance and information about combat activities are provided in this section, and staff should familiarise themselves with these and apply them to their unique set of circumstances. The rules of the governing bodies of sport may not always be appropriate to schools, and schools should adjust their practice where necessary. (See **Chapter 1, Section 2, 1.2.10–1.2.14**, and Chapter 2, Section 5, 2.5.60–2.5.61.) Links to websites can be followed to access additional information relating to safe provision of combat activities.

4.3.5   It is advisable to **inform parents** about decisions to introduce combat and martial arts activities into a school programme.

4.3.6   All combat and martial arts activities should be appropriate to the age, ability, strength, stamina and experience of the students involved. A progressive scheme of work is essential. Basic **skills and rules** should be taught before competitive combat is introduced. Rules need to be applied fully and consistently.

Staff competence

4.3.7   As the potential for injury can be high, staff appointed to teach combat and martial arts activities in schools should be **competent** to do so safely.

      For more information about staff competence, see Chapter 2, Section 2, page 68.

4.3.8   Coaches should hold a **valid licence** to coach the relevant combat or martial arts activity. Schools need to check whether the school insurance will cover any combat and/or martial arts activities on offer. The school should check that the coach also has the personal insurances required.

4.3.9   Schools may choose to contact the relevant national, regional and/or county professional body to help determine a coach's **suitability** to deliver combat or martial arts activities in schools.

Demonstrations involving students

4.3.10   Careful consideration and forethought should be given to whether adults should perform dynamic **demonstrations using students**, and to ensure that technical guidance is provided without placing any student in an unsafe situation. Static demonstrations are acceptable.

4.3.11   Students should be carefully matched for demonstrations. Staff should not compete with students.

For more information, see Chapter 2, Section 8, pages 155 **(matching students) and** 158 **(staff participation in student activities).**

Technique

4.3.12   Correct instruction is important where strike pads are used to practise punching and kicking, both in the way the pads should be held and the impact allowed.

4.3.13   Students should be taught how to land safely (eg break falls) before take-downs and throws are practised, and mats need to be used.

Equipment

4.3.14   The wearing of **glasses** is not recommended in these activities. The use of sports goggles is suggested where required. Where students are unable to purchase these, schools may wish to make them available. If this is not possible, the staff member needs to manage the student safely within the activity or provide an alternative activity.

For more information, see Chapter 2, Section 11, 2.11.45–2.11.49, pages 188–189.

4.3.15   **Gloves** should be worn, to avoid potential soft-tissue damage, where relevant to the activity (eg boxing and fencing).

4.3.16   It is recommended that **weapons** are not used in martial arts in the school context and are preferably only introduced in the club situation. Where hazardous equipment such as fencing foils are permitted, they should be made secure and stored in a safe place that prevents unauthorised access.

4.3.17   **Mats** should:

- be inspected regularly

- comply with BS EN requirements for the specific activity; gymnastics mats are inappropriate and should not be used as they are likely to separate during activity.

For more information about mats used in martial arts activities, see Chapter 2, Section 12, 2.12.29–2.12.30, page 198.

Combat arenas

4.3.18   These should:

- be sited in a clear area away from walls and other obstacles

- be large enough to allow safe activity, ie floor area and ceiling height

- be level, even and clean, with a non-slip surface

- provide secure footing

- be sufficient in size to accommodate the group.

Personal responsibilities of students

4.3.19   Students should be made aware of their **personal responsibilities** in terms of their own and others' safety in combat and martial arts activities. They should learn to take increasing responsibility for ensuring that they:

- warm up appropriately for the activity

- participate according to the rules

- accept the official's decisions

- respect their peers, coach and working environment

- avoid being excessively competitive

- avoid losing their temper during activity

- contribute to risk assessments

- wear appropriate clothing, footwear and personal protective equipment (PPE) for the specific activity

- tie long hair back

- cut their nails short

- remove potentially hazardous personal effects

- do not chew food, sweets or gum when participating.

Mixed-gender practice

4.3.20   This is allowed in some combat and martial arts sports (eg fencing, taekwondo and judo), but mixed-gender competition is not allowed.

Guidance on specific combat activities

Boxing

4.3.21   Boxing involves two participants of similar weight fighting each other with gloved fists in a series of 1–3-minute rounds. Technical points are scored according to the accuracy, frequency and direction of blows landed on the opponent. If there is no stoppage before an agreed number of rounds, a winner is determined through a points accumulation. If the opponent is knocked down and unable to get up before the referee counts to 10, or if the opponent is deemed too injured to continue, a knockout is the result.

4.3.22   The British Medical Association (BMA), as a body of medical experts, does not support the teaching or coaching, or any participation in the sport of boxing due to evidence indicating detrimental effects on health.

4.3.23   Schools may wish to consider non-contact versions of boxing only. Wherever non-contact boxing is introduced to the curriculum, schools should ensure that all parents and students involved are aware of, and accept, the inherent and obvious risks. Parents can then make the decision as to whether their child progresses to contact boxing within a club situation.

4.3.24   England Boxing's development pathway is designed to ensure that the correct safety standards are upheld and applied in all settings. It has developed 'Standards for coaching Olympic-style non-contact boxing in schools' (http://goo.gl/nnN3eD).

4.3.25   England Boxing has introduced non-contact versions of boxing for primary and secondary students (eg for primary level at some School Games events).

4.3.26   Also at primary level, simple, fun, non-contact activities concentrating on stance and movement are introduced. No gloves or additional equipment is worn.

4.3.27   At secondary level, England Boxing has introduced 'BOX' training for teachers. This is a fitness boxing course that provides a qualification for delivering fun fitness sessions incorporating Olympic-style boxing techniques that focuses on high quality glove and pad work. This qualification can support teachers to deliver these activities within the curriculum or as an after-school club.

4.3.28   Secondary aged students (over 14) can also access the Junior Boxing Organiser Sports Leaders UK award, one of the add-on modules to the Junior Sports Leader or Community Sports Leader award.

4.3.29   If taking part in contact versions of the activity, students should be advised to wear the recommended items of equipment **at all times**, including a mouth guard, protective hand bandages, gloves, cup protectors, force-absorbent headgear and a shirt to absorb sweat. Women boxers are also required to wear breast protectors. All equipment should meet national requirements.

4.3.30   Schools engaging **boxing coaches** to work with them should be clear about what qualifications they are looking for.

4.3.31   An England Boxing **Full Coach** (Level 2 equivalent) is the minimum required to lead a session. The **Assistant Coach Award** (Level 1), as it suggests, only permits the coach to assist in a session delivered by a full coach.

4.3.32   Schools should be aware that attendance at a **Boxing Tutor course** or **England Boxing Boxing Leader Course** does not qualify candidates to lead sessions. They can only assist the delivery of sessions under the direct supervision of an England Boxing Full Coach or higher.

Useful websites

Amateur Boxing Scotland:	www.amateurboxingscotland.co.uk
England Boxing (ABAE):	www.abae.co.uk
England Boxing Disability Development Plan:	http://goo.gl/lEHi1S
Irish Amateur Boxing Association:	www.iaba.ie
Welsh Amateur Boxing Association:	http://welshboxingassociation.org/

Fencing

4.3.33   The rules and safety requirements of British Fencing, the relevant governing body of sport, need to be strictly observed.

4.3.34   The three common forms of fencing are **epee, foil and sabre**. Safety measures need to be thoroughly addressed in order to minimise the risks involved in these potentially dangerous activities.

4.3.35   The majority of fencing injuries are caused by broken blades. All swords should be regularly checked by knowledgeable staff. It is essential that only swords in **good condition** are used. Others should be condemned or taken out of use until repaired.

4.3.36   The **points of swords** need to be covered with purpose-made protective tips.

4.3.37   **Pistes** (playing areas), for both competition and practice, need to be well **spaced out** at least 1.5 metres apart. There should be a clear **run-off** at each end for the safety of participants and spectators.

4.3.38   Students should be taught the basic safety requirements. They should **never**:

- run in the salle (fencing hall) (unless under the direction of a teacher or coach and then never holding a weapon)

- point a weapon at anyone not wearing a mask and correct clothing

- mishandle equipment

- use a blade that shows signs of 'softness' or is badly bent or kinked

- fence against anyone whose blade shows signs of 'softness'

- carry a weapon other than by the pommel with the point towards the floor or by gripping the point with the weapon hanging down vertically, other than when practising or fencing

- remove masks until told to do so by the coach.

4.3.39   Students under the age of 10 should fence with weapon blades of size 0, and those under 14 should normally fence with weapon blades of size 3 or smaller, corresponding to the competition requirements for their age. Adult-sized blades (size 5) are normally to be used by all fencers of 13 years and older.

4.3.40   Adequate **body protection** is essential and should be worn **at all times**, both for practice and competition. Students should only participate in fencing activities if they are wearing:

- a plastron – a partial jacket worn under the main jacket on the weapon arm side of the body

- a mask, complete with bib and effective back spring or 'contour-fit' secured at three points (top and sides of mask) that fits correctly; sub-standard masks are unacceptable; all masks with a back spring need to be fitted with safety back straps

- a jacket long enough to cover the waistband of the trousers by at least 10cm when in the en garde position (ready to fight)

- gloves with a gauntlet to cover the cuff of the jacket sleeve, and protect the wrist and arm by extending halfway up the sword forearm to ensure a safe overlap

- breeches, mandatory during competition but optional during practice; if trousers are worn, any opening pocket needs to be taped, sewn or zipped closed

- knee-length socks, if wearing breeches, that are always covered by the bottom of the breeches so no bare skin is shown

- shoes with a sole that grips the floor adequately.

4.3.41　In addition, it is compulsory for women to wear breast protectors, and strongly recommended that girls wear breast protectors from the age of 10 or from the onset of puberty if earlier.

4.3.42　Right-handed fencers need to wear right-handed garments, which have openings on the left side, and vice versa for left-handed fencers, or they can wear jackets that zip at the back.

4.3.43　Protective clothing should be labelled denoting a **safety rating** in *newtons (N)* with a minimum for non-electric fencing of 350N for jacket, plastron and breeches. Where electronic scoring apparatus is used, the plastron should be rated 800N for over-13s.

4.3.44　Any **electrical equipment** used for scoring should be stored safely and observed carefully while in use.

GO/FENCE

4.3.45　This is the soft form of fencing using foam or plastic swords and a simple plastic face mask.

4.3.46　Guidelines for GO/FENCE are as follows:

- Check plastic foils have a large rubber button firmly affixed at the tip, that the plastic guard and blade have no cracks, and the guard is fitted securely.

- Check there is no excessive bend in the blade and that any slight curvature is in the correct direction, ie downwards (see inside guard for the word 'Thumb' and an arrow indicating where to place the thumb – the blade should be straight, but if not, a slight downward curve is allowable).

- Check the integrity of the plastic mask by ensuring all rivets are in place, especially around the visor, and that the elasticated back strap is properly fixed to the plastic and that the Velcro fastenings are intact and secure.

4.3.47　Ideally, participants in GO/FENCE activities should wear a long-sleeved top and tracksuit or jogging bottoms. A cloth-covered foam protective tabard for the chest is also recommended, especially for girls.

Useful websites

British Disabled Fencing Association:　www.bdfa.org.uk

British Fencing:　www.britishfencing.com

England Fencing:　www.englandfencing.org.uk

GO/FENCE:　http://gofence.com

Welsh Fencing:　www.welshfencing.org

Self-defence

4.3.48　There are a number of different self-defence styles and activities, some of which include weapons. In many cases, a range of combat and martial arts moves are combined to achieve successful control, restraint and self-protection.

4.3.49　Self-defence training for students will usually cover aspects of personal safety awareness skills, as well as physical self-defence techniques. Schools should check that any self-defence or self-protection training they offer is suitable for the age group in question.

Wrestling

4.3.50   The rules and philosophy of the internationally agreed freestyle form of wrestling (ie Olympic-style wrestling) are formulated to enable two wrestlers to engage in hard physical combat without pain and/or injury.

4.3.51   Schools that provide wrestling for students list the many benefits it offers as improving strength, stamina, flexibility and coordination, as well as helping to develop confidence, discipline and respect for others.

4.3.52   A trained and experienced mat chairperson should be positioned at the edge of the mat during competitions. They should intervene immediately if any move or hold performed is likely to cause pain. School staff/coaches should adopt the role of mat chairperson during practice sessions.

4.3.53   Moves that put pressure on, or twist, the neck are **extremely hazardous** and should not be taught.

4.3.54   Wrestlers aged under 17 are not allowed to execute any form of **full nelson**. A scissor lock with the feet crossed on the head, neck or body is forbidden. Students under the age of 11 are not allowed to use any form of nelson or bridging. The nelson is not allowed to be used in female wrestling.

4.3.55   Clothing should be close-fitting without being too restrictive. Swimming costumes are ideal for training, but shorts are unsuitable and should not be worn. Specifically designed wrestling singlets are recommended for competition.

4.3.56   Suitable **support protection**, in line with wrestling rules, should always be worn by male and female students. Protective arm and knee pads may be worn, and the use of ear guards should be encouraged.

4.3.57   **Footwear** for beginners should be free of metal lace tags or eyelets, and have smooth soles.

4.3.58   The wrestling **area** normally covers 12 metres by 12 metres (depending on the level), with smooth mats, in good condition, firmly secured together and meeting the Federation Internationale des Luttes Associées (FILA) standards.

4.3.59   No outside footwear should be worn on the mats. Disinfecting mats before or after every session can prevent the spread of germs and disease.

4.3.60   The minimum ceiling height should be as for judo, at 3.5 metres high, with no objects hanging below this height. Any potentially hazardous walls should be padded.

Useful website

British Wrestling Association: www.britishwrestling.org

Guidance on specific martial arts activities

Aikido

4.3.61   Aikido is a martial art that involves neutralising an attack by using holds and locks that are usually taught by modern/practical or classical/ceremonial methods.

4.3.62   Dangerous locks, holds or movements are **not** appropriate to be taught or practised in schools' programmes.

4.3.63   Students should wear a loose tunic and loose-fitting trousers such as tracksuit trousers. The traditional Japanese Gi (loose white trousers and belted jacket) is also suitable.

4.3.64   Requirements for mats, mat space per person and ceiling height are the same as for judo.

 For more information about mat space and ceiling height, see 4.3.73–4.3.75 below.

4.3.65   Mat space per person increases and additional ceiling clearance is required if weapons are used. This should only be in a club situation.

4.3.66   Aikido has no recognised governing body of sport in England.

Useful website

British Aikido Board: www.bab.org.uk

Disability martial arts

Useful websites

Adaptive Martial Arts Association: http://adaptivemartialarts.org

Disability Martial Arts Association: www.dmaa.org.uk

Judo

4.3.67   Judo involves two participants in a contest where the object is to throw the opponent largely on to their back with considerable force and speed. This scores 'ippon' (one point or 10 scores) and ends the contest. It is also possible to score ippon by pinning the opponent to the mat for a period of 25 seconds. In addition to the sought-after ippon, smaller scores are given for less successful throws and hold-downs broken before the 25-second limit.

4.3.68   It is essential that students are taught the various **ways to submit** and that they understand how important it is to accept submission and to stop applying technique immediately.

4.3.69   Students should not practise throwing techniques while others are practising groundwork skills.

4.3.70   Strangle and arm locks are **not** appropriate to be taught as part of a school's programme of tuition.

4.3.71   Whenever possible, judogi (**judo suits**) should be worn in practice. These are mandatory in competition.

4.3.72   Only **bare feet** are permitted on the tatami (judo mat).

4.3.73   A minimum **ceiling height** of 3.5 metres is needed, with no objects hanging below this level.

4.3.74   The recommended **mat area** is one metre by one metre for young children, increasing to two metres by one metre for adults. More space may be required, depending on the type of activity and intensity of practice or 'randori'.

4.3.75   The edge of the mat area should be at least two metres away from any walls, projections or open doors.

4.3.76   GCSE syllabuses provide useful guidance for the organisation of judo activities.

Useful website

British Judo Association: www.britishjudo.org.uk

Karate

4.3.77   Karate is a Japanese, weapon-free martial art based on scientific principles that encompass physical culture, character development, self-defence and sport.

4.3.78   There are many different karate organisations in the UK. It is essential that only coaches from **approved organisations** be appointed to lead karate sessions in schools. Details of approved organisations can be obtained from national sports councils or county sports partnerships.

4.3.79   One hour is the **maximum time** recommended for curriculum karate sessions, and 90 minutes is the maximum time recommended for extracurricular sessions. Sessions should emphasise technical competence and comprise:

- a safe, effective and relevant warm-up and cool-down (see Chapter 2, Section 9, page 170)

- fundamental techniques (kihon)

- formal exercise (kata)

- sparring (kumite).

4.3.80   **Non-contact sparring** should be introduced initially, with careful progression to touch contact. Reckless fighting should never be allowed.

4.3.81   Face masks and body armour should be worn at competition level.

4.3.82   Three square metres per student is required when practising fundamental techniques (kihon) and $4m^2$ per student when practising formal exercises (kata).

4.3.84   GCSE and A Level syllabuses can provide useful guidance for the organisation of karate activities.

Useful websites

Disability Karate Federation: www.disabilitykarate.co.uk

English Karate Federation: www.englishkaratefederation.com

Scottish Karate Association: www.scottishkarateassociation.co.uk

Welsh Karate: www.welshkarate.org.uk

Ju-jitsu, kendo, kung fu and tang soo do

4.3.85   As the potential for harm in these activities is high, school staff are recommended to discuss with the employer their inclusion in a school programme.

Useful websites

British Council of Chinese Martial Arts: https://bccma.com
British Ju Jitsu Association: www.bjjagb.com
British Kendo Association: www.britishkendoassociation.com
UK Tang Soo Do Federation: www.uktsdf.org.uk

WTF taekwondo

4.3.86   Taekwondo is described as a martial art and a full contact combat sport. The Korean martial art of taekwondo appeals to young people as it is characterised by fast, high, spinning kicks and energetic movements, often in sequence. In addition, participants learn to apply powerful hand and joint-locking techniques.

4.3.87   Holds and locks should be taught safely, with students made aware of the potential for injury.

4.3.88   Students need to be matched according to gender, size, weight, age, experience and ability when sparring.

 For more information about matching students in groups, and mixed-gender and mixed-age sport, see Chapter 2, Section 8, pages 155–157.

4.3.89   Headgear and shin protectors of the correct size and that meet recommended standards should be worn.

4.3.90   At competitive levels, mouth guards, body protectors, groin guards and shin protectors are also compulsory.

4.3.91   Mats should be joined together securely so they do not move apart.

Useful websites

British Taekwondo: www.britishtaekwondo.org.uk
British Taekwondo Council: www.britishtaekwondocouncil.org

© Coachwise/SWpix

Chapter 4/Section 4: Dance activities

The dance context

4.4.1   Dance is a creative activity that uses movement with imagination through the processes of composing, performing and appreciating. Dance provides unique learning opportunities within schools in that it is a vehicle for young people to physically express and communicate their ideas, identity and culture, and their understanding about themselves, others and the society in which they live. Dance can contribute to students' physical, aesthetic, artistic, creative, cultural and social development, and can also play an important role in promoting physical and emotional health and well-being.

4.4.2   Different dance styles and techniques emphasise particular movements, use of the body, relationships with gravity and other stylistic elements. Students should be provided with opportunities to acquire and develop both safe and effective technique and approaches to working creatively. Although dance may seem relatively low risk in comparison to other physical education, school sport and physical activity (PESSPA) activities, comprehensive and informed risk management remains essential.

General safe-practice issues

4.4.3   Fundamental principles of safe practice (**Chapter 1**) and principles of safe organisation and management (Chapter 2) should be understood and applied to all school provision of dance. A helpful summary of these is provided in Table 6, Chapter 2, pages 64–67. More specific guidance and information about dance are provided in this section, and staff should familiarise themselves with these and apply them to their unique set of circumstances. Links to websites can be followed to access additional information relating to safe provision of dance.

Floor area

4.4.4   Guidance about appropriate **floor area** can be found in Chapter 2, Section 13, page 216. In addition, One Dance UK provides some useful information for those involved in designing new dance studios, which includes safety advice about floor area, floor surface, ventilation, heating and accessibility: http://goo.gl/9zQGgM

Space

4.4.5   Different dance styles can require **varying amounts of space**. Some South Asian and African styles, for example, may require limited space, while 'creative dance' or contemporary dance may require larger areas, especially if lots of travelling is involved.

4.4.6   The NDTA recommends a minimum of three square metres for each primary student and five square metres for each secondary student in order to enable them to move safely and freely when engaged in dance sessions as part of the PESSPA programme.

Footwear

4.4.7   Decisions about the appropriateness of **bare feet for dance** should be based on information in Chapter 2, Section 10, 2.10.22, page 176, and should consider the following:

- **Level of impact** – how much high-impact activity is involved (eg jumping or stamping)? (See Chapter 2, Section 9, page 162, for more information.)

- **Competence of the students** – to what extent can they perform high-impact actions with safe technique (eg good take-offs and landings)?

- **Type of contact with the floor by the feet** – do the dance actions involve lots of skipping (eg traditional English/Scottish country dancing); 'shuffling' and 'sliding' (eg 'hip-hop'); slides, spins and turns (eg jazz dance)? These can be quite abrasive for bare feet.

- **Repetition and duration involved** – how often are the dance actions performed, especially those that might be abrasive for bare feet or that are high impact?

- **Resilience of the floor surface** – is the floor sprung, partially sprung or concrete?

- **Cleanliness, condition and temperature of the floor** – has the floor been used by those wearing outdoor shoes? Is the floor damaged, gritty, dirty or cold?

Safe exercise practice

4.4.8   Staff should be well informed about, and able to apply effectively, the principles of safe exercise practice when completing risk assessments of specific dance exercises and movements, especially in relation to:

- warming up and cooling down

- developing and monitoring safe, effective and correct dance technique (eg knees in line with toes when bending, correct spinal alignment in different moves, avoiding moves/exercises that put stress on the neck, lower back or knees)

- developing safe technique for lifting or supporting others' weight (when appropriate)

- helping students to develop flexibility, muscular strength and endurance and cardiovascular fitness for dance

- meeting the basic psychological needs of the pupils, and providing effective and appropriate feedback in a safe and healthy psychological environment

- providing adaptations for pupils with additional needs

- providing opportunities for rest and recovery based on the demands of the dance activity.

For further information about safe exercise practice, see Chapter 2, Section 9, page 160, and student learning about safe exercise practice, see Chapter 3, Section 5, page 320.

Also see One Dance UK's Industry Standards at http://goo.gl/9Sf8Xx

Equipment

4.4.9   **Music** and IT equipment is often used to promote learning in and through dance. Staff should ensure that:

- all electrical and IT equipment, such as CD players, is subject to **PAT testing** (see Chapter 2, Section 12, page 210)

- the volume of the music allows their students to hear staff instructions and peer conversations relevant to safe practice, procedures and learning

- the use of music does not adversely effect the ability of students to access learning (eg those with hearing impairments or autism/autistic spectrum disorder [ASD]/Asperger's syndrome (see Chapter 2, Section 14, page 235).

Mirrors

4.4.10   Any mirrors in dance studios need to be made of toughened shatterproof glass.

Useful websites

One Dance UK: www.onedanceuk.org

One Dance UK is the new industry body formed from the bringing together in April 2016 of four key dance organisations:

- Association of Dance of the African Diaspora (ADAD)

- Dance UK

- National Dance Teachers Association (NDTA)

- Youth Dance England (YDE).

Chapter 4/Section 5: Games activities

© Alan Edwards

The games context

4.5.1 Games include all team or individual activities or **'sports'** in which players use a range of tactics and strategies to overcome opponents in direct competition. Depending on the demands of each particular game, and the level at which it is played, the degree of challenge faced will vary.

4.5.2 Participation in competitive games not only benefits physical health but can also benefit social and emotional health and well-being by building traits such as confidence, a sense of belonging, a sense of achievement, an ability to work effectively with others and resilience.

4.5.3 Curriculum games are sometimes categorised as invasion games (eg football, hockey, basketball, rugby, netball), net/wall games (tennis, badminton, volleyball), and striking and fielding games (rounders, cricket, softball). In addition, target games such as archery and golf have become increasingly popular in schools.

General safe-practice issues

4.5.4 Fundamental principles of safe practice (**Chapter 1**) and principles of safe organisation and management (Chapter 2) should be understood and applied to all school provision of games activities. A helpful summary of these is provided in Table 6, Chapter 2, pages 64–67. More specific guidance and information about games activities are provided in this section, and staff should familiarise themselves with these and apply them to their unique set of circumstances. The rules of the governing bodies of sport may not always be appropriate to schools, and schools should adjust their practice where necessary. (See **Chapter 1, Section 2, pages 1.2.10–1.2.14**, and Chapter 2, Section 5, 2.5.60–2.5.61.) Links to websites can be followed to access additional information relating to safe provision of games activities.

Alternative versions of specific games

4.5.5 It is possible to access alternative versions of many games activities played in school or club settings. This is particularly useful when:

- introducing a game to younger or less able students

- making a game more inclusive and accessible to a wider range of participants

- less space is available for learning

- fewer participants are available.

4.5.6 Where applicable, information regarding alternative versions of games is included in the guidance on specific games activities below.

4.5.7 Where 'outdoor' games are played indoors (as a result of poor weather or limited facilities), it is important that adjustments are made to ensure the safety of those involved. Consider:

- clearly marking the reduced playing area, and making players aware of this

- ensuring adequate run-off areas are available

- reducing team numbers

- considering any necessary changes to the rules of the activity.

Information regarding playing areas can be found in Chapter 2, Section 13, page 216.

4.5.8   Whichever version of a game is used, it is essential for the safety of all involved that physical education, school sport and physical activity (PESSPA) staff know and apply the rules of the activity they are supervising, teaching or officiating, whether in an educational or club context. Similarly, students should be taught to manage any risks within the different types of games activity, and be encouraged to always play within the spirit and rules of the game, to reduce levels of risk to themselves and others.

Participation in wheelchair games activities

4.5.9   Participating in games activities in wheelchairs can require the wheelchair user to reach, bend and transfer in and out of the wheelchair. These movements will cause a change to normal balance, centre of gravity and weight distribution of the wheelchair.

4.5.10   Proper positioning is essential for safety. When reaching, leaning, or bending sideways or forward, it is important to use the casters as a tool to maintain stability and balance. Chairs used for different wheelchair games should conform to all safety specifications including protective horizontal bars and footrests.

4.5.11   It is important that students who are regular wheelchair users (and those using chairs as a requirement of participation) determine and establish their particular safety limits and confidence by practising bending, reaching and transferring activities before attempting to participate in games activities.

4.5.12   In activities where wheelchair users are playing alongside ambulant participants, both need to be mindful of entering each other's space. It is common practice for the playing space to be 'zoned', or players restricted to specified areas of the space to achieve this safely.

4.5.13   A number of wheelchair games activities are mentioned in this section. This is by no means a complete representation of the opportunities available.

The role of governing bodies of sport in organising games events and activities

4.5.14   Governing bodies of sport play a central role in developing games activities. They are responsible for establishing the rules, regulations and conventions of their respective activities. This **informs the guidance** that afPE provides to support teachers in ensuring safe practice. Where games activities, tournaments and events are organised by governing bodies of sport, their rules and regulations will be enforced. Where activities are organised by schools or other non-governing body of sport organisations, school rules will apply. Where governing bodies of sport are involved in delivering activities at events organised by schools or other agencies (eg the School Games), organisers are advised to ensure that both schools and governing bodies of sport are clear about which rules should be applied.

4.5.15   For some activities listed, court specifications are discussed and explained. For full details of **pitch and court specifications and dimensions**, refer to the governing body of sport websites provided at the end of each section and also information provided by Sport England (2015) 'Comparative Sizes of Sports Pitches and Courts':

* outdoors: https://goo.gl/vN8jYk

* indoors: https://goo.gl/vkzJXA

For more information about floor areas and pitch sizes, see Chapter 2, Section 13, page 216.

Guidance on specific games activities

Invasion games

4.5.16   In 'invasion games', the objective is to attack and defend parts of the playing area, with the aim of scoring more goals or points than the opposition. They include fast-moving activity, frequently involve physical contact and, in some games, hard implements. Consequently, the most common causes of accidents include:

- unintended collision with other players

- being struck by a hard implement or ball

- poor application of technique, such as when tackling.

Association football/soccer

4.5.17   Since the start of the football season 2015–2016, The Football Association (FA) allows boys and girls to play in the same teams up to the under-18 age limit. This can also apply in competitive situations, but individual league or competition organisers should be consulted directly for confirmation.

4.5.18   Schools can make their own decision regarding this, applying matching principles such as size, ability, confidence and previous experience.

For more information about mixed groupings, see Chapter 2, Section 8, page 156.

4.5.19   Studded and bladed boots should be maintained to an appropriate safety standard.

For more information about footwear, see Chapter 2, Section 10, page 176.

4.5.20   The wearing of shin pads at all times is recommended. Where students do not have shin pads, staff should manage the situation to ensure the safety of all participants.

For more information about PPE, see Chapter 2, Section 11, page 183.

4.5.21   The FA permits the wearing of glasses (spectacles) up to under-14 years old, at the discretion of the official.

The information found in Chapter 2, Section 11, page 183, **and** Chapter 2, Section 10, page 179, **supports schools to develop their own policy in relation to this.**

4.5.22   Goalposts, netting and corner flags should be checked regularly for safety.

For more information about checking equipment prior to use, see Chapter 2, Section 12, page 192.

Useful websites

English Schools Football Association:	www.esfa.co.uk
The Football Association:	www.Thefa.com
Football Association of Wales:	www.faw.org.uk
Irish Football Association:	www.irishfa.com
Northern Ireland Schools Football Association:	www.nisfa.co.uk
Scottish Football Association:	www.scottishfa.co.uk
Scottish Schools Football Association:	www.scottishfa.co.uk/ssfa/
Welsh Schools Football Association:	www.welshschoolsfa.co.uk

Futsal and five-a-side football

4.5.23   These games are normally played indoors on a flat, smooth, non-abrasive surface. Five-a-side may also be played outdoors within a restricted, enclosed area. Where futsal is played outside, it would usually be on artificial grass. The main difference in futsal is the absence of rebound boards, which are more common in five-a-side games.

4.5.24   Players should wear soft-soled trainers. All players, including the goalkeeper, are recommended to wear shin pads, and would be required to do so in activities organised by The FA.

 For more information, see Chapter 2, Section 10, page 176 **(footwear) and** Chapter 2, Section 11, page 183 **(PPE).**

4.5.25   The rules of futsal regarding accumulated fouls contribute to safety by discouraging teams from being overly physical or disputing the decisions of the two referees.

Useful website

Futsal and five-a-side:	http://goo.gl/RWBEN7

Wheelchair football

4.5.26   For power chair users, The FA promotes the use of lap seat belts. Leg, feet and chest straps should be used if normally worn. Other safety equipment may include helmets, headrests and other assistive or protective technology normally used by the student. Where possible and practical, schools should aim to implement these recommendations.

Useful websites

Disability football:	http://goo.gl/8Qecez
Wheelchair football:	http://goo.gl/24uSuo

Basketball

4.5.27   Basketball goals can be wall-hinged, wall-mounted fixed, ceiling drop down, socketed or portable, and may be used for match play or recreational practice. Schools need to consider the use of the court and basketball goal systems available in order to make suitable choices.

4.5.28   Where match or game play takes place on marked courts, the court perimeter should be free from hazard with a safe zone of at least 1.05 metres around the edge. Protruding **obstacles** should be removed or made safe behind and in line with the backboards. The overhang (measured from the front of the post to the front of the backboard) should be 1.2 metres and to the centre of the ring 1.575 metres.

4.5.29   Where such space is not available, careful officiating and management of the situation are essential. When wall-mounted boards are used for cross-court games, participants should be warned to avoid collisions with the end walls, and to refrain from using feet against the end wall to help achieve height.

4.5.30   Where boards are freestanding or socketed in playground or court areas, padding can be used around the post to reduce the impact of collisions.

4.5.31   Players should keep fingernails short and well trimmed.

Useful websites

Basketball Northern Ireland: www.basketballni.com

Basketball Scotland: www.basketball-scotland.com

Basketball Wales: www.basketballwales.com

England Basketball: www.englandbasketball.com

Wheelchair basketball

4.5.32   The court should have a flat, hard surface free from obstruction. The seated team bench personnel should be at least two metres from the playing court.

4.5.33   Players should keep fingernails short and well trimmed.

4.5.34   Body padding may be worn, and glasses are allowed.

Useful website

British Wheelchair Basketball: http://goo.gl/cyOcqt

Gaelic games

4.5.35   Posts should be checked regularly for safety.

    For more information about checking equipment prior to use, see Chapter 2, Section 12, page 192.

4.5.36   In all hurling games and practice sessions, the governing body has made it mandatory for all players up to and including under-21 'grade' to wear a mouth guard, and **helmet** with a facial guard.

4.5.37 Gaelic Athletic Association policy with regard to the use of hurling helmets is that they should comply with IS 355 (ie the official hurling helmet specification that was set out by the National Standards Authority of Ireland [NSAI] in 2006).

Useful website

Gaelic Athletic Association: www.gaa.ie

Handball

4.5.38 A safe, non-slip playing area should be maintained, particularly in attacking areas where perspiration from players making contact with the ground may constitute a hazard.

4.5.39 The court perimeter should be free from hazard with a safety zone surrounding the playing court of at least one metre along the side-lines and behind the goal lines. Protruding obstacles should be removed or made safe behind the lines of the court.

4.5.40 Schools should be working towards goalposts complying with governing body of sport safety standards. Goalposts (fixed or portable) should be made **secure** at all times in such a manner that they cannot fall forwards or backwards for any reason. They should be checked regularly for safety.

For more information about checking equipment prior to use, see Chapter 2, Section 12, page 192.

4.5.41 The normal **playing time** for teams should be adhered to:

- 16 years and above is two halves of 30 minutes with a half-time break of 10 minutes.

- 12–16 years is two halves of 25 minutes with a 10-minute half-time break.

- 8–12 years is two halves of 20 minutes with a 10-minute break.

4.5.42 In festivals and tournaments, the playing time equivalent of two full-length matches played in one day should not be exceeded.

4.5.43 Single-period playing times of up to 10 minutes are frequently played by teams in the 8–12 years age group. In the 12–16 age group, teams frequently play single periods of 12–16 minutes.

Useful websites

British Handball Association: www.britishhandball.com

England Handball: www.englandhandball.com

Scottish Handball: www.scottishhandball.com

Hockey

4.5.44 Playing surfaces, whether grass or synthetic, need to be true and flat.

4.5.45 Goalkeepers need to be suitably equipped and protected with:

- pads and kickers

- gauntlet gloves

- body protectors

- a full helmet

- a throat guard.

4.5.46　The wearing of shin pads and mouth guards should be encouraged at all times. They are highly recommended for match play and competitive practices, and mandatory at junior representative level.

 For more information about PPE, see Chapter 2, Section 11, page 183.

4.5.47　Players should seek to develop and exercise good stick and ball control at all times. Controlled pushing should be well established before the introduction of hitting.

4.5.48　Goalkeepers should try to remain on their feet whenever possible.

Useful websites

England Hockey:　　www.englandhockey.co.uk

Hockey Wales:　　http://hockeywales.org.uk

Scottish Hockey:　　www.scottish-hockey.org.uk

Ulster Hockey:　　www.ulsterhockey.com

Quicksticks hockey

4.5.49　Players should be encouraged to comply with the wearing of personal protective equipment (PPE) (mouth guards and shin pads) from an early age. While the ball used in Quicksticks hockey is softer than the regular hockey ball, accidents to the mouth area are generally as a result of lack of control of another player's stick.

Useful website

Quicksticks:　　www.playquicksticks.co.uk

Lacrosse

4.5.50　Teachers should ensure all school team sticks are legal and safe for use. Under governing body of sport rules, from the start of the 2015–2016 season, umpires and coaches must have a stick check before every game at every level to ensure player safety.

4.5.51　Governing body of sport kit requirements include:

- padded gloves/gauntlets to protect hands and wrists (optional for women in field play)

- head protection (for men's lacrosse)

- protective goggles (that meet manufacturer's specifications)

- mouth guards.

4.5.52　All goalkeepers should be suitably protected with PPE for both the head and body.

4.5.53　POP is the lacrosse game for primary schools. It is a non-contact version of lacrosse that uses plastic-headed sticks and oversized lacrosse balls.

Useful websites

English Lacrosse: www.englishlacrosse.co.uk

Lacrosse Scotland: www.lacrossescotland.com

Welsh Lacrosse Association: www.waleslacrosse.co.uk

Netball

4.5.54   The court should be level and flat, with no loose objects, such as grit or wet leaves, on it or the surrounding area. Where netball is played on the same area as tennis, check that holes used for net posts have covers in place.

4.5.55   Goalposts should be checked regularly for safety. They should be slotted into the ground. Portable goalposts should be placed on the centre point of each goal line with none of the base protruding on to the court. The use of post protectors is encouraged.

 For more information about checking equipment prior to use, see Chapter 2, Section 12, page 192.

4.5.56   There should be at least two metres of space between adjacent courts.

4.5.57   Players should keep fingernails short and well trimmed.

4.5.58   During competitive matches, **gloves** may only be worn at the discretion of the umpire.

Useful websites

England Netball: www.england-netball.co.uk

Netball Northern Ireland: www.netballni.org

Netball Scotland: www.netballscotland.com

Welsh Netball: www.welshnetball.co.uk

High 5 netball

4.5.59   Court specification and safety, and post safety are as for netball above.

4.5.60   High 5 netball can be played with mixed-gender teams so care needs to be taken with matching opponents.

Useful website

High 5 netball: http://goo.gl/d6pQnx

Rugby football (league and union)

4.5.61   A suitable playing surface is essential and should be soft enough to safely accommodate falls during tackles.

4.5.62   Goalposts and corner flags should be checked regularly for safety.

 For more information about checking equipment prior to use, see Chapter 2, Section 12, page 192.

4.5.63   Recommended PPE:

- The Rugby Football Union (RFU) states that mouth guards are mandatory for representative matches above school level. Otherwise, they are recommended. Schools should encourage the use of mouth guards at all times.

- RFU-approved padded head protection is permitted.

- Soft shoulder padding is permitted.

For more information about PPE, see Chapter 2, Section 11, page 183.

4.5.64   The RFU recommends that glasses (spectacles) should not be worn when playing rugby beyond the under-eight years age band.

4.5.65   **Contact** versions of the game should only be introduced and managed by suitably experienced staff and coaches following recognised teaching progressions, guidelines and the regulation of the governing bodies of sport for rugby union – England Rugby (RFU) – and rugby league – the Rugby Football League (RFL). Teachers should not teach or officiate contact rugby until they are competent to do so. Where they are not competent, additional professional learning should be completed.

4.5.66   Schools are advised to follow governing body regulations that permit players to play in teams one school year group above their own. This might result in teams including players of three different ages. For example, a year six team could incorporate players from year five, resulting in players' ages spanning 9–11 years old. In special circumstances, players can be permitted to play in a team two school year groups above their own. Age bandings (eg under-nines, under-11s) are determined by a player's date of birth in relation to the playing season. In all cases of students playing above their age group, appropriate assessment should be carried out, and parents should be informed and their consent gained.

For further information relating to England Rugby's Age Grade Rugby, see http://goo.gl/ljsPky

For Ireland, see http://goo.gl/SKjXru

For Scotland, see http://goo.gl/glOR00

4.5.67   In exceptional circumstances, a player over 12 years of age may play on a mixed-gender team where no other option for continuing to play rugby exists. Parental consent and medical agreement should be sought in these cases.

4.5.68   A player should not participate in mixed-gender teams once they have reached the age of 15.

Useful websites

Irish Rugby:	http://goo.gl/CEfiQl
RFL:	www.rugby-league.com
RFU:	www.englandrugby.com
Scottish Rugby:	www.scottishrugby.org
Welsh Rugby Union:	www.wru.co.uk

Touch rugby

4.5.69   This is a version of rugby where tackling is replaced by touching or tapping the opponent.

4.5.70   Teams can be mixed so matching needs to be carefully managed.

 For more information about mixed-gender activities, see Chapter 2, Section 8, page 156.

Useful website

Touch rugby:	http://englandtouch.org.uk

Tag rugby

4.5.71   The **non-contact** element must be enforced throughout the game. The ball carrier is not allowed to run directly into defenders, and defenders are not allowed to block the progress of the ball carrier.

4.5.72   Hand-offs, or use of hand, elbow or ball to block or shield a 'tag' are not allowed.

4.5.73   As a mixed-gender game, matching needs to be carefully managed.

 For more information about mixed-gender group activities, see Chapter 2, Section 8, page 156.

Useful website

Tag rugby:	www.tagrugby.org

Wheelchair rugby

4.5.74   Contact between wheelchairs is permitted, but players should not exceed the reasonable force required when challenging an opponent for position or for possession of the ball. Players are expected to make an effort to avoid dangerous contact by slowing down, stopping or changing direction if necessary.

Useful website

Great Britain Wheelchair Rugby:	http://gbwr.org.uk

Ultimate frisbee

4.5.75   When played outdoors, a field similar in size to a football pitch is used. The last 18 metres at either end of the field are the 'end zones'. A goal is scored when a player throws the frisbee to a member of their team standing (or more likely running) in the end zone they are attacking.

4.5.76   Ultimate frisbee is also played indoors with some variations in the rules. The indoor playing area is ideally 35–40 metres long and 15–20 metres wide. In school, the distance from the end zone to the end wall should be at least a metre to reduce the likelihood of collision with the end wall.

4.5.77   When playing ultimate frisbee, participants spend a great deal of time looking up. For this reason, it is important to:

- check the grass playing surface for damage, such as animal holes, and holes from sports posts

- be aware of any obstacles indoors and out, such as posts or boundary markers

- ensure that the end zone areas are kept clear at all times.

4.5.78   This can help to prevent injury or collision.

4.5.79   As this is a self-refereed sport, delays can occur in fouls being called, leaving a period of time of potentially unsafe situations. When teaching students in schools, this should be considered so that participants are aware of the implications in their own play.

Useful website

Ultimate frisbee: www.ukultimate.com

Net/wall games

4.5.80   In net/wall games, the objective is for players to send a 'projectile' (eg ball or shuttlecock) towards an area that is defended by an opponent, and to make it difficult for the defender to return the projectile. In some of these games, the areas being defended are separated by a net (eg badminton, tennis, volleyball), and some games use a wall to rebound the ball (eg squash, fives).

4.5.81   The most common causes of accidents are:

- being struck by a racket or fast-moving projectile

- tripping or slipping

- collision with obstacles, equipment or another player

- crossing a court when it is in use.

Badminton

4.5.82   There should be sufficient space on court to accommodate group practice and to avoid students playing over post bases.

4.5.83   Suitable **lighting** should permit clear visibility of the shuttle in flight.

4.5.84   Nets should be free from holes and tears. Posts should be regularly checked for safety. Portable posts should be transported, stored and positioned safely.

 For more information about checking equipment prior to use, see Chapter 2, Section 12, page 192.

4.5.85   Equipment should be in good condition. Rackets with broken strings should not be used.

Useful websites

Badminton England: www.badmintonengland.co.uk

Badminton Ireland: www.badmintonireland.com

Badminton Scotland: www.badmintonscotland.org.uk

Badminton Wales: www.badmintonwales.net

Squash and racketball

4.5.86   Protective **eye shields** are advisable to protect against eye injury.

4.5.87   Short-lever rackets are recommended for beginners.

4.5.88   Squash is played in a confined area. A **maximum** of six students per court is recommended for coaching and practice sessions.

4.5.89   Safe procedures should be established for door opening, and entering and leaving the court.

4.5.90   Players should only progress to doubles play when a high standard of singles play has been achieved.

Useful websites

England Squash and Racketball: www.englandsquashandracketball.com

Irish Squash: www.irishsquash.com

Scottish Squash and Racketball: www.scottishsquash.org.uk

Squash Wales: www.squashwales.co.uk

Tennis

4.5.91   If tennis posts are removed, **caps** should be used to cover the holes, particularly on multi-use areas.

4.5.92   Broken wire in surround **fencing** is particularly hazardous, and students should maintain a safe distance (indicated by use of barriers or cones) until it has been repaired.

4.5.93   Courts should be arranged in the same **direction** of play in order to avoid the possibility of a player being hit by a ball from another game.

4.5.94   Students should keep alert to play and other players at all times, and avoid standing in direct proximity to someone who is about to hit a tennis ball.

4.5.95   Students should be encouraged to check regularly that the playing area is clear of loose tennis balls before starting any practice or game. Stepping on a loose tennis ball can result in tripping or 'turning' an ankle.

4.5.96   A full-sized tennis court may be used safely by more than four players for rallying practices if players can demonstrate an acceptable level of safety awareness.

4.5.97   When practising smashes or serves, appropriate space should be allowed between students, and the ball should be directed towards empty spaces on the court.

4.5.98   When practising the smash, it is inadvisable for feeders to be positioned directly in front of the player who is performing the smash. Any students who are 'waiting' for their turn to smash should remain alert and off the court.

4.5.99   Players should be discouraged from:

- looking round at a doubles partner who is serving

- jumping over a tennis net

- attempting to play strokes outside their designated playing area.

Useful websites

Tennis England: http://goo.gl/5cWv0O

Tennis Ireland: www.tennisireland.ie

Tennis Scotland: http://goo.gl/lX0eo2

Tennis Wales: http://goo.gl/HROmis

Short tennis (short court or Mini Tennis)

4.5.100   This version is played in a more restricted space than the full game, usually half a tennis court or a badminton size court, so players need to be aware of others in their area.

4.5.101   Shorter rackets, light or slower balls and lower nets (approximately 80cm in the middle) should be used.

Useful website

Mini Tennis: http://goo.gl/DODY4M

Wheelchair tennis

4.5.102   The game of wheelchair tennis follows the same rules as tennis except the wheelchair tennis player is allowed two bounces of the ball. The wheelchair is regarded in the rules as part of the body.

4.5.103   Care regarding the safe use of the wheelchair as set out on page 394, in this section, applies.

Useful website

LTA tennis for the physically impaired: www.tennisfoundation.org.uk

Volleyball

4.5.104   Volleyball posts and nets should be checked regularly for safety.

 For more information about checking equipment prior to use, see Chapter 2, Section 12, page 192.

4.5.105   Schools should aim to acquire volleyball posts that comply with governing body of sport safety standards. Posts (fixed or portable) should be made **secure** and stable at all times in such a manner that they cannot fall on occasions when players make contact with the net. Weighted posts can be made secure by **retaining wires** attached to adjacent walls above head height.

4.5.106   Bases should not protrude on to the court.

4.5.107   Free-standing or weighted posts are not acceptable for competitive matches.

4.5.108   All lights above the court should have guards fitted.

4.5.109   When practising smashes or serves, appropriate space should be allowed between students, and the ball should be directed towards empty spaces on the court.

4.5.110   When practising the smash, it is inadvisable for feeders to be positioned directly in front of the player who is performing the smash. Any students who are waiting for their turn to smash should remain alert and off the court.

4.5.111   Balls should be rolled back during match play and carried back when both sides of the court are used for practice.

Useful websites

Northern Ireland Volleyball: www.nivb.com

Scottish Volleyball Association: www.scottishvolleyball.org

Volleyball England: www.volleyballengland.org

Volleyball Wales: www.volleyballwales.org

Sitting volleyball

4.5.112   Correct manual handling techniques should be applied when helping players to move from a wheelchair to the floor.

4.5.113   A range of different size and weight balls may be used according to ability.

Useful website

Sitting volleyball: https://goo.gl/WpO4Ta

Striking and fielding games

4.5.114   Striking and fielding games are usually played in teams. The objective is for the batting team to strike a ball, using a bat and attempt to run between two points before the fielding team can retrieve and field the ball to stop play. Examples of striking and fielding games include cricket, rounders and softball.

4.5.115   Consequently, the most common causes of accidents include:

- being unintentionally struck with a fast-moving hard ball

- being unintentionally struck with a bat or stick

- collision with another player or an item of equipment.

Cricket

4.5.116   The wicket – grass or synthetic – should be reasonably true and well maintained.

4.5.117   Practice netting should be free of gaps, holes and tears, positioned so players in adjacent areas are not at risk, and preferably include roof netting.

4.5.118   Batsmen (a term applied by governing bodies of sport to male and female players), wicketkeepers and fielders close to the bat should wear appropriate PPE, including helmets.

 For more information about PPE, see Chapter 2, Section 11, page 183.

4.5.119   Rules administered by the cricket governing bodies of sport relating to **close-in fielding** by junior players should be strictly enforced.

4.5.120   Bowlers should bowl in a controlled order and always ensure that the batsman is fully ready before bowling.

4.5.121   Waiting batsmen should observe from a safe position.

4.5.122   Where cricket nets are used indoors, the netting needs to completely surround the practice area so that balls hit with power cannot escape the net and hit someone close by involved in another activity. A suitable space should be left between nets and other activity areas to allow for billowing when a ball hits the net at speed. Care needs to be taken when retrieving balls from cricket netting and should only happen when bowling has been halted.

Useful websites

Cricket Ireland: www.irishcricket.org

Cricket Scotland: www.cricketscotland.com

England and Wales Cricket Board: www.ecb.co.uk

Welsh Cricket Association   www.cricketwales.org.uk

Kwik Cricket

4.5.123   The correct equipment, moulded plastic bats, balls and stumps should be used.

4.5.124   As plastic balls are used, helmets are not required.

Useful website

Kwik Cricket: http://goo.gl/DAjhv4

Rounders, softball and baseball

4.5.125   Rounders posts should be of **appropriate height**, and have secure bases and rounded tops.

4.5.126   Catching mitts/gloves should be worn as appropriate for baseball and softball.

4.5.127   Backstops (the catcher) in baseball and softball should consider the use of head and body protection, extra padding in their glove and a helmet.

4.5.128   The ball should not be pitched/bowled until all players are fully ready.

4.5.129   While waiting for their next turn, or after being out, batsmen should wait in clearly marked areas at a safe distance away from the batting line.

4.5.130   Rounders bats should be **carried** by batsmen when running between bases and never thrown down.

4.5.131   Backstops should take care to position themselves so as to avoid backswing.

Useful websites

Baseball Softball*UK*:   www.baseballsoftballuk.com

Rounders England: www.roundersengland.co.uk

Target games

4.5.132   In target games, the objective is to aim a 'projectile', often at great speed, towards a designated scoring area. Target games include archery and golf.

4.5.133   Consequently, the most common causes of accidents include:

- other players, spectators or passers-by inadvertently wandering into the path of the projectile

- waiting players standing too close to the person who is 'launching' the projectile and being struck by an implement

- a lack of skill causing the projectile to go off line and possibly into an area where others are standing.

Archery

4.5.134   Archery in schools should always be organised and supervised by suitably qualified and experienced personnel.

4.5.135   If an area of the school field is used for target practice, extreme care should be taken to ensure that archers are positioned a sufficient distance from any other groups using the field, buildings, roads or other facilities. Targets should never be set where archers are aiming towards other archers or towards other groups using the area.

4.5.136   Participants need to be clear about rules regarding retrieving arrows, and the commands that permit this.

 Chapter 4, Section 2, page 371, guidance about athletics throwing events provides useful information about safe practices and procedures.

4.5.137   Bows should always be pointed towards the ground, even when not containing an arrow.

4.5.138   Students should always check behind them before drawing an arrow.

4.5.139   Arrows should never be fired high into the air.

4.5.140   Students should remain in a clearly marked waiting area until it is their turn to shoot.

Useful websites

Archery GB: www.archerygb.org

Disability archery: http://goo.gl/vkq2Ky

Golf

4.5.141   A golf course or driving range provides much lower risk facilities for practising golf than a school field.

4.5.142   If a school field is used as a facility for beginner golfers, extreme care should be taken to ensure that participants are positioned a sufficient distance from any other groups using the field, buildings, roads or other facilities. Students should never hit towards other golfers, other groups using the field, buildings, roads or other sport facilities.

4.5.143   When a net is being used for practice:

- a well-maintained special net with fine mesh that is at least 2.5 metres high and hangs clear of any supports should be used

- only light (airflow) balls should be used if students are practising on both sides of the net

- suitable protective mats should be used when indoors.

4.5.144   When practising in group situations, care needs to be taken to ensure that all players have sufficient space and can hit the ball in a safe direction.

4.5.145   Individual players should always ensure they have sufficient personal space around them to swing their club safely.

4.5.146   Balls should only be retrieved (where applicable) on a given signal after all players have completed their shots.

 Chapter 4, Section 2, page 371, guidance on athletics throwing events provides useful information about safe practices and procedures.

4.5.147   Careful supervision is essential to ensure participants' actions and behaviour do not create a hazard for other students.

Useful websites

England Golf: www.englandgolf.org

Golfing Union of Ireland: www.golfnet.ie

Golf Union of Wales: www.golfunionwales.org

Scottish Golf Union: www.scottishgolf.org

Tri-Golf and Golf Xtreme

4.5.148   Both adaptations of the game use purpose-made equipment that comprises lighter clubs, reduced-flight balls and Velcro targets.

4.5.149   Great care needs to be taken to ensure that the different types of clubs are not mixed up during storage. It is wise to store plastic Tri-Golf equipment separately from metal clubs.

4.5.150   Metal clubs should not be accessible to students who have not been taught to use them safely.

Useful website

Golf Foundation: www.golf-foundation.org

Disability golf

4.5.151 Schools may wish to make students aware that the R&A, as a governing body for golf, has adjusted rules for disabled golfers, allowing for a caddy and supervisor on the course. The caddy can carry the bag or push the trolley and handle the clubs, but not have input into the game. The supervisor cannot touch the bag or clubs, but has full input into the game. Some golf clubs are beginning to implement these rules. England Golf also has an established programme for players with a range of disabilities. Schools may wish to implement a version of this rule to assist students with disabilities to participate safely.

Useful website

R&A: http://goo.gl/4PtNM7

Other games activities

4.5.152 Some games are used as 'fun' activities, and in all cases, staff should be satisfied that students:

- have sufficiently mastered the skills required before putting them into a competitive situation

- continue to concentrate on skilful play as well as having fun.

4.5.153 The most common causes of accidents include:

- students inadvertently colliding with each other or an obstacle

- slipping or falling.

Benchball

4.5.154 Clear guidance should be given regarding:

- how many students are allowed to stand on a bench

- where participants should stand if they are not on a bench.

4.5.155 Benches used should be checked to be in good condition, and positioned away from other apparatus.

Dodgeball

4.5.156 Players must take care to avoid throwing the ball above shoulder height of their opponent.

4.5.157 While players may wear glasses in school for dodgeball, the likelihood of the ball hitting the face is fairly high. Where glasses can be removed, this is recommended, or alternatively, sports goggles may be considered.

 For more information, see Chapter 2, Section 11, 2.11.45–2.11.48, pages 188–189.

4.5.158 Balls should be made of rubber or foam.

Useful websites

UK Dodgeball: www.ukdba.org

British Heart Foundation Ultimate Dodgeball: https://goo.gl/hwvXZm

Relay racing and tag games

4.5.159   Clear boundary markings are necessary for tag-type activity.

4.5.160   In relays, walls (windows and doors) are unsuitable as turning points due to the likelihood of wrist injuries from hands being used to decelerate runners, or cuts from broken glass. Lines and marker discs placed an appropriate distance from the wall can provide a safe alternative.

4.5.161   Care needs to be taken that students are sufficiently competent and confident to perform specific skills before they are used in competitive relay or tag games.

VX sport

4.5.162   This activity contains elements of several sports, including dodgeball, lacrosse and hockey. Aspects of safety pertinent to those sports would apply here.

4.5.163   Players should be able to control the VstiX and cannot strike the ball or another player with it.

Useful website

VX England: www.vxengland.org

© Alan Edwards

Chapter 4/Section 6: Gymnastics activities

The gymnastics activities context

4.6.1   Gymnastics involves moving the body with control and precision, and is often described as body management through the use of functional movement. Gymnastics activities can include a variety of movement experiences both off and on apparatus that include transferring weight, flight, balance and rotations. Gymnastics activities in schools help students to develop locomotor and balance skills, as well as body and spatial awareness, coordination, flexibility, agility, muscular strength and endurance and bone strength.

General safe-practice issues

4.6.2   Fundamental principles of safe practice (**Chapter 1**) and principles of safe organisation and management (Chapter 2) should be understood and applied to all school provision of gymnastics activities. A helpful summary of these is provided in Table 6, Chapter 2, pages 64–67. More specific guidance and information about gymnastics activities are provided in this section, and staff should familiarise themselves with these and apply them to their unique set of circumstances. The rules of the governing bodies of sport may not always be appropriate to schools, and schools should adjust their practice where necessary. (See **Chapter 1, Section 2, 1.2.10–1.2.14,** and Chapter 2, Section 5, 2.5.60–2.5.61.) Links to websites can be followed to access additional information relating to safe provision of gymnastics activities.

Safe exercise practice

4.6.3   Staff should be well informed about the principles of safe exercise practice, and able to incorporate them into their gymnastics activity sessions in relation to:

- warming up and cooling down

- developing and monitoring safe, effective and correct joint alignment (eg knees over toes when bending, correct spinal alignment in different moves, avoiding moves/exercises that put stress on joints, especially the neck, lower back or knees)

- developing and monitoring safe, effective and correct technique to minimise the risks associated with high impact (eg safe jumping and landing technique) and appropriate use of control (eg ensuring that all movements are 'stoppable')

- developing safe technique for supporting others' weight (when appropriate).

For further information about safe exercise practice, see Chapter 2, Section 9, page 160.

Guidance on specific gymnastics activities

Curriculum gymnastics

4.6.4   For the purpose of this resource 'curriculum gymnastics' refers to movement challenges that develop body management and locomotor skills. Curriculum gymnastics helps students to acquire precision of movement and quality of response in the creative contexts of balancing, inverting, climbing, rolling, jumping, landing, transferring weight, stepping and managing the body in flight. Skills and creative sequences are developed using the floor, mats and/or small and large gymnastics apparatus.

4.6.5   Staff teaching curriculum gymnastics should be competent to do so and should work at a level at which they feel confident about their own experience and expertise.

For more information about competence, see Chapter 2, Section 2, page 68.

4.6.6   An appropriate British Gymnastics (BG) advanced level teaching or coaching award is strongly advised for staff wishing to offer formal gymnastics in primary or secondary schools, through an out-of-hours club and/or when seeking to involve students in, and prepare them for, competitive involvement: https://goo.gl/G3CkDe

4.6.7   On no account should any school gymnastics session ever be left **unsupervised**. In the event of the member of staff needing to resolve any emergency or organisational problem, all gymnastics activity should stop until the member of staff deems it safe to continue.

4.6.8   It is recognised that work on apparatus presents higher risks than floor or mat work, with the majority of recorded incidents typically involving falls or misjudged descents from gymnastics equipment. However, work at a low level (ie on the floor or when using benches and mats) requires equally rigorous risk management.

4.6.9   Most **primary schools** deliver curriculum gymnastics through a task-centred or problem-solving approach, building in some direct teaching where progress and safety issues require a specific focus. The ability of staff to set realistic and appropriate movement challenges based on the existing abilities of their students is key to safety in this approach.

4.6.10   In **secondary schools**, where initial teacher education (ITE) programmes have provided sufficient and appropriate training, specialist physical education staff may be able to teach more formal gymnastics skills, typically associated with vaulting and agility, that may lead to acrobatic, artistic, rhythmic, tumbling and cheerleading gymnastics genres. A sound knowledge of technical progression relating to the skills involved in a specific gymnastics genre is essential to safe practice.

4.6.11   Physical **support** may be necessary in the learning of more complex skills, usually to prevent under- or over-rotation. Guidance on physical contact should always be followed.

For more information about physical contact from adults in student activities, see Chapter 2, Section 8, page 157.

4.6.12   Sensible and appropriate progression would typically involve the development or consolidation of skills using the floor or mats, followed by application and further consolidation of the skills on apparatus.

4.6.13   The frequency, intensity and duration of **training sessions** for students progressing towards competitive situations need to reflect the physical and mental maturity of those involved.

4.6.14   Reasonable adjustments to tasks, and clear support and guidance can create a safe learning environment to enable students with special educational needs and disabilities (SEND) to participate fully.

See also disability gymnastics in this section, page 416.

4.6.15   **Barefoot work** is preferable for curriculum gymnastics where the surface is appropriate.

4.6.16   Sprung floors used exclusively for gymnastics lessons provide optimum levels of safety and are the most conducive to barefoot work.

4.6.17   Soft-soled, flexible gymnastics slippers are also appropriate to enable the 'feel' of a movement. Thick-soled training shoes are not suitable. Socks should never be worn on a polished surface.

4.6.18   **Clothing** should allow free, unrestricted movement without being loose. Very loose clothing may snag on equipment and cause injury.

4.6.19   **Apparatus** should conform to appropriate standards, and be purchased from reliable sources and stored in a manner that allows ready access. **Equipment** should be maintained in good order, and removed if damaged or condemned. The condition of apparatus and equipment should be monitored regularly by a member of staff responsible for, and experienced in, the teaching of gymnastics, and checked visually by the teachers and students prior to commencing work.

4.6.20   Organisation of lessons needs to take account of accommodating large groups in a limited space, such as with compact apparatus arrangements or alternating periods of observation with practical involvement.

4.6.21   Students should be involved in **moving and assembling apparatus** from the earliest ages in a manner appropriate to their age, ability, physical development and safety awareness.

This requires simple manual handling skills to be taught and closely monitored by the teacher.

For more information, see Chapter 2, Section 12, 2.12.9, page 192, **and Chapter 3, Section 8, page 341.**

4.6.22　Many primary schools make use of BG's **Key-Steps** Gymnastics competition framework. The equipment required to meet the different levels of competition does not differ from that recommended for use in primary schools. At the highest level (Y6 Option 3) of the vaulting element, the use of regular 25mm gymnastics mats is sufficient for safe landing, providing correct landing technique has been taught and mastered by the students.

4.6.23　**Inspection** of gymnastics equipment and apparatus should take place at least annually by a specialist company.

For more detailed information on gymnastics equipment inspection, see Chapter 2, Section 12, page 206.

Useful website

British Gymnastics:　　www.british-gymnastics.org

Freestyle gymnastics

4.6.24　Freestyle gymnastics (FreeG) is a combination of gymnastics skills and elements of acrobatic tricks, kicks and leaps, regulated by BG.

4.6.25　It is intended for indoors only, within a supervised and approved indoor environment, such as a school hall, gym or sports hall.

4.6.26　The activities can be carried out using existing school gym equipment, but purpose-made additional equipment specifically designed for FreeG has been developed: http://goo.gl/GE1vFB

4.6.27　It is recommended that school staff wishing to deliver FreeG are:

- a qualified specialist physical education teacher who has completed the Level 2 BG Freestyle Gymnastics module

or

- a qualified teacher (non-physical-education specialist) who holds a Level 2 BG Gymnastics award, and who then completes the Level 2 BG Freestyle Gymnastics module

or

- a teaching assistant or other member of school staff deemed competent by the school who holds a Level 2 BG Gymnastics award, and who then completes the Level 2 BG Freestyle Gymnastics module.

4.6.28　Where a coach is used to deliver FreeG in club settings or schools, they should hold at least a Level 2 gymnastics qualification, plus the Level 2 Freestyle Gymnastics award.

Useful website

FreeG: https://goo.gl/Vew7oO

Disability gymnastics

4.6.29   BG has recently launched a new disability programme – 'I'm In' – which supports the participation of disabled people in gymnastics. Hub sites have been appointed as specialist centres to train and develop staff so that they are competent to work safely with people with disabilities. BG aims to increase the number of opportunities for disabled people to take part in safe, high quality gymnastics programmes by enabling more clubs and more trained staff to work with disabled gymnasts.

Useful websites

Disability gymnastics: https://goo.gl/o9nEQq

I'm In: https://goo.gl/p7JeOT

Trampolining

 For further information, see Chapter 2, Section 12, page 201.

4.6.30   Trampolining is a higher risk gymnastics activity that involves participants performing gymnastic moves with control, quality and precision in the air, propelled from a trampoline bed. Skills can include simple shapes (pike, straddle, tuck) and can involve degrees of rotation (eg back drops, half turns, somersaults) and twists. Skills are combined to form routines (comprising up to 10 bounces) in which the participant performs one skill per bounce.

Trampoline qualifications

4.6.31   Staff teaching trampolining are strongly advised to be able to show up-to-date and appropriate **qualifications and expertise** that demonstrate knowledge of the basic skills, techniques and mechanics of the moves they are helping students to learn.

4.6.32   Courses organised or approved by BG are recommended. Where alternatives to governing body of sport qualifications are offered, the employer needs to determine clearly the standards and expertise offered by alternative agencies before agreeing to accept them.

4.6.33   BG's Teachers' Trampoline Awards are currently in two parts. Part one must be successfully completed before the individual embarks on part two. The two parts can comprise a four-day training course. Part one allows the teacher to teach up to but not including rotational trampoline skills. Part two covers teaching somersaults.

4.6.34   Training for the Teachers' Trampoline Awards can be accessed by:

- specialist physical education teachers with qualified teacher status (QTS)

- specialist physical education trainee teachers

- non-physical-education teachers with QTS (or registration) who have gained at least the Level 2 BG Trampoline Coach Award.

4.6.35   Holders of Teachers' Trampoline Awards are **not automatically eligible** to coach trampolining in a non-school setting such as a community club.

4.6.36   It is recommended that staff who have completed the Teachers' Trampoline Award or BG trampoline coaching awards attend a **refresher course** every three years. The employer's policy regarding this should be checked. Staff should not agree to teach trampolining if they feel that their knowledge and practice are not up to date.

Useful website

BG trampoline training courses: https://goo.gl/gKDNHB

Choosing the appropriate size trampoline

4.6.37   Trampolines suitable for use in schools vary in size, and in the thickness of the bed webbing. The potential for higher performance is increased the larger the trampoline, and the narrower the bed webbing.

4.6.38   Models of trampoline include the:

- Continental Sports 77 series (smaller) (in line with Nissen and Ceetex 77)

- Continental Sports 99 series (in line with the Universal sports GM Models, the Nissen GM, Goliath, the Euro Grandmaster and the Ceetex GM)

- Continental Sports 101 series (larger) (in line with Nissen and Ceetex GMEX).

4.6.39   The bed webbing options are 6mm (higher performance), 13mm or 25mm (standard performance). It is the combination of the two aspects that determines the suitability of the trampoline for the level of performance required. Based on this, a high performance trampoline for competition purposes is likely to be a 101 series with a 6mm by 6mm or 6mm by 4mm bed.

4.6.40   When making a choice, schools need to consider all the potential users. If a trampoline has shared use with a community club, it makes sense to address the needs of both. While a 77 series trampoline with a 25mm or 13mm bed may be suitable for school use, this may not be adequate for the needs of a club. It is recommended that schools always consider the highest performance level of potential use as it is possible for students in a physical education lesson to safely work on a higher performance trampoline, but not advisable for a higher performer to work on one with a lower specification.

4.6.41   For the reasons outlined above, the 99 series trampoline with a 13mm bed is a popular choice in schools. It is suitable for secondary age students who may achieve a high performance level. Where shared use is not a concern, or where storage space is limited, the 77 series with a 13mm bed may be more suitable as it is smaller in frame, but still adequate for secondary students.

4.6.42   Where the trampoline is used with younger students or for rebound therapy (see page 419), the 77 series with a 25mm bed is recommended.

Positioning and assembling trampolines

4.6.43   See information in Chapter 2, Section 12, page 201.

Using students as spotters

4.6.44   While the use of matting down the sides of the trampoline is recommended (see Chapter 2, Section 12, page 203), one or two student spotters may also be positioned at each side. It is essential that anyone fulfilling this role is suitably strong, mature, responsible and trained in spotting.

4.6.45   Spotters should:

- not distract the performer by giving vocal encouragement

- pay attention to the trampolinist at all times when spotting – this is essential for personal safety, whether assisting a faller or not

- move out of the way of the falling trampolinist if the spotter feels unsure or unable to assist (ie a trampolinist falling with great momentum); experienced trampolinists can sometimes make adjustments more successfully themselves to reduce the impact of a fall.

4.6.46   Where a spotter is capable of assisting a falling performer, they should:

- reach as high as possible, to contact the chest or shoulders of the faller

- make contact with the faller as early as possible if this will reduce the momentum of the faller

- only attempt to slow down the performer.

Safe teaching

4.6.47   On no account should students ever be left **unsupervised**.

4.6.48   Suitable **clothing** is similar to that used in gymnastics, with a long-sleeved top advised to prevent friction burns when performing a front drop.

4.6.49   Non-slip trampoline **slippers** are advised to prevent toes entering the gaps in the webbed bed. Cotton or wool socks are acceptable. However, nylon socks on a webbed nylon bed may not provide adequate traction.

4.6.50   Only one student at a time should normally be allowed on the trampoline. Work should only begin when everyone is appropriately positioned and ready.

4.6.51   Rebounding should take place as near to the **centre** of the bed as possible and at a height that enables the maintenance of full control.

4.6.52   Should **loss of control** occur, the student should be taught to flex at the knee and hip joints on the very next contact of the feet with the bed to deaden the bounce.

4.6.53   Teaching should emphasise the basic skills, correct techniques and quality of movement, with **graduated progression** according to the ability, confidence and responsible attitude of the individual student, avoiding unnecessary risks and over-rapid progress. Skills should be learnt and consolidated in isolation before being combined into routines.

4.6.54   Basic straight jumps should be mastered before any performer progresses to rotational movements.

4.6.55   Typically, **beginners** should work for about 30 seconds, gradually increasing to about a minute, but should stop if tired or if they are losing concentration.

4.6.56   With experience, staff can safely **supervise a number of trampolines** at once. In such instances, the importance of appropriate positioning in order to maximise observation and allow frequent scanning of the whole activity area cannot be overemphasised. Appropriate positioning enables prompt intervention and advice to be provided where necessary.

4.6.57   It is recommended that trampolining activities are carried out with smaller groups, dependent on the number of trampolines and qualified teachers available. In some instances, where staff are very experienced and students at a level where they can work independently, it may be acceptable for half the class to be doing trampoline-related practices on the floor while the teacher is supervising the other half of the students on the trampoline.

4.6.58   Safe practice is compromised where one teacher supervises half the class working on the trampolines as well as the other half doing a different activity, even when this is in the same space.

4.6.59   Any competition or display routine should consist only of movements successfully **practised and consolidated** as a result of learning and practice. It is not acceptable to place students at risk by changing their routines in a bid for higher marks during a competition.

4.6.60   **Tag-on-type games**, in which students in turn add a movement to the routine, are not recommended as they may encourage students to jump beyond their ability or endurance.

Working on trampolines with students with SEND

4.6.61   Trampolining, trampoline therapy and rebound therapy are names given to activities using a trampoline bed that can provide **stimulus and therapeutic benefit** for students with a range of SEND. These activities can help to promote balance, movement, fitness, sensory awareness, communication and relaxation.

4.6.62   These forms of therapy do not constitute trampolining, and the usual qualification requirements for staff teaching trampolining would not apply, though teachers should be **trained in the particular therapeutic discipline**, particularly when they share the trampoline bed with the student to adjust the effect of weight and speed for control between movements. Staff should also be fully up to date with procedures such as the safe assembly and folding of the trampoline.

4.6.63   The teacher or therapist should assess the need for **safety matting and end decks** (see Chapter 2, Section 12, 2.12.53, page 203) when working with non-ambulant students. Similarly, they should consider whether or not the potential benefit of floor mats would be outweighed by the tripping hazard, and the restriction of access for mobile hoists and wheelchairs.

4.6.64   Very careful risk assessments should be made before enabling individual students with SEND to progress from therapeutic activities to developing recognised trampoline skills.

 For information regarding students with Down's syndrome working on a trampoline, see Chapter 2, Section 14, page 239.

Trampoline parks

4.6.65   These are large warehouse areas with a number of trampoline beds linked together in a 'patchwork' arrangement. Such facilities have become very popular for young people and provide opportunities for high levels of activity.

4.6.66   As outlined in this resource, staff teaching trampolining to students at school are recommended to have a formal qualification, and to develop the skills required progressively and safely. Activity at these centres, while monitored, is largely recreational, with participants being free to choose the extent of their activity. For this reason, the centres require a waiver to be signed for participants who are under 18 years old. Schools cannot sign waivers on behalf of pupils, and neither can they ask parents to sign waivers for children while the children are under the school's duty of care.

4.6.67   Taking these principles into consideration, it is not recommended that schools arrange visits for students to these centres as a school organised trip.

Useful websites

BG trampolining: https://goo.gl/rJaJkn

Continental Sports: http://goo.gl/uWbner

Trampette work

 For further information, see Chapter 2, Section 12, page 201.

4.6.68   Basic trampette skills are the same as those for trampolining, except that forward travel occurs, and landing takes place on a thick, weight-absorbing mattress.

4.6.69   Jumping from a double-footed take-off **on the floor** should be well developed before progressing to the trampette.

4.6.70   Beginners should approach the trampette in an unhurried and controlled manner from a short approach of only a few steps. Each trampette skill should be thoroughly practised and consolidated before progressing to the next stage.

4.6.71   Appropriate support for the skill being practised should be provided. Support should provide a physical 'check' for the students as they land, preventing them from pitching forwards or falling backwards. Responsible students may be trained to provide this support.

4.6.72   **Rotational skills** in the horizontal or vertical plane during flight from a trampette are potentially dangerous and should never be attempted by beginners. The same applies to forward rolls after landing.

4.6.73   **Direct supervision** is required where somersault actions are being learnt. These are more safely learnt on a trampoline using an overhead support rig, followed by competent support when transferred to the trampette until the movements are thoroughly consolidated.

4.6.74   The use of single trampettes is recommended. Using double trampettes (where two or more precede the final action of flight and landing) is only suitable for advanced performers.

4.6.75   Trampettes should always be inclined and not flat when approached from the floor.

4.6.76   When a trampette is used as part of one activity within a gymnastics lesson, close attention should be paid to the performance of basic trampette skills. Frequent observation and maintaining control of the class as a whole are essential.

4.6.77 It is recommended that trampettes are not used during vaulting activities. Students who are not specifically trained or sufficiently skilled in their use find it difficult to cope with the additional height and rotation provided.

4.6.78 The use of trampettes as a piece of gymnastics equipment is not recommended within primary curriculum lessons. Some schools have introduced mini rebounder sessions. Staff should be trained in the use of this equipment.

 For more information about trampoline and trampette activities in primary schools, see Chapter 2, Section 12, page 204.

4.6.79 Appropriate **footwear** is needed when using trampettes with webbed beds.

Chapter 4/Section 7: Health-related physical activities

The health-related physical activities context

4.7.1   Health-related physical activity (HRPA) is physical activity associated with health enhancement and disease prevention. All UK countries highlight the importance of HRPA in their national curriculum orders and have made learning about healthy active lifestyles (HAL) (albeit under different titles) an inclusive learning entitlement.

4.7.2   Learning about HAL involves students developing the knowledge, understanding, motor skills, social and emotional competences, positive attitudes and confidence necessary to feel empowered to make informed decisions about the role of lifelong physical activity in promoting health and emotional well-being in their own and others' lives.

4.7.3   All physical education, school sport and physical activity (PESSPA) activities have the potential to be health-related. In addition, specific exercise and fitness activities are increasingly used in both primary and secondary schools as contexts for learning about HAL. Such activities include various types of circuits, exercise to music/'aerobics' activities (including step and zoomba), Pilates, skipping and yoga. Many secondary schools also promote learning about HAL in a fitness room environment (ie using cardiovascular machines, fixed resistance equipment and free weights). Given the increasing range of health-related physical activities currently included in PESSPA programmes, it is important that staff are very clear about the safe practice and principles to monitor and apply.

General safe-practice issues

| 4.7.4 | Fundamental principles of safe practice (**Chapter 1**) and principles of safe organisation and management (Chapter 2) should be understood and applied to all school provision of HRPA. A helpful summary of these is provided in Table 6, Chapter 2, pages 64–67. More specific guidance and information about HRPA are provided in this section, and staff should familiarise themselves with these and apply them to their unique set of circumstances. Links to websites can be followed to access additional information relating to safe provision of HRPA. |

Safe exercise practice

 See information in Chapter 2, Section 9, page 160.

4.7.5   Staff should be well informed about the principles of safe exercise practice and able to effectively apply them when completing risk assessments of exercise and fitness activities, especially in relation to:

- warming up and cooling down

- developing and monitoring safe and effective technique (eg knees over toes when bending, correct spinal alignment, avoiding moves/exercises that put stress on the neck, lower back or knees)

- ensuring that exercise and fitness activities are developmentally appropriate for all students.

Equipment

4.7.6   **Mats** should be available for any exercises that require kneeling, sitting or lying on the floor (eg resistance exercises working against body weight, or cool-down stretches). Lightweight, portable, individual exercise mats are ideal for this purpose. However, **exercise mats should never be used in other activity areas as substitutes for proper gymnastics mats**.

4.7.7   **Music** is often used as an accompaniment for specific HRPAs (eg aerobics and circuits).

4.7.8   Staff should ensure that:

- **all electrical equipment** such as CD players has been PAT tested (see Chapter 2, Section 12, page 210)

- the volume of the music allows their students to hear staff instructions and peer conversations relevant to safe practice, procedures and learning

- the use of music does not adversely effect the ability of students to access learning (eg those with hearing impairments or autism/autistic spectrum disorder [ASD]/Asperger's syndrome). See Chapter 2, Section 14, page 235.

Guidance on specific health-related physical activities
Fitness testing

4.7.9   Fitness testing is common practice in the majority of secondary schools and an increasing number of primary schools, and involves the administration of a range of simple tests that measure the components of health-related fitness (eg cardiovascular fitness, strength, endurance, flexibility) and performance-related fitness (eg agility, balance, power, reaction time). Examples of tests commonly used include the abdominal curl conditioning test, Cooper Run, Multistage Fitness Test ('beep test'), and sit and reach test.

4.7.10   It is recommended that any form of fitness testing carried out with students in curriculum time should be **positive**, meaningful, relevant, **developmentally appropriate**, and part of a planned, progressive programme of study, the primary aim of which is to promote healthy, active lifestyles (afPE [2015] 'Health position statement', http://goo.gl/IHCYrZ

4.7.11   afPE advocates that fitness testing is **not good use** of the limited curriculum physical education time in primary schools.

4.7.12   For fitness testing to be seen as part of a PESSPA programme that promotes the health, safety and well-being of all young people, staff would be wise to consider:

- the appropriateness of the fitness tests chosen

- the implementation methods used

- over-use of fitness testing as a means for promoting and enhancing students' participation in physical activity.

4.7.13   Maximal tests, such as the Multistage Fitness Test ('beep test') and abdominal curl conditioning test, were designed **for elite adult performers**. The appropriateness of these tests for safe use with young people and children is questionable.

4.7.14   Maximal tests are problematic for use with mixed ability groups of students because:

- they can impose inappropriate physiological demands

- self-imposed and peer pressure can encourage exercise beyond safe limits

- screening is required prior to such tests

- close and continuous monitoring is essential.

4.7.15   Fitness tests that are individualised and developmentally appropriate are recommended for curriculum use. Such tests might include:

- maximal tests that allow students to pace themselves during the time or distance allowed (eg **time/distance runs** and timed/paced muscular or **endurance tests**)

- **sub-maximal tests** (eg taking a pulse rate after 2–3 mins of paced step-ups), which make more appropriate demands on developing systems and provide more information for learning about fitness components.

Fitness room activities

4.7.16   Fitness rooms provide a variety of exercise opportunities that enable individuals to develop all components of fitness 'under one roof'. Fitness room equipment might include cardiovascular (CV) machines (eg rowing machines, stationary cycles and treadmills), fixed resistance machines (eg shoulder press, chest press and leg extension machines) and free weights such as dumbbells, barbells and kettlebells.

Staff qualifications and training

4.7.17   Fully qualified specialist physical education teachers are deemed to be suitably qualified to teach students in a fitness room, although additional professional learning is strongly recommended. All staff teaching, coaching or supervising students in a fitness room should be competent to do so. An assessment of competency should confirm that they are:

- well informed and up to date in terms of knowledge about safe exercise practice for young people (see Chapter 2, Section 9, page 160)

- sufficiently experienced and confident in using a range of fitness room equipment

- able to lead, demonstrate, monitor and correct safe exercise practice in the context of fitness room activities.

4.7.18   If any of these competencies require further update or development, it is recommended that additional appropriate professional learning is undertaken, such as:

- internal training within school, where colleagues have the necessary expertise

- a relevant professional development training course (eg Promoting Effective Learning about Healthy Active Lifestyles in Fitness Rooms at KS 3 and 4 – developed by www.learningabouthal.co.uk and certificated by YMCA Fitness Industry training)

- UKCC Level 2 Gym Instructor qualification (eg http://goo.gl/0fo3IX).

Fitness room equipment and layout

4.7.19   Fitness rooms should always be locked when not in use, to **prevent unauthorised access** to potentially dangerous equipment.

4.7.20   All CV machines, fixed resistance machines and other specialist equipment should be checked regularly by a company competent in working with the equipment.

4.7.21   Many fitness rooms do not have equipment appropriate for school use. In situations where facilities are shared with the community (ie dual use), schools often make compromises when using adult equipment with young people. Equipment 'donated' from another leisure provider should be checked thoroughly to establish whether it is appropriate for use with students.

4.7.22   In cases where adult-oriented machines cannot be adjusted sufficiently to accommodate the needs of specific students, alternative exercises (eg using resistance bands or light dumbbells) should be provided and the adult equipment not used.

4.7.23   Too much equipment packed into a fitness room can be a potential safety hazard and also result in the space being ineffective as a learning environment.

4.7.24   Where possible, a school fitness room should have some floor space available for:

- mats to be placed for floor exercises (eg stretches, abdominal curls)

- mats, dumbbells, exercise balls, resistance bands/tubing to be used

- students to sit while being addressed as a whole group.

For more information about fitness room facilities, see Chapter 2, Section 13, page 221.

Age-related issues about student use

4.7.25   Many local authorities (LAs) or private providers set age restrictions for the use of their fitness room facilities. Reasons given for this are often linked to insurance barriers.

4.7.26   Current guidelines indicate that it is not only safe for adolescents to take part in well-supervised, developmentally appropriate resistance exercise programmes, but that there are many health benefits to be gained from doing so. The British Association of Sports and Exercise Sciences (BASES) recommends that:

> *facilities and equipment should be designed to suit the needs of individuals; be well supervised and led by suitably qualified staff; young people should be helped to understand the place of resistance exercise in a balanced programme of health-enhancing activity.*

> Stratton, G., Jones, M., Fox, K.R., Tolfrey, K., Harris, J., Maffulli, N., Lee, M. and Frostick, S.P. (2004) 'BASES position statement on guidelines for resistance exercise in young people', *Journal of Sports Sciences*, 22 (4): 383–90.

4.7.27   For this reason, schools should not hesitate to seek to use fitness rooms with students aged 11–18 providing that the above guidance can be met.

The 'BASES position statement on guidelines for resistance exercise in young people' leaflet is available to purchase from 1st4sport.com: http://goo.gl/3Yk64V

Safe learning in the fitness room

4.7.28   A fitness room is a high risk environment. Depending on the size of the facility, staff may need to consider how the lesson can be organised to manage the learning safely. Where lack of space presents a hazard, staff may decide to discuss with the leadership team ways to reduce the group size.

4.7.29   Fitness room activities should always be **supervised appropriately**. Students should be provided with an adequate introduction to all fitness room exercises. This should include:

- information concerning how to adjust CV or resistance machines to ensure joints can work in correct alignment

- a practical demonstration showing safe and correct technique

- teaching points explaining correct joint alignment (eg knee, wrists, spine, elbows)

- information about how to start and stop exercising safely

- essential safety points (eg only the person using the CV machine is to adjust the controls; keep hands away from pulleys and weight stacks; place free weights equipment safely and in readiness for the next person).

4.7.30   Some exercises using a barbell or heavy dumbbells require **spotters**. It is recommended that only teachers with specific training/qualifications in 'spotting' technique (eg UKCC Level 2 Gym instructor or 1st4sport Level 2 Certificate in Coaching Weight Lifting or 1st4sport Level 2 Award in Instructing Weight Lifting – see page 429 in this section) or significant personal experience of spotting, should attempt to teach exercises that require the use of spotting skills.

4.7.31   Where schools are considering allowing older students (year 12 or 13) to use the fitness room with remote supervision, this should in the first instance be discussed and agreed with their employer. Parents should be informed that the opportunity is being offered to their child. Procedures should be put in place to manage this arrangement appropriately. These may include students:

- having experience of, and being deemed competent by a staff member to use, the equipment in the facility

- signing in and out of the facility

- not using the facility alone

- being restricted in the equipment they use (eg free weights may not be used)

- agreeing and signing up to a code of conduct for use of the facility

- understanding the emergency procedures, should assistance be required

- being intermittently supervised by staff.

Staff personal use of school fitness rooms

4.7.32   Schools that have their own fitness rooms may decide to allow staff to use the room in their own time. Where this is an option, staff need to be aware that they use the facility at their own risk, but regardless of this fact, they will still be expected to observe the safety requirements and code of conduct.

4.7.33   Staff should:

- be inducted on how to use the machines, even if they have attended fitness room inductions elsewhere; ideally, a trained member of the physical education staff or a qualified fitness instructor (UKCC Level 2 or above) should deliver this induction

- complete a participatory agreement, declaring that they have no known medical conditions for which fitness room activities could be harmful, and confirming that they have been advised of the code of conduct and emergency procedures

- be advised not to exercise alone, although they do not need to be directly supervised

- understand that if exercising unsupervised, they are only covered by occupier's liability (ie that the facility and equipment are safe for the purpose they are being used for, as long as they are being used correctly)

- understand that if exercising with supervision, they may also be covered for third-party liability arising from negligence on the part of the supervisory staff.

4.7.34   The school should inform its employer that staff are using the facility in this way.

High intensity training

4.7.35   High intensity training (HIT) is a form of resistance training that focuses on performing high quality resistance exercise repetitions to the point of muscular failure. This is not recommended for use with students in PESSPA.

High intensity interval training

4.7.36   High intensity interval training (HIIT) is a version of CV interval training that involves short intervals of extremely intense CV exercise, followed by short, sometimes active, recovery periods.

4.7.37   While HIIT is a suitable training method for some young people, it is not recommended in mixed ability PESSPA sessions (for further information, see 4.7.42).

Resistance exercise

4.7.38   Resistance exercise involves contracting muscles against a resistance. It has benefits for students of all ages as it develops muscular strength and endurance, and promotes healthy bone growth and development. Resistance exercise includes weight-bearing activities (eg climbing, throwing, pushing, pulling and travelling on different body parts), body-weight activities (resistance exercises working against resistance personal body weight as in push-ups and squats), resistance training or weight training (using external resistance provided by equipment such as elastics, tubing, fixed resistance machines, dumb-bells and kettlebells) and weightlifting (which uses external resistance usually provided using barbells and free weights).

4.7.39   Common causes of accidents in resistance exercise include:

- inappropriate equipment in an unsafe environment

- excessive loadings

- programmes not being developmentally appropriate

- lack of supervision by appropriately qualified and competent professionals.

4.7.40   BASES (Stratton et al, 2004) recommends that:

- resistance exercise programmes are individualised to meet the needs of each participant

- well-supervised resistance exercise is led by suitably qualified staff to reduce the risk of physical injury and psychological harm.

Isometric resistance exercises

4.7.41   These are static strength exercises in which muscles contract or 'tense' but without movement about joints (eg 'the plank' or 'wall sit'). These exercises are commonly used in circuits and, with secondary students, can be effective in developing strength and endurance in muscles in the position in which the exercise is performed.

4.7.42   If staff are using isometric exercises in their programmes with students, it is wise to:

- make accurate **risk assessments** of each exercise using the principles of safe exercise practice (see Chapter 2, Section 9, page 160)

- check that students are able to perform **'isotonic'** (dynamic/moving) resistance exercises (eg squats, abdominal curls, push-ups) for the same muscle groups with safe and correct technique, and showing a good level of core stability

- avoid challenging students to perform isometric exercises to the point of extreme fatigue or 'failure' – this can prove extremely uncomfortable, distressing and demeaning for some individuals, is at variance with the principles of safeguarding and is not necessary in order to gain physical health benefits from performing such exercises.

Weightlifting

4.7.43   Weightlifting is associated with the sport of Olympic weightlifting, which involves the performer working against resistance using techniques such as the 'snatch' and 'clean and jerk'. Weightlifting, as a form of resistance training, can be beneficial to older secondary students' health when delivery is planned, programmed and monitored by appropriately qualified and competent professionals.

4.7.44   All staff teaching weightlifting in schools should have a **relevant qualification**. The 1st4sport Level 2 Award in Instructing Weight Lifting can be accessed by:

- specialist qualified physical education teachers

- physical education trainee teachers.

4.7.45   All staff teaching weightlifting who are not qualified teachers should have at least a 1st4sport Level 2 Certificate in Coaching Weight Lifting.

4.7.46   Holders of the 1st4sport level 2 Award in Instructing Weight Lifting are not **automatically eligible** to coach weightlifting in a non-school setting such as a community club.

4.7.47   Mats for lifting weights are for the purpose of protecting the equipment and facilities from unnecessary damage. A **platform** is a specific piece of flooring apparatus/matting used for the sport of weightlifting that provides a hard surface to stand on (for stability) while performing the exercise, and soft surfaces either side for dropping the weights in a manner that is safe and protective for the facility and equipment.

4.7.48   The **ceiling height** of the facility used should be a minimum of three metres for safety reasons when lifting weights above the head.

4.7.49   Weights should be 450mm in diameter to ensure the barbell has a safe minimal height from the floor, to allow for weightlifting activities. Exposed metal weights are to be avoided, and a rubber or plastic-covered weight is suggested.

4.7.50   Barbells should be available that are appropriate for use by young people. A variety of bars are available (eg technique bars weighing around 5–12kg and lighter bars from 15kg – known as the women's bar – with a bar shaft diameter of 25mm).

 Standards for bars can be found on the International Body for Weightlifting website: www.iwf.net

4.7.51 Mixed **footwear** can be used for weightlifting, depending on the standard of the participant. This may include the use of a sports shoe or a weightlifting-specific shoe. A weightlifting shoe will provide additional tension while ensuring appropriate support of the ankle, specific to the sport's demands.

4.7.52 British Weight Lifting recommends that there should be an emphasis on skill mastery and technique development, rather than just weight lifted, until the age of 13 years.

4.7.53 BASES (Stratton et al, 2004) recommends that:

- high intensity resistance exercise is avoided during periods of rapid growth

- rest and resistance exercise are alternated where the training stimulus involves considerable overload

- a 48-hour recovery period follows heavier resistance exercise programmes.

Useful website

British Weight Lifting: www.britishweightlifting.org

Other exercise and fitness activities

Exercise to music

4.7.54 An increasing number of exercise to music genres are currently used in school PESSPA programmes, including aerobics, body pump, step and zoomba.

4.7.55 It is wise for physical education staff who are teaching exercise to music within the school programme to:

- have appropriate personal experience of taking part in these activities (eg in community classes)

- carry out thorough risk assessments of all exercises to be used in terms of safe exercise practice and developmental appropriateness.

 For further information about safe exercise practice, see Chapter 2, Section 9, page 160.

4.7.56 Staff wishing to access additional training in exercise to music can consider:

- CYQ Level 2 Certificate in Fitness Instructing (Group Exercise to Music) – http://goo.gl/esdUX4

- a relevant professional development training course (eg Promoting Effective Learning about Healthy Active Lifestyles through Aerobics and Circuits at KS 3 and 4 – developed by www.learningabouthal.co.uk and certificated by YMCA Fitness Industry training).

4.7.57 Exercise to music has no recognised governing body of sport.

Indoor rowing

4.7.58 It is wise for staff leading indoor rowing within a school programme to:

- provide adequate supervision

- organise for safe and secure storage of ergos (ergometers – the rowing machine equipment)

- teach safe lifting and transport techniques if moving ergos

- check that ergos are correctly assembled and in appropriate working order before use

- check that ergos are positioned appropriately (eg to allow sufficient space for the rower to work safely, to avoid obstructing fire exits)

- check that students are wearing appropriate clothing (eg no loose, long baggy tops that might get caught in the mechanism, no jewellery)

- check that students are wearing training shoes

- include an effective warm-up and cool-down

- be sufficiently competent and knowledgeable to ensure that high quality technique is developed and maintained

- make well-informed decisions concerning when it is appropriate for students to progress to competitive challenges.

4.7.59   British Rowing makes the following recommendations in British Rowing (2016) 'Guidance on on-water and indoor rowing by school children', https://goo.gl/DtGrpZ:

- Appropriate, correct, suitable coaching and learning of 'The British Rowing technique' provide the basis for performance and enjoyment of the sport, and allow the rower to be safe, providing their spine and other injury risk areas with proper protection.

- The drag factor should be kept low for all rowers but especially for beginners and younger participants.

- The session length and content must be suitable for the ability and training age of the rower.

Useful websites

British Rowing: www.britishrowing.org
Indoor Rowing for Young People: https://goo.gl/RkXFRw

Kettlebells

4.7.60   A kettlebell is a cast-iron weighted ball with a handle attached to the top of it. Kettlebell 'workouts' comprise a range of explosive exercises that challenge all of the major muscles, strengthen the core, burn fat and build power.

4.7.61   It is wise for physical education staff who are teaching kettlebell exercises within the school programme to:

- have appropriate personal experience of performing kettlebell workouts (eg in community classes)

- carry out thorough risk assessments of all exercises to be used in terms of safe exercise practice and developmental appropriateness.

 For further information about safe exercise practice, see Chapter 2, Section 9, page 160.

4.7.62   Some organisations offer professional development for teaching kettlebell exercise. These courses are sometimes restricted to qualified UKCC Level 2 fitness instructors or those with appropriate practical experience of working with kettlebells. In many cases, qualified specialist physical education teachers can access them.

Useful website

Kettlebells: http://goo.gl/2EXqcZ

Skipping

4.7.63   Skipping is a high-impact exercise activity that is commonly included in PESSPA programmes in many primary schools and some secondary schools. It also remains a very popular playground activity. Skipping can develop CV fitness, muscular endurance and bone health, as well as agility, balance, coordination and creativity.

4.7.64   The floor should be smooth, flat, dry and clear of any articles that might cause tripping. Wooden sprung floors or rubberised surfaces offer more resilience than tarmac or concrete and are therefore safer if skipping is to be performed regularly. Skipping on mats should be avoided.

4.7.65   Skippers should have sufficient space around them to avoid hitting others with the rope as it turns. There should also be sufficient space overhead, if working indoors, to avoid bringing down light fitments and other objects from the ceiling.

4.7.66   Skippers should be encouraged to check that the space around and above them is clear before they start to skip.

4.7.67   Skipping in supportive footwear with shock-absorbing soles (eg training shoes) is recommended. Avoid skipping in socks or bare feet.

4.7.68   Good landing technique should be taught, monitored and encouraged to ensure that impact is minimised by reducing the height of the jump, bending the knees and landing on the ball of the foot followed by touching the heels gently on the ground.

4.7.69   A thorough and progressive warm-up and cool-down should be included in every skipping session.

 For more information about safe exercise practice, see Chapter 2, Section 9, page 160.

4.7.70   Staff should avoid exposing students to long-duration or excessive amounts of jumping as this may cause unnecessary stress to bones and joints. During a skipping session, it is wise to intersperse jumping activities with non-jumping activities.

4.7.71   Skipping is not appropriate, safe or comfortable for all students, and care should be taken when working with young people who are obese or very sedentary, or who have SEND in terms of integrating them safely and appropriately.

Useful website

British Heart Foundation Jump Rope for Heart Campaign: https://goo.gl/bsk6zN

Yoga and Pilates

4.7.72   **Yoga** is an ancient form of exercise that focuses on strength, flexibility and breathing to boost physical and mental well-being.

4.7.73   **Pilates** is similar to yoga, but focuses on using both the mind and body to achieve optimum performance. The stabilising or 'core' muscles of the body are conditioned and strengthened using sequences of movements that use gravity and body weight as forms of resistance.

4.7.74   It is wise for physical education staff who are teaching yoga or Pilates exercises within the school programme to:

- carry out thorough risk assessments of all exercises to be used in terms of safe exercise practice and developmental appropriateness (for further information, see Tables 13–16, Chapter 2, Section 9, page 161)

- undertake additional training in children and young people's yoga or Pilates

- work alongside a fully qualified yoga/Pilates teacher, trained in working with children or young people as appropriate.

4.7.75   It can also be helpful if the member of staff has personal experience of taking part in these activities.

4.7.76   Pilates has no recognised governing body of sport.

Useful website

British Wheel of Yoga: www.bwy.org.uk

Useful websites

afPE Health Position Paper: http://goo.gl/IHCYrZ

British Heart Foundation National Centre for
Physical Activity and Health: www.bhfactive.org.uk

Learning About Healthy Active Lifestyles Ltd: www.learningabouthal.co.uk

Register of Exercise Professionals: www.exerciseregister.org

YMCA Fitness Industry Training: www.ymcafit.org.uk

Chapter 4/Section 8: Outdoor and adventure activities

The outdoor and adventure activities context

4.8.1 Outdoor and adventure activities (OAA) recognise the benefits of environmental education and adventure, which encourage students to take responsibility for their own actions in appropriately challenging situations. These opportunities offer learning through 'real' experiences and have the potential to develop skills for life. OAA include:

- **local/low-level outdoor activities** such as problem-solving activities, introductory orienteering, low-level climbing, excursions in normal lowland countryside, and team-building activities, which can develop trust, communication and leadership skills using simple equipment in safe, controlled environments

- **outdoor adventure activities (often conducted off site)** such as rock climbing, sailing, potholing, canoeing and abseiling, in which the spirit of adventure needs to be balanced against responsibility for the well-being and safety of those participating.

General safe-practice issues

4.8.2 Fundamental principles of safe practice (**Chapter 1**) and principles of safe organisation and management (Chapter 2) should be understood and applied to all school provision of OAA. A helpful summary of these are provided in Table 6, Chapter 2, pages 64–67. More specific guidance and information about OAA are provided in this section, and staff should familiarise themselves with these and apply them to their unique set of circumstances. The rules of the governing bodies of sport may not always be appropriate to schools, and schools should adjust their practice where necessary. (See **Chapter 1, Section 2, 1.2.10–1.2.14,** and Chapter 2, Section 5, 2.5.60–2.5.61.) Links to websites can be followed to access additional information relating to safe provision of OAA.

Provision of local/low-level outdoor and adventure activities

4.8.3 Most schools are able to deliver outdoor and adventure activities both within the school site and the immediate locality. The level of demand and risk in such activities can be relatively low.

4.8.4 In such circumstances, the technical demand on staff is such that experience is often a key component of competence, along with knowledge of the locality and the school's system for managing groups off site.

4.8.5 Where the activity makes **basic demands** on students and staff, such as using the school and its immediate local environment (eg problem solving, orienteering using the school grounds or walking in local lowland countryside), competence through experience and relevant training is often the only requirement of the employer, combined with a plan that meets the needs of the group and identifies significant issues.

4.8.6 The organisation, planning and risk management of these types of activity can be covered both within a school's policy and as part of normal lesson planning. The Department for Education (DfE), in its health and safety advice for schools, points out that schools are not required to complete a risk assessment every time they undertake an activity in the locality during the school day: DfE (2014) 'Health and safety: Advice on legal duties and powers for local authorities, school leaders, school staff and governing bodies', https://goo.gl/GyphRM

4.8.7 Where an initial risk assessment is carried out, it should stipulate the required levels of expertise.

4.8.8   Employers should set out their requirements for staff competence and arrange periodic monitoring to ensure good practice.

 Guidance on planning visits and activities can also be found on the Outdoor Education Advisers' Panel (OEAP) website: www.oeap.info

Provision of outdoor and adventure activities (often off site)

4.8.9   Competent leadership and appropriate safety management are essential in delivering safe, high quality outdoor and adventure activities.

4.8.10   Before leading an outdoor adventure activity, an individual needs to ensure that they meet their employer's criteria for competence and planning requirements for the activity. Assessing competence can take into account a number of factors (see Chapter 2, Section 2, page 68). In the case of specific OAA, competence may include:

- holding a governing body of sport leadership/coaching award at an appropriate level – governing bodies of sport regularly update and develop their awards, resources and current best practice relating to safe organisation, leadership and risk assessment

- being approved by a suitably competent technical adviser, where available, who is appointed by an employer and recognised as suitably qualified by the relevant governing body of sport.

4.8.11   The qualifications matrices produced by the Adventure Activities Licensing Authority (AALA) provide further information about qualifications to lead or advise on specific outdoor adventure activities, including qualifications appropriate for technical advisers: http://goo.gl/KXBolp

4.8.12   Schools seeking competent leaders to deliver outdoor and adventure activities may also require them to have:

- relevant recommended qualifications and skills related to particular environments required by their employer (and the relevant governing body of sport if applicable) including basic first aid and training in how to manage an emergency

- recent experience or knowledge of the intended location, taking into account weather conditions/forecasts and other variables

- clear educational objectives for the activities planned

- a good knowledge of the students for whom they will be responsible

- knowledge of the fitness and experience of students to help them to match the proposed activity to them

- proven qualities of leadership and responsibility that are evident from other aspects of their work

- a flexible approach to altering a plan appropriately if conditions dictate

- the capacity to react effectively if things do not go to plan

- the ability to say 'no', despite student protestations, if circumstances make the original plan unworkable

- the necessary mental and physical fitness to undertake the proposed activity

- the ability to establish safe supervision levels, taking into account all relevant variables

- a positive track record in active supervision

- the ability to recognise, and remain within, the extent of their competence.

Organisation and planning

4.8.13   The organisation and planning required for outdoor and adventure activities can vary according to whether the activity takes place on site/locally or further afield. Some employers provide detailed guidance for the delivery of outdoor and adventure activities. Where this is the case, employees must follow this. Where the employer does not provide this guidance, or where additional guidance is required, the leader should refer to alternative guidance such as that offered in this resource, and by appropriate governing bodies of sport.

4.8.14   If possible, the skills required for specific outdoor and adventure activities should be introduced to students within the school setting prior to off-site participation.

4.8.15   A suitable **risk assessment** that meets the employer's requirements should be carried out covering all aspects of the trip. This is the responsibility of the member of staff leading the visit.

> **i** For further information about risk assessment, see Chapter 1, Section 6, page 29, and Chapter 2, Section 6, page 128.

4.8.16   The school leader and other staff, where appropriate, should have **recent knowledge and experience** of off-site venues or locations, and it is highly recommended that some staff make a **preliminary visit** prior to the commencement of the activity.

4.8.17   Where a preliminary visit is not possible, it is advisable that local knowledge is sought and risk assessment is carried out on arrival to determine whether a planned activity can proceed.

> **i** See Chapter 2, Section 6, page 128, for further information about planning trips and visits.

4.8.18   Where off-site visits require transport, the school leader should plan and assess the transport as an equally important part of the visit.

> **i** For further information about transport, see Chapter 2, Section 17, page 286.

4.8.19   Any employer's requirements for effective supervision, including adult:student **ratios** when taking groups off site, must be observed at all times. Staff may decide to work with smaller groups where students have additional needs. On some occasions, recommendations from governing bodies of sport regarding ratios should be taken into account, but those of the employer always take priority.

4.8.20   Where no employer requirements are set, supervision should be determined through an informed risk assessment, taking account of the range of variables. There are a number of different approaches to such an assessment. The OEAP provides one example using the acronym SAGED as a way of remembering the issues to consider:

- **S**taffing requirements – Trained? Experienced? Competent? Ratios?

- **A**ctivity characteristics – Specialist? Level of demand? Insurance issues? Licensable?

- **G**roup characteristics – Prior experience? Ability? Behaviour? Special and medical needs?

- **E**nvironmental conditions – Like last time? Impact of weather? Water levels?

- **D**istance from support mechanisms in place at the home base – Transport? Residential?

To access a range of useful OEAP documents, see http://goo.gl/edTDL3

Information presented in Table 38, page 440, and the exemplar off-site risk assessment template in Chapter 1, Section 6, pages 48–56, can also be used.

4.8.21   In anticipating the possibility of changed circumstances, the school leader should make sure that supervision is always sufficient to ensure safety by having realistic **contingency plans**.

4.8.22   While not legally required, it may be wise for at least two responsible adults to accompany a group off site to allow for dealing with unanticipated events. An **assistant leader**, capable of fulfilling the leader's role or managing the group until help arrives, should be identified where there is more than one member of staff with the group. Employers' requirements and the risk assessment will have a bearing on the decisions made.

4.8.23   **Mixed groups** benefit from having staff of each gender, particularly for overnight stays. The needs of the students should be assessed to determine whether same-gender staff are required. Where a mixed-gender staff is not possible, parents should be informed so they can decide whether to consent to their child participating.

4.8.24   If students are to use their own clothing and equipment (eg for camping), this should be checked to ensure it is appropriate before the group leaves the school, and before the activity commences.

4.8.25   All members of the school leadership team should be **aware of the visit plans**, and trained to manage an emergency.

4.8.26   Where a leader operates alone for an off-site visit, effective communication with the school is essential, and the group should be trained in what action to take in the event of the leader being incapacitated, and be deemed able to take this action if required.

4.8.27   Relevant **information** should be accessible at the school or base to enable effective emergency action if required. This should include:

- contact information (eg school and parent emergency communication)

- activity location

- expected time of arrival and return (and action to take if the group fails to return on time)

- equipment carried

- names and number of students and staff

- agreed procedures to be followed in the event of an accident or emergency.

4.8.28   An effective communication system with school should be available while the group is away.

4.8.29   Discipline must be maintained at all times, and staff must be prepared to intervene if students take potentially unsafe action.

4.8.30   It is accepted practice, and an integral part of high quality provision, for students participating in activities such as the Duke of Edinburgh's Award scheme to undertake carefully planned expeditions under progressively **remote supervision**, providing they have been trained to do so. Before taking part in more independent activities, students should first demonstrate sufficient skill, experience and maturity under the supervision of a competent leader.

4.8.31   Once the leader is satisfied that the students have acquired the necessary skills and have the necessary confidence, physical ability and judgement, the withdrawal of the direct supervision should be a gradual **four-stage process**, evolving through:

- accompanying the group

- shadowing the group

- checking regularly at agreed locations

- checking occasionally at agreed locations.

4.8.32   Staff should always consider apprehensions and the level of ability of individual students, and avoid putting undue pressure on individuals to progress when they do not feel ready. Adequate safeguards and progressive steps should be put in place by relevantly qualified and experienced staff before proceeding with activities in these situations.

4.8.33   Where remote supervision is considered, students need to:

- be clearly briefed

- be informed of potential hazards

- be left in no doubt as to action to take in the event of emergencies

- carry suitable emergency equipment to deal with foreseeable incidents

- be able to contact the leader if required.

4.8.34   If **external providers** contribute with school staff to the activity programme, roles and responsibilities should be identified and understood.

4.8.35   When external agents or **tour operators** are used, schools should follow their employers' requirements for engaging their services. Systems should be in place to ensure that tour operators:

- are reputable

- meet relevant statutory requirements, including financial bonding arrangements

- are able to fully satisfy the school's duty of care expectations.

4.8.36   The Learning Outside the Classroom (LOtC) Quality Badge gives assurance that providers meet nationally recognised standards. Providers holding the badge, and the amount of their insurance, can be checked at http://lotcqualitybadge.org.uk

4.8.37   When dealing with commercial agencies, some knowledge of the Package Travel, Package Holidays and Package Tours Regulations 1992 and the Package Travel Directive 2015 will enhance safe planning.

 For information about sports tours, see Chapter 2, Section 6, page 131.

Table 38: Planning checklist for off-site OAA

Long-term planning should:	Medium-term planning should:	Short-term planning should:
• meet employer's requirements with regard to OAA • be supported by consultation with the educational visits coordinator (EVC) where one exists • allow sufficient time for necessary planning and coordination and, where appropriate, visit approval • clarify necessary staff competence, availability (eg enforced staff-substitution arrangements) and staff:student ratios • identify timescales covering important aspects of the itinerary, which might include: – a preliminary visit to the intended location – EVC clearance and submission of any necessary paperwork (eg risk assessment), as required by the employer – a detailed plan for the proposed trip, with timescales – written information to parents if it is an optional activity, including outline plan, consent forms, educational aims and a proposed programme of activities – expectations and codes of behaviour – times of meetings and information evenings if these are relevant to the event	• establish a schedule for the supervision of students • provide for contingency arrangements in the event of accident, illness or inability to participate in the proposed programme • establish the necessary equipment requirements and ensure equipment is: – in good condition – fit for purpose – correctly sized to fit the students involved • ensure students are emotionally prepared and physically fit for the proposed activity	• provide for flexibility on the day, taking into account variables such as weather, the presence of other groups and the disposition of the group in question • include ongoing consideration of: – the educational aims of the event – staff:student ratios and appropriate supervision arrangements for the group – the capabilities, individual needs and physical state of students and staff – the development of weather systems as the day progresses – site-specific issues relating to the proposed venue – transport logistics and travelling times • enable the adult in charge to: – follow accepted current good practice in the conduct of the activity – provide an appropriate level of challenge for the range of individuals involved – ensure the group is adequately clothed and equipped

(continued)

Long-term planning should:	Medium-term planning should:	Short-term planning should:
– any finance details and student costs – travel arrangements, including the management of breaks in the journey – any accommodation details with arrangements for mixed-gender groups – information concerning personal insurance and the limit of the school's liability – appropriate equipment lists – Disclosure and Barring Service (DBS) checks – designation of approved-adult status, where relevant – responsibilities and supervision arrangements for the duration of the trip – meal arrangements – individual needs, such as diet, educational and medical information – an accurate register of participants and appropriate adult:student ratios – contingency arrangements for when adverse circumstances prevent the planned programme from taking place – anticipation of staff changes and their effects on continuity – agreed and workable emergency procedures – an effective communication system with the school – ensuring an appropriate level of challenge for participants with a progressive approach to skill acquisition • allow sufficient time for the submission of plans to the leadership team and, where appropriate, school governing body for approval.	• take account of the weather forecast, and pre-empt contingency arrangements affected by this • identify workable accident-reporting procedures.	– ensure the group is adequately briefed on the plan for the day – take into account the medical background of students and staff, and ensure prescribed medication, such as asthma inhalers, is accessible – ensure accessories such as watches and jewellery are removed if they pose a danger or are liable to be damaged; long hair is tied back and spectacles secured if necessary – check any equipment used is fit for purpose – monitor and take account of changes in the physical and mental state of students during activities – carry out the plan, unless unforeseen circumstances dictate otherwise, so the group can be located in the event of an emergency – ensure emergency equipment is adequate and readily accessible – consider the experience and abilities of other members of staff, clearly define roles and responsibilities, and delegate only appropriate levels of supervision – consider communications systems and emergency procedures in the event of an accident – modify the activity as necessary to ensure safe participation.

Guidance on specific local/low-level outdoor and adventure activities

Team building and problem solving

4.8.38   Problem-solving and team-building activities can develop trust, communication and leadership skills using simple equipment in safe, controlled environments.

4.8.39   Students are encouraged to think both logically and critically, as well as creatively, when problem solving. Staff experience and an active approach to risk management during the activity are important to safety. Sensible precautions can reduce risk without stifling initiative, enterprise and excitement.

4.8.40   Some problem-solving activities can appear contrived and innocuous on occasions (eg 'crossing an imaginary swamp using mats'), and students may not fully appreciate the real risks involved. Despite this, participants should always be required to act in a safe manner and take responsibility for their own and others' well-being.

4.8.41   Where activities may require working some distance above the ground, students may need protective equipment, such as helmets. Students' clothing and equipment for such activities should provide an acceptable level of protection.

4.8.42   Consideration should be given in the risk-assessment process to the appropriateness of all equipment to be used in problem-solving activities. This is particularly important when using equipment that has not been designed specifically for the task. Due consideration should also be given to the nature and size of the equipment relative to the capabilities of the group and individuals concerned.

4.8.43   Students should be adequately **briefed** on the potential hazards of the activity, and the parameters within which they may act independently should be carefully defined. The hazards and consequences of overtly competitive activities should be fully considered.

4.8.44   If the activity involves **independent** work, staff should be positioned to manage potential hazards at specified locations such as busy roads, entrances, exits and near deep water.

4.8.45   Activities that involve students physically supporting each other should be carefully managed in terms of groupings, safe and effective technique, and time given for familiarisation and practice.

Orienteering

4.8.46   Many schools establish introductory orienteering activities and short courses on the school site, and some develop this into the immediate locality.

4.8.47   Holders of British Orienteering's qualification Teaching Orienteering Part 1 or 2 (depending on location and level of delivery) or competent adults with experience of orienteering are both competent to deliver a basic introduction to orienteering in the school grounds, local parks or small areas of woodland with clear boundaries and observable paths.

 For more information on British Orienteering teaching qualifications, see https://goo.gl/Y5gMsv

4.8.48   On-site orienteering routes should take account of the hazards relating to car-park areas, boundaries and particular aspects of the school site. Beyond the school site, prior **permission** should be sought from any landowner – the existence of orienteering maps does not necessarily indicate a right of access.

4.8.49   Wherever possible, the orienteering course should avoid students crossing busy roads or negotiating major geographical hazards (eg crags or areas very close to deep water). Safe and appropriate route planning is an essential part of the risk-management process.

4.8.50   **Clothing** should be appropriate to the prevailing weather conditions and type of orienteering course. Complete coverage of the arms and legs is strongly advised when participating in thick vegetation and woodland.

4.8.51   **Footwear** should be suitable for the course terrain and weather conditions.

4.8.52   All students should carry a whistle or other means of calling for help if orienteering in areas where they will be out of sight of the leaders. Where mobile phones are carried, loss of signal reception should be anticipated.

4.8.53   Students should be briefed with clear ground rules. All foreseeable hazards should be identified and brought to their attention.

4.8.54   A **call-back signal** and prearranged cut-off time should be agreed and understood by all participants. Escape instructions may be issued to enable students to retreat safely to a prearranged point.

4.8.55   Inexperienced students should take part in pairs or small groups and remain together.

4.8.56   If groups are to be **unaccompanied**, consideration should be given to:

- educational aims

- the potential hazards associated with proposed routes

- the potential threat from other people

- emergency procedures in the event of injury or getting lost

- a realistic cut-off time

- the boundaries of the course.

4.8.57   Only experienced and relevantly trained students should take part in **night-time orienteering**, except on the most straightforward sites (eg school grounds or fully enclosed areas of limited size).

4.8.58   Procedures for locating students who get lost should be handled by the leader.

4.8.59   First aid kits must be available when working off site.

 For more information about travelling first aid kits, see Chapter 2, Section 15, page 252.

Useful website

British Orienteering: www.britishorienteering.org.uk

Traversing walls and bouldering

4.8.60   Low-level traversing and bouldering walls are becoming more common, particularly in primary schools. Adjustable holds are attached to a wall, enabling students to manoeuvre along the wall at very low heights. Low-level traversing and bouldering do not involve the use of ropes, and require a minimum level of leadership expertise while offering challenging situations to the students involved.

4.8.61   Traversing walls for beginners should incorporate low **holds** to enable less confident students to complete very low-level traverses. Expert advice should be sought before making adjustments to the holds in order to provide a range of routes along the wall to accommodate a range of ability and confidence.

4.8.62   Sufficient space should be provided so that climbers have the opportunity to look at the location of holds and devise their own route along the wall without the pressure of others crowding them.

4.8.63   Clear safety rules should be established before low-level traversing begins. It is good practice for the leader to involve the students in devising the safety rules.

4.8.64   Consideration needs to be given to the control and supervision of all group members. Dependent on the age group, dedicated supervision of low-level traversing may be required both in curricular and extracurricular time. Where this is the case, the individual supervising the low-level traversing wall should not be expected to supervise other activity areas at the same time.

 For guidance regarding safety surfaces for climbing and bouldering walls, see Chapter 2, Section 13, page 220.

Useful website

Mountain Training (skills and awards):   www.mountain-training.org

Parkour/freerunning

4.8.65   Parkour or freerunning is the non-competitive physical discipline of training to move freely over and through any terrain using only the abilities of the body, principally through running, jumping, climbing and quadrupedal movement. Both terms are used interchangeably to ensure that an English-speaking audience understand the French term.

4.8.66   The activity aims to develop the functional strength and fitness, balance, spatial awareness, agility, coordination, precision, control and creative vision that are required to achieve the movement while at the same time aiming to build confidence, determination, self-discipline and self-reliance, and a responsibility for one's actions.

4.8.67   As a specialist, **higher risk activity**, teachers wishing to teach parkour during curriculum time or as an extracurricular activity are recommended to undertake the Parkour UK 1st4sport **Introductory** CPD Award in Teaching Parkour/Freerunning. This enables them to deliver the activity **indoors** using appropriate equipment and/or purpose-built equipment/facilities.

4.8.68   At the next level, the **Intermediate** CPD Award in Teaching Parkour/Freerunning includes information about delivering parkour indoors and **outdoors**, in curriculum and extracurricular time. This does not qualify teachers to teach or coach in an external or community setting.

4.8.69   Training awards are also available for teaching assistants and lunchtime supervisors to assist a teacher, and achieving and leading awards are available for students.

4.8.70   In cases where external coaches are used to deliver parkour/freerunning as part of the school programme, schools should be looking for an individual to hold at least the Parkour UK 1st4sport Level 2 Certificate in Coaching Parkour/Freerunning. In addition to this, they should be registered with the Parkour UK Parkour Professionals Register, which assures proof of occupational competence and insurances of £10million. It is also recommended that a DBS check and/or update service number is supplied.

4.8.71   In most cases where parkour/freerunning is taught in schools, it may take place in school gyms or sports halls. It can be taught outdoors, dependent on the type of qualification that is held by the teacher/coach.

4.8.72   Existing indoor physical education equipment can be used, or purpose-built parkour equipment/facilities can be purchased from a number of suppliers. Equipment should comply with the relevant BSI British Standard for parkour equipment – BS10075:2013 (or any replacement of this standard).

4.8.73   Students should wear training shoes and comfortable physical education kit.

4.8.74   In preparation for learning parkour moves, staff should ensure that students have been taught correct techniques for jumping and landing, rolling and some vaulting, and that they understand how these contribute to safe exercise practice.

Useful website

Parkour/freerunning: www.parkouruk.org

Walking in lowland country

4.8.75   Venues should offer levels of educational, environmental and/or activity challenge appropriate to the abilities, confidence and experience of the group. Lowland areas could include walking in urban streets or country parks and fields.

4.8.76   **Staff competent** in the activity should carefully choose appropriate venues, and plan routes, taking into account all variables. Where lowland walking develops into more remote and challenging journeys, it is advised that the group leader holds the Mountain Training Lowland Leader Award.

 For information about the Mountain Training Lowland Leader Award, see http://goo.gl/CGHG56

4.8.77   Even at low levels, **the weather** can change quickly and significantly, causing increases in wind speed and rainfall intensity, and reductions in temperature. Wind chill and topographical funnelling effects (ie effects of geographical features on weather conditions) should also be anticipated by staff when choosing appropriate venues.

4.8.78   **Planning** should include:

- suitable stops for rests

- an estimated time for completing the journey

- consideration of equipment needs

- a level of demand appropriate to the abilities and experience of the group

- possible hazards and how they might be managed

- emergency procedures that may need to be implemented.

4.8.79   Each **group member** should carry or wear suitable clothing and equipment to ensure their comfort. This will typically include:

- waterproof and windproof clothing

- food and drink

- appropriate spare clothing

- appropriate footwear.

4.8.80   In addition, the **group** should carry equipment to allow them to deal with emergencies. This will typically include:

- a first aid kit, which must be carried when off site

- map and compass, where appropriate

- emergency procedures aide-memoire

- mobile phone (plus a contingency where reception is not available).

4.8.81   Low-level walking may be an appropriate context for groups to be **remotely supervised**.

 For more information about remote supervision of DoE expeditions, see 4.8.30 in this section.

Useful website

Mountain Training (skills and awards):   www.mountain-training.org

Camping

4.8.82   There are various forms of camping, ranging from 'standing camps', which involve the use of some permanent on-site facilities, to lightweight camping and backpacking expeditions, which demand greater levels of skill and knowledge. It is essential that potential hazards relating to camping sites and associated activities are identified at the planning stage.

4.8.83   When leading camping in the school locality or hills, staff should be appropriately experienced, trained and, if relevant, qualified for the terrain, in accordance with Mountain Training guidelines.

4.8.84   All sites should be thoroughly **risk assessed** by an appropriately experienced person and the necessary control measures put in place.

4.8.85   If the party is to camp **near water**, group leaders should be familiar with the issues relating to water safety.

4.8.86   Sufficient space should be left between tents to allow free movement and prevent the spread of fire.

4.8.87   Sites close to mines and quarries, busy main roads and steep ground should be avoided wherever possible.

4.8.88   All rubbish should be taken away and disposed of thoughtfully.

4.8.89   A first camp should be held under controlled conditions, located near permanent shelter and close to vehicle access.

4.8.90   **Contingency plans** for alternative routes, venues or activities, in the event of bad weather, should be agreed at the planning stage.

4.8.91   Group leaders should ensure that students receive **adequate training** in key aspects of camp craft, including effective pitching of tents for anticipated weather, the importance of hygiene, the safe packing and carrying of loads and a 'minimum impact' approach to the environment.

4.8.92   Careful thought needs to be given to the training and supervision required for safe use of stoves, including:

- the type(s) of **stove** used

- safe placement of stoves

- fuel storage

- safe refuelling, ie:

    - after the stove has cooled

    - in a ventilated area

    - when other nearby sources of ignition have been extinguished.

4.8.93   Students should be taught how to prepare and store food safely, and to clean utensils with consideration for the environment and hygiene.

4.8.94   Menu planning should reflect the need for:

- healthy nutrition

- cooking convenience and hygiene

- fuel efficiency

- palatability.

Useful websites

Mountain Training (skills and awards):   www.mountain-training.org
OEAP: www.oeap.info

Bushcraft/Forest Schools

4.8.95   Bushcraft and Forest Schools involve students taking part in engaging, motivating and achievable tasks and activities in a woodland environment. The philosophy of Forest Schools is to encourage and inspire individuals of any age to develop social and emotional skills and competencies through positive outdoor experiences. Activities should be adapted to students' ability levels and educational needs, and the weather and terrain. Activities linked to the prescribed curriculum and personal and social development include hide and seek, shelter building, tool skills, lighting fires, building dens and environmental art.

4.8.96   A Forest Schools Level 3 practitioner award (or equivalent) is advised as the standard for leading Forest School sessions. However, competent adults with some experience of Forest Schools may be able to deliver basic activities in the school grounds, local parks or small areas of woodland with clear boundaries and observable paths.

4.8.97   Where Forest Schools take place outside school grounds, prior **permission** needs to be sought from the landowner, and the site must be risk assessed and prepared before use. Appropriate boundary setting is an essential part of the risk-management process.

4.8.98   Wherever possible, the Forest School area should not be close to busy roads or major geographical hazards (eg crags or deep water). Where there is access to the public, appropriate procedures should be in place to ensure student safety.

4.8.99   **Clothing** should be appropriate to the prevailing weather conditions and type of activities being undertaken. Complete coverage of the arms and legs is strongly advised when participating in thick vegetation and woodland.

4.8.100   Where Forest School activities take place over a number of sessions, a progressive plan of activities should be developed.

4.8.101   Students should be briefed with clear **ground rules**. All foreseeable hazards should be identified and brought to their attention.

4.8.102   A **briefing area** (often with a circle area and fire pit) is recommended as a focal point for starting and finishing activities.

4.8.103   Fire making and tool use are practised in Forest Schools in a traditional woodland manner and should be carefully introduced by demonstration and supervised throughout. Supervision and monitoring of tools and fires are essential. However, students should be encouraged to think about and assess their actions, and become aware of safety issues in order to manage risk.

4.8.104   For all activities, consideration should be given to:

- educational aims
- the potential hazards associated with the environment and activities
- the potential threat from other people
- emergency procedures in the event of injury or getting lost.

4.8.105   If appropriate, **escape instructions** may be issued to enable students to retreat safely to a prearranged point.

4.8.106   Procedures for locating students who get lost should be handled by the leader.

4.8.107   First aid kits must be available for all off-site activities.

For more information about travelling first aid kits, see Chapter 2, Section 15, page 252.

Useful websites

Bushcraft Specialist Interest Group: http://goo.gl/a035F6
Forest Schools Association: www.forestschoolassociation.org

Guidance and information on specific outdoor and adventure activities (often off site)

4.8.108   These activities should be planned and organised as independent activities but could be part of a progressive programme of OAA.

4.8.109   School staff leading **higher-risk activities** must follow their employers' requirements for competence, qualification, experience and management. It is recommended that teachers planning to provide challenging adventure activities for students should regularly check the latest guidance provided by the relevant OAA governing bodies, and ensure that staff who are leading students are qualified to the appropriate level of challenge and/or specialist experts are used.

For information about provision of OAA (often off site), see page 436.

4.8.110   Where activities are led by an **external provider**, the provider assumes responsibility for risk assessing its **services and provision**. School staff should understand and be satisfied with these as part of their overall assessment of the provider, and take responsibility for risk assessing those elements of the visit falling directly under their supervision. **Overall duty of care remains the responsibility of the school (employer) and cannot be delegated to the service provider.**

For information about duty of care, see Chapter 1, Section 4, page 15.

4.8.111   The websites of governing bodies of sport for specific activities will provide up-to-date guidance and information on relevant coaching, leading and personal performance awards, recommended supervision levels, current best practice and risk-assessment considerations. The OEAP has developed a provider statement form that can be used to ensure that the provider has appropriate arrangements in place: http://goo.gl/Ef4zjG

4.8.112   This form is not necessary if the provider already holds a LOtC Quality Badge.

4.8.113   Latest DfE Guidance (February 2014) states:

> *When planning an activity that will involve caving, climbing, trekking, skiing or water sports, schools must currently check that the provider holds a licence as required by the Adventure Activities Licensing Regulations 2004. These regulations apply to adventure activities that take place in England, Scotland and Wales but these arrangements may be subject to change in the future.*

> DfE (2014) 'Health and safety: Advice on legal duties and powers for local authorities, school leaders, school staff and governing bodies', https://goo.gl/GyphRM

4.8.114   The **AALA** ensures that, for licensable activities (those identified within the categories of trekking, climbing, caving and water sports), activity providers follow good safety management practices, which should allow young people to experience exciting and stimulating activities outdoors without being exposed to avoidable risks of death or disabling injury.

For more information on the AALA and activity licensing, see http://goo.gl/Pgibil

4.8.115   If a provider holds the LoTC Quality Badge, this demonstrates that they hold such a licence if it is required, and it also demonstrates that they meet equivalent standards for any other adventure activities they offer.

4.8.116   A statement issued in January 2016 by the Health and Safety Executive (HSE) confirmed that the licensing arrangements for adventure activity providers in England, Wales and Scotland were to remain as they currently stand – providers of activities in the scope of the current arrangements must still hold a valid licence.

Water-based outdoor and adventure activities

4.8.117   Group leaders are strongly recommended to ensure at least one member of the party is trained in lifesaving and first aid. They should have practical experience of the waters in which the activity will take place.

4.8.118   An accurate weather forecast and knowledge of local water conditions (eg susceptibility of the venue to flooding, tide times, and the effects of wind on tide and sea states) should inform the risk assessment.

4.8.119   Students need to be adequately equipped and clothed for the prevailing weather conditions. Appropriate footwear should be worn.

4.8.120   Where appropriate, students should be adequately dressed for immersion. In such cases, wetsuits, helmets and buoyancy aids should be worn, even in shallow water.

For information regarding the use of wetsuits, see the British Outdoor Swimming Association website: http://goo.gl/tsCG4y

For information regarding water safety, see the Royal Lifesaving Society website: http://goo.gl/Oql5Li

Angling

4.8.121   Angling is popular with many young people. It can provide opportunities to develop an awareness of environmental issues, address conservation matters and promote respect for other water users.

4.8.122   Angling can take place in many environments, including:

- fast-flowing rivers

- meandering streams

- ponds, lakes and reservoirs

- from the seashore

- on the open sea.

4.8.123   When fishing from a **boat**:

- it should be fit for purpose and appropriately licensed

- it should not be overloaded, and there should be sufficient space

- there should be a method to retrieve anyone who falls overboard

- that is hired, the boat should conform to the requirements laid down by the Maritime and Coastguard Agency (MCA) and other relevant agencies

- staff members should be vigilant at all times.

4.8.124   Students need to be adequately equipped for the prevailing weather conditions. Appropriate footwear (usually wellingtons) should be worn.

Useful websites

Angling Trust – Angling Course for Schools and Teachers: www.anglingtrust.net

Environment Agency fishing information: https://goo.gl/SO9jsn

Canoeing, kayaking and paddle sports

4.8.125   Canoeing and kayaking take place in a wide variety of contexts and environments, from open boating to flat-water marathon racing and offshore sea kayaking.

4.8.126   Group leaders should hold a governing body of sport qualification that is appropriate and relevant for the specific craft and environment. Governing body of sport qualifications are divided into two areas: coaching and personal skills/leadership. Specialist knowledge (for kayaks and canoes) is available in the following areas:

- racing

- slalom

- wild-water racing

- surfing

- open canoeing

- polo

- freestyle

- sea kayaking

- white-water kayaking

- flat water.

Useful websites

British Canoe Union (BCU):	www.bcu.org.uk
Canoe England:	www.canoe-england.org.uk
Canoe Association of Northern Ireland:	www.cani.org.uk
Canoe Wales:	www.canoewales.com
Scottish Canoe Association:	www.canoescotland.org

Combined water/rock activities

4.8.127   Combined water/rock activities are adventure activities where those hazards associated with the rock environment may, at times, combine with those of the water environment. Some activities involve participants jumping into the sea from height, and seeing aspects of the coast that are not normally seen. These include:

- gorge walking

- sea-level traversing and coasteering

- canyoning

- adventure swimming

- river running.

Useful websites

British Caving Association:	www.british-caving.org.uk
British Mountaineering Council:	www.thebmc.co.uk
HSE/ AALA Guidance note 6.06 – Combined water/rock activities:	http://goo.gl/HSlozF
HSE AALA Note 6.20 – Coasteering:	http://goo.gl/DbtboV
International Coasteering Federation:	www.coasteering.org

Dinghy sailing

4.8.128   Sailing is a long-established adventure activity that has become a core component of outdoor education. It offers opportunities for developing physical skills, self-confidence and self-esteem, and is used frequently for team building, leadership and management-development programmes.

Useful websites

National School Sailing Association:	www.nssa.org.uk
Royal Yachting Association (RYA):	www.rya.org.uk
RYA Northern Ireland:	www.ryani.org.uk
RYA Scotland:	www.ryascotland.org.uk
Welsh Yachting Association:	www.welshsailing.org

Improvised rafting

4.8.129   Improvised rafting using barrels and planks as building materials is an outdoor activity that is often used for team building and management-development programmes.

 For information about team building and problem solving, see page 442 in this section.

4.8.130   For improvised rafts, group leaders should be experienced in construction techniques. Rafts may distort when placed on the water, and care will be needed, during design and construction, to anticipate the effect of this.

4.8.131   Students should be made aware of the hazards involved in lifting and handling the construction materials, which should be fit for purpose. Clear **communications** will be necessary to ensure safe lifting and handling techniques are used. Construction and safety guidelines should form part of the initial briefing. At the construction stage, helmets may be useful.

4.8.132   A **capsize or break-up** of the improvised raft should be considered a real possibility, and an action plan established to rescue anyone in the water. On stretches of open water, an appropriately staffed **safety boat** may be required where individuals could have difficulty reaching the shore in the event of capsize. Where safety boats are to be used, appropriate procedures should be followed. Safety boat 'kill cords' should be used, and the instructor should carry a knife.

4.8.133   Students should be dressed adequately and safely for immersion – wetsuits, helmets and buoyancy aids should be worn, where possible, even in shallow water. The risk of entrapment needs to be anticipated and managed appropriately.

Useful websites

OEAP: www.oeap.info

HSE AALA Note 6.08 –
Improvised Rafting: http://goo.gl/Lct70g

Rowing

4.8.134   Rowing as an indoor activity at school has become very popular. Schools need to carefully manage the transition between the indoor and outdoor activity, using specialist qualified providers, where required, and ensuring that students appreciate the additional safety aspects of the outdoor activity.

 For information on indoor rowing, see Chapter 4, section 7, page 430.

Useful website

British Rowing: www.britishrowing.org

Sub-aqua activities

4.8.135   Underwater exploration often begins with snorkelling, but the proficient use of scuba equipment significantly enhances the levels of enjoyment, challenge and opportunities for sub-aqua activities farther afield. Due to the specialist nature of sub-aqua activities, only recognised and fully **accredited teaching centres** should be used to deliver diving programmes.

Useful websites

British Sub-Aqua Club: www.bsac.com

Professional Association of Diving Instructors: www.padi.com

Surfing and windsurfing

4.8.136   These activities are frequently offered as part of an activity programme for water-based residential activity trips. Appropriate buoyancy aids should be provided and competent instructors used. Where instruction takes place in the sea, the instructors should ensure that students are taught about tidal activity, currents and staying safe in the surf.

Useful websites

Royal Life Saving Society UK: www.lifesavers.org.uk

RYA windsurfing: http://goo.gl/KE9b2n

Surf Life Saving Association of Great Britain: www.slsgb.org.uk

Surfing GB: http://surfinggb.com

White-water rafting

4.8.137   White-water rafting involves paddling purpose-made inflatable rafts on white-water rivers. School staff should ensure that raft guides are appropriately qualified for the level of river.

Useful website

BCU: www.bcu.org.uk

Land-based outdoor and adventure activities

Caving and mine exploration

4.8.138   Underground systems, other than show caves and tourist mines, present many of the challenges and adventure opportunities associated with climbing and water, and these, along with darkness and confined spaces, make the underground experience uniquely challenging and exciting. Well-organised underground activities can provide numerous educational opportunities for personal and group development.

Useful website

British Caving Association: www.british-caving.org.uk

Climbing and abseiling

4.8.139   Climbing and abseiling require degrees of balance, agility, strength, endurance and mental control that are dependent on the standard of routes selected at the chosen venue. The activities also require that individuals take responsibility for their own and others' safety in what can be potentially hazardous environments.

 For information about indoor climbing, traversing and bouldering walls, see Chapter 2, Section 13, page 219.

Useful websites

British Mountaineering Council: www.thebmc.co.uk

Mountain Training: www.mountain-training.org

Mountaineering Council of Scotland: www.mcofs.org.uk

Mountaineering Ireland: www.mountaineering.ie

National Indoor Climbing Award Scheme: www.nicas.co.uk

Cycling and mountain biking

4.8.140   Great care should be exercised when planning and organising cycling activities. Risk assessments should take into account the levels of technical difficulty, objective dangers, overall distance (including height gain and loss), escape routes and whether a leader with a mountain-biking qualification will be required (and available) to ensure acceptable margins of safety.

4.8.141   The competence of the group should be assessed before taking to the road or trail, and this assessment should take place in controlled conditions in a safe area. **Venues** should be chosen that take account of the fitness, ability and experience of the group.

4.8.142   Cyclists should be briefed on key safety measures. These will normally include:

- bike controls

- body positions when ascending and descending

- braking

- skid control

- riding as part of a group at different speeds

- specific venue hazards, including traffic or weather variables.

4.8.143   They also need to be forewarned of **hazards** relevant to the planned route. These might include:

- very steep descents

- difficult bends

- unusually rough terrain

- other unusual riding surfaces

- other potential track users.

4.8.144   Such situations should be managed according to the ability of the group, whether on or off-road. Safe progressions with appropriate levels of challenge and development should characterise the session. Safe braking distances should be maintained between each bike.

4.8.145   **Weather** variables will have effects on the riding surface. Wind strength and direction, wind chill and the possibility of frozen ground will impact on progress and safety margins.

4.8.146   **Bikes** should:

- be roadworthy, with all parts in good condition

- have tyres that are appropriately inflated for the nature of the riding

- have wheels that are locked in place and not buckled, with hubs running smoothly

- have correctly adjusted brakes that are capable of stopping the cyclist effectively

- be correctly sized with securely adjusted handlebars, brake levers and saddle

- have correctly adjusted and smooth-running gears

- be fitted with suitable lights (if appropriate)

- have safe stowage and pannier systems (if appropriate).

4.8.147   Cyclists should wear **clothing**, and carry equipment, suitable for the activity, venue and conditions. This will normally include:

- gloves

- properly fitted and sized helmet

- appropriate footwear – trainers are normally acceptable, but it should be remembered that riders can be susceptible to cold feet when wet

- long sleeves and full-length, close-fitting trousers

- waterproof/windproof top (in warm weather, it is usual to carry this in a rucksack; otherwise, riders may suffer from overheating).

4.8.148   It is wise to consider wearing high-visibility clothing/armbands whenever possible.

4.8.149   Each **group** should carry equipment to deal with foreseeable emergencies. Depending on the route and other variables, this will normally include:

- first aid kit, which must be carried when going off site

- group shelter

- puncture repair/maintenance kit

- tyre pump

- map and compass

- emergency procedures aide-memoire

- mobile phone

- water.

4.8.150   Consideration needs to be given to the **position of staff** in the group when riding. This 'position of most usefulness' may involve the leader dismounting to check individuals at certain points.

4.8.151   Cycling frequently involves transporting bikes and students by minibuses and trailers. The legal requirements in respect of minibuses must be observed.

For more information about transport, see Chapter 2, Section 17, page 286.

Useful websites

British Cycling: www.britishcycling.org.uk

Cycling UK mountain-biking and cycling courses: http://goo.gl/3ihtlq

Scottish Cycling: https://goo.gl/xSJ14m

4.8.152   The British Cycling Guidelines for Coaching Cycling provide information on bike, helmet and clothing checks a British Cycling coach should perform prior to activities. This is a coaching-specific document as it is recommended that those delivering cycling activities should be appropriately trained.

To view the British Cycling Guidelines for Coaching Cycling, see https://goo.gl/XQOKyP

4.8.153   British Cycling offers a Cycling for Schools workshop for people delivering sessions in a school environment, which covers the guidelines set out above and gives delegates ideas on how to deliver fun, engaging and safe cycling activities.

For more information on Cycling for Schools, see https://goo.gl/53by1F

Horse riding and pony trekking

4.8.154   Horse riding and pony trekking are popular activities with many young people, and provide an excellent context, particularly for some students with special educational needs and disabilities (SEND). Schools should use only approved riding schools, trained horses and qualified staff when offering equestrian activities.

4.8.155   School staff should discuss the needs of their students with the riding school to ensure the standards of rides chosen are appropriate for the needs of the group, and reflect prior experience.

4.8.156   Horses and riders should be relevantly equipped in line with British Horse Society (BHS) standards and guidelines.

4.8.157   Staff **ratios** should reflect the:

- demands of the terrain

- needs of the group

- risk assessment requirements of the riding centre.

4.8.158   Clear, comprehensive and concise guidance from the centre's staff should be given to all responsible adults if they are to lead particular horses.

Useful websites

Association of British Riding Schools: www.abrs-info.org

British Horse Society: www.bhs.org.uk

Riding for the Disabled: www.rda.org.uk

Ropes courses

4.8.159   High- and low-level ropes courses have become very popular in recent years, both for recreational visits and as part of school adventure programmes. Despite the high potential for risk, there is no specific regulation of the ropes course industry in the UK.

4.8.160   Ropes courses are currently out of the scope of the Adventure Activities Licensing Regulations and, as such, **do not require a licence for this activity.**

4.8.161   New guidelines have been published to help providers to comply with EN 15567:2015 – the standard for the installation and operation of new and existing ropes courses. Staff should satisfy themselves that any centre visited complies with this standard.

4.8.162   Schools should discuss with providers ratios of staff required, and agree the number of instructors that will accompany a group, and what type of supervision they will provide. This will be based on a range of variables including the type of visit (recreational or instructional), experience of instructors, ability and experience of participants, weather conditions, aims of the session and the demands of the particular course.

4.8.163   It is very important that the guidance presented in the document listed below is understood before visiting these centres.

Useful website

HSE AALA Guidance note 6.05 – UK Ropes Course Guide: http://goo.gl/McJv3v

Skating

4.8.164   The advice in this section applies to ice, roller and in-line skating.

4.8.165   In preparation, a pre-visit inspection of the location by the leader is highly recommended, and information to parents should explain the nature of the risks inherent in visits to skating rinks.

4.8.166   The **skating surface** should be:

- even

- free from obstructions

- regularly checked

- maintained and inspected before use.

4.8.167   For taught sessions, skating should be supervised by school staff, and a competent instructor should always be present. Leaders should have previous experience of skating at rinks and leading groups in similar environments. Where possible, it is advisable for beginners and advanced skaters to skate in separate groups.

4.8.168   When teaching, many leaders introduce the acronym **SLAP**, which means skaters should be:

- **s**mart:

  - always wear protective gear

  - master the basics, including stopping and turning

  - skate at a speed that is safe and appropriate for the level of competence

- **l**egal:

  - observe the venue's protocol for overtaking

- **a**lert:

  - skate in control at all times

  - watch out for hazards

  - be vigilant for changes to the skating surface

- **p**olite:

  - announce an intention to pass

  - always yield to novices and pedestrians

  - accept the need to skate thoughtfully and with care.

4.8.169   For recreational skating, the terms and conditions of the particular commercial venue must be observed. The group should observe any local requirements for direction of skating. This is usually an anticlockwise direction, skating on the right and passing on the left.

4.8.170   Students should wear suitable **clothing** that provides adequate protection. Beginners should wear gloves. Helmets may be required in certain circumstances. Elbow and knee protection is advisable. Ice/roller boots should provide firm ankle support.

4.8.171   In-line skating is increasing in popularity, and guidance should be sought from the relevant local authority (LA) or employing organisation for its policies on skating in public areas and/or on highways.

Useful websites

British Artistic Roller Skating: www.british-roller-skating.org.uk

Federation of Artistic Roller Skating: www.fars.co.uk

National Ice Skating Association: www.iceskating.org.uk

Skiing and snowboarding

4.8.172   Skiing and snowboarding can encourage students to develop a wide range of physical skills and qualities, including general fitness, coordination, balance and strength. Foreign residential visits, as cultural experiences, also offer wide-ranging opportunities for personal and social development in challenging new environments.

4.8.173   The wearing of **ski helmets** has become compulsory in several countries. Employers may have their own policy regarding this. afPE endorses the principle of wearing safety helmets when skiing.

> **For more information about ski helmets, see** Chapter 2, Section 11, page 187.

Useful websites

British Association of Snowsport Instructors: www.basi.org.uk

OEAP guidance on overseas visits: http://goo.gl/E17oDV

OEAP snowsport visits guidance: http://goo.gl/Y8gvZJ

Snowsport England: www.snowsportengland.org.uk

Snowsport Scotland: www.snowsportscotland.org

Snowsport Wales: www.snowsportwales.net

Triathlon

4.8.174   Triathlon (combining swimming, cycling and running) has grown in popularity in recent years. Students can be introduced to the activity through school events, and can compete from as young as eight years old.

4.8.175   The British Triathlon website listed below provides clear rules and regulations to be followed during all three aspects of this event.

> **For safety information about:**
>
> *   **open water swimming, see Chapter 4, Section 1, page 366**
>
> *   **cycling, see Chapter 4, Section 8, page 455**
>
> *   **running activities, see Chapter 4, Section 2, page 374.**

Useful websites

British Triathlon   www.britishtriathlon.org

HSE AALA Guidance note 6.12 –
Off-road Cycling Leader qualifications: http://goo.gl/Zfh2dm

Outdoor and residential centres

4.8.176   Many schools use outdoor and residential centres to provide students with experience of the outdoors, and opportunities to work with specialist staff. Centres may be run by LAs, charitable bodies or commercial/private agencies.

4.8.177   Centres offering activities that are subject to licensing under the **Adventure Activities Licensing Regulations 2004** (see page 449 in this section) must demonstrate to the licensing authority that they meet acceptable standards of safe practice in those activities. Accredited centres are issued with a unique licence number, which gives assurance that the provider is following sound safety-management practice.

Centres that hold a current AALA licence are listed on the AALS website: http://goo.gl/TVkdEX

4.8.178   The AALA scheme does not cover OAAs offered by voluntary associations to their members, by schools to their students, or provision for young people accompanied by their parents. However, its guidance on safety in the outdoors is appropriate to schools' provision. Alternatively, the LOtC Quality Badge, Adventuremark or accreditation by a relevant governing body of sport provides the same assurance that recognised safety-management practices are being followed by the provider.

4.8.179   While centre specialist staff are responsible for technical aspects, school staff maintain overall duty of care for their students. (See **Chapter 1, Section 4, page 15**.) Clarity of role and responsibility is essential.

4.8.180   Prior to booking at a centre, checks should be made by the school to ensure:

- the centre is appropriate for the students and planned learning outcomes
- the education credentials, staff competence and reputation of the centre are sound
- whether an AALA licence is held and, if so, what it covers
- fire and emergency procedures are satisfactory
- which facilities and services are offered
- whether sole use is possible or shared use with other groups will occur
- insurance arrangements are appropriate and acceptable
- who is responsible for what and when
- regular meetings with centre staff are scheduled to resolve issues and evaluate progress.

4.8.181   Any unsatisfactory issues should be resolved before booking.

4.8.182   Where there are insufficient school staff to accompany each activity group under instruction, school staff should organise a system of ongoing monitoring of all groups and specialist staff leading the activities so that all groups are observed each day.

4.8.183   Where school staff have concerns about any unreasonable or unnecessary risk, including the behaviour of the group affecting its safety, they should approach the specialist staff, and measures should be taken to ensure the continued safety and well-being of the students.

Overseas OAA expeditions

4.8.184   Challenging overseas expeditions are an area of growth in adventure activities, with significant issues involving insurance, quality assurance of activities and providers, and communication with school.

4.8.185   When organising such trips, schools should establish strong ongoing relationships with the parents of those participating to ensure that all aspects of preparation and planning are understood and completed in good time.

See also Chapter 1, Section 6, page 29, and Chapter 2, Section 6, page 128.

Useful websites

Adventure Activities Licensing Authority (AALA):	http://goo.gl/bCJUvI
Adventuremark:	www.adventuremark.co.uk
Association of Heads of Outdoor Education Centres:	http://ahoec.org
British Activity Providers Association:	http://goo.gl/7pFoyi
British Mountaineering Council:	www.thebmc.co.uk
Council for Learning Outside the Classroom:	www.lotc.org.uk
eduFOCUS:	www.edufocus.co.uk

(offers a managed online service called EVOLVE, which is specifically designed to enable the efficient processing of educational visit proposals)

Expedition Providers Association:	www.expeditionprovidersassociation.co.uk
Foreign and Commonwealth Office:	www.fco.gov.uk
Handsam:	http://handsam.co.uk

(offers an online 'School trip learning outside the curriculum organisation and management system' that aids the planning, administration and coordination of off-site visits)

HSE School Trips and Outdoor Learning Activities – Tackling the health and safety myths:	http://goo.gl/C5igZw
LOtC Quality Badge:	www.lotcqualitybadge.org.uk
Mountain Training (skills and awards):	www.mountain-training.org
Outdoor Education Advisers' Panel:	www.oeap.info

(provides the following downloadable information and guidance sheets:

- Guidance document on adventurous activities
- Outdoor learning cards scheme for training in leading local/low level adventure activities and outdoor learning
- Managing and delivering outdoor learning and off-site visits
- A guide to risk management
- Identifying the level of planning and risk assessment needed for different types of visit
- Responsibilities of a visit leader and assistant leader
- Pre-visits
- Preparing for and handling emergencies
- Duke of Edinburgh's Award expeditions
- Using external providers and facilities
- Self-organised visits and the package travel regulations
- Assessing competence in this area of work
- Guidance for visit leaders
- Visit leader checklist
- The role of an educational visits coordinator)

Royal Geographic Expedition Advisory Service:	www.rgs.org
Young Explorers' Trust:	www.theyet.org

Case law used in the text

Case law is law established by the outcome of former court cases and is based on decisions that judges have made.

In this resource, case law and information used to illustrate 'a case in point', included in **Chapters 1** and **2**, help readers to understand how the law is applied to real physical education, school sport and physical activity (PESSPA) situations.

Learning gained from relevant case law should inform and improve safe practice in PESSPA, and this is reflected within each updated version of this resource.

Table 39: Case law used in the text

No.	Title	Issue	Section	Paragraph
Chapter 1: Fundamental principles of safe practice				
1	Woodbridge School versus Chittock (2002)	Range of reasonable options in teaching	1: Teaching safely, teaching safety	1.1.13
2	R versus Essex County Council (2012)	Inadequate supervision due to lack of guidance on safe management	2: Health and safety law	1.2.3
3	McErlean versus Governors of St Bride's Primary School (2014)	Employers' duty of care to their employees	2: Health and safety law	1.2.4
4	Williams versus Eady (1893)	Standard of care	4: Duty of care	1.4.9
5	Lyes versus Middlesex County Council (1962)	Standard of care as a teacher	4: Duty of care	1.4.10
6	Gower versus LB of Bromley (1999)	In loco parentis applies to all in schools	4: Duty of care	1.4.12
7	Stokes versus Guest, Keen and Nettleford (Bolts and Nuts) Limited (1968)	Higher duty of care	4: Duty of care	1.4.14
8	Bolam versus Friern Hospital Management Committee (1957)	Standard of care as a teacher	4: Duty of care	1.4.17
9	Shaw versus Redbridge LBC (2005)	Regular and approved practice typical of profession	4: Duty of care	1.4.19

(continued)

No.	Title	Issue	Section	Paragraph
10	Woodland versus Swimming Teachers' Association, Stopford Direct Swimming Services, Maxwell, Essex County Council and Basildon District Council (2011)*	Duty of care non-delegable	4: Duty of care	1.4.28
11	Blairford versus CRS Adventures Ltd (2012)	Non-foreseeable risk	4: Duty of care	1.4.38
12	Bolton versus Stone (1951) and Harrison versus Wirral MBC (2009)	Rare event means no liability	4: Duty of care	1.4.39
13	R versus Leisure Connection Ltd (2013)	Failing to follow own procedures	5: Policy and procedures	1.5.10
14	Inquest into student killed by polar bear (2014)*	Failure to follow procedures and actions highlighted in the risk assessment	5: Policy and procedures	1.5.27
15	Edwards versus National Coal Board (1949)	Definition of 'reasonably practicable'	6: Risk assessment	1.6.10
16	R versus Chargot and Ruttle Contracting (2008)	Common sense approach to risk	6: Risk assessment	1.6.14
17	R versus Porter (2008)	Real not hypothetical risk situation	6: Risk assessment	1.6.22
18	Uren versus Corporate Leisure (UK) Ltd and Ministry of Defence	Failure to carry out a 'considered and conscientious risk assessment'	6: Risk assessment	1.6.31
19	Liverpool City Council versus the Adelphi Hotel (2010)	Inadequate risk assessment	6: Risk assessment	1.6.36
20	Flint versus Cornwall Academies Trust (2015)	General rather than specific risk assessment as satisfactory safe management	7: Risk management	1.7.6
21	R versus HTM (2008)	Foreseeability as to the likelihood of injury occurring	7: Risk management	1.7.15

(continued)

No.	Title	Issue	Section	Paragraph
Chapter 2: Teaching safely – principles of safe organisation and management				
22	Jones versus Manchester Corporation (1958)	Management responsibility to deploy competent staff	2: Competence, qualifications and professional learning	2.2.8
23	R versus Thornton Grammar School (2014)	Lack of adequate training	2: Competence, qualifications and professional learning	2.2.9
24	Denbighshire County Council versus McDermott (2005)	Clear instructions	2: Competence, qualifications and professional learning	2.2.16
25	Smolden versus Whitworth (1996)	Officials must apply rules of sport correctly	2: Competence, qualifications and professional learning	2.2.26
26	Wooldridge versus Sumner (1962)	Officials have a duty of care for spectators when on pitch	2: Competence, qualifications and professional learning	2.2.27
27	Kenyon versus Lancashire County Council (2001)	Injury caused by incorrect tuition	2: Competence, qualifications and professional learning	2.2.57
28	R versus Kite (1996)	Management responsibility to employ competent staff	2: Competence, qualifications and professional learning	2.2.70
29	Norfolk County Council versus Kingswood Activity Centre (2007)	Staff not trained adequately	2: Competence, qualifications and professional learning	2.2.73
30	van Oppen versus the Clerk to the Bedford Charity Trustees (1988)	Parental responsibility to insure students	3: Insurance	2.3.33
31	R versus Drake (2011)	Teacher abusing position of trust	4: Safeguarding	2.4.8
32	R versus Brooks (2007)	Teacher abusing position of trust	4: Safeguarding	2.4.9
33	R versus Thompson (2008)	Teacher abusing position of trust	4: Safeguarding	2.4.10
34	R versus Lister (2005)	Teacher abusing position of trust	4: Safeguarding	2.4.11

(continued)

No.	Title	Issue	Section	Paragraph
35	Hattingh versus Roux (2011, South Africa)	Dangerous and illegal play	4: Safeguarding	2.4.21
36	R versus Weston (2012)	Dealing with violent behaviour during play	4: Safeguarding	2.4.22
37	Gravil versus Carroll (1) and Redruth RFU Club (2) (2008)	Vicarious responsibility	4: Safeguarding	2.4.23
38	R versus Chapman (2010)	Dangerous play	4: Safeguarding	2.4.24
39	R versus Stafford (2009)	Golf rage	4: Safeguarding	2.4.25
40	R versus Ellis (2003)	Not communicating risk	5: Programme management	2.5.12
41	Heffer versus Wiltshire County Council (1996)	Staff to check student confidence and provide appropriate progression	5: Programme management	2.5.30
42	Jones versus Hampshire County Council (1997)	Failing to judge the readiness to progress	5: Programme management	2.5.31
43	R versus Manningtree High School (2013)	Working beyond ability	5: Programme management	2.5.32
44	Anderson versus Portejolie (2008)	Working beyond ability	5: Programme management	2.5.41
45	Woodroffe-Hedley versus Cuthbertson (1997)	Not following established procedure	5: Programme management	2.5.48
46	Shaw versus Redbridge LBC (2005)	Regular and approved practice typical of profession	5: Programme management	2.5.49
47	Woodbridge School versus Chittock (2002)	Range of reasonable options in teaching	5: Programme management	2.5.50
48	Moore versus Hampshire County Council (1981)	Reintegration into lessons after absence	5: Programme management	2.5.57
49	Dickinson versus Cornwall County Council (1999)	Consider in planning that possibility becomes foreseeable after one instance	6: Sports fixtures, festivals, tours and club links	2.6.26

(continued)

No.	Title	Issue	Section	Paragraph
50	Secondary School Athletics (2015)*	Failure to follow procedures for managing groups during high risk activities	8: Group management	2.8.9
51	Jones versus Cheshire County Council (1997)	Exceeding set ratios	8: Group management	2.8.12
52	Harris versus Perry (2008)	Constant supervision not essential	8: Group management	2.8.15
53	McDougall versus Strathclyde Regional Council (1995)	Constant supervision not essential	8: Group management	2.8.18
54	R versus Aberdeen City Council and Aberdeenshire Council (2012)	Inadequate supervision and ineffective group management	8: Group management	2.8.19
55	Secondary fitness room activities (2011)*	Adequate instruction and supervision	8: Group management	2.8.22
56	Burton versus Canto Playgroup (1989)	Leaving a minor to manage young students	8: Group management	2.8.34
57	Palmer versus Cornwall County Council (2009)	Inadequate ratios	8: Group management	2.8.35
58	Orchard versus Lee (2009)	Students owe staff a duty of care	8: Group management	2.8.36
59	Mountford versus Newlands School (2007)	Playing out of age group	8: Group management	2.8.46
60	Affutu-Nartay versus Clark (1994)	Teacher taking full role in game	8: Group management	2.8.61
61	A versus Leeds County Council (1999)	Ensuring control of movement	9: Safe exercise practice	2.9.19
62	Farmer versus Hampshire County Council (2006)	Footwear for activity	10: Clothing, footwear and personal effects	2.10.33

(continued)

No.	Title	Issue	Section	Paragraph
63	Villella versus North Bedfordshire Borough Council (1983)	Footwear for activity	10: Clothing, footwear and personal effects	2.10.34
64	R (ex parte Roberts) versus the Chair and Governors of Cwnfelinfach Primary School (2001)	Jewellery	10: Clothing, footwear and personal effects	2.10.50
65	Begum versus the Head Teacher and Governors of Denbigh High School (2006)	School's right to set uniform policy	10: Clothing, footwear and personal effects	2.10.51
66	Watkins-Singh versus the Governing Body of Aberdare High School and Rhondda Cynon Taff Unitary Authority (2008)	Covering or removal of religious artefacts in PESSPA	10: Clothing, footwear and personal effects	2.10.52
67	G (a child) versus Lancashire County Council (2000)	Duty to inform parents about critical information	11: Personal protective equipment	2.11.11
68	Steed versus Cheltenham Borough Council (2000)	Faulty goalposts	12: Equipment	2.12.13
69	Hall versus Holker Estate Co Ltd (2008)	Goal netting not secured, causing injury	12: Equipment	2.12.14
70	Clarke versus Derby City Council (2015)	Supervising equipment handling where a high risk of injury is clearly present	12: Equipment	2.12.64
71	Greenwood versus Dorset County Council (2008)	Injury folding trampoline	12: Equipment	2.12.65
72	Beaumont versus Surrey County Council (1968)	Inadequate disposal of faulty equipment	12: Equipment	2.12.99
73	Bassie versus Merseyside Fire and Civil Defence Authority (2005)	Dusty floor as slipping hazard	13: Facilities	2.13.9

(continued)

No.	Title	Issue	Section	Paragraph
74	Sutton versus Syston Rugby Club Ltd (2011)	Standard of inspection expected	13: Facilities	2.13.22
75	Jones versus Monmouthshire County Council (2011)	Tripping hazard	13: Facilities	2.13.23
76	Douch versus Reading Borough Council (2000)	Undulating playing surface	13: Facilities	2.13.24
77	Taylor versus Corby Borough Council (2000)	Unsafe facility	13: Facilities	2.13.25
78	Futcher versus Hertfordshire Local Authority (1997)	Compacted sand causing long-jump injury	13: Facilities	2.13.26
79	Jones versus Northampton Borough Council (1990)	Not informing participants of hazard	13: Facilities	2.13.27
80	Morrell versus Owen (1993)	Facility unsafe for participants	13: Facilities	2.13.36
81	Managing the climbing wall (2014)*	Sufficiently competent to operate facilities	13: Facilities	2.13.54
82	Faithful versus Kent County Council (2015)	Clear communication of the needs of students with SEND	14: SEND and medical conditions	2.14.12
83	Sloan versus the Governors of Rastrick High School (2014)	Risk assessment of needs when working with students with SEND	14: SEND and medical conditions	2.14.24
84	R versus Taverham High School (2013)	Importance of sharing information about student with SEND	14: SEND and medical conditions	2.14.32
85	Hippolyte versus Bexley London Borough (1994)	Following school policy	14: SEND and medical conditions	2.14.38
86	Felgate versus Middlesex County Council (1994)	Adopting well recognised practice	15: First aid	2.15.62

(continued)

No.	Title	Issue	Section	Paragraph
87	CMG (a minor) versus Rhondda Cynon Taf County Borough Council (2014)	Trust your professional judgement regarding injury reporting	15: First aid	2.15.70
88	Liddell versus City of York Council (2015)	Importance of recording detailed accounts of accidents at the time	15: First aid	2.15.73
89	School rugby (2011)*	Second impact syndrome	15: First aid	2.15.89
90	R versus Unwin (2011)	Importance of reputable transport companies	17: Transport	2.17.81

*These cases are presented within the text as 'A case in point'.

Frequently asked questions

The frequently asked questions (FAQ) found in **Chapters 1** and **2** of this resource are provided to help readers apply the content to everyday physical education, school sport and physical activity (PESSPA) situations. These questions represent those frequently asked by practitioners and can also develop a deeper understanding of issues already covered within the text.

Table 40: FAQ used in the text

No.	Title	Section	Paragraph
	Chapter 1: Fundamental principles of safe practice		
1	What is meant by 'a duty of care'? Can I be blamed (sued) if a child gets hurt while they are my responsibility?	4: Duty of care	1.4.37
2	I have recently started my first teaching job. There doesn't appear to be any health and safety policy available to look at. Should I ask to see one?	5: Policy and procedures	1.5.28
3	I have been asked to produce a physical education policy for my school. How should I go about this? Do you have a template to help me?	5: Policy and procedures	1.5.29
	Chapter 2: Teaching safely – principles of safe organisation and management		
4	I am a qualified secondary physical education specialist. Do I need a formal fitness industry qualification in order to teach my students in a fitness room facility?	2: Competence, qualifications and professional learning	2.2.56
5	Can an HLTA or cover supervisor teach a practical physical education lesson?	2: Competence, qualifications and professional learning	2.2.72
6	As a physical education teacher, I have been asked to take a group of students to a sports event on a Saturday. Does my school insurance cover me to do this?	3: Insurance	2.3.32
7	I currently teach in a secondary school and am moving to a new post in further education. Will I need to have a new DBS check carried out?	4: Safeguarding	2.4.46
8	I have heard that school staff should not assist students in applying suncream. Some younger students struggle to manage this on their own. Should they be helped?	5: Programme management	2.5.72

(continued)

No.	Title	Section	Paragraph
Chapter 2: Teaching safely – principles of safe organisation and management (continued)			
9	I understand that I need to carry out a risk assessment for away sports fixtures with other schools. Is it necessary to do this for every fixture?	6: Sports fixtures, festivals, tours and club links	2.6.6
10	I will be taking a group of students from my school to compete in a school sports tournament next week. The organisers of the tournament have provided consent forms, which they would like the parents of my students who are taking part to sign and return. Is this necessary? My school collects consent from parents at the start of each year to cover all trips and activities that the students may attend during that year. On the basis of this, can I inform the tournament organiser that all consents have been received?	7: Parental consent	2.7.12
11	At the end of term, we like to raise money for charity by having a staff versus students sports event. How is this practice viewed?	8: Group management	2.8.60
12	Is there a list of exercises that are 'unsafe' for students in schools?	9: Safe exercise practice	2.9.10
13	Should I include static or dynamic stretches in warm-ups?	9: Safe exercise practice	2.9.20
14	My year two class seem flexible enough. Do they need to stretch in warm-ups and cool-downs?	9: Safe exercise practice	2.9.21
15	I have a student who frequently fails to bring his kit for PESSPA activities. How can I try to address this? Should I provide him with kit?	10: Clothing, footwear and personal effects	2.10.32
16	My primary school is considering making the wearing of mouth guards compulsory in all hockey sessions, both within the curriculum and at extracurricular clubs. Is this something we can do?	11: Personal protective equipment	2.11.18
17	At what height is it safe to allow my year four students to work on the climbing equipment?	12: Equipment	2.12.34
18	Should I place mats at the base of the climbing equipment?	12: Equipment	2.12.35
19	A community gymnastics club has approached us and asked if they can hire the school sports hall to run public gym sessions. We are happy to do this, but what is the best way to arrange it?	13: Facilities	2.13.105

(continued)

No.	Title	Section	Paragraph
Chapter 2: Teaching safely – principles of safe organisation and management (continued)			
20	Who can push a wheelchair?	14: SEND and medical conditions	2.14.23
21	I have been told that it is compulsory for me to undertake training in the use of EpiPens. Is this correct?	14: SEND and medical conditions	2.14.37
22	Do schools need to have a specific policy about concussion?	15: First aid	2.15.93
23	We are running a large school PESSPA event and want to adopt a correct and manageable approach to photography. What should we consider?	16: Digital technology	2.16.21
24	At some sporting events, parents and other spectators are asked to register their intention to take photographs. Is this necessary/good practice?	16: Digital technology	2.16.22
25	Who can drive the minibus?	17: Transport	2.17.52

Glossary of terms

Table 41: Glossary of terms

accident	An event that results in harm/injury.
aquatic activities	For example, swimming, water safety activities, lifesaving, diving and open-water swimming.
British Standards (BS)	Advisory and not regulatory standards of quality for goods and services produced by the British Standards Institute (BSI) group. Where any personal protective equipment (PPE) is involved in an injury, these standards are considered to be a benchmark.
case in point	Use of case law and information from legal inquiries and hearings to illustrate key principles and help readers to apply the theory to actual situations.
case law	Law established by the outcome of former court cases and based on decisions that judges have made.
Clubmark	Cross-sport accreditation scheme for community sports clubs, used in England, Northern Ireland, Scotland and Wales. An accredited club is recognised as a safe, rewarding and fulfilling place for participants of all ages, as well as helping parents and carers know that they are choosing the right club for their young people.
coaches	Those who are qualified to coach specific sports.
code of conduct	This sets out the expectations placed on individuals (eg by the school) in a specific context or situation.
combat activities	Activities that are characterised by one-on-one combat in which a winner is determined against a set of rules.
concussion	A brain injury that can occur after a blow or other injury to the head or body **that** involves the brain being shaken against the inside of the skull. Concussion is known to have potential dangers both at the time of injury and in later life.
cover supervisors	Adults employed to supervise groups doing pre-prepared work. They may not have any expertise in physical education, school sport and physical activity (PESSPA).
competence	Appropriate and relevant experience, expertise and/or qualifications to undertake specific responsibilities.
contingency planning	A course of action planned to respond effectively to a significant future event or situation that may or may not happen (eg deterioration in weather conditions).
cool-down	Helps the body and mind recover safely and effectively after taking part in PESSPA activities.

(continued)

curriculum gymnastics	Movement challenges that develop body management and locomotor skills, and help students acquire precision of movement and quality of response in the context of balancing, inverting, climbing, rolling, jumping, landing, transferring weight, stepping and managing the body in flight.
developmentally appropriate	How appropriate a PESSPA activity/task is for the physical, social or emotional maturation of the child or young person.
direct supervision	Involves a member of staff working alongside students or support staff in order that they can intervene at any time, as necessary.
duty of care	A moral or legal obligation to ensure the safety and/or well-being of others.
dynamic risk assessment	Carried out before an activity or event and while it is taking place, identifying and responding to unforeseen issues, such as an unsafe response to a task, sudden illness, changes in climatic conditions or ineffective officiating. Sometimes referred to as ongoing or continuous risk assessment.
education, health and care plan	A plan for students with specific special educational needs and disabilities (SEND) that considers what would help the individual to access PESSPA within the curriculum and as part of an extracurricular programme.
employer	Has overall legal responsibility and accountability for all health and safety in schools – school employers are dependent on the type of school and can be a local authority, governing body, proprietor or board of trustees.
European Standards (EN)	Advisory and not regulatory standards of quality for goods and services. Where any PPE is involved in an injury, these standards are considered to be a benchmark.
forethought	An element of competence for teaching safely that involves forward planning, anticipating what may happen, and thinking about where harm is likely.
generic risk assessment	Considers the general principles that apply to an activity, wherever it may take place. A generic risk assessment is usually the starting point and is generally provided in a **written format** by the employer, governing body of sport or similar organisation.
governing body of sport	Independent, self-appointed organisation that governs its sport through the common consent of the sport.
hazard	Something with the potential to cause harm.
head teacher (HT)	The most senior teacher, leader and manager of a school.
health-related physical activity (HRPA)	Physical activity associated with health enhancement and disease prevention.
higher duty of care	That held by a professional with specialist expertise, qualifications or responsibility whose level of expected care is based on those with the same expertise within the same profession.

(continued)

higher level teaching assistant (HLTA)	Does all that regular teaching assistants do, and has an increased level of responsibility. For example, HLTAs might teach classes on their own, cover planned absences, and allow teachers time to plan and mark.
incident	An adverse event resulting in an **undesired situation** or **'near miss'** where no injury occurred, but there was the potential to cause injury.
Key Stage 1	Students aged 5–7 years (now covered by the Foundation Phase in Wales, which includes students aged 3–7).
Key Stage 2	Students aged 7–11 years.
Key Stage 3	Students aged 11–14 years.
Key Stage 4	Students aged 14–16 years.
must	Used only where the situation described relates to a statutory requirement, or where the employer sets out what must be followed by the employees.
national governing body of sport	This is a governing body of sport that has submitted a whole sport plan, which details how it will use Sport England investment to help it increase the number of people playing its sport and nurture talent.
negligence	May be defined as 'careless conduct which injures another and which the law deems liable for compensation' – Frederick Place Chambers (1995) *Negligence at Work: Liability for Injury and Disease*. St Albans: XPL Publishing. ISBN: 978-1858110-31-8.
near misses	Incidents that have occurred in a PESSPA session, in which an individual could have suffered harm but fortuitously did not.
organiser's event risk assessment	An event risk assessment, completed by the organiser, that takes account of venue issues and the organisation of the planned event.
parent	Any person, a natural parent or not, who has care and parental responsibility for a child or young person, ie the child lives with, and is looked after, by that person, irrespective of their relationship.
PESSPA activities	Include all practical learning contexts that are part of physical development activities, physical education lessons, organised sport and/or physical activity sessions beyond the curriculum, both in school settings and the community.
PESSPA sessions	Include physical development activities, physical education lessons, organised sport and/or physical activity sessions beyond the curriculum both in school settings and the community.
personalised learning	Involves matching the tasks to the students to enable progress at appropriate pace within lessons, over a series of lessons and throughout a programme of study – sometimes referred to as differentiated learning.
personal protective equipment (PPE)	Any device worn or held by an individual for protection against one or more health and safety hazards. The most common forms of PPE used in schools include mouth guards, shin pads, helmets, padding and swimming goggles.

(continued)

physical activity	A broad term referring to all bodily movement that uses energy. It includes all forms of physical education, sports and dance activities. However, it is wider than this as it also includes indoor and outdoor play, work-related activity, outdoor and adventurous activities, active travel (eg walking, cycling, rollerblading, scootering) and routine, habitual activities such as using the stairs, doing housework and gardening.
physical contact	In a safeguarding context, this is 'intentional bodily contact initiated by an adult with a child'.
physical education	Planned, progressive learning for all students that takes place within the school curriculum and involves both 'learning to move' (ie becoming more physically competent) and 'moving to learn' (eg learning through movement and the development of a range of competencies beyond physical activity, such as cooperating with others). The context for the learning is physical activity, with children experiencing a broad range of activities, including sport and dance.
Post-primary	Term used in Northern Ireland for 'secondary'.
programmed aquatic activities	Activities with formal structure, supervision, control and continuous monitoring from the poolside. (Also see unprogrammed aquatic activities.)
progression	**Staged development** of knowledge, skills and understanding in accordance with confidence, ability and successful prior experience.
professional learning	Teachers engage in this to stimulate their thinking and professional knowledge, and ensure their practice is critically informed and up to date.
Quality mark	afPE's benchmark and industry standard for high quality PESSPA in schools for students aged 5-16 years.
regular and approved practice	Practice that is **common and widely practised** as safe as opposed to an idiosyncratic practice adopted by individuals or organisations.
remote supervision	Involves a member of staff supervising a group of students without being directly present at all times. Decisions to supervise less directly should not be taken lightly and may be implemented only in appropriate circumstances, and would need to consider carefully the necessity of remote supervision, as well as student behaviour, age and ability.
risk	The likelihood of harm occurring from a hazard.
risk assessment	A judgement about whether a situation is safe within established practice and procedures, or whether additional precautions are required.
risk management	Risk management is the process of identifying, quantifying and managing the risks that an organisation faces.
risk-benefit analysis	Comparison of the level of risk against the benefits. It aims to balance acceptable risk with appropriate challenge and, in doing so, considers whether the benefits of participation outweigh the likelihood of harm or injury occurring.

(continued)

risk protection arrangement scheme	A government scheme that aims to protect academy trusts against losses due to any unforeseen and unexpected event.
safe exercise practice	Physical activities that are developmentally appropriate, and performed with appropriate control and correct joint alignment while minimising any undue stress associated with high impact.
safeguarding	Action that is taken to promote the welfare of children and protect them from harm.
safe practice in PESSPA	Where the risks for those involved in PESSPA sessions are deemed to be acceptably low.
scheme of work	A written long- or medium-term plan that informs lesson planning, fulfils the statutory requirements of any curriculum, and meets local circumstances and needs. A scheme of work typically comprises detail such as progressive learning targets, essential techniques and skills, suggestions for assessment, suggested requirements for prior learning, cross-curricular learning, and relevant safe-practice information.
school sport	Structured learning that takes place beyond the curriculum but within school settings. The context for learning is physical activity that has the potential to develop and broaden the learning that takes place in physical education, and form vital links with community sport and activity. Sometimes referred to as extracurricular or out-of-school-hours learning.
second impact syndrome	Second impact syndrome (SIS) is a very rare condition in which a second concussion occurs before the first concussion has properly healed. SIS can result from even a very mild concussion that occurs minutes, hours, days or weeks after the initial concussion.
should	Used in this resource to illustrate regular and approved practice.
STEP framework	A framework for making adjustments to the learning environment in terms of **s**pace, **t**ask, **e**quipment and **p**eople in order to provide appropriate differentiated challenge for all students in relation to achieving learning outcomes.
staff	Adults who may be deemed competent to lead PESSPA sessions in schools with the approval of the head teacher. This commonly includes qualified/registered teachers (with or without specialism in physical education), HLTAs and sports coaches.
students	All children and young people attending school.
PESSPA subject leaders	All those responsible for managing physical education in an educational establishment.
support staff	A term used for all adults without qualified/registered teaching status (QTS) who contribute to the teaching of students in schools (eg HLTAs, cover supervisors, physical education apprentices, volunteers and sports coaches). Support staff do not include trainee teachers.

478

(continued)

trainee teachers	Those undergoing training that leads to qualified/registered teacher status (QTS).
un-programmed aquatic activities	Sessions in water without a session structure but with supervision and continuous monitoring, in most cases from the poolside (also see programmed aquatic activities).
venue risk assessment	A risk assessment completed by the manager/owner/host that identifies the hazards, evaluates the risks and establishes appropriate controls to make the **venue** safe for the purpose for which it is being offered or hired out to the user group.
warm-up	Prepares the body and mind safely and effectively to take part in PESSPA activities.

Abbreviations

Table 42: Abbreviations used in the text

AALA	Adventure Activities Licensing Authority
ABAE	England Boxing – **Amateur Boxing Association** of **England** (ABAE) reformed in 2013 and became **England Boxing**
AED	Automated external defibrillator
afPE	Association for Physical Education
AP	Appointed person (first aid)
ARP	Accident report point
ASA	Amateur Swimming Association
ATSPRA	Aquatic Therapy Shallow Pool Rescue Award
BASES	British Association of Sports and Exercise Sciences
BMA	British Medical Association
BG	British Gymnastics
BHFNC	British Heart Foundation National Centre for Physical Activity and Health
BS	British standard Kitemark of quality for goods and services
BS EN	The UK version in English of a European harmonised standard
BSI	British Standards Institute
CCEA	Council for the Curriculum, Examinations and Assessment (Northern Ireland)
CE	Conformité Européene – certifies that a product has met EU health, safety and environmental requirements, which ensure consumer safety
CPR	Cardiopulmonary resuscitation
CPSU	Child Protection in Sport Unit
CSP	County sports partnership
DBS	Disclosure and Barring Service
DfE	Department for Education
EA	Education Authority (Northern Ireland)

(continued)

EAL	English as an additional language
EAP	Emergency action plan
EFAW	Emergency First Aid at Work
EN	European standards
EU	European Union
FA	The Football Association (England)
FAQ	Frequently asked questions
FAW	First Aid at Work
HAL	Healthy active lifestyles
HASWA	Health and Safety at Work etc Act 1974
HIV	Human immunodeficiency virus
HLTA	Higher level teaching assistant
HRPA	Health-related physical activity
HSC	Health and Safety Commission
HSE	Health and Safety Executive
HT	Head teacher
IHPE	Institute of Health Promotion and Education
ITE	Initial teacher education
LA	Local authority
LOtC	Learning outside the classroom
LSCB	Local safeguarding children board
MiDAS	Minibus Driver Awareness Scheme
MREGS	Management of Health and Safety at Work Regulations 1999 and 2002
NC	National curriculum
NEELB	Northern Ireland Education and Library Board (now the Education Authority – EA)
NI	Northern Ireland

(continued)

NOPs	Normal operating procedures
NPLQ	RLSS UK National Pool Lifeguard Qualification
NRASTC	National Rescue Award for Swimming Teachers and Coaches
NSPCC	National Society for the Prevention of Cruelty to Children
OAA	Outdoor and adventure activities
OEAP	Outdoor Education Advisers' Panel
OEAP NG	Outdoor Education Advisers' Panel National Guidance
PAT	Portable appliance test
PCV	Passenger-carrying vehicle
PESSPA	Physical education, school sport and physical activity
PIE	Preventing, informing and educating – afPE model that can be used to support the application of safe-practice principles (teaching safely and teaching safety)
PoS	Programme of study
PPA	Planning, preparation and assessment
PPE	Personal protective equipment
PSHE	Personal, social and health education
PSOPs	Pool safety operating procedures
PSV	Public service vehicle
PUWER	Provision and Use of Work Equipment Regulations 1998
QTS	Qualified teacher status
R	Regina (more commonly stated as 'the Crown')
RFL	Rugby Football League (governing body for rugby league in the UK)
RFU	Rugby Football Union – known as England Rugby (governing body for rugby union in England)
RIDDOR	Reporting of Injuries, Diseases and Dangerous Occurrences Regulations 2013
RLSS	Royal Life Saving Society

(continued)

RPA	Risk protection arrangement
RoSPA	Royal Society for the Prevention of Accidents
SAPs	Standard accident procedures
SEND	Special educational needs and disabilities
SIS	Second impact syndrome
SoW	Scheme of work
STA	Swimming Teachers' Association
STEP	An acronym to describe simple features of a learning environment (space, task, equipment, people) that can be adapted to meet the needs of different learners
TPs	Teaching points
TS	Teachers' standards
UKA	British Athletics
UKCC	United Kingdom Coaching Certificate

Index

Note:

- Fig indicates figure; Tab table.

- Numerals in parentheses are page numbers. They are used where there is no paragraph number.

Professional Learning to Support Safe Practice: in Physical Education, School Sport and Physical Activity 2016

This professional learning opportunity is designed to help staff to feel confident when dealing with health and safety issues in school PE. It aims to reduce the concerns that many staff have about the responsibilities and risks associated with teaching and managing an exciting PE programme, and encourages them to design challenging lessons, and know that they are safe. Part of the day is used to look at a simple approach to risk assessment in PE as recommended by the Association for Physical Education (afPE), and helps staff to consider key elements of a PE policy.

The training will reflect the updates and new additions in the recently published Safe Practice: in Physical Education, School Sport and Physical Activity 2016, and delegates will be helped to familiarise themselves with the new publication.

Course Outcomes*

- *You will become familiar with the latest afPE publication Safe Practice: in Physical Education, School Sport and Physical Activity 2016.*
- *You will have a sound understanding of H & S principles in relation to planning and monitoring school PE and Sport*
- *You will feel more confident in your teaching in the knowledge that you are applying key H & S principles*
- *You will be able to appreciate the importance of knowing and applying policies and procedures in your school, and contribute towards developing these where required*
- *You will enable students to recognise how they also play a part in taking responsibility for their own safety and ensure the safe inclusion of all pupils*
- *You will be familiar with an approach to risk assessment in PE and sport in school.*

*Based on a full day course.

The style of delivery is through group work, discussion and collaborative activities, designed to put delegates at their ease, and allow them to become conversant with the information whether or not they have any prior knowledge.

Appropriate Audience:

Teachers, Head Teachers, Governors, Coaches, Teaching Assistants, School Health and Safety Leads, Local Authority Health and Safety Leads.

Tutor: Angela James

Angela James is a physical activity consultant, and is currently the health and safety and safeguarding officer for afPE the PE subject association. afPE offers its members access to health and safety advice and guidance via both phone and email. Angela is also joint author of afPE's Safe Practice: in Physical Education, School Sport and Physical Activity 2016.

Book a Course:

A range of courses are advertised on the afPE website (www.afpe.org.uk), however, should you wish to book a bespoke course please contact our Professional Learning Team on **01905 855584** or email **cpd@afpe.org.uk**.